The

Call

to

Read

The
Call
to
Read

Reginald Pecock's
Books and Textual Communities

KIRSTY CAMPBELL

University of Notre Dame Press
Notre Dame, Indiana

Library of Congress Cataloging-in-Publication Data
Campbell, Kirsty, 1977–
    The call to read : Reginald Pecock's books and textual communities / by
Kirsty Campbell.
        p.   cm.
    Based on the author's thesis (doctoral)—University of Toronto.
    Includes bibliographical references (p.   ) and index.
    ISBN-13: 978-0-268-02306-5 (pbk. : alk. paper)
    ISBN-10: 0-268-02306-9 (pbk. : alk. paper)
    1. Pecock, Reginald, 1395?–1460?   2. Theology—England—History—
Middle Ages, 600–1500.   3. Christian literature, English (Middle)—History
and criticism.   4. England—Church history—1066–1485.   I. Title.
    BX4705.P4C36   2010
    282.092—dc22   2010024327

∞ *The paper in this book meets the guidelines for permanence and durability*
of the Committee on Production Guidelines for Book Longevity of the Council
on Library Resources.

To those who have believed in me—

my wonderful husband, Eric;

my supportive parents, Helen and Iain;

and my amazing mentor Suzanne

Contents

Acknowledgments

I would like to express my gratitude to a number of institutions and individuals who supported me as I wrote this book. The project took root during my doctoral studies at the University of Toronto's Centre for Medieval Studies. It began as a dissertation under the supervision of Suzanne Akbari, an exceedingly generous teacher, inspiring mentor, and intelligent scholar. The study took new shape through the support of James Simpson, who provided stimulating discussion and opportunities for me to present my work to other scholars. I am grateful to Ruth Harvey, a generous scholar whose wise counsel has shaped my work in many ways. I would also like to thank Brian Stock, Alexandra Gillespie, and Will Robins, without whose support and encouragement this book would never have been written.

I wish to thank the Centre for Medieval Studies and the School of Graduate Studies at the University of Toronto for supporting my research through fellowships, travel scholarships, and a postdoctoral teaching fellowship. I am particularly grateful for the unrivaled resources at the Pontifical Institute for Medieval Studies Library at the University of Toronto. I would also like to acknowledge my gratitude to my warm and supportive colleagues at Yeshiva College, who have brought new insights and fresh perspective to my scholarship.

I am grateful to those who have given me the opportunity to present my ideas about Pecock at international workshops and conferences. I wish especially to thank Steve Partridge, Erik Kwakkel, Alastair Minnis, James Simpson, Fiona Somerset, Stephen Lahey, and Joseph Grossi. Audience members, fellow presenters, and organizers at these conferences offered thoughtful feedback that has motivated and challenged me.

I would like to thank the Marquess of Bath at Longleat House, Warminster, Wiltshire, Great Britain, for permission to print extracts from MS Longleat 4. I am also grateful for the assistance of the curator of the Longleat Historic Collections, Kate Harris.

I have normalized the spellings in all quotations of Middle English works in accordance with the guidelines of Henry Ansgar Kelly's helpful article "Uniformity and Sense in Editing and Citing Medieval Texts," which appeared in *Medieval Academy News*, Spring 2004.

The anonymous reviewers at the University of Notre Dame Press have provided invaluable feedback and suggestions to improve this book. I am grateful for the time and effort they took to help me widen my perspective and focus my thinking on important aspects of Pecock's work. I am overwhelmed by their generosity and diligence. I would also like to thank the editorial team at the University of Notre Dame Press for their diligence and professionalism in bringing this book to publication; Elisabeth Magnus copyedited this book with careful, insightful attention. Thank you, Elisabeth.

I have dedicated this book to the people who believed I could write it. I thank each of them for their constant dedication and support. I would also like to express my gratitude here to Miriam, whose patient counsel was instrumental in bringing this book to publication.

Abbreviations

BF   Reginald Pecock, *Book of Faith*, ed. J. L. Morison (Glasgow: James Maclehose and Sons, 1909).

Donet   Reginald Pecock, *The Donet*, ed. Elsie Vaughan Hitchcock, EETS, o.s., 156 (1921; repr., New York: Kraus Reprint, 1971).

Folewer   Reginald Pecock, *The Folewer to the Donet*, ed. Elsie Vaughan Hitchcock, EETS, o.s., 164 (1924; repr., New York: Kraus Reprint, 1981).

MED   Kurath, Hans, and Sherman M. Kuhn, eds., *Middle English Dictionary* (Ann Arbor: University of Michigan Press, 1964–81).

PMM   Reginald Pecock, *The Poore Mennis Myrrour*, appendix to *The Donet*, ed. Elsie Vaughan Hitchcock, EETS, o.s., 156 (1921; repr., New York: Kraus Reprint, 1971).

Repressor Reginald Pecock, *The Repressor of Overmuch Blaming of the Clergy*, 2 vols., ed. Churchill Babington, Rerum Britannicarum Medii Aevi Scriptores 19 (London: Longman, Green, and Roberts, 1860).

Reule   Reginald Pecock, *The Reule of Crysten Religioun*, ed. William Cabell Greet, EETS, o.s., 171 (1927; repr., Millwood, NY: Kraus Reprint, 1987).

Introduction

Reginald Pecock's Books and His Textual Community

Fifteenth-century England was a time of intense debate and speculation about the nature of the religious life, the role of the church in
Christian society, and the faith of the ordinary Christian. Questions
once voiced and discussed by churchmen in places beyond the reach
of ordinary lay folk were asked in vernacular writings that circulated
among men and women of all walks of life. Controversy about the
authority of the Bible, for example, as a supreme source of Christian
knowledge raged in both the secular and sacred realms. Questions
about the proper way to interpret the Bible, the best way to educate
the Christian laity in matters of faith, and proper modes of interaction
between the pious laity and God's ministers were on the minds of
many, as we can observe from the contents and concerns of sermons,
tracts, treatises, and manuals. Thinking about these kinds of issues
was stimulated in large part by the Lollard heresy, which flourished
openly in the fourteenth century and underground in the fifteenth
and threatened to change the very structure of the Christian community and the practice of Christian religion. Churchmen like John
Mirk, John Capgrave, John Audelay, Reginald Pecock, the anonymous
author of *Dives and Pauper* and the Longleat sermons, and other
anonymous writers were all invested, in various ways, in finding an
appropriate response to the Lollard heresy and in revitalizing orthodoxy through vernacular writings aimed at lay readers. The kinds of

questions that the Lollards brought forth, about sacred doctrine, the role of the Bible, and the authority of the church, stimulated orthodox churchmen to seek answers, accommodations, and solutions that would acknowledge and engage with Lollard concerns without tearing the Christian community apart. The range of responses offered by people like Audelay, Capgrave, and Pecock helps us to see the fifteenth century as a dynamic rather than a dull time, in which writers, poets, and preachers were stimulated to come up with new ideas about the best way to structure Christian behavior and belief.

Until recently, we have been so fixated on the repressive, restrictive official responses to the Lollard heresy that we have not been able to open our eyes to the way that the threat of heterodoxy drove people like Reginald Pecock and John Capgrave to find alternative means of unifying the Christian community and engaging the laity in the practice and learning of their faith. In their critique of contemporary literary history, Stephen Kelly and Ryan Perry write that scholarly attention to Lollardy has limited our understanding of the religious works written in the aftermath of the English heresy: "The scholarly attention paid to the circulation of Wycliffite ideas and of the Wycliffite Bible itself distorts, we contend, the scene of fourteenth and fifteenth century theological speculation in England. Scholarship has presented us with a camera obscura, in which either the influence on religious writing of Wycliffite thought is pictured as all-pervasive or Wycliffitism is perceived as an ideological fiction propagated by the authorities in order to legitimate a tightening of secular and/or ecclesiastical control."[1]

Certainly in Pecock's case, the influence of Wycliffite ideas was not all-pervasive, even though he spent time and effort countering Wycliffite claims; rather, Wycliffite culture galvanized his thinking and made him reach for new ideas about lay religion, ideas from sources as diverse as Aquinas, Aristotle, and Wyclif himself. Scholars such as Kathryn Kerby-Fulton are beginning to paint a new picture of the religious and literary scene of late medieval England, which can be better understood as a dynamic intellectual culture where diversity of thought was possible and customary, as people of all kinds pressed in different ways against and beyond traditional orthodoxies.[2]

The changing picture of late medieval religious culture in England is witnessed by the words used to categorize its literature. The term *vernacular theology* itself has experienced a shift: first coined by A. I. Doyle in 1953 in his famous but unfortunately unpublished "Survey of the Origins and Circulation of Theological Writings in English in the 14th, 15th, and Early 16th Centuries," the term was used provocatively by Nicholas Watson in his seminal 1995 article "Censorship and Cultural Change" to differentiate a body of challenging and intellectually explorative fourteenth-century religious writing from a very different kind of writing produced in a climate of censorship in the fifteenth century.[3] More recently, the term has been used by a wide range of scholars working to "draw our attention to the richness and variety of vernacular literary production under the umbrella of religion."[4] In the 2006 journal *English Language Notes* a cluster of articles by Elizabeth Robertson, Daniel Donoghue, Linda Georgianna, Kate Crassons, C. David Benson, Katherine Little, Lynn Staley, James Simpson, and Nicholas Watson suggest diverse new ways of understanding the religious writing of late medieval England and demonstrate "the insights to be gained" from viewing vernacular theology as a "capacious category," even suggesting that "the plural, vernacular theologies, is surely more apt."[5] In writing this book, it is my aim to present the corpus of Reginald Pecock as one of the most fascinating and important bodies of work for our understanding of his cultural moment and of just how "capacious" vernacular theology could be.

Indeed, viewing Pecock's corpus as one of many vernacular theologies of late medieval England helps us to avoid the pitfall Linda Georgianna warns against, of reducing the category "to a coded term for various binaries—English versus Latin, or theology versus moral instruction, or the like."[6] Understanding Pecock's accomplishment requires that we recognize his vernacular theology as an innovative body of work written in English in which moral instruction, philosophical truth, devotional exercises, and theological doctrine mingle together, stimulated by the teachings of thinkers ranging from Aristotle to Aquinas to Wyclif, in order to assist all Christians in their efforts to follow the "Reule of Crysten Religioun" while living in this world. Written in the vernacular, the surviving books facilitate access to theological and philosophical training, not for "suche lay men whiche schulden mowe leerne and vndirstonde tho writingis if they weren maad in Latin" (*Folewer*, 7), but for those who cannot read Latin. By noting that some laymen can read Latin while others "kouthe not studie and undirstonde hem if they were maad in Latin," Pecock suggests that within his London milieu we cannot be certain of a clear division between Latinate clerics and laymen literate only in English. While it certainly is true that Pecock is introducing new material and doing new things in the vernacular, we must be careful, as Ian Johnson warns, to avoid using words like *appropriation* to describe work like that of Pecock, given that such vocabulary, based on "seeing medieval vernacular textuality in terms of its competition against colonial, clerical Latin culture and its sources," can obscure the "common ground between Latin and English texts/culture, let alone their rich intertextual relations."[7] Pecock's decision to use the vernacular as a vehicle for transmitting the learning of moral philosophy from the university environment to a wider audience does not necessarily mean that he was educating and empowering lay readers alone. While Pecock generally speaks of his readers as members of the laity, he also notes, as I point out in chapter 1, that his books are useful for young scholars and university clerics in disciplines outside theology. As increasing numbers of scholars help us to better understand the different dimensions of vernacular theology during this once-neglected period of literary history, I offer this study of Pecock's books to give us a better idea of the plurality and sense of possibility that characterized fifteenth-century culture. The term *vernacular theology* provides what Linda Georgianna calls "a tool of critical analysis" that can be particularly useful in understanding Pecock's accomplishment.[8] His vernacular theology is one that draws on approaches to teaching from the university setting, that has its source in Aquinas's great synthesis of reason and faith, that extends and innovates traditions of teaching pastoral theology in English going back to Lateran IV, that shares some of Lollardy's "intellectual terrain," that fosters cohesion among clergy and laity instead of promoting "the acquisition of religious knowledge as a zero-sum game wherein every gain by the laity is registered as a loss for clerical authority," that provides for the whole Christian soul not only food for thought but fruits for meditation and devotion, and that offers new ways of understanding doctrine as meaningful Christian practice for those living in the here and now.[9]

The contents of Pecock's writings are the subject of this book. An extensive study of Pecock's works and thought has not emerged since the 1980s, when Charles Brockwell published a monograph on Pecock.[10] The most significant work on Pecock to emerge since then is Wendy Scase's immensely important biography, a work that fills in many gaps in our knowledge about Pecock's life and career but offers less in the way of detailed analysis of Pecock's writings.[11] In her biography, Scase tells us that Pecock was born in Wales, probably around 1390, and educated at Oxford. After his BA and MA, he studied theology at Oriel College, probably from 1416 to 1424. His first position was the rectory of St Michael's, Gloucester, which he resigned when he was appointed master of Whittington College, a position he held from 1431 to 1444, as I discuss in detail in chapter 1. He was made bishop of St. Asaph in 1444 and then of Chichester in 1450. In 1447 Pecock preached a sermon in London that offended many important secular and spiritual authorities; his books and his views became controversial from then on. During the 1450s his position became tenuous as he was examined and forced to revoke his heresies, positions on doctrine that could "uncharitably be rendered" as heretical views, such as his notion that it was not necessary to believe in Christ's descent into hell, the Holy Ghost, the Catholic Church, and the communion of saints.[12] He made a public recantation and died several years later, having been deprived of his bishopric as well as his books and his writing materials.

In addition to this valuable biography by Scase, a few articles have been published over recent years that examine Pecock's writings in relation to questions about translation, authorship, heresy, and biblical hermeneutics. This work has highlighted the significance of Pecock's writings in our understanding of late medieval debates about these subjects.[13] In doing so, they have demonstrated the need for a book-length study that assesses Pecock's place in fifteenth-century intellectual, religious, and literary culture.

The first two functions of this book, then, are to fill the gap in our knowledge about Pecock's writings and to better clarify where he stands within his fifteenth-century context, in terms of the contribution he offers to debates about lay religion and to the tradition of teaching religion to the laity. Throughout this book I draw comparisons between Pecock's teachings and a range of material written in the vernacular and read by the pious laity in fifteenth-century England. This material includes translations, didactic treatises, guides to contemplation, devotional tracts, pastoral compilations, and polemical writings: reference will be made to works such as *The Abbey of the Holy Ghost*, Hilton's *On the Mixed Life*, Saint Edmund of Abingdon's *Mirror*, *Jacob's Well*, *Book to a Mother*, *The Testimony of William Thorpe*, *A Ladder of Foure Ronges*, *Contemplations on the Dread and Love of God*, and *The Book of Margery Kempe*. This field of comparison will help to illuminate the ways that Pecock's writings adapt, extend, and even innovate contemporary approaches to the teaching of doctrine, prayer, contemplation, and the moral life.

The contribution that Pecock makes to late medieval thought helps us to see that the institutional response to the Lollard heresy, which has dominated scholarly inquiry until recently, is simply one on a spectrum of possible responses. The sweeping legislation of Archbishop Arundel, with the Constitutions of 1409, reacted to the problem of heresy among both laity and clergy in the Christian community by forbidding people to read, think, and discuss certain things. I will discuss the relationship between the Constitutions and Pecock's corpus in more detail in chapter 2, but for now I would like to highlight the fact that Arundel thinks big: rather than seeking answers to the questions raised by the Wycliffite heresy, he attempts to shut down thinking on these matters entirely. As Nicholas Watson points out, the Constitutions were a set of laws put in place in 1409 that were designed to put an end to Lollardy.[14] The Constitutions were meant to reinforce orthodox doctrine and thinking by censoring academic discussions of theological matters, by forbidding the writing and reading of English translations of scripture without episcopal approval, and by strictly regulating the activities of preaching and teaching. Some preachers were denied the right to share with the laity religious knowledge that extended beyond the material outlined in Pecham's 1281 Constitutions, legislation that had constituted an innovative and exciting attempt at reforming religious instruction after the council of Lateran IV by ensuring that all Christians should receive vital spiritual instruction through "sermons covering the fourteen Articles of Faith, the Decalogue, the two Evangelical Commandments, the Seven Works of Mercy, Deadly Sins, Principle Virtues, and Sacraments."[15] Much religious instruction in the vernacular that circulated in late medieval England can be seen as a development of the "elaborate and unusually sophisticated" program of instruction laid out by Archbishop Pecham and his council; it appears, however, that one of Arundel's answers to heresy was to limit circulation and production of works that took their stimulus from this syllabus of instruction but offered education beyond the subjects approved in 1281.[16]

Restricting the practice of religion and the learning of the faith in these ways was certainly a powerful response to the problem of crisis in the Christian community; how effective this legislation was is another matter. A number of critics, including Fiona Somerset, Shannon McSheffrey, and Vincent Gillespie, have rejected the notion that Archbishop Arundel's Constitutions of 1409 had any real impact on the production and reception of stimulating and exciting religious writings.[17] McSheffrey points out, for example, that upper-class lay readers were allowed to hold on to their Bibles despite the new legislation.[18] The survival of just under 250 copies of the Wycliffite Bible from this period also tells us that the decree against owning the Bible may not have been observed. Vincent Gillespie's recent work on the "post-Arundel" period argues that the career of Archbishop Chichele may be a more important consideration than Arundel's legislation for examining the production of literature in the fifteenth century that was dedicated to the renewal and reform of orthodoxy.[19] For Kate Crassons, "the vibrant life of medieval dramatic performance" provides an example of a "distinctive mode of vernacular theology" in which questions and issues thought to be polemical and dangerous were talked out in innovative ways, undisturbed by Arundel's decrees.[20] These scholars share the view that Arundel's legislation may not have had such a drastic effect on the vernacular theologies that were produced and read in the fifteenth century. What I would suggest is that Arundel's legislation can be seen as one response among many to the problem of heresy and crisis in Christian society. If people like Pecock were still looking for effective methods of combating heresy and fortifying orthodoxy in the mid–fifteenth century, we can be sure that Arundel's Constitutions were not entirely successful in wiping out the independent thought of the laity, that the crisis of heresy in the Christian community was not over, and, more importantly, that there was room for alternative thinking on ways of reinstating orthodoxy.

I would even suggest that there are certain resemblances between the sweeping changes that Arundel proposes and the sweeping changes that Pecock proposes. Pecock also thinks big. He is concerned not only with the spread of heresy but with laxity of devotion, basic misunderstanding of the faith among the majority of the laity, rampant superstition, singular practices that have no rational basis, and overwhelming disrespect for the learned clergy. He, too, looks for a solution to these threats to the health and vitality of the Christian community that will be just as powerful as Arundel's legislation in reinforcing the authority of the clergy and in wiping out error. His solution, however, comes in the form of a mass educational program, or what I will describe as the construction of a textual community centered on his books. Rather than placing certain topics out of bounds, Pecock invites all to contemplate them in a carefully structured and directed process of schooling in his corpus of instructional materials. In his system, members of the laity are challenged to think in new ways about religious faith and to apply their intellects in new and active ways to their belief system—a system that they have customarily absorbed passively. They are taught new means of expressing and engendering devotion for God. In short, the way that they think about and practice religion will be changed. Pecock's changes are in the form of education: a systematic, uniform, and universal program of education that will control problems like heresy and superstition without resort to censorship or repression.

Pecock thinks big when he mandates the reform of teaching and preaching in Christian society. He stridently calls for reform throughout his corpus, announcing that the time has come to usher in more productive methods of teaching, to change the way doctrine is presented to the laity, and to strengthen the rational foundations of belief among both clergy and laity. This renewal demands the participation of fellow clerics within the community, and Pecock is not particularly meek in asking for it. Indeed, he is intensely critical of the practices of other teachers and preachers. He says, for example, that it is "ful un-seemly" in preachers to present themselves as "reulers and reformers and enformers" of the lay people only to neglect their flock (*Folewer*, 10). This neglect stems from their abandon of "argumentis of resoun" (*Folewer*, 10). Those who neglect the teaching of moral philosophy abuse their "greet autorite and overte over the heerers" (*Folewer*, 10). This criticism of fellow divines echoes throughout Pecock's corpus. He does not mince words in criticizing the practices and learning of fellow clergy. For example, Pecock warns lay readers that they should not blindly rely on their teachers for their understanding of the nature of faith and law but should instead learn how to examine "pure certain groundis wherby it schal be certain that it is so feith or lawe" (*Folewer*, 34). The best way to avoid being "bigilid" is to demand more sophisti-cated teaching, "though men crie upon thee ful lowed, seying 'this is feith' and 'that is feith', and 'this is lawe' and 'that is lawe'" (*Folewer*, 34). It seems to me that in his eagerness to spread his forms of teach-ing, Pecock steps on the toes of other clerics like him in the London community. His frequent comments about his detractors, and his criti-cisms of their lack of learning, all reinforce the observation of Wendy Scase that Pecock's "enmities were to prove costly."[21] Scase argues that a "major motive behind Pecock's downfall was political," that the decision to try him for heresy was part of a larger effort to demon-strate the power of temporal princes over the church by exerting "royal authority over the archbishop and prelates in the cause of cor-recting a cleric."[22] Though the impetus for Pecock's downfall may have been the decision of the temporal authority to make an example of him in order to exalt the authority of the Lancastrian monarchy, it also seems clear that Pecock himself had created a strong opposition among clerics who were happy to support his prosecution.[23] Perhaps he would have had more support among his fellow clerics if he had tempered his criticism in his earnest zeal for reform. In his devotion to his project of revolutionizing Christian pedagogy, Pecock may have underestimated his opposition, or the power of his "inpugners whiche laboren by gile and wile to make her inpugnacioun seme good before the multitude of lay men, and at temporal lordis eeris, and at multi-tude of clerkis not scolid in divinite, or not profundely endewid in di-vinite" (*Donet*, 8). Having more support among the multitude of laymen, clerks, and temporal lords might have ensured a more secure future for Pecock's pedagogical initiatives.

Pecock makes it clear that we should take seriously this project of Christian pedagogy when he tells readers that it is divinely inspired. In his prologue to *The Reule of Crysten Religioun*, Reginald Pecock describes the dream vision that made him decide to write the book. He claims that he was visited by a multitude of beautiful ladies, who arranged themselves in seven companies and identified themselves as the daughters of God. These "ful comely and faire" women addressed Pecock in this way: "Man, we ben treuthis of universal philosophie comprehending lawe of kinde and lawe of feith. We ben out of the lond of resonable soulis longe time exilid. We ben thilke whiche schulen schewe to thee in desirose longing, and teche how thou schalt boothe knowe, serve and have thy final eende, perpetual joie and al thyn hertis feeding" (*Reule*, 32). Having told Pecock that their seven companies comprised all the learning and knowledge that he would need to live a proper spiritual life, as well as to "teche and counseile al othere to live cristenly," the lovely ladies told him that they wanted to win some lovers for God with the power of Pecock's pen (*Reule*, 34). They asked him to write a work that would give them textual form and so offer to vernacular readers a source of religious truth that would be so "ful and sufficient to almankinde" that no other study of "goostly philosophie and cristen divinite" would be necessary (*Reule*, 35). The resulting product was, of course, *The Reule of Crysten Religioun*, a book that educates Christian readers of late medieval England in the nature, benefits, punishments, and moral law of God, the wretchedness and wickedness of humanity, and remedies for mankind's sins and failings.

The contents of Pecock's surviving corpus of six vernacular religious books can be described in the same way, as a written record of these truths of universal philosophy "comprehending lawe of kinde and lawe of feith" (*Reule*, 32). Though other books in his oeuvre are written for more specific purposes, like correcting particular errors of belief, his works all share the goal of presenting to readers those truths that are necessary for our salvation, which we know by reason and by faith. Pecock tells us in the introduction to *The Reule of Crysten Religioun* that many of his books are written with the same purpose:

the *Reule* and "the othere bookis to this present book perteiningly knitte to and annexid," which include the *Bifore Crier, The Donet, The Filling of the Foure Tablis, The Book of Divine Office,* and *The Enchiridion,* as well as "othere mo bookis" that he lists elsewhere, offer an abundance of knowledge and instruction "which can not so esily be leerned in other bokes, neither in sermouns or prechingis, neither by mennis spekingis" (*Reule,* 9). To achieve this goal, of providing each individual reader with all the "kunning" he will need "forto be a good cristen man," and thus offering to lay readers a religious education that is unprecedented in its scope, Pecock spends a good part of his career, from the early 1430s to the late 1450s, producing vernacular writings on subjects such as the sacraments, the priesthood, the Bible, the writings of the church fathers, and God's moral law (*Reule,* 35). In addition to providing an immense resource of religious information, Pecock's writings train readers in rational modes of thought and argument. As he presents readers with knowledge about the soul, about sin, and about God's moral law, he educates readers in principles of logic and argumentation so that they can process and understand this knowledge rationally.

In their content, Pecock's books of religious instruction are similar in many ways to Thomas Aquinas's *Summa theologiae,* a vast encyclopedic work treating subjects such as the existence of God, the nature of the created world, the ultimate goal of human life, the nature of virtue and sin, free will, the nature of human emotion, and the sacraments. Pecock's works range over the same topics as Aquinas's *Summa,* under the seven main topics of the nature of God, God's benefits, God's punishments, God's moral law, man's wretchedness, man's wickedness, and remedies for man's wickedness. In the same way that Aquinas merges the philosophical teachings of Aristotle with the doctrine of the medieval church, Pecock brings cogent analysis of the moral life together with instruction on the sacraments and the articles of faith. Pecock's books admittedly are less complex than Aquinas's *Summa:* his section in the *Reule* on God's nature and essence focuses on God's qualities of goodness, infinity, and mercy, for example, without examining the finer points of God's existence, essence, and operations covered in the first book of the *Summa.* It is noteworthy, however, that both Pecock and Aquinas base their account of the moral life, not on the seven virtues, the seven vices, or other popular groupings, but on the order of being. Mark Johnson says that the moral section of Aquinas's *Summa*, the *Secunda pars*, was intended to answer questions of the "'how' and the 'why' of the moral life": "The goal of the *Secunda pars* was to answer those questions, by discovering some unifying notion that would encompass the moral life based rather upon the nature of the reality under consideration—the human person—than upon some preexistent order, traditionally handed on because of its link to, say, confession."[24] Pecock's moral teaching is similarly based on questions about how we know what we know about God, how God has blessed us with gifts and benefits, what makes us sin and indulge in vice, and what we can do to merit heaven.

Important differences between Pecock's approach to moral instruction and that of the *Secunda pars* of the *Summa* tell us that Pecock's project is not to simplify and translate the teachings of Aquinas. For example, Pecock's teaching is arranged differently from that of Aquinas: Pecock blends teaching on the sacraments with teaching of moral philosophy in his treatment of subjects like God's law, God's benefits, and God's nature, instead of treating the sacraments in a separate and final book. Despite these differences, however, there are extraordinary points of resemblance between Pecock's systematic approach to lay religious education and Aquinas's *Summa*. For example, as I suggest in chapter 5, both Aquinas and Pecock treat the moral life by establishing first principles and then abstracting from these principles more specific rules of conduct. Though Pecock's teaching on God's moral law is not organized into categories corresponding to the virtues of faith, hope, charity, prudence, justice, fortitude, and temperance, he covers the same particular subjects, like usury, worship, and friendship, within his own system. The scholastic method of dialectical inquiry in Aquinas's *Summa*, described as "the basic analytical method applied to all areas of study and used to elucidate the meaning of textual points, to harmonize seeming contradictions and to adjudicate logically between differing interpretations of matters arising from a text," is also featured in Pecock's program for lay education.[25] As readers pass from the *Donet* to the *Reule* and finally to the *Folewer*, as the moral instruction becomes more detailed and sophisticated, alternative approaches to particular issues and alternative interpretations of matters arising from scripture are considered and brought to bear on Pecock's own teaching. Jeremy Catto argues that "most of what Pecock taught is the standard orthodox teaching of the schools, given a Thomist direction by his insistence on the primacy of the intellect."[26] The similarities between the *Summa* and the interlocking system formed by the *Reule*, the *Donet*, and the *Folewer* make Pecock look like a fifteenth-century scholastic thinker, drawing on authoritative traditions of teaching from the academic world to provide the laity with a new way of thinking about Christian belief and conduct.

Regrettably, there is not enough space in this study to do justice to the complicated question of the influence of Aquinas and other scholastic thinkers on Pecock's corpus of vernacular writings. I limit myself in this book to a brief comparison in chapter 5 of the approach to moral instruction in Pecock's pedagogical system and in Aquinas's *Summa*; a fuller examination of the sources of Pecock's moral instruction will be part of a book-length study I have begun on moral philosophy in the literature and the schools of late medieval England.

Though a careful examination of the relationship between moral philosophy in the *Summa* and in Pecock's corpus cannot be carried out here, it is useful to keep in mind the similarities in scale between Pecock's resources for vernacular instruction and Aquinas's *Summa*. Both offer comprehensive, wide-ranging instruction on everything a Christian needs to know about doctrine and devotion; what makes Pecock so innovative is that he makes this knowledge accessible to lay readers who lacked the kind of training in the arts that university students would have had before they learned moral philosophy and theology through works like Aristotle's *Ethics*, Aquinas's commentary on the *Ethics*, and the *Sentences* of Peter Lombard. Indeed, I would suggest that Pecock's educational corpus constitutes an attempt to transfer the rudiments of a university education in the arts to the vernacular, through his instruction on terminology, on rules of logic, and on the syllogism, and through his attempt to condense the most important teaching on Christian morality and doctrine in his books. Such a project would have uses beyond the streets of London: Pecock reminds us in several places that his books are intended not just for the laity but also for university students. His books, as they travel back and forth, will help to blur the boundary between the lay world and the academy, providing knowledge for both intellectually minded laymen and "clerkis being yonge biginners in scole of divinete" or "clerkis not leernid moche in comoun philosophie, in metephisik and in the highest party of divinite" (*Reule*, 86). For Oxford scholars engaged in the study of civil law or medicine, for example, or for undergraduates in the faculty of arts who would not complete an MA or go on to further studies in the faculty of theology, Pecock's books would act as useful primers on philosophy and theology. They would also provide accessible introductions for those just starting out in the study of theology. They would help to round out the studies of "othere clerkis of othere facultees not having time and leisour to studie in highest metaphisik and divinite" (*Reule*, 86), or, in other words, of other students who would not have time to pursue the same course of studies that Pecock pursued at Oxford, first in natural philosophy, moral philosophy, and metaphysics, and then in the Bible, Lombard's *Sentences*, and commentaries on the *Sentences* by theologians such as Aquinas, to earn his MA probably in 1416 and his Bachelor of Theology from Oriel College by 1424.[27] The information provided in the *Reule* on God and "persoonis in godhede" constitutes "scole ynough for ever" and is perfect training for those who seek doctrine in order to "be stirid to love god and to have fervent wil forto serve god" (*Reule*, 86).

It can be argued that Pecock capitalizes on current trends in Oxford's faculty of theology in his efforts to transfer an entire discipline of thought into the vernacular for diverse readers interested in learning doctrine that would increase their love for God. In his work on the theological curriculum at Oxford University, Catto notes that practical moral theology was the going concern in the fifteenth century. He says that this period was not one of great innovation at Oxford: "There is little evidence of the engagement of minds in theological controversy which had been obvious when Scotus, Bradwardine or Wyclif had lectured in the schools."[28] Pecock's own corpus of practical moral theology was likely influenced by these currents at Oxford: rather than engaging in theological speculation, he too focuses on practical questions about the moral life that were relevant to lay readers. These practical questions were the focus of study among monks, friars, and parish clergy, many of whom would pass on this learning to the lay population in the form of sermons. Catto remarks that the "moral and topical questions" that interested theologians at Oxford in the fifteenth century would have given "their academic work, especially if it were diffused in sermons, a broad social relevance."[29] Pecock took this initiative one step further by providing books of instruction that enabled the laity to study for themselves "the accumulated pastoral theology of the schools," including knowledge of the sacraments, faith, prayer, contemplation, virtue, and vice.[30]

The books that Pecock offers to lay readers, constituting a comprehensive guide to the Christian faith, are like nothing else available in the vernacular in fifteenth-century England. The third purpose of this book is to assess the position that Pecock's vernacular writings occupy in the context of late medieval reading culture. I am interested primarily in what Pecock has to say about the role that reading plays in the spiritual and intellectual lives of the laity and in religious reform in late medieval England. I am fascinated, in particular, by the fact that Pecock's corpus of religious books offers something new to late medieval reading culture, something that partly grows out of inherited ideas from the scholastic period and from fourteenth-century writers like Walter Hilton but partly emerges as an entirely new solution to problems of heresy and laxity of devotion among the laity. In this book, I examine what Pecock tells us about the role his books will—and should—play in the lives of his intended audience of lay readers, and I argue that this should open our eyes to the diversity of opinion in this period about the shape religious reform could take, about what was possible for, and appropriate for, lay readers, and about how the reading of books could revitalize and stabilize religious devotion in a culture that was heading toward Reformation.

One of Pecock's particularly interesting contributions to late medieval reading culture, for example, is his notion that the private, silent reading of the individual layman and laywoman fosters an engagement with "communal structures" rather than disengagement.[31] As I argue in chapters 2 and 3, Pecock's project of invigorating Christian society as a whole starts with the training of each individual in theology, moral philosophy, and rational modes of thought. While he advises "alle thy cristen peple" to take his *Reule of Crysten Religioun* "with hisse purtenauncis," or companion books, "into use of ful bisy, ech day studying, leerning and comuning and afterward thereupon re-membring, and if not in ech day, yitt in holy daies, and that as bisili as peple ben in werk daies y-occupied aboute worldis winning" (*Reule*, 13), he does not mean for readers to neglect the "leeful occupaciouns aftir that men ben therto by goddis grace able, callid and assigned," such as "marchaundising for the comoun profite" (*Donet*, 214). As Cynthia Baule points out, scholarly debate over the growth of private, as opposed to public, reading in late medieval England tends to em-phasize that private reading is "abstract, silent, and disengaged with personal interaction."[32] Private reading fosters the growth of interi-ority and self-reflection, while public reading brings members of a community together through the warmth of "human contact seen in the relationship between speaker and hearer."[33] Just as Baule suggests that Capgrave's *Life of Saint Katharine* "complicates the distinction between public and private reading," making it clear that the "relation-ship between the oral and written can only be understood through the investigation of specific texts and contexts," I suggest in chapter 3 that Pecock's advocacy of very bookish spiritual and pedagogical practices among the laity does not necessarily result in their withdrawal from the outside world or the separation of the individual from the com-munity.[34] Rather, private study in Pecock's corpus stimulates the growth of self-reflection and self-examination among lay readers at the same time as it ties individuals to the community, fostering com-munication and human contact.

For example, though his readers can meditate on his teaching in the "solitude of private chambers," their engagement with the self is followed by and fulfilled in dialogue, discussion, and "felawlik comu-nicacioun" among members of the community, which fosters "group identity."[35] This communal engagement, which I discuss in chapter 7, is possible because Pecock's books are designed to train readers in ra-tional modes of thought and argument, creating a level playing field for a sort of academic discussion between clerical and lay members of the community. It is significant that the role models that Pecock pro-vides for his lay readers are learned clerics who devote serious labor to study for the purpose of spreading God's truths in service to the Christian community, rather than contemplative monks whose reading is a form of withdrawal from the world. For Pecock's readers, solitary reading is not a "prelude to an immediate encounter with the Divine" but a prelude to dynamic human interaction and vital discussion within the community of the faithful.[36]

Furthermore, Pecock's readers are not isolated or distanced from Pecock himself in the experience of solitary study. Because Pecock's personality and presence inform the text to such an extent through his interjections, directions to readers, references to his own experiences, and bold assertions about the difference between the texts that he has authored and other inferior books, I would argue that his writing does not foster a major separation between author and audience. The voice of the teacher is constantly heard, guiding the lay reader through the reading experience; as I suggest in the conclusion to this book, this may be a conscious effort to prevent the lay reader from confronting the text in an undirected way and an effort to control the reading process. Pecock's constant presence in the text encourages a connection between author and reader, preventing the reader from feeling a sense of disengagement and distance in the solitary reading experience. Pecock's emphasis on the value of solitary, bookish spiritual practices among the laity is particularly interesting, considering that he is writing at a time when lay studiousness and lay reading of vernacular religious texts created "anxieties" among Pecock's contemporaries.[37] Directing the lay folk to study and learning could open the door to uncontrolled lay speculation on religious doctrine: Karen Winstead observes the appearance of "anti-intellectual currents" in late medieval England, noting that some churchmen "worried that modeling intellectual piety to a laity not equipped to pursue it might lead to heretical speculation."[38] She adds, "Amateur lay 'theologians,' however orthodox, might undermine ecclesiastical authority through their pesky questions."[39] Pecock does not share the anxiety of some of his contemporaries that private reading among the laity leads to the loss of clerical control over the formation of Christian belief. Indeed, he suggests that solitary study of the right kinds of texts can bring individual members of the laity back under the supervision, authority, and control of the learned clergy, allowing the clergy to shape the development of faith and understanding in subtle yet powerful ways. Learning may provoke lay questioning, but the provision of a uniform corpus of teaching materials on the matters most important to know also means an opportunity to direct lay speculation and lay thought in productive ways, and thereby to provide stronger roots for orthodox belief.

It is my view that Pecock's books are designed to help construct a community of articulate and intellectual lay readers who will develop certain habits of thought and behavior such as an aptitude for learning, respect for learned clergymen, and the development of dialogue and amicable relations within the community. I believe that when Pecock looks around him, at members of his London community, at the reading material that is currently circulating, and at the state of lay devotion, he sees an opportunity to change the way things are done and thought in terms of sharing God's word, structuring piety, and understanding religious truth. He sees a moment that is ripe with possibility and ready for change. He sees the chance to woo individuals to God in new ways and to create different norms of behavior and belief through the production of a vast corpus of materials that will form the basis for a new kind of religious community. These kinds of ambitions are rampant in the century after Pecock's death as Catholic and Protestant reformers alike envision new ways of structuring patterns of belief and forms of conduct. Pecock's own ambitions show that this kind of dynamism of reformist thought was not lacking in the fifteenth century.

Since the concept of textual community informs my reading of Pecock's works, I should clarify what I mean by it before proceeding further. This term, coined by Brian Stock, has been variously applied by medievalists to the literature of medieval England. While Stock invented the term to "interpret the beliefs and activities of small, isolated, heretical and reformist groups in medieval Europe," it has since been used to describe the communal gestation of a work as well as a kind of subculture of people who are brought together by virtue of owning or having access to a certain book.[40] For Felicity Riddy, for example, "A textual community may be a social community, but it is also the community of those who do not know one another but who read the same book; a community of the living and the dead."[41] For Stock, textual communities are actual groups of people who recognize themselves as such, "microsocieties organized around the common understanding of a script," who normally see themselves "as small units within the whole: they are the dissenters and reformers, whose social dramas are played out against the backdrop of a larger world."[42] According to my reading of Stock's work, a textual community is a group of people brought together by their common interpretation or reading of a particular text; this interpretation may be suggested to them by a charismatic leader, an *interpres* figure, whose literacy enables him to understand the text and then "pass his message on verbally to others."[43] The interpretation becomes the common possession of the group itself, however, through the discourse of the group. Stock writes that textual communities take their authority from this common understanding rather than from the inherited traditions of the past. Members of the group understand their chosen text—the Gospels, perhaps—in a way that differs sharply from how it has been read before. For Stock, it is this break with traditional norms that distinguishes a textual community from a reading community: the differing interpretations of a textual community "issue in rule-bound patterns of behaviour that break with what has come before."[44] As Stock writes, "By a process of absorption and reflection the behavioural norms of the group's other members were eventually altered."[45] The members are self-consciously part of a group, and they feel themselves to be different from others who understand texts like the Bible according to traditionally and perhaps institutionally established meanings; their own interpretations of the text justify and authenticate different types of group experience.[46] The connection of one member to another, through a common understanding of a text, transcends "backgrounds, professional allegiances, and antecedent beliefs."[47] Paul Strohm suggests that the Lollards like those who gathered with John Claydon to read and hear the tract *Lanterne of Light* are a "splendid example" of Stock's textual community.[48]

There are some fundamental differences between Stock's definition of textual community and my use of his concept to better understand Pecock's project. While Stock is interested in real textual communities, men and women brought together by contact with particular texts, I am interested here in an imagined, ideal textual community—that conceived by Pecock as the intended audience for his corpus. In chapter 1, in my investigation of what we know about

Pecock's audience, I distinguish between this imagined community and the actual readers of his historical audience, using the concepts of the intended reader, the historical reader, and the implied reader. This investigation is speculative, in large part, because we know so little about the reception of Pecock's works.[49] Unfortunately, I can offer no historical accounts of members of Pecock's textual community who were interrogated by authorities and found to be influenced in important ways by common interpretations of his texts. I can, however, present both internal and historical evidence that helps us to understand some of the factors that may have influenced the reception of Pecock's books, and some of the possible responses that his works may have elicited. As I will note in chapter 1, Pecock's envisioned textual community is much broader than the particular community of London merchants that we can definitely connect with him. When Pecock declares that his works must be read by all Christian people, it is clear that he does not see his readers as a small "unit" within the whole of Christian society.[50] His intention is to reform Christian society as a whole, starting at the level of the individual. My use of the concept of textual community also differs from Stock's to take account of the fact that Pecock's textual community is more textual. In Stock's definition of textual community, only one literate is necessary—the *interpres* who understands the text and passes on his understanding of it to the other members of the community.[51] Pecock's envisioned textual community is far more text based: his readers are the members of the group, and though Pecock envisions that his books will have a life beyond the private study, in the form of oral readings and dialogue within the community, he is ultimately determined that even poor members of society should have access to copies (at least in the form of extracts) of his books. Oral transmission alone is not what Pecock intends.

As I demonstrate, however, Pecock's envisioned textual community has much in common with Stock's definition, and this is why I find his concept so useful. First, Pecock's readers are to be brought together by their reading of his books. These books offer an alternative source of religious knowledge that is partly a reading or interpretation of two other texts: the Bible and the book of reason. These two sourcebooks provide the *materia* for the creation of Pecock's *Reule of Crysten Religioun:* Pecock tells his readers that the writing of this book was inspired by the daughters of God, truths of universal philosophy "comprehending lawe of kinde and lawe of faith" (*Reule*, 32). Throughout his instruction in this book, on the seven essential matters of religious truth, Pecock is careful to specify which truths are rooted in the book of reason and which are rooted in the Bible. The law of kind, or book of reason, offers truths relating to God's moral law that we can discover solely through the use of our rational faculties: these include our knowledge of man's moral nature, the nature of the intellect and the soul, the kind of behavior that God expects from mankind, and our natural inclination to search for God—all truths that were discovered by the ancients like Aristotle. The Bible offers truths "into whos knowing men mowe not come by laboure of natural resoning, whiche trouthis and articles ben therefore knowun of us by feith oonly" (*Reule*, 10): these include knowledge about the nature of heaven, about Christ's life on earth, and about the sacraments, which God shares with us through the Bible. The doctrine of the Trinity is an example of a truth regarding God's nature that we cannot discover on our own: to teach the matter of "the thre persoonis and the propirtees of tho thre personnis in godhede," Pecock must "bringe forth auctorite of feith writun in holi scripture" because this is a matter in which "resoun may make no proof of certeinte or of sufficient likelihood if al feith be deducid and leid aside" (*Reule*, 23). Pecock interweaves truths from both sources in his treatment of subjects like God's benefits, God's punishments, and God's moral law. For example, in his discussion of God's benefits, he directs readers first to the knowledge about benefits that can be gleaned from the book of reason and second to the knowledge that can be derived only from the Bible. By transmitting to readers the most essential truths that God has transmitted to us through the book of reason and the Bible, Pecock provides a comprehensive resource of knowledge for a full Christian education. In terms of their content, then, it can be said that Pecock's books do not contain radically new interpretations of Christian belief or moral philosophy; instead, they condense the most important truths for Christians to know from the two most authoritative books available.

What makes Pecock's works innovative, instead, is his organization of this knowledge. As I noted above, for example, Aquinas, in his *Summa theologiae*, saves the sacraments for the last book, while Pecock treats them variously under the topics of God's moral law, which we know by faith, and God's benefits, which we know by faith. Pecock organizes moral teaching into a new system of four tables, replacing the Decalogue, which presents doctrine in an insufficient manner. The articles of faith are also presented differently in Pecock's system: while the institutional church delivers articles of faith to the laity in a "nakid forme," Pecock provides rational evidences that help readers to "conceive, perceive, and trowe the same thing" (*Reule*, 91). By condensing the most important matters for all to know in a kind of *summa theologiae*, which asks lay readers to learn and understand religion differently, Pecock proposes a break with traditional teaching of Christian doctrine: the four tables, the seven matters, and the teaching of articles of faith completely reform the way that moral precepts and Christian faith are learned by the laity. For example, Pecock's readers learn the twelve articles of the Creed from Pecock's teaching on matters such as God's nature and benefits. The articles of belief in the Creed "touching the godhede and touching his benefete in making creatures" are taught in various different places in Pecock's books, according to his own system of seven matters of Christian knowledge (*Donet*, 103). Pecock takes a completely new approach to the organization of doctrine and the articles of belief, offering readers sources for learning Christian behavior and belief that are different from the "comoun rekening of the vii deedly sinnis" (*Donet*, 105), the teaching on the "vii giftis of the holy goost," the teaching of "sacramentis of cristis ordinaunce in the newe lawe" (*Donet*, 117), and the "comoun foorme of the x comaundementis" (*Donet*, 145), all of which must be replaced by Pecock's forms, despite the fact that these "doctrines, scolis and prechingis ben so famose, and so moche apprised and sett by of clerkis and of the lay partie" (*Donet*, 102).

Passing on a message, in textual form, from his own understanding of the Bible and the book of reason, Pecock can be seen as a kind of charismatic *interpres* figure who presents to other members of the textual community the truths that they need to know in new forms.

When the universal truths of philosophy and faith visit Pecock in a dream vision described above, they enable him to hear a message, as "so many reformers, heretics, and mystics" did.[52] What he hears is not exactly new doctrine, or truths that diverge in a major way from orthodox belief. What Pecock does differently is to present these truths to lay readers, whose reading material does not customarily contain extensive teachings on moral philosophy, such as teachings on the passions, on moral vices, on the various powers of the soul, on involuntary and voluntary deeds, on "meenal" virtues, on the distinction between "kunningal" virtue and moral virtue, and on the difference between "sciencial" faith and "opinional" faith. He also provides detailed teaching on the Christian faith, on theological questions including the difference between "grace moving or stiring" and "grace allowing or accepting" (*Reule*, 1), the importance of Christ's sacrifice for securing man's salvation, the relations between the persons of the Godhead, and the difference between making amends for sin and moving God, in his infinite mercy, to pardon sin. Pecock's task is to inscribe truths of philosophy and faith in vernacular books, offering readers a new way of understanding the Christian codes of conduct that they have been taught through systems like the seven deadly sins and the Ten Commandments. When the universal truths tell Pecock to approach the teaching of religion in this new way, they assure him that it will help him to win more lovers for God. Pecock's divinely approved rational treatment of doctrine must help to create a common understanding of doctrine and faith among the laity that breaks with the inherited traditions of the past.

Pecock also breaks new ground in the emphasis he puts on his readers' intellectual development. Rather than relying passively on the opinions of the *auctores* and the teachings of the church, readers must learn to work through processes of argumentation themselves in order to distinguish between heterodox and orthodox belief: we can see Pecock insisting on this approach to religious instruction in his lack of citations of authoritative texts and his extended arguments from reason. The authority of the community comes from training in the book of reason rather than from inherited interpretations of religious truths. Though the beliefs of members may not be different from orthodox doctrine, the way of arriving at these beliefs, through logical analysis rather than passive acceptance and memorization of doctrine provided by the clergy, is different.

Pecock's readers will feel themselves to be part of a group by learning his seven matters and four tables alongside one another, in schools, in public congregations, in small councils, and even in the home. As I suggest in chapter 2, Pecock's plans for formal lay education in his corpus create the setting in which the textual community will come together as a group. His readers are invited to be self-conscious of their participation within the group: Pecock often makes clear the distinction between the kind of person who is a "scoler" in his corpus (*Donet*, 126)—someone who is considered part of a group of "greet wittid and leerned lay men" (*Donet*, 161) or of "wise and discreet cristen peple" (*Reule*, 365)—and the kind of person who is mired in error, caught up in superstition, or idling in the infantile stages of intellectual development (*Folewer*, 13). Scholarly readers are literate, capable, and accustomed to thinking through difficult matters, and Pecock never ceases to insist upon this readerly identity throughout his introductions to his books. His readers' backgrounds, antecedent beliefs, and professional allegiances are transcended in their textually organized education: Pecock's scheme for education embraces poor men who can afford only extracts of his books (*Donet*, 177) and rich men of the clergy and laity who can get involved in both the learning process and the production of copies of Pecock's books, "yvel and weel disposid men of the lay partie" (*Reule*, 19), men and women, boys and girls.

It is important to note, however, that these people may not share the sense of group identity to the same degree as Lollard communities that Shannon McSheffrey has studied. McSheffrey notes that individuals in these groups were "connected to one another by their common participation in clandestine gatherings, who willfully and collectively differentiated themselves from the majority (and, in their eyes, godless) Church."[53] She warns, though, that "the cohesiveness of these groups of heretics should not be exaggerated" and that many "drifted in and out."[54] Members of Pecock's textual community are invited to willfully differentiate themselves from a number of godless others—those who have been misled by Wyclif and his followers, those who say their prayers like inarticulate babies and old men, those who spew passages of the Bible without proper understanding, and those who do not even understand the meanings of the words they throw around in debate with clerics. Pecock encourages readers to see distinctions between the well-trained, rational reader and the foolish, dull-witted, even godless other.

Finally, Pecock proposes spiritual and intellectual practices that constitute changes and refinements to everyday ways of doing things, from prayer to public worship to communal interactions. As I suggest in chapter 5, the processes of learning in Pecock's books are a kind of "ritual of self-definition," especially in terms of the way that readers are expected to learn scholastic modes of thought and rational argumentation. Stock writes that these rituals of self-definition are "processes of conversion, initiation, and confirmation" that help to form the ideas "that make a group cohere."[55] In the case of Pecock's textual community, systematic training in his corpus, through various levels of study, is a kind of process of conversion that turns the lay reader into a "scoler" in divinity. Pecock's texts also propose new forms of communication and cooperation between lay and clerical members of the community. Pecock attempts to foster the "horizontal energies of group consciousness" by bringing laity and clergy together in the activity of learning—energies that are "essential" to Stock's definition of textual community.[56]

By understanding how Pecock's envisioned textual community works, we can better understand how lay reading practices can revitalize and stabilize orthodox religion by affecting modes of thought, patterns of behavior, forms of communal engagement, the development of interiority and self-reflection, the formation of individual identity, and the development of group identity. Lay reading practices, rooted in Pecock's corpus of vernacular materials, can change the structure of Christian belief and practice. The intention of this book is to draw together these insights, offered both directly and indirectly throughout Pecock's writings, about the power of books and learning to change the very fabric of the Christian community.

The seven chapters that form the body of this book focus on the following subjects: Pecock's historical and implied textual communities, the structure and foundations of the textual community, the nature of reading practices within the textual community, the books at the center of the textual community, and the relations among members of the textual community. The first chapter offers observations on the nature of Pecock's audience and the possible responses that his books may have elicited. The second chapter is on the educational system and processes on which the textual community depends: I examine the significance of Pecock's plan for systematic, uniform, and formal religious education. The third chapter looks at the place that this theological training occupies in the lives of lay readers by analyzing Pecock's treatment of the mixed life. The fourth, fifth, and sixth chapters focus on the uses of books. Chapter 4 is about the role of Pecock's books in the devotional life, particularly in practices of ritual reading and meditative reading. The fifth and sixth chapters consider the structure, nature, and aims of two very different reading experiences by examining, respectively, the role of the book of reason and of the Bible in Pecock's textual community. Chapter 5, on the book of reason, considers the role that Pecock's books play in training readers to learn God's moral law. Chapter 6 describes the much more limited role and use of the Bible in the textual community. In the seventh chapter, I focus more broadly on Pecock's understanding of the relationship between the clergy and the laity within his idealized textual community. The book concludes by considering the significance of Pecock's oeuvre within his cultural moment.

Perhaps what interests me most, in this study of Pecock's vernacular theology, is Pecock's sense of the power of books like his to influence relations in society, to change belief systems, to shape behavioral patterns, and to alter modes of cognition; what interests me is the way that his books are set up to achieve all of this. I argue that Pecock's attempt to educate lay readers is more than an effort to supply religious instruction: it is an attempt to establish and unite a community of readers around his books, to influence the way that these readers behave and relate to one another, and to change the way that they understand the world and their place in it. Indeed, Pecock is convinced that conformity to orthodoxy and religious renewal depend on this very textual, bookish project: it is his aim to harness the power of texts to change the way that the laity conceives of religion.

Pecock's Audience

This chapter considers the question of Pecock's audience. As Paul Strohm notes in his work on Chaucer's audience, there is general acceptance within literary studies that "a literary work achieves its meaning in the interaction between a text on the one hand and an audience on the other" but that any discussion of audience must first consider the question: "*Which* audience?"[1] This chapter examines evidence for Pecock's intended audience, his historical or actual audience, and his implied audience. The intended audience is perhaps most easily identified, because Pecock provides lengthy prologues to his works identifying the readers he is attempting to reach. Within the category of his intended audience, there may be a difference between the audience Pecock *hopes* to reach and the audience he knows he can reach. The historical audience is harder to reconstruct, since readers of Pecock's works do not appear on record. We lack documentation like wills that could tell us about patterns of ownership, and we lack evidence of Pecock's possible influence on subsequent publications of vernacular theology. Indeed, we lack most of the books that Pecock claims to have written, and we can only speculate about the identity of the *opuscula* referred to in his trial documents. The performance of various searches for Pecock's books in the province of Canterbury and at Oxford may be the reason why so few books remain, and it seems likely that anyone who successfully hid Pecock's books from the authorities would have been sure to avoid making reference to these forbidden books in official documents such as wills.[2] It is difficult, therefore, to get a sense of Pecock's reception among an actual audience. My procedure will be to investigate the question of his historical audience by balancing two kinds of evidence: Pecock's direct observations of the tendencies and capacities of London lay readers, and historical evidence documenting Pecock's involvement with various kinds of people in London society. This analysis will point in the end to a possible or likely actual audience for Pecock's corpus among the London mercers, and it will briefly explore some of the factors that influenced this audience's "horizon of expectations."[3] Finally, I investigate Pecock's implied audience, defined by Strohm as "a hypothetical construct, the sum of all the author's assumptions about the persons he or she is addressing."[4] Implied readers are those who will respond to the work in an ideal fashion—those who can follow its directions, share its assumptions, get its jokes, and understand its allusions. The investigation of implied audience will draw on Iser's theory of aesthetic response, which "focuses on how a piece of literature impacts on its implied readers and elicits a response"—I will examine what kinds of responses are elicited by Pecock's habit of multiplying illustrations of moral truths.[5]

Intended Audiences

We meet Pecock's intended readers in his prologues. His opening statements divide his corpus into two different kinds of books intended for two different types of audience. *The Repressor of Overmuch Blaming of the Clergy* and *The Book of Faith* open with polemic, addressing members of the laity who have descended into errors that include criticizing the clergy, refusing to accept the clergy's teachings on faith, and refusing to accept any teachings other than the Bible on moral matters. These errors belong to a group among the lay people that he labels Lollards: they are the holdouts from a "wickidli enfectid scole of heresie among the lay peple in Ynglond which is not yit conquerid" (*Repressor*, 89). Pecock says in conclusion to the first part of the *Repressor* that he writes it "for to convicte and overcome tho erring persoones of the lay peple whiche ben clepid Lollardis, and forto make hem leve her errouris" (128). Similarly, *The Book of Faith* is written to draw back, "fro lengthe and breed of erring, and of untrewe wyde wandring," the "sones and doughtris" of God's "hole chirche" (*BF*, 114). Did such Lollards still exist in the London community, as Pecock suggests? According to Wendy Scase, "London was often named by Lollard suspects as the place where they learned their heresy. James Wyllis, tried in 1462, said he had lived in the London parish of St Martin in the Fields."[6] Anne Sutton writes, "In 1428–29 the clergy were promoting a crusade against the Hussite heretics and there were extensive investigations of Lollard sympathizers. The particular heretical assertions under investigation were that no Christian should fight or kill the heretics of Bohemia, and that all property should be held in common." Sutton says that the trial of a London priest who was imprisoned for these particular beliefs after a number of authorities from a number of parishes testified against him would have been talked about widely in the London community: "The households of mercers in these parishes must have talked of little else." Sutton remarks, "It is worth noting that these investigations occurred just before Pecock's arrival at Whittington College in 1431; they may have persuaded him of the need to convince the London laity of their errors."[7] If trials like this one reminded Pecock that London had not been cleansed of Lollard error, then we can surmise that there was a real audience in London of people he describes in the prologues to his polemical works.

Pecock's other remaining books of instruction, *The Reule of Crysten Religioun*, *The Donet*, *The Folewer*, and *The Pore Mennyis Mirroure*, are for a wider audience. Pecock intends these books for both "weel disposid cristen men of the lay partie" and "yvel disposid men of the lay partie" (*Reule*, 19). They have a broader goal of teaching all Christians in belief and practice and are not limited to those with heretical leanings. A wide range of people are embraced in the prologues to the works listed above: Pecock aspires to embrace "alle . . . cristen peple" within his readership, and he reminds us in more than one prologue that he expects a diverse audience of varying abilities, literacy, and intentions (*Reule*, 13). Interestingly, this diverse audience includes clergy as well as laity, children as well as adults, women as well as men, and the poor as well as the rich. It is difficult to determine whether Pecock's emphasis on universality points to an audience that he dreamed of reaching or an audience that he knew he could reach. I believe that Pecock was indeed ambitious and set high goals for his works, but I also believe that it was possible for his works to reach such an audience in fifteenth-century England, given the increased access to cheaper books facilitated by "the vital presence of a flourishing book trade in London during the century leading up to Caxton," the rising interest among wealthy Londoners in providing schools for the education for children, the increased efforts to provide books for poorer clergy through the institution of libraries like that at the Guildhall, the records of book ownership confirming interests among both men and women in religious books, and Pecock's own connections to poorer members of the London community through his involvement, to be discussed shortly, with some important London institutions.[8] I would suggest, therefore, that Pecock was a dreamer with his two feet firmly planted on the ground and that we should take him at his word when he talks about the universality of his intended audience.

Historical and Implied Audiences

Knowing that Pecock intended his works for a broad, inclusive reading public, we must ask whether this vision had any basis in reality. What kinds of people read the works that Pecock wrote in London from the 1430s to the 1450s? How literate were they? What sorts of expectations and knowledge did they bring to bear on their spiritual reading practices? Unfortunately, as I have already said, we do not have historical evidence that allows us to confirm whether Pecock's actual, historical audience included the wide range of people he intended to reach. We cannot confirm, for example, whether his works were actually read by children in London's grammar schools at St. Paul's, St. Martin le Grand, St. Mary Arches, St. Anthony's Hospital, and St. Dunstan in the East.[9] It is easier to get a grasp on the readers that Pecock tells us more about: these are the members of the London laity that he has observed through personal contact. I suggest that an important source of information about Pecock's actual historical audience is Pecock himself: Pecock's corpus of religious writings in the vernacular is rare in that it contains a profusion of remarks and reflections about what readers do with texts, what kinds of texts readers prefer, and what habits readers have developed. But how should we read such statements about the capacities, dispositions, and tendencies of the readers he envisions? Certainly they can be read, at one level, as an effort to shape the ideal reader. Poking fun at bad readers and mocking the wrong sorts of reading practices serves to exclude certain kinds of readers and include readers who will receive the work in a way that Pecock can control to some extent. Reflections and directions on reading might be Pecock's way of limiting his audience to people "in the know," those who already see themselves as the critical, orthodox, and intellectually engaged readers he hopes to train. These statements can be read, then, as an effort to distinguish his audience members from other kinds of readers in order to create a sense of solidarity among his readers as they embrace Pecock's particular way of doing things; perhaps comments that praise certain modes of reading and study could prompt feelings of loyalty to his methods of teaching belief and behavior through the four tables and the seven truths.

However, it is also possible to attempt to reconstruct, as much as possible, Pecock's historical audience by comparing some of the internal evidence about readers and reading practices with historical evidence for the reading public in fifteenth-century London. In a recent article entitled "The Canterbury Tales and London Club Culture," Derek Pearsall addresses the complicated question of what we know about Chaucer's actual audience—its nature, tastes, and practices—while stressing that scholars investigating the historical reality of a writer's audience must find a balance between internal evidence of "implied audience" and external, historical evidence.[10] The overt, direct comments that Pecock makes about laymen he has observed in his community must be balanced with relevant external evidence drawn from currently proliferating studies of London, by scholars such as Wendy Scase, Caroline Barron, Anne Sutton, Vincent Gillespie, Amy Appleford, and scholars working on the "Geographies of Orthodoxy" project, Ryan Perry and Stephen Kelly. The current surge of scholarly interest in medieval London is increasing our understanding of the social and intellectual context in which Pecock produced most of his writings for the laity and where he continued to work even once he had accepted the bishoprics of St. Asaph in 1444 and Chichester in 1450.[11] My purpose here is not to add to our knowledge of Pecock's historical context but to gather relevant details from existing historical research about his intellectual and social environment, in order to tease out some of the implications of what Pecock has to say about his audience: I sketch a picture of an actual historical audience of literate men, probably many of whom were mercers, who worked closely with representatives of the clergy on projects for civic development. I suggest that despite Pecock's insistence on the importance of the individual reader's task of committing himself to serious study, we must also consider that members of the reading public in fifteenth-century London did not encounter books in a void; rather, they experienced books in a particular social and historical environment, within a discursive space of personal relationships, discussion, debate, and "comuning" (*Reule*, 13).

After sketching the best possible picture of Pecock's actual reading public, I turn to a second way of assessing his implied audience. In this final section, I look more closely at the kind of evidence Pearsall investigates: Pearsall discovers a particular tone of voice in some of Chaucer's pronouncements about general truths and off-the-cuff asides, which seem to be directed at "a clubbable coterie of men . . . with appeals to their way of thinking, their prejudices, their sense of humour."[12] I will examine Pecock's use of illustrations and examples with this question in mind to see if it is possible to detect any signs that the readership implied by the text can be identified with particular groups in London society.

There is internal evidence to suggest that Pecock's actual audience included London mercers. Arguing that books containing difficult matter should be accessible to laymen, Pecock observes that those who "take homlines with mercers of london" will be persuaded that such men are capable of handling truths about the Trinity (*Reule*, 94). He says, "If a man bise hym silf weel aboute, he schal weel knowe that the lay peple muste nedis and schulen be drive to forto conceive herder and derker trouthis with harder and darker evidencis in plees of lond, in plees of dette and of trespace, in rekeningis to be maad of receivers and rente gaderers in the account of an audit, yhe in bargeyns making of greet marchaundisis and in rekeningis making therupon" (93–94). These observations suggest a familiarity with the business world of mercery, and they suggest that Pecock had mercers in mind when producing his corpus of educational materials. On a side note, I think that Pecock's use of the word *homlines* to describe a relationship between clergy and laymen is particularly fascinating, since it suggests that familiarity, intimacy, and friendliness between clergy and laymen have an important role in shaping the contents of religious writings in the vernacular and determining what sorts of works will be put into circulation. A similar statement about the subtlety of wit that "ech wiis greet mercer" must employ in "rekeningis and bargeyns making" indicates that Pecock's reading public may have included mercers (21). Finally, Pecock's observation that merchants' servants have been reading his books implies that his books had certainly made their way into mercers' households by the time he was writing the *Folewer* in the early 1450s. The son says, "Now late in Londoun a book of yowre writing which the kunningist and wiisist clerkis in Ynglond maken ful mich of and preisen it mich, and in which they finden noon yvel, was scornid and reprovid of mercers servauntis, whanne the book came into her handis and was of hem rad" (*Folewer*, 176). This statement is interesting for two reasons: first, it seems to suggest that Pecock had submitted his book to learned members of the clergy, which would indicate an awareness of a need for ecclesiastical approval before publication; and second, it suggests that Pecock's work has found an audience in the homes of mercers, whose servants have also had the chance to access it.

Historical research by the scholars Wendy Scase, Caroline Barron, Anne Sutton, and Jean Imray confirms that Pecock was indeed familiar with London mercers and therefore supports the notion that his historical audience would have contained the men whose literacy and mental acuity he admires. He was connected with a group of men that oversaw the distribution and management of the estate of the wealthy London official Richard Whittington (d. 1423). The documentation surrounding the Whittington foundations gives us a sense of the circles in which Pecock moved, of the "network of pious and powerful Londoners" who actively shaped religious culture in fifteenth-century London through their support and management of institutions like chapels, libraries, and almshouses.[13]

Whittington's money came from a financial career "which encompassed three spheres of activity: as a mercer, as a royal financier and as a wool exporter."[14] His executors chose to entrust the foundations of his posthumous philanthropy to the mercer's company, the guild of silk and linen merchants that experienced a "golden age" in the fifteenth century in terms of prosperity and control over London.[15] The charitable distribution of the estate, which Imray argues represents "the combined achievement of the founder and his executors," included the foundations of an almshouse, which was to support thirteen poor men and women, and a college of priests (Whittington College), housing five secular chaplains, at St. Michael Paternoster in Riola.[16] Both foundations were completed in 1424.[17] Another important foundation probably thought up by John Carpenter was the Guildhall Library.[18] Whittington's executors were leading figures in London, including chief executor John Carpenter, common clerk of London (1417–38); John White, the master of St. Bartholomew's Hospital and former parson of St. Michael's; John Coventry, a mercer and mayor from 1425 to 1426; and a scrivener, William Grove.[19]

Pecock was involved in the administration of these establishments. He was selected, probably by Carpenter, as rector of St. Michael Paternoster and master of Whittington College from 1431 to 1444. He entered this post in a customary celebration that involved the mercers: Scase notes an item of expenditure in the Mercers' Wardens' accounts for the hire of a ferry to bring Pecock to Lambeth for his presentation in 1431 as the new master of Whittington College and rector of St. Michael Paternoster Royal.[20] While he was master of Whittington College, which was "a very young institution," he was involved in formal processes arranging for legal recognition of the institution.[21] Sutton says, "Pecock was almost certainly involved in the formal issue of the statutes of the college by Act of Parliament, letters patent and other legal acts, which made everything watertight in 1432; he was a feofee, and presumably took an active hand in the making of the ordinances of the almshouse, of which the first set were dedicated in a verse to the wardens of 1442–43."[22] Pecock's post as master of Whittington College would have brought him into contact with members of the mercantile community. Sutton suggests that Pecock was just one of a "string of academic priests at Whittington

College with whom intellectually minded mercers . . . could have fraternized."[23] Such fraternization between laymen and doctors of theology is revealed by the evidence, cited by Sutton, of a dispute between a priest and a mercer over a matter of astronomy that involved the input of an "impressive list of clerics and academics."[24]

As Scase points out, however, Pecock's associations with London mercers did not end with Whittington College. The church where he was rector was used by the guild of the cutlers, which undoubtedly brought Pecock into contact with practitioners of this craft. Furthermore, "Evidence of his involvement in the wider community is given by the bequest of John Wockyng, vintner of London to Reginald Pecock, clerk, Andrew Mitchell and Robert Fytlyng, citizens, in 1440."[25] He was also involved in a project in the 1440s that "brought certain London citizens and clergy . . . together with members of the court." This project was the "foundation of a chapel dedicated to the Virgin Mary and the Nine Orders of Angels at Isleworth, Middlesex, just north of Syon Abbey." A hospital was also founded in association with this chapel, for the "relief of nine poor old men and a religious guild of brothers and sisters called the Guild of the Nine Orders of Holy Angels by Syon."[26] The Guild of All Angels was the kind of organization that brought together in close relationships members of the clergy and the laity. Vincent Gillespie writes, "From 1446 onwards, Syon also had strong links with the influential Guild of All Angels in nearby Isleworth, a guild with close connections to the world of the London common-profit books." The connection that this guild facilitated between Syon and prosperous Londoners like Colop and Carpenter suggests to Gillespie that Syon was "permeable and hospitable to the outside world."[27] The circles that Pecock moved in included men who were responsible for the government of London and who were prepared to cross traditional boundaries between the secular and spiritual estates to increase the prosperity of their city in both secular and spiritual terms. Pecock's references to cutlers and mercers in his books can be seen against this historical background of his association with a range of London citizens.

Historical evidence therefore confirms the possibility that Pecock's actual historical audience contained important officials like Colop and Carpenter, members of the mercers' guild and the cutlers' guild, and members of the mercantile community who liked to engage in debate with their spiritual leaders. Internal evidence suggests that Pecock's selection of moral lessons was sometimes made with this mercantile audience in mind: in the discussion of the role of ignorance and constraint in committing sin, the son asks for clarification on the question of interest promised under constraint. Why, he asks, is it morally acceptable for a man who has borrowed twenty pounds from another man, and agreed "undir covenaunt" to render back the twenty plus four more pounds, to "sewe and constreine the leener forto restore to him the iiii pound" even though the borrower promised, without being constrained, and "with deedis and wordis withoutforth," to provide the interest? (*Folewer*, 144). In response to this complicated question, the father opposes usury. He says that by refusing to help the poor man out of his poverty without imposing usurious interest, the rich man constrains the poor man to pay interest, since it is a "grettir yvel" to the poor man to remain in "poverte and need" than to pay "the usure of iiii pound" (145). He says:

> The riche man, knowing the poor man to be in need for to borewe, and the same riche man being of power, without hurt or damage, forto releve his need, and yit, nilling it helpe and releve, holdith by what in him is the same poor man in the same neede. And so by as miche as the seid riche man holdith the poor man in thilk poverte and need, in lasse than the poor man wole borewe of him undir covenaunt to paie the valew borewid and usure overplus, he constreineth the poor man to paie thilk usure by threatening of grettir yvel, which is that he wole not ellis helpe the poor mannis neede, and that ellis by as miche as in him is he wole holde the seid poor man in his poverte. (145)

The rich man, threatening the poor man with the greater evil of poverty, is at fault. Lenders who constrain borrowers in this way should not have "lordschip upon the usure paied to hem" (145). The borrower can get his interest back, however, by lying: he should "defende him ayens the tyranrie and constreining of the leener" by inwardly objecting to the usury (145). If he inwardly objects, yet agrees outwardly, then he is justified in reclaiming the interest. However, if he knows how to object inwardly, yet fails to do so, he cannot reclaim the interest. If he forgets how to "withdrawe and hide his inward consent" and ends up consenting to the usury, then he can legitimately reclaim the usurious interest (145).

Interestingly, Pecock then argues that rules about usury should be found "in lawe of kinde and of resoun, without nede of positiif lawe to be maad therupon" (146). He promises to treat usury in more detail in his book "of usure," but this statement alone indicates that Pecock wanted to supply readers with more rational arguments and logical ways of thinking about usury so that they would properly understand it. Pecock does not find sufficient answers for the son's questions in the teaching on usury supplied by "eny positiif statute of the al hool chirch or of the pope him silf" (146). His planned recourse to the law of nature betrays a sense of inadequacy in the church's laws. Sutton says that a London mercer would have been well aware of the "moral guidelines" on usury outlined by the church, knowing that "usury carried no pardon." She continues: "His local clergy would have seen to it that he knew that the Lateran Council of 1139 had deprived lay usurers of the ministry of the Church and that the Council of 1179 had declared war on usury."[28] Apparently Pecock thought that the laity needed more comprehensive teaching on usury in the form of books; this is yet another example of his impulse to share the learning of the university with the lay community. Catto notes that usury was a recurrent topic in the faculty of theology at Oxford, in witness to the interest in practical moral theology there in the fifteenth century. Catto cites as evidence a notebook owned by a Merton fellow, *De usuries et restitutionibus*, that preserves some questions on this topic and treats it by considering "real situations: dowry-bargaining, cattle-marketing and the sale of corn futures, together with the rights to usurers' wives."[29] Pecock's brief instruction on usury in the *Folewer* is similarly practical, advising readers about how they should compose themselves internally and externally when embarking on a transaction requiring them to pay usury. This example demonstrates Pecock's efforts to transfer the learning of the schools to a mercantile environment not through preaching but through the medium of books, which can be read and reread, consulted regularly by laypeople facing moral dilemmas in everyday life. This sort of teaching would have been important for a man like Richard Whittington, who helped to punish usurers in the London usury trials of 1421, in which the majority of cases were successfully prosecuted. Sutton remarks that "usury was held to harm the city's commercial reputation with men and God" and that the successful prosecution of several mercers was a "sign that the city authorities were determined to give a sharp shock to the business community."[30] Pecock's brief discussion on usury in the *Folewer* seems to suggest that he felt another kind of sharp shock was needed, this time in the form of proper teaching on the subject, which would make men see usury clearly in the light of reason instead of through the form of legal rulings and prohibitions.

Pecock's moral teachings are made concrete to inhabitants of London through his examples, which call upon readers' knowledge of local geography and public sites like London bridge, "Poulis Cros" (*Repressor*, 338) and "the greet chirche of Seint Poul in Londoun" (*Repressor*, 330, 332), London crafts and occupations such as sporiers and cutlers (*Repressor*, 50), London festivals (*Repressor*, 28, 29), and major events in London history, which I will discuss shortly. He also draws upon readers' knowledge of international affairs, such as the "rewful and wepeable destruccioun of the worthy citee and universitee of Prage, and of the hool rewme of Beeme" (*Repressor*, 86), and the king's "conquest of his lond of Normandy and of Fraunce" (*Repressor*, 90). Most of his references to place, however, describe a London setting. For example, to demonstrate what opinion is, Pecock uses several examples including one particular to London, saying:

> Opinioun is a trowing wherby we assenten to eny thing as to be a treuth, by cause of likly evidencis. . . . Though no persoon seye eny thing therto forto witnesse it be trewe: as is this trowing wherby we trowen that this day schal be a reiny day for that his morowning was reed, or that to morrow schal be a faire day for that his eventide is reed, or that he whiche is now chosen to be meyre of Londoun is richer than he is which is not yit chosen to be aldirman of Londoun, by cause it is oft wonid that greet inquerry and aspie ben afore had among wise men who is riche and who is not, and how riche oon is and how riche an other is for to be aldirman and meyre or no. (*Folewer*, 54)

As Sutton notes, the wealth of leaders chosen to govern London was an important factor in determining whether they could be successful in the job. She says, "Aldermen, as the wealthiest men of London, were expected to give generously whether to the king (they frequently shouldered a loan between them) or in the way of charity."[31] The men who elected city officials considered not only their moral standing but also their fortunes: "The ordinance of 1397 had laid down that candidates for vacant aldermanries were to be reputable and discreet, and fit both in morals and in worldly goods to be judges and aldermen of the city."[32] Barron notes that expenses for these civic officials were so onerous that some were "anxious to avoid office."[33] Similarly, the mayor had to be wealthy and "impressive enough to impose order within the city and to carry weight with the great men of the realm outside it."[34] His term was a year, and it was "an expensive year." Knowing who was rich and who was not would certainly be a major fact in electing these officials. Pecock's use of this example to define the meaning of faith calls upon common knowledge among Londoners about the elections of their city leaders.

Pecock's use of examples that pertained to a particular audience of Londoners provides internal evidence for a historical audience of London citizens. Another interesting example that draws upon an audience's knowledge of the contemporary scene occurs in Pecock's teaching on the passions in the *Folewer*. Discussing the problem of anger, Pecock digresses to tell readers about a particular sermon (his famous sermon preached at St. Paul's Cross) that he preached in London. He states that by proceeding in "undirneming and blaming certein prechers . . . sharply and not without profis," he provoked the people's anger (104). The people "beere hem anentis the seid precher as wiilde, unresonable beestis in many kindis cruely, unmanly, uncurteisly and untrewly. . . . And in special they clateriden herinne so unwiisly that he schulde be thane out of charite" (105). Having endured the clattering and rage of the people, Pecock notes that "therayens suffrance is oon remedie into time peple chaunge and falle fro her furie" (105). Time heals, but in the meantime he must bear the accusations and criticisms. Scase discusses the preaching controversy that Pecock "ignited" by this sermon preached at St. Paul's Cross probably on Sunday, May 15, 1447.[35] Pecock's reference to this sermon, which stirred up major controversy among leading churchmen in London, is indignant and tinged with a sense of victimhood. He casts himself as the wronged party, misunderstood and attacked without cause. This may constitute an appeal for readers, familiar with the event, to take his side. The story seems designed to garner the audience's pity and support by describing Pecock's opponents generally as "the people" who degenerated into vicious beasts instead of identifying the learned and powerful priests, doctors of theology, and rectors that he also offended. The sermon is said to have provoked "inquietationem" in many minds, especially "in ista civitate London."[36] By failing to explain the sermon's conclusions in the *Folewer*, and by describing it rather vaguely as a corrective aimed at bringing about reform, Pecock avoids stirring up more controversy while making an appeal for his audience's sympathy. This would work best if his audience members were familiar with the events he describes.

My sense here that Pecock is drawing on his audience's common knowledge of previous events is supported by his use of an example that refers to another recent event in London history. To illustrate the difficulty of changing the hearts of these furious people, he mentions a contemporary event that enraged the people, causing them to be "brimly sett in an outragiosenes": "It was hard and impossible forto redresse anoon the furie and madness of the peple spokun and doon at the toure hil of Londoun and in the cite for the brenning of a preest doon there, not withstonding that greet bisines was doon therayens by autorite of the king, and diverse solempne sermons weren made for the redressing therof, neuertheles with mich unthank and reproof and casting therfore upon the prechers whil the time of the furie and madness durid" (*Folewer*, 108). This example appears to assume common knowledge of the execution of the Lollard priest Richard Wyche in 1440.[37] The public outcry that Pecock describes is registered by the establishment of a shrine, set up by Wyche's followers at the site where his ashes were buried, "where they made prayers as to a saint."[38] Christina von Nolcken describes Wyche as "one of the most long-lived and probably one of the most influential of the fifteenth-century Lollards." He had several run-ins with the authorities in 1410, 1417, and 1419, but it was not until 1440 that he was "convicted as a relapsed heretic before the bishop of London, and on

17 June he and his servant Roger Norman were burned on Tower Hill."[39] Pecock's reference must be to Wyche, and it is tempting to speculate about just what Wyche was preaching when he served as vicar in Kent and Essex between 1420 and 1440. Perhaps Pecock's knowledge of Wyche and his teachings shaped his response to the Lollards in the *Repressor* and the *Book of Faith*. In any case, what is noteworthy about this example is that it draws upon knowledge of major local events that would have still been present in the communal memory in the 1450s, when the *Folewer* was published.

Historical evidence confirms that the subjects and examples discussed in Pecock's moral instruction were particularly pertinent for an audience of London citizens, including mercers. Historical evidence also confirms that these mercers were both interested in and capable of reading books of religion. Pecock observes the considerable mental powers and literacy of the mercers, saying, in the introduction to the *Folewer*, that he is familiar with laymen who are literate in English and laymen who are literate in Latin (7). The *Folewer* is written for the former, but this observation indicates that Pecock had associates within the lay community with competency in both languages. Though English and French literacy were more common, Latin literacy was required for those mercers' assistants, or beadles, who had scribal duties and handled formal documents.[40] Sutton says that "every mercer needed to read, write, and count" and that "it is unlikely any boy would have been accepted for apprenticeship, at the usual age of fourteen to sixteen, if he had not already acquired the rudiments."[41]

Book ownership also confirms high rates of literacy and bookishness among London mercers. Sutton writes of a "high incidence of mercer book-ownership," listing a broad variety of books owned by mercers, including copies of *Piers Plowman*, *The Pricke of Conscience*, psalters and books of hours, lives of Christ, saints' lives, and works by Hilton.[42] The contents of the common-profit books, discussed below, included works by Hilton, the *Speculum ecclesie*, the *Pore Caitiff*, and commentaries on the psalms.[43] The contents of a group of devotional anthologies from fifteenth-century London include treatises on faith, charity, and prayer, as well as commentaries on the Lord's Prayer, the Ten Commandments, and the seven deadly sins.[44] In their research for the "Geographies of Orthodoxy" Web-based project, Stephen Kelly and Ryan Perry discuss a number of devotional anthologies produced in London in the first half of the fifteenth century: MSS Bodley 789, Bodley 938, Westminster School MS 3, Laud Misc. 174, and Laud Misc. 23. These manuscripts all contain pseudo-Bonaventuran translations, but Kelly and Perry argue that the rest of their contents define these manuscripts as "politically unstable."[45] The composition of these manuscripts, mixing orthodox lives of Christ with reformist texts, tells us that the London book trade catered to readers who wanted books like Pecock's: books written in a reformist tone that offered material to stimulate pious devotions and curious minds. When examining the horizon of expectations among London readers, then, we must consider that audiences may have cultivated tastes for religious texts that asked probing questions about the nature of the church and the practice of religion. Pecock's own calls for reform would not have seemed entirely radical to such readers.

Sutton observes that the wills reveal an emphasis on pious books "rather than frivolous romances," but she is careful to note that is it impossible to construct from these references to book ownership a clearly defined religiosity among the mercers: "The inner piety of mercers, from Whittington down, is in the final analysis unfathomable, but the evidence supports what common sense might suggest: a few had profound convictions and the rest muddled through."[46] Among the books left by mercers to relatives are some books of philosophy, which are particularly noteworthy in this study because of Pecock's continual emphasis on the need for more teachings on moral philosophy. In her discussion of the books bequeathed by mercers in wills, Sutton cites only one reference to books of philosophy: "A contemporary of Whittington and one of the circle of pious book-lovers, a warden and the scribe of the 1404 ordinances, Martin Kelom, left books of grammar, philosophy and theology as well as English books to his son."[47] It is unclear whether these books of philosophy and theology would have contained similar teachings to Pecock's corpus, but this ownership of books of philosophy is still interesting, given what Pecock has to say in the introduction to the *Reule* about the light of philosophy being out (31–36).

The will of Whittington's chief executor, John Carpenter, contains hints of a broader interest among the London elite in moral philosophy.[48] Carpenter mentions "that book 'cum Secretis Aristotelis,'" better known in the medieval period as the *Secretum secretorum*.[49] The will also mentions a book in French called *De corpore pollecie*, which may be Christine de Pizan's *Livre du corps de policie*, a book concerned with moral and political governance.[50] This work does not make connections, as Pecock does, between moral philosophy and theology, but it does address some concerns about social behavior and moral governance that are familiar to us from a reading of Pecock's works, such as the importance of obedience within the social hierarchy and the need to control the passions. Two works attributed to Seneca are mentioned: the *Seneca ad Callionem* and the suppositious *Seneca de quatuor virtutibus cardinalibus*.[51] I am unaware of a work by Seneca "ad Callionem," which Thomas Brewer claims exists in Cottonian MSS. Vespasian E xii (13) fol. 115b,[52] but I wonder if this work has been confused with the treatises dedicated to Seneca's brother Gallio, *De ira* and *De vita beata*.[53] Carpenter's will also mentions the *Speculum morale regium*, which Brewer believes was a part of Vincent de Beauvais's thirteenth-century encyclopedia *Speculum maius: Naturale, doctrinale, morale, historiale*.[54] The volume on morals contains teaching on human acts, the passions, law and grace, the theological and cardinal virtues, the gifts, fruits, and beatitudes, sin, the seven vices, and penitence.[55] This book comes closest of any book on Carpenter's list to Pecock's moral philosophy and makes problematic Pecock's assertion that moral philosophy has been lost and neglected. However, the fact that John Carpenter owned a book on moral philosophy does not necessarily lead to any certain conclusions that other mercers were commonly interested in the subject. As a prominent and wealthy man who held high office and discharged important duties like the distribution of Whittington's estate, Carpenter is not exactly representative of the middle-class London laity.

The references to book ownership in the wills of London citizens provide important information for establishing a horizon of expectations among such readers. Hans Robert Jauss says, "The first reception of a work by the reader includes a test of its aesthetic value in comparison with works already read." This comparison arises from "a pre-understanding of the genre, from the form and themes of already familiar works, and from the opposition between poetic and practical language."[56] Pecock's reformist tone may have had a familiar ring to readers of the London devotional anthologies studied by Kelly and Perry, but the works customarily read by members of Pecock's audience, according to Pecock himself, offer markedly different approaches to moral instruction. Pecock's self-appointed task is to bring the truths of moral philosophy into light, into the vernacular, and into the lay community. For university students at Oxford who read both Aquinas's *Summa* and Aristotle's *Ethics*, Pecock's discussions of subjects like constraint, ignorance, moral virtues, worship, faith, and penance would have seemed familiar, if somewhat simplified. From my own reading of other works of religious instruction available to lay readers in fifteenth-century England, it seems that Pecock does not have much company on his mission to transfer this particular branch of learning from a university environment, from the sophisticated theological works of Aquinas and Scotus on the will, the *habitus*, the moral and intellectual virtues, and so on, to the busy streets of London.

If, according to Jauss, the reception of this scholastic discourse would be influenced by its comparison to works already read by London's reading public, and if John Carpenter's ownership of the *Speculum morale* is not taken as indicative of widespread tastes among London citizens, it would seem that Pecock's works would be received as a new approach or a new form for religious instruction that reimagines "what the Church might be and how it might overcome a crisis of confidence, of government, of authority."[57] While his reformist impulses make his voice familiar, his efforts to restructure Christian society through education in moral philosophy make Pecock's voice different. It is likely that the reading habits of London citizens gave them a common knowledge of various literary or aesthetic conventions used in reformist religious literature; it might even be possible to outline a list of common *exempla*, images, literary forms, motifs, and topoi in these kinds of works. It is likely, for example, that readers would be familiar with the convention of understanding the difference between contemplative and active lives through the biblical story of Mary and Martha, a story that Pecock himself draws on in the *Reule*. The dialogue form would be familiar to readers of popular works like *Dives and Pauper*, as well as to Lollard readers. Similarly, the convention of the dream vision prologue in the *Reule* must have been a fa-

miliar device, yet it is important to note that Pecock drops this convention quickly and does not develop it in a sustained way. It may be
the case that Pecock was attempting to draw in readers with this conventional device, to "wowe the more multitude" (*Reule*, 36), through
recognition of the familiar, only to supplant the conventional with
something entirely different. He used the familiar only to destabilize
it. Jauss argues that a literary work, even one claiming to be new,
"predisposes its audience to a very specific kind of reception by an-
nouncements, overt and covert signals, familiar characteristics, or
implicit allusions. It awakens memories of that which was already
read," thereby helping to create in the reader a "specific emotional
attitude."[58] Though Pecock does at times draw on conventions that
would have been familiar to a London reading public, the ways that
his works depart from conventional approaches are more noteworthy:
his forms of the seven matters of religious truths and the four tables of
moral law are new. His instruction on careful distinctions, within the
four tables, on the differences between honoring, praising, worshiping, and veneration is much more similar to Aquinas's distinctions in
the *Summa theologiae*.[59] He himself notes that his audience members
are not familiar with the discourse of moral philosophy that his books
impart: though they have sufficient intellect to comprehend the matters of his books, they lack the terminology. The prominent, clever
men of London are not familiar with "the signifying of the wordis," of
the discipline of moral philosophy, but Pecock has structured his corpus with this in mind, providing definitions of terms and concepts
throughout (*Reule*, 21).

So there is internal evidence that Pecock was writing at least in
part for an actual audience of London mercers who were literate and
interested in books of reformist piety but probably unfamiliar with
sophisticated distinctions between "eendal" and "meenal" virtues
(*Folewer*, 175–76). What else does Pecock tell us about the audience
for his books in fifteenth-century England? Is there any internal evidence pointing to other factors that would have affected their reception of his books? As Jauss suggests, it is important to consider the
influence of "already familiar works" in the construction of an audience's "horizon of expectations."[60] What else helped to construct a
horizon of expectations in the London reading public?

Reception of a literary work is influenced by what an audience has previously read, but in the late medieval context, what audience members had previously read was not necessarily limited to books they had read independently, in private study. Reflecting on the phenomenon of late medieval "publication," Felicity Riddy remarks that we need to "stop thinking of the manuscript era as one in which books belonged to the intimate sphere."[61] She argues that a useful "approach to the problem of 'publication' might be via a publicness that is not a realm of consumption but of talk." What she defines as "the space of talk" is admittedly "one of the most inaccessible areas for us in studying the past," but "this should not allow us to ignore the existence of a public sphere of discussion, debate, news, gossip, and rumour, in which things were generally spoken of and generally known, a discursive rather than a spatial publicness."[62] Sutton suggests that this kind of talking may have taken place after weekly sermons: "Many Londoners owned books, and, as orthodox lay people, were prepared to discuss their weekly sermon; rich parishioners were able to demand that their parson live up to their expectations and listen to their opinions as churchwardens."[63] If books become known through talk, then talk can shape awareness of genre, form, style, language, motifs, and conventions, thus influencing the audience's horizon of expectations. In other words, the reception of new books is shaped by the horizon of expectations constructed through talk about previous books. As well, talk about books can affect the cultivation and development of taste within the reading public, as some books are talked about with appreciation and others neglected entirely.

If a horizon of expectations can be shaped by previous reading, seen in this context of reading through communal interactions, then we must search for evidence of this public discourse. It is difficult, without evidence, to theorize about the impact that public conversations about books would have had on the reception of Pecock's works by members of the London laity, but this does not mean that we should discount the importance of the public sphere in the production of a horizon of expectations among the pious reading public in the fifteenth century.

First, the internal evidence. The role of talk in shaping an audience's reception of new works is at stake in Pecock's dream vision experience in which the daughters of God visit him to complain of being supplanted by dangerous, erroneous books (*Reule*, 31–36). The daughters of God lament that clerks have written "manie grete volumes and bookis" that are "mighty and famose in the world" (33). They are so often discussed and so well known that "ther is no man holde a clerke but if he can of hem be a talker, no man worthy to sitte in cumpanie but if of hem he can be a dadelar, no man worthy or acceptable to preche but if he be of his sermoun by hem a florischer" (33). Knowledge of books is a form of intellectual capital, defining who is worthy and authoritative and who has the power to define and establish rules for belief and behavior. What troubles Pecock here is that reading the wrong kinds of books has led to unprofitable conversation, or communing in the Christian community, which in turn leads to the possibility that his own books will not be well received. He hopes that his fellow clerics will spread the word about the benefits his books offer, in order to influence people to read his books and receive them in the right way—with gratitude. He encourages his fellow churchmen not just to distribute his books "abrood to manye," once they are approved, but also to make "fame and noise . . . to the seid lay peple of suche bokis" (*BF*, 116). If his books can enter the space of talk, if the clergy can provoke the laity to read his books through "fame and noise," then perhaps more people will read them for themselves. Furthermore, once people have read his books, his books will enter the space of talk in the form of "comuning" (*Reule*, 13). Pecock is hopeful that this communing will shape the audience's horizon of expectations in new ways, producing in this audience an appreciation for the reasonable truths of scholastic discourse.

There is additional internal evidence pointing to the importance of interpersonal exchanges in establishing a horizon of expectations for a London audience. In the *Donet*, Pecock suggests that personal relationships between clergy and laity are an important factor in shaping the way that an audience will receive a particular work. According to Pecock, the popularity of some approaches to moral instruction is tied to the personal charisma or authority of the clergy and their intimate connections to members of the lay community. Pecock says that the reason for the popularity of commentaries on the Ten Commandments is "the usage and custom of such attendaunce into which the peple is brought and lad thorugh long time by her prechers and techers" (176). Preachers and teachers play a formative role in transmitting particular approaches and not others. People grow attached to certain ways of thinking about faith and morality, to certain ways of orienting themselves in their spiritual lives, because they grow accustomed to their preacher's way of doing things. A work's weight and influence depend on the personal bonds of loyalty that the laypeople feel for their spiritual teachers and preachers. Pecock says in the *Reule* that the laypeople have been led into heresy by clerks, "namelich Johan Wiccliffe and hise disciplis," not because they thought too much about doctrine but because of "the affeccioun whiche the comoun peple hath to the persoonis, and what for the truste to the leving of thoo persoonis" (96). The intimate connection between the people and these spiritual leaders accounts for their deviance from orthodoxy, demonstrating the power of personal relationships and common ties to influence the way that religious thought develops and changes and the way habits of belief are formed in particular communities.

Though neither of these comments refers directly to reading habits among the laity, they do help to give us an idea of the power of collaboration and exchange between laymen and clerics to shape religious belief and to influence the reception of religious literature. One form of historical evidence for "talk" about books within the public sphere is the documentation of relationships among laity and clergy. We do not have records of conversations about books, but we do have records that point to significant and productive relationships among mercers and clerics like Pecock. Close relationships between clergy and laity are at the foundation of various schemes for book circulation in fifteenth-century London, including that envisioned by Pecock in his *Book of Faith* as well as the common-profit book scheme studied by Wendy Scase.[64] The London common-profit books were financed from the estates of donors who sought prayers for their souls in exchange for books. London executors like John Colop and John Gamalin were assigned the task of distributing the property of testators in the form of alms and "convert[ing] bequests into books; their names are inscribed in common-profit books indicating their status as donors."[65] According to Scase, the scheme for producing books for the "poorer lay people" from the goods of more wealthy laymen (a shearman and a grocer) resembles patterns of book lending among the clergy, which provided for the use of books among the poorer secular clergy and which ensured continued circulation instead of ownership. She argues that similarities between the two types of book-lending scheme suggest that "the Colop scheme was formulated in an informed awareness of the pattern among clerics, and in awareness of the principles behind it."[66] Scase does not reflect further on the way that this awareness developed among London executors like John Colop and John Gamalin, but it seems clear that the adaptation of the clerical scheme points to close relationships between clergy and laity in which talk about religious books would have been prominent.

Talk about religious literature may also have been a part of relationships between the laity of London and the contemplatives at Syon monastery. The recent work of scholars on Syon confirms the importance of the role played by personal ties between men of the secular and spiritual worlds in the cultivation of religious practices among the laity in London. Manuscript studies by Vincent Gillespie and A. S. G. Edwards show that such personal bonds had a major impact in determining which texts would circulate in the lay community and which forms of teaching would take root there. Both Edwards and Gillespie mention one particular manuscript (University of Notre Dame MS 67) that was produced in the London area and was owned by John, fourth Baron Scrope of Masham, and his wife Elizabeth Chaworth.[67] Gillespie argues that one of the works in this manuscript, the *Mirror to Devout People* (or *Speculum devotorum*), was probably written by a Carthusian monk of Sheen for a Brigittine sister of Syon before its readership was expanded to include "well-connected lay people like Elizabeth Chaworth/Scrope, whose husband's family had numerous connections to Syon and other metropolitan nunneries."[68] The path that this manuscript traveled from Sheen into the lay community indicates, to Gillespie, that although the Carthusian scribes at Sheen intended their books for the "small, local, and tightly defined" audience of Syon, Syon was likely a "conduit through which their works reached a wider readership."[69] Gillespie postulates: "I suspect that in London the main such conduit, and a notably leaky one, was in fact Syon. I also suspect that, with or without the conscious consent or permission of the Carthusians over the river, the special circumstances of the Syon brethren and the special configuration of the double convent at Syon led to books originating at Sheen being propelled into much wider circulation."[70]

Now, Gillespie notes that more work needs to be done on the role of the Syon brethren in influencing book circulation in London, noting, "I suspect that Syon's intervention in the transmission of English spiritual writing was more decisive than has yet been realized or established."[71] He does help us to understand how such intervention might have been possible by providing some historical information from the library catalog and the *Regula salvatoris* about the function of the brethren at Syon, noting that they, unlike their brothers at Sheen, were actively involved in cultivating lay piety through sermons and perhaps individual counsel. Gillespie shows that the Syon brothers were "opynly to preche" on solemn festivals, that they were "bounde to expoune iche sonday the gospel of the same day in the same messe to all herers in ther modir tonge," that they may have been expected to accept confession from outside the house, and, most interestingly, that "there is also some evidence to suggest that they acted as spiritual directors for well-placed laymen and women, as Symon Wynter did for Margaret, Duchess of Clarence."[72] They managed the flow of visitors who "flocked to the indulgence sermons" as Syon's fame increased, and they "seem to have offered collegial hospitality to priests and laymen who wished to work in the library."[73] The connection that Gillespie's work points to between the Syon brethren and the London textual community is another important source of information about the role that discourse between these two groups played in influencing the horizon of expectations among the London laity.

It seems clear, then, that the reading audience in Pecock's London would have experienced books, developed tastes, and adopted habits of interpretation in a world that extended beyond the private study: the reception of books was shaped by friendships, associations, conversations, and debates within the community. A man like John Carpenter, who owned a diverse selection of books, would have developed forms of piety and belief in the experience of reading these books, but the experience of interpreting these books and thinking about what these books meant to him must have included discussions about the contents, assumptions, and meaning of these books in conversation with his friend and possible mentor Richard Whittington, in debate with academically trained priests of the college that he oversaw, in discussion with intellectually minded mercers, who had similar interests in circulating edifying and spiritually nourishing books, and in association with the monks at Syon, who would have provided yet another viewpoint on the spiritual life. The diverse perspectives he must have seen by engaging with these different groups could all have been brought to bear on his reception of Pecock's books.

In this final section, I look closely at Pecock's method of teaching moral truths through examples and illustrations in order to explore possible ways in which his books may have influenced their implied readers and elicited particular responses. Pecock's habit of multiplying illustrations of moral truths invites readers to make connections among these examples in a way that brings together diverse aspects of their experience in society. For example, arguing that the lay people must receive faith from the clergy, Pecock states that the clergy are the rightful successors of the apostles. Pecock says, "This argument takith his strenthe herof, that in waast schulden eny persoones be ordeinid successouris to othere former persoones, as in waast schulde a king now living succede to his fadir, in making the lawe of the lond be kept, but if the peple now living were bounde forto obeie to him in hise comaundis aboute the lawe keping, as they were bounde forto obeie to his fadir . . . though the fadir of this king were moche holier man than this is" (*BF,* 183). In the same way, monks owe obedience to their abbot's successor even if "the predecessoure were an holier man than is his successoure," and "in liik maner it is bitwix the citeseins of Londoun and the meirs of Londoun" (183). These examples can be seen as a way of reminding the mercers within his audience of their place in a larger community. Pecock's teaching encourages readers to draw on a broad basis of knowledge of the world around them—the world of business, of profit, of government, and of the ecclesiastical establishment—to understand the Christian code of conduct.

The grouping of three different examples in confirmation of an argument is a technique Pecock commonly uses, and it may imply a mixed audience drawing on different kinds of experience. In his discussion of God's moral law, he outlines four tables of truths derived from reason about ethical conduct, prescribing how each person ought to behave toward God, self, and neighbor. While Pecock is not in the habit of providing examples for every truth, the examples that he does include are important evidence in an examination of his implied audience. For example, he teaches temperance by saying that each individual must cultivate bodily health and strength in a desire to serve God, using his own body and the things of this world only in so far as he needs them to serve God. Things like food, drink, and sleep are to be used as means rather than enjoyed as ends. A man must take care of his bodily health and never recklessly "hindere his bodily helthe or strengthe and schorte his bodily liif withoute getting therby so greet a goostly good which ellis schulde not be getun, or without voiding of so greet a moral harme" (*Reule*, 267). A person can sacrifice bodily health if it means avoiding a major moral harm, or reaching a spiritual goal, but in needlessly sacrificing the body a man sins "by greet indiscrecioun, fforwhy he werith out the meenis ordeined into the getting of an eende other wise than as by hem the eende is best or moost plenteousely getun" (267).

To illustrate this moral truth, Pecock draws parallels between spiritual and worldly profit. Pecock says that a miller should wear out his horse by working it hard for ten years, rather than keeping it going for twenty, if it means more profit. He says,

> If a man have bought an hors forto drawe aboute his mille, and if this man knowe certeinly or miche likely that by the setting of this hors so bisily and so traveilosely a werk wherby he schal be worun out and spend out into deeth wiithinne x yeris, ther schal more corn be grounde than schulde be grounde if the same hors were cherissched in his labour so that the hors schulde haue xx winter; certis ther were noon indiscrecioun in this man, but ther were in him greet discrecioun forto in such greet a winning were and spende out his hors withinne x yeer, rather than to cherische him into lasse winning forto live xx winter. (268)

Just as the miller uses his possessions to win the most profit, the Christian should use his fleshly means in a way that secures the most spiritual profit. Three additional examples illustrate Pecock's point in this passage. The first is the example of a man walking "and journeying from London to Seint Albons" who spies a falcon worth twenty pounds: catching the falcon will secure a major profit, which makes it prudent to "leve the plein esy wey and renne over heggis and stilis and thornis, boisschis and breris a long time, . . . al though he werie or hurte sum what his body" (267). The second is the example of a man who can win a hundred pounds of gold by walking for twenty days. Even though he will wear out his new pair of shoes with all the walking, it would be an "indiscrecioun" to "so miche cherische the peire of schoon that therefore the hundrid pound schulde be not getun" (268).[74]

Pecock's examples show how readers should use the things of this world, such as their own flesh and their material possessions. As I will demonstrate in chapter 5, Pecock's use of analogies asks readers to abstract from their observations of common life philosophical principles about the nature of ethical living, encouraging them to see fundamental connections between the principles that operate in human relationships and human experiences and the higher principles of moral philosophy. Here I wish to stress that Pecock's habit of listing several examples that would appeal to different kinds of life experience implies a diverse audience, one that could include men from various walks of life in fifteenth-century London. His use of references to London mayors, aldermen, and citizens, as well as London geography and recent London history, suggests an effort to take an abstract religious discourse of moral philosophy and bring it into a local context. Pecock's teaching on morality requires that readers grasp abstract truths about the nature of the will, the workings of the passions, and the formation of a moral habit, but he ties these truths through his concrete examples to a more localized religiosity. The abstract truths of moral philosophy, from the world of Latin learning, receive expression in a vernacular writing to provide moral teaching that is locally situated in the world of fifteenth-century England. Ulrike Wiethaus helps to make sense of this phenomenon with his statement that the relationship between Latin and vernacular literatures reflects "complex negotiations between a transregional, and highly expansive, social structure (the Church) and geographically specific and locally bound Christian communities."[75] Pecock brings the teaching of moral philosophy out of its learned, Latin environment of the university, drawing on readers' contemporary thought-world to help them understand the workings of moral decisions. This bringing together of the concrete and the universal constitutes an effort to train readers to think at an abstract level by thinking through their own experiences.

Pecock's method of listing various examples that appeal to different levels within his audience is a reminder to us that Pecock's audience was not necessarily limited to London readers. References to London are mixed with other more general references to things like a man climbing a tree and a man walking along an unspecified riverbank. This may imply that Pecock is ensuring with his plethora of examples that his work would have an appeal beyond the readership that would recognize the precise local allusions. Certainly his marshaling of readers' knowledge of local customs and local places would make his works resonate within the broader context of the production, at the same time, of texts celebrating London life, memorializing London customs, and confirming the importance of civic institutions like Carpenter's *Liber albus*.[76] In the context of works like the *Liber albus*, Pecock's references to local institutions bring together ethical training with the cultivation of civic pride.[77] But we must not look only at Pecock's London examples. His habit of providing alternate illustrations of moral truths shows us that he was working carefully to ensure that his works could have a broader appeal beyond the mercers of London. Our inability to access other elements of his audience should not close our eyes to the potential his works had to reach a larger audience. Pecock's layering of examples tells us that an important way to reach this audience was to bring diverse people together, through their various experiences, to share in reflection on the same fundamental Christian truths.

Using an author-centered perspective, we can understand Pecock's use of diverse examples as an attempt to embrace "alle cristen peple." We can also consider Pecock's plethora of examples from another perspective, that of reader-oriented criticism, to understand what sort of response this method may have elicited from a specific reader, such as a London mercer. How would this particular form of teaching affect a man like John Carpenter? Answering this question must start with Wolfgang Iser's theory of aesthetic response. Iser's theory is not intended for didactic, religious texts like Pecock's, but his thoughts about the way that eighteenth-century novels elicit particular responses from readers can provide us with ways of thinking about just what kind of participation is demanded from readers of Pecock's texts. Iser describes the literary text as follows: "Firstly, it differs from other forms of writing in that it neither describes nor constitutes real objects; secondly, it diverges from the real experiences of the reader in that it offers views and opens up perspectives in which the empirically known world of one's own personal experience appears changed."[78] Pecock's teaching on what constitutes the moral life offers the reader views and perspectives in which the known quantities of his own life, his self, his world, and his community appear changed. Readers are taught to examine themselves in light of moral philosophy, to develop new categories of thought for processing everyday experiences by learning about them in the context of the inclinations of the will, the development of a *habitus*, and the ways in which the will is constrained from acting virtuously. It is the goal of this teaching to get the reader to reorient his understanding of himself and his world around Pecock's moral truths. I would argue, therefore, that far from showing the reader a description of the world he knows, Pecock's books offer up a radically altered picture of the familiar and the everyday.

Pecock's instruction in moral philosophy provokes readers to see their everyday lives from a new vantage point, and it does this by helping the reader to understand universal, abstract truths about the moral life through vivid, concrete examples. Pecock's works invite the reader's participation in visualizing how these abstract truths apply to real situations described by Pecock and in reflecting further on how these truths apply to personal situations that are not inscribed in the book. Iser says, "Every literary text invites some form of participation on the part of the reader" because the reader fills in "the indeterminate sections or gaps of literary texts"; he "removes them by a free play of meaning-projection."[79] Iser borrows Roman Ingarden's concept of "schematized views" to suggest that "literary objects come into being through the unfolding of a variety of views which constitute the object in stages and at the same time give a concrete form for the reader to contemplate."[80] For example, the reader must work out the connection among several plot threads that are running simultaneously but are dealt with one after the other. The connection among these threads is made not by the author but by the reader, who fills in the gaps made by the interruptions within the plot line. Such gaps "offer a free play of interpretation for the specific way in which the various views can be connected with one another. These gaps give the reader a chance to build his own bridges, relating the different aspects of the object which have thus far been revealed to him."[81] I would argue that Pecock's provision of diverse examples to illustrate abstract moral truths provides readers with different possible views of that moral truth, with the result that a reader may build bridges connecting these different perspectives on a moral truth to his own perspective on his moral life.

The ethical training that Pecock's books offer constitutes a psychological journey that enables the reader to understand himself by constantly adjusting his perspective of himself as a universal Christian man, equipped with a rational soul, a free will, and powerful passions, and as a London businessman, rooted in a particular corner of the mundane world. He must synthesize diverse ways of understanding himself, reconciling the abstract moral self with the particular self that is part of a particular community and that is occupied with particular problems and habits. The reader must learn to alternate, continually, between the universal and the concrete because this alternation constitutes the moral life: the Christian must interpret the significance of his actions in the mundane world in light of his understanding of the functions of the will, the inclinations of the passions, and the trajectory of the soul. This requires that he make connections between his private self, his public self, and his moral self.

As a London mercer learns to examine his conscience through intense reflection on the four tables of moral principles, he is prompted to think not only of his own individual experience but also more broadly of his experience within a larger society. It is important to note here that the four tables are provided as a tool for confession, a kind of handbook for penance that is oriented around moral philosophy. Study of the four tables should produce deep contemplation of one's actions and intent, helping the reader to see where he has erred. The way that this teaching is illustrated, then, through contemporary examples, serves to bring the private and the public together as the reader's sense of himself as an individual struggling to lead a virtuous life is connected to his sense of himself as a member of a community. Reading Pecock's examples provokes a sense that all experiences can converge on this text: for example, in the instruction on rightful obedience to a ruler's successor, the binding together of an example about mayors and citizens with an example about kings and their subjects and another example about abbots and monks reminds a London reader that he is part of a larger society. If he has connections with monks, as mercers did with the monks at Syon, or if he has connections with royalty, as mercers did through organizations like the Guild of All Angels, then these examples will speak to his sense of himself as a member of a diverse society in which all are bonded together in the pursuit of the common good. Most importantly, Pecock's examples show the reader that the moral life of the individual cannot be separated from the individual's public identity: the shaping of one's spiritual self must and can take place in the everyday world, in productive contact with other people, and not in an enclosure.

This kind of inclusive reading experience is crystallized in Pecock's *Reule*. The reading program fashioned by the *Reule* prevents division within Christian society by fostering a sense of belonging within a community for those who use the *Reule* in their personal devotions. I discuss the devotional nature of Pecock's corpus in chapters 3 and 4, but here I wish to demonstrate that the *Reule* constructs a reading practice that brings all Christians together in uniform, standardized praise of God. It is important to note that the doctrine in the *Reule* is presented in the "foorme of preising" (*Donet*, 203). Pecock defines praise as "a declaring of a persoonis dignitee by wordis therof in speking," and since "al thilk 'book of cristen religioun,' thorugh alle hise ii parties, goith upon Goddis dignities and Goddis worthinesses and goodnessis, and that in ful faire and swete and devoute maner, thou nedist not haue a fairer, a fruitfuller, a devouter foorme to preise God therby" (203). Readers who wish to praise God "by rehercels of doctrine and of cleer knowing upon Goddis worthinessis and dignitees and goodnessis" should read "by worde withouteforth in the seid book, 'the reule of cristen religioun,' thorugh eny of hise ii parties" (203). This kind of rehearsal of doctrine that runs on God's worthiness is exemplified by the beginning of a passage on God's infinite nature:

Lord, though al thou be knowun for preiseable and loveable for
that thou art a greet worthy being, a goodnes, a majeste, mighte,
wisdom and love (with othere more noble condiciouns rehercid),
yitt thou art not knowun for over wonderfully and over excel-
lently preisable and loveable but if it be knowun that ech of these
condiciouns is unmesurable and infinite. . . . Therefore teche us,
Lord, of al necessarie trouthis—clerist techir, gladdest enformer,
freest graunter, largist giver—teche us by sum ensaumple or in
sum other wise to have a conseit upon the over excellent wondir-
fulness of infinitnes and of unmesurabilnes, in which hangith the
over greet hight of thy preisabilnes and loveabilnes, and the grettist stiring and mowing to preise thee and love thee, drede thee,
and by keping of thy lawe serve thee, that may be for oure derke-
nesse, freelnes, and feebilnes. (*Reule*, 49–50)

What is important to note here is that teaching about God's infinite "loveabilnes" is formulated not as information about God, addressed to the reader, but as praise of God, directed at God himself
from the speaking voice of the text. This is Pecock's standard practice
in educating readers about God's nature, his benefits, his punishments, and his moral law. Instead of saying to readers, "God will show
infinite mercy to mankind," for instance, Pecock phrases his teaching
as a direct address from a corporate voice to God, saying, "Lord God,
thou hast the vertu of mercy, and not oonly thou hast the vertu of
mercy but thou hast the grettist mercy possible to be, and as greet as
may be of us thought to be, fforwhy thy mercy is unmesurable and
infinitely greet" (*Reule*, 161).

The parts of the *Reule* that teach about God are rehearsals of clear
doctrine, to be voiced as spoken prayer in the first-person plural, a
corporate voice: Pecock recommends reading "the seid preisingis" of
God when occupied in "outward" or voiced prayer, using the book as a
kind of script (*Donet*, 206). These rehearsals of doctrine can be useful
as well in inward prayer during private meditation, which Pecock constructs as an activity requiring thoughtful contemplation of the seven
matters of the *Reule* (*Reule*, 160). As I demonstrate in chapter 4, it is
important to note that these seven matters constitute the basis of
Pecock's reformed liturgy in other books to which he refers readers:

they are intended as a universal script for Christian devotional practices, both public and private, lay or clerical. Pecock says, "Miche
higher and plesauntir wolde thilke occupaciouns [of singing and reading in praise and prayer to God] be if it ranne upon cleer to be
undirstonde and upon worthy and digne maters of thy nobiltees, of
thy benefetis and of thy lawis as they ben in the i and secunde parties
of this present book tretid, and as they ben in the 'book of divine
office' and in 'the encheridioun' by preising and preying fourmed"
(*Reule*, 416). The recital of God's nature and benefits is to be the basis
not only of individual lay prayer and meditation but also of corporate
and monastic prayer, bringing together diverse members of the community (416). This corporate voice can also be heard in the prayers
that open and close each of the treatises of the *Reule*. For example, the
second treatise opens with a prayer addressing God as "al reverent, al
loveable, al desirable to plese and al dreadful to offende," thanking
God for ministering and giving "likingful and delectable" truths
which are "swettir to us than gold and topazion," and asking God for
more knowledge by appealing to his "reverent, loveable, worschipful,
incomprehensible, and unquytable greetnes" (100). The majority of
the prayers that preface and close the teaching in the *Reule* use this
communal voice, drawing readers and speaking voice together in a
prayer for the provision of instruction. The speaking voice of Pecock's
Reule is not that of a teacher, addressing readers directly and providing
information about divine truth, but more a corporate voice, which the
reader can inhabit.[82] It is the voice of "we Christians," a community—
beginning with Pecock and the reader, both described significantly as
seekers of God's truths—which comes together to acknowledge
God's gifts and goodness with reverence (*Reule*, 337). The social
framework implied by the conflation of speaking voice and reader
embraces the laity, the enclosed religious, and the clergy, who should
use the *Reule* in study and devotions. This voice does not have a dis-
tinctly clerical or lay identity; instead, it is that of the "parfiit and an
ordinat zelatour of thy lawe keeping, whether he dwelle in religioun
or out of religioun": this is the voice of God's chosen people, "creatures" that are "trewe servauntis and kinde lovers," who "shapen and
disposen" themselves "not feinedly and feintly" in serving and loving
God (423–24).

This chapter has addressed the following three questions: Who were the members of Pecock's historical audience? What factors would have influenced their reception of his works? What possible responses could Pecock's works have elicited from his historical audience? I have argued that we can be fairly certain that Pecock's audience contained London mercers; I have suggested that their horizon of expectations was shaped by the books they had previously read and the interpersonal relationships they shared; I have pointed to the possibility that Pecock's use of examples and his use of a common voice could have prompted a sense of community, a sense of inclusiveness, and a sense that who you are as a pious, ethical Christian before God is connected to and does not have to be separated from who you are within your wider community. I suggest, throughout this book, that although Pecock was intent on training the Christian laity at the level of the individual, one by one, within his program of vernacular religious education, he was always thinking about this individual within the context of an ideal, imagined textual community. This community, as I stated in the beginning of this chapter, embraces women and men, children and adults, clergy and laity, and well-meaning and not-so-well-meaning people. Though we can certainly locate a real, local textual community for Pecock's works in the recent historical studies of the London circles in which he moved, we must also consider the importance of the universal community of "alle cristen peple" that his books could possibly bring together.

The Religious
Education of the Laity

In late medieval England, the production of religious literature in the vernacular constitutes a massive transfer of *clergie*—of knowledge and learning—from the clergy to the laity. Most scholars agree that this process started with Archbishop Pecham's innovative and ground-breaking program, in 1281, of mass education requiring priests to preach and expound "the fourteen Articles of Faith, the Decalogue, the two Evangelical Commandments, the Seven Works of Mercy, Deadly Sins, Principle [sic] Virtues, and Sacraments."[1] Pecham's syllabus provided impetus for the concerted development of lay instruction in pastoral theology throughout the fourteenth and fifteenth centuries. Vincent Gillespie writes, "The fifteenth century witnessed an extensive and consistent process of assimilation by the laity of techniques and materials of spiritual advancement, which had historically been the preserve of the clerical and monastic orders."[2] Over 250 copies of the Wycliffite Bible, mostly in fragments, are produced during this period. This is a time when, as Sarah Beckwith notes, "the mechanisms for the transmission of 'theology' were expanding, and conventionally theological questions, or questions hitherto restricted to a clerical milieu, were being disseminated beyond the clergy in the vernacular, and hence understood and received in different ways."[3] The significance and the extent of this transmission of religious culture are witnessed by the use of the term *vernacular theology*, by

Nicholas Watson, to characterize ambitious works like *Piers Plowman*, which grapple with complicated questions about salvation, divine justice, and divine mercy in a language that was accessible to lay readers.

Works of religious instruction, like manuals of pastoral theology, commentaries on the Decalogue, the deadly sins, and the Pater Noster, and other didactic compilations form a large part of these "materials of spiritual advancement" that moved freely between clergy and laity in the fifteenth century. Scholars like Vincent Gillespie argue that these kinds of works—particularly pastoral handbooks and manuals like Mirk's *Instructions for Parish Priests*, and the *Speculum Christiani*, a work that "enjoyed enormous popularity in the fifteenth century"—provide us with an important source of information about the religious education of the laity in late medieval England.[4] Indeed, Gillespie suggests that though "there has been an understandable tendency to concentrate on the pulpit as the cornerstone of the didactic edifice," it is just as important to pay attention to the "developing lay taste for manuals" of religious instruction and to the "increasingly varied demands made upon their resources."[5] Alexandra Barratt concurs that much more work can be done (particularly on questions of audience, purposes, and uses) on didactic poems and prose works that "in their various ways, cover—fully or partly—the official teaching curriculum for the laity of the medieval Church," which included the Lord's Prayer and Creed, the fourteen Articles of Faith, the Decalogue, the two Evangelical Commandments, the seven works of mercy, the deadly sins, the principal virtues, and the sacraments.[6] In his study of medieval education, Nicholas Orme has suggested that religious instruction in the late Middle Ages was imparted through the religious and moral literature that "gave knowledge of God, narrated Christian history, taught virtues, and censored sins," as well as through sermons and any other public opportunity at which the priest gave public instruction, and through the informal education of young children in the principles of morality and the basic Christian prayers and precepts.[7] Didactic works that modeled themselves in various ways on the "standard instructional programme" of the Church helped readers—both clerical and lay—to learn and memorize basic doctrine, perhaps providing a resource for teaching others as well as a tool for private meditation.[8]

The writings of Reginald Pecock are an important part of this picture because he made it his task to expand mechanisms for the transmission of theology to the laity by writing books of religious instruction and by devising innovative plans for lay education. Indeed, what is extraordinary about Pecock's involvement in the transmission of religious culture to a lay milieu is both his participation in this transmission—that is, the production of sophisticated, challenging religious writings in the vernacular—and his ideas about the need for this transmission to be more regulated, systematic, and universal. In short, Pecock envisioned the religious education of the lay members of the Christian community in ways that had never been imagined before. On the one hand, Pecock's determination to educate the laity properly in theological matters is in keeping with larger contemporary efforts, across the orthodox and heterodox continuum, to increase and improve religious education. On the other hand, Pecock's notions of the most effective way to carry out this education extend well beyond traditional methods of educating parishioners in essential pastoral theology. Of course, it must be admitted that as far as we know, his program of lay religious education was not implemented, nor did it influence subsequent scholars interested in Christian pedagogy. The fact that his ideas were not put into practice, however, does not make them less interesting: what I hope to do here is to draw attention to the visionary nature of Pecock's thought, which helps to show the possibility of dynamic, progressive thinking in the fifteenth century, a fascinating period of transition and reform that has long been neglected or disdained by scholars. Pecock's scheme for lay education shows that while he had his finger on the pulse of the intellectual culture in fifteenth-century England, his determination to preserve orthodoxy and eradicate heresy drove him to new ways of thinking about the best way to instruct the Christian laity, which are quite different from ideas about education current in this period.

As is customary in pastoral manuals and didactic treatises of late medieval England, Pecock emphasizes the importance of education as a charitable duty. Pecock lists the education of the laypeople under the various governances of God's moral law pertaining to the duties of each Christian to his neighbor, which include the duties of a teacher to his pupils, of a master to his apprentice, of a priest to his parishioners,

of parents to their children, and of "sovereigns and overers" to "sug-
getis and undirlingis" (*Reule*, 288). In Pecock's view, one of the most
important duties of the clergy is the spiritual education of the laity: he
suggests that the various points of God's moral law (which are presented and organized most logically and effectively by Pecock's system
of four tables) must be "sadly and diligently discussid" and learned
"afore alle othere thingis" (363). It is also the role of parents to teach
children the seven matters of religious knowledge that Pecock has
devised, which cover "what God is, and whiche ben his benefetis, and
whiche ben his punischingis, and whiche is his lawe and service,
whiche ben oure natural wrecchidnessis, whiche ben oure wickidnes-
sis, and whiche ben remedies ayens booth hem" (11). Pecock instructs
that "as soone as the childe comith to yeeris of discipline," the parents
must "teche him to knowe thee, God, thy benefetis and thy lawis,
forto love thee and to serve thee and forto knowe thy punischingis, his
owne natural wrecchidnes and his wickidnes and remedies ayens hem
booth, and to drede ther ayens forto wille or to wirche" (320). These
kinds of comments about the importance of religious instruction as a
charitable activity are typical of contemporary treatises of religious
instruction like the *Speculum Christiani*, which opens with the following thoughts on teaching: "Techinge es that eche body may enforme
and teche his brothir in every place and in conable time, os he seeth
that it be spedful. For this es a gostly almesdede, to which every man
es bounde that hath cunninge."[9] Pecock's sense of the urgency of the
clergy's task to educate the laity is also in keeping with the writings of
the Lollards, who are just as keen as orthodox writers to see the clergy
fulfill their mission of spreading God's word. The Lollard writer of
the sermon *Omnis plantacio* castigates clerics who refuse to share the
dense and nutritional bread of God's word with a lay audience, saying, "Hou cruel they ben to the peple in goostly almesse they shewen
opunly ynow, in that that they hiden the breed of Goddis word so
streitly fro the hungry peple."[10] We can say very broadly, then, that
Pecock's sense of education as one of the Christian acts of charity is in
keeping with contemporary feeling.

What distinguishes Pecock from other writers of didactic tracts,
however, is his sense that his books have an important role to play not
simply in educating individual readers who are interested in more ac-

tively cultivating their spirituality but also in the task of extending God's truths to all the corners of the world. As well as providing an immense resource of Christian learning for both the "weel disposid cristen men of the lay partie" and the "yvel disposed men of the lay partie" (*Reule*, 19), Pecock offers tools for the conversion of the non-Christian: his books are designed to spread the Christian message, through proper methods of education, well beyond his local community. Pecock aims his *summa* of religious knowledge beyond the "lewed and menliche lettred men and wymmen" addressed by manuals like *A Myrour to Lewde Men and Wymmen* to include "painemis, hethene men" (pagans, heathen men) who live "oonly undir the lawe of kinde" and must be shown "motives and argumentis by meenis of resoun" to lessen their potential "horroure or abhominacioun to cristen feith" (*Reule*, 29).[11] In a manner similar to Aquinas in his introduction to the *Summa contra Gentiles*, Pecock claims to provide this grand source of learning not only for members of the Christian community but also for those outside the borders of Christendom. Pecock adopts the same strategy of Aquinas, of appealing to natural reason where possible rather than starting from principles of faith in his teachings. Aquinas says that it is "necessary to have recourse to natural reason, to which all are compelled to assent," because some of his intended readers, "like the Mohammedans and pagans, do not agree with us as to the authority of any Scripture whereby they may be convinced."[12] Pecock's voiced intention to teach heathen men may well be a trope of authorship—a rhetorical device meant to heighten the importance of his work for those within the Christian community, as a weapon in the arsenal of Western Christendom. Pecock's sense of a larger mission for his books, however, in providing effective teaching for masses of believers and nonbelievers distinguishes him from writers who have more moderate goals in mind than providing a kind of standard and comprehensive resource of Christian theology.

Second, Pecock provides not just one didactic treatise that imparts the essentials of doctrine but a whole system of interrelated religious manuals that are to be read at different stages of the learning process. Rather than simply conveying knowledge to readers, Pecock devises a plan to take them from the basics to a higher level of understanding, training their minds at the same time as he passes on religious knowledge. Though only six books of his corpus survive, namely, *The Reule of Crysten Religioun*, *The Donet*, *The Folewer to the Donet*, *The Repressor of Overmuch Blaming of the Clergy*, *The Book of Faith*, and the *Poore Mennis Myrrour*, Pecock continually refers to a number of additional books such as the *Bifore Crier*, *The Filling of the Foure Tablis*, and *The Book of Divine Office*, which are meant to be read with the others: they are "perteiningly knitte to and annexid" to the books that have survived (*Reule*, 9). In the *Reule*, Pecock describes the various books of his corpus as the various colors of a painting that are layered on top of each other to provide the final picture; readers must progress through the easier texts before moving on to more complex and sophisticated modes of instruction (367). "Children" and "simple men and wymmen of witt" start with the *Donet* (*Folewer*, 2), where knowledge about virtue and vice is taught "biginningly" (*Folewer*, 4). Doctrine is presented to readers differently in the *Donet* than in the following books, the *Reule* and the *Folewer to the Donet*: it is outlined in a simple way to ensure that "aftir al this the leerners be the more able to leerne and conceive" the matters of the subsequent books (*Folewer*, 14). Before the reader attempts the more difficult *Folewer*, he should try the *Reule* and "ocupie his witt therinne by long leisers of yeeris unto time he be more able to undirstonde derk and hard maters" (*Folewer*, 14). In his introduction to the *Folewer*, Pecock encourages readers to hone their intellectual faculties and study until they can understand difficult matters: he suggests that learners will "profite, into time, by lenger exercising and using of her wittis in leerning" until the time when "her wittis growe up into clerer light and into larger receivabilnesse" (13). In this passage, Pecock makes it clear that the reading experience has important pedagogical goals that extend beyond the acquisition of religious knowledge: by creating a massive corpus of educational materials that work together in this way, Pecock provides the tools for a kind of standard curriculum for lay readers who wish to school themselves in his methods. This suggests a need for the system of lay religious instruction to be reformed in a fundamental way, by defining religious education as a distinct process that must be standardized and formalized.

It is also clear in Pecock's introductory prefaces to these books that there is a particular way of proceeding through his books that works best. His corpus of materials is not a pile of books that readers should thumb through indiscriminately, looking for subject matter that interests them. Rather, there is an approved method of learning, much the same as that followed in the degree programs charted for young scholars of divinity in the universities. In the *Folewer*, Pecock gives instructions for the best way to proceed but also outlines a different approach for those who do not have the "corage" and "leiser" to read all of the difficult passages (5): he directs these readers to certain key passages, ensuring that they will at least have the most important, general knowledge on moral virtues. Pecock is not content, therefore, to let the reader explore his books in a haphazard and subjective manner; instead, there is a formal procedure to be followed to ensure that each reader receives the most profit. Furthermore, Pecock guides his readers carefully through his corpus, providing ample references to other passages and other works that will clarify and fill out his teaching on various subjects. These frequent cross-references suggest that he envisions readers treating the reading process as more of an academic exercise: readers are to work through his works in a systematic way, rather than "lukyng in haly bukes" more randomly.[13] Of course, this is inherently a more controlled system and shows a degree of caution in allowing readers freedom to move easily from one train of thought to another. In her study of the "polytextual reading" program offered in books of hours, Sylvia Huot argues that the illustrations, glosses, and marginal annotations allowed readers to construct the meaning of the text on their own, choosing to follow one line of thought or another. Huot says, "Such readings could be both edifying and entertaining, free-wheeling or strictly orthodox, according to the inclinations and mood of the reader."[14] Pecock's directed program makes it less likely that readings in his corpus will be so "freewheeling." That Pecock views the reading of his books as a formal kind of study mirroring that of the universities is made clear by his notion that the reading experience will be completed by consultation with learned clerics, in which the lay reader asks for help in puzzling through difficult matters. The challenging nature of Pecock's books ensures that the learned cleric will be called upon to provide instruction to his fellow layman.[15]

The third thing that sets Pecock apart from the authors of other kinds of devotional or didactic treatises, like the English adapter of the *Horologium sapientiae*, is his desire to replace, rather than add to, an ample supply of religious reading material that is currently available for readers of the vernacular in late medieval England. The English translator and adapter of Suso's *Horologium sapientiae* (ca. 1330) introduces his vernacular version of it, *The Seven Poyntes of Trewe and Everlasting Wisdom* (1419), with a brief account of why he decided to produce the translation. He says that he almost decided against it because of the "multitude of bokes & tretees drawne in Englische," but he continued regardless, partly because "the kinde of manne in this life hath likinge in chaunge and diverse thinges, bothe bodilie and gostlie, and summe folke delitene in one & summe in another."[16] The writer suggests that a varied population of readers calls for a varied stock of reading material; some books will satisfy certain readers while other books will give spiritual delight and comfort to others. In the interest of appealing to the taste of readers who might prefer Suso's work to another, he decides to add this alternative source of spiritual knowledge to a growing heap of English religious writings. He indicates that his book is one of many religious works that are available in the fifteenth century, drawing a picture of an abundant supply of reading material for those interested in enriching their spiritual lives.

Pecock does not want to add to this diverse supply of books; instead, he wants to replace it with his own corpus, which will provide abundant variety and sufficient teaching within itself. Pecock expresses the desire to standardize the reading material of the laity, rather than to contribute to a broad range of reading material, when he criticizes other methods of religious instruction and suggests that his own methods are far superior. Indeed, profitable and useful books like his, of moral philosophy, are those that register and give witness to the moral truths of God's law that are printed first on the inner book of reason.[17] These kinds of books should be multiplied to fill the Church of St. Paul's in London, "out of which inward book and writing mowe be taken by labour and studying of clerkis mo conclusiouns and treuthis and governauncis of lawe of kinde and of Goddis moral lawe and service than mighten be written in so manie bokis whiche schulden fille the greet chirche of Seint Poul in Londoun" (*Repressor,* 30–31). Pecock wants to draw readers to books like his and away from their beloved treatises on subjects such as the Ten Commandments and the deadly sins. As I noted in chapter 1, Pecock feels that the popularity of treatises on topics such as the Ten Commandments, the seven sins, and the five wits, which do not treat doctrine as sufficiently, stably, or logically as Pecock's works, is directly related to "the usage of custom of such attendaunce into which the peple is brought and lad thorough long time bi her prechers and techers" (*Donet*, 176). People are creatures of habit, and they are accustomed to reading works that offer inferior (because less substantial) teaching. Pecock is certain that if preachers and teachers were to introduce his works to these readers and bring his superior system of moral teaching "into usage and custom" for "eny notable time," the people would "cleeve and leene to the foorme of the iiii tablis as moche or more than they cleeven and leenen now to the foorme of moyses tablis, and to the othire foormes joined therto of the vii deedly sinnes, of vii werkis of mercy, of v wittis, and so forth" (*Donet*, 176). In Pecock's system of instruction, the lay reader must learn the doctrine of the Creed and the commandments, for example, by understanding the philosophical principles of these rules for belief and behavior rather than by memorizing points of religious instruction in the way that is suggested by pastoral manuals that present these points within a "useful mnemonic framework."[18] Presumably, then, Pecock intends his works to compete for the attention of lay readers with popular compendia of religious instruction such as the *Book of Vices and Virtues*, the *Speculum vitae*, *The Myrour to Lewde Men and Wymmen*, *Speculum Christiani*, and other treatises offering more "easily memorable formulations of basic doctrine" and to "guide the Christian soul in his rejection of sin and his progress in a life of service to God."[19] Pecock attempts to renew the religious education of the laity by replacing the current tools of religious instruction—which have in his view become codified and fixed—with his own system. He calls for a new approach, based on scholastic logic and moral philosophy, to the task of guiding the lay Christian in his moral and spiritual life.[20]

It is also apparent that Pecock feels that he is competing with preachers for the ears and minds of audiences: in his *Folewer to the Donet* he reproves preachers "whiche helden hem clerkis" and yet dismiss rational methods of teaching, saying "fy in resoun, fy in argumentis"

(10). He hopes that these preachers will leave this error, which is "ful unsemely in prechouris, whiche leten hem silf in pulpit to be reulers and reformers and enformers of worthy peple, as by greet autorite and overte over the heerers, be so derk and so unsufficiently feling" (10). He bases his own teaching on rational argumentation so that "such errour growe not in time to come in persoones whiche mowe be preservid therfro by this present writing" (10). The need for Pecock to save and protect the worthy people, through this "present writing," from preachers who have great authority over them reinforces the distinction between Pecock's approach to teaching and that of others at the same time as it conveys an urgent need to cast away old customs and methods and to install Pecock's works in their place. This, of course, implies that there should be one, universal approach to the religious teaching of the laity: lay education must be standardized and consistent. Every sin, whether it exists in "man or woman, preest or prince or comuner, monke or frere or nunne," is covered by Pecock's moral teaching on the virtues, in his four tables; his teaching is therefore pertinent to all of these people (*Reule*, 363). This impulse toward standardization of a curriculum and a teaching method distinguishes Pecock from writers like the adapter of Suso's *Horologium sapientiae*, who depicts himself as a contributor to a varied supply of teaching materials rather than as the creator of a set syllabus.

The fourth and final thing that distinguishes Pecock's books from other didactic treatises is the place that they will occupy in the school system: Pecock outlines a plan to endow universities, colleges, and schools that will have his works on the curriculum. To ensure that "alle kindes of moral vertues or of goddis servicis" are learned by clerics, adults, children, monks, friars, and nuns, it will be necessary first "to founde and endewe by liiflood universitees and therin colleges that therby clerkis or leernid men be brought up into leerning and kunning forto edifie and to teche othere in the vii principal maters of this present book" (*Reule*, 363). This system is self-sustaining: founding universities and colleges with Pecock's works on the curriculum will ensure that teachers are properly equipped to teach the seven principal matters of Pecock's *Reule*, which in his opinion should be "taken of alle thy cristen peple into use of ful bisy, ech day studying, leerning and comuning and afterward thereupon remembring" (13).

The teachers of both clergy and laity will be educated in Pecock's ped-agogical systems, and they will pass on this learning in several ways: "in chaier of scole or in pulpit of chirch or in eny counceil giving or in eny doute or questioun assoiling apart to oon or ii or fewe herers out of open congregacioun of peple" (363). To ensure that these matters are taught in schools, it will be necessary to find sources of funding for the schooling of children, both "mawlis or femawlis" (363). Pecock's works are to be taught, therefore, at the very lowest and very highest levels of education. To make this teaching possible, it will be necessary to ensure an ample supply of his books, to "finde greet let-trid men and leernid men to write and profiitable bookis" (363). These same men will also "teche in scolis, or to go aboute to preche openly and solempnely in pulpet or to teche and answer openly and not solempnely out of pulpet" (363–64). This passage clarifies Pecock's views about the role his books can play in innovating systems of teaching in books, as well as in the pulpit, in schools, in open con-gregations of people, in councils, and in universities and colleges.

Pecock's desire to change the curriculum at the elementary level is indicated by his comment about the teaching of his seven matters "in scolis" and in "chaier of scole," as well as his statement that the *Donet* is intended for both children and beginners.[21] As Orme testifies, "ele-mentary education" started with the reading of the basic prayers in books containing the elements of the faith."[22] He writes that "in the absence of any real textbooks or readers specially designed for elemen-tary instruction . . . service books provided a useful substitute": the Psalter and the matins book, for example, gave children practice in recognizing words and learning to read, at the same time as prepar-ing them for "performing religious devotions later in life."[23] Jo Ann Hoeppner Moran writes that the curriculum would also include books owned by teachers, citing the example of a grammar master at Lincoln in 1410 who owned two English tracts on the Ten Commandments and one on the seven deadly sins; she cites another example of an ele-mentary text that includes the alphabet, the seven works of mercy, the Ten Commandments, and the seven deadly sins.[24] The primer was also a common text for this first stage of education, if available to stu-dents and teachers. In her recent study of devotional literature, Mary Erler describes primers as follows: "The book's core was the hours of the Virgin; these were preceded by a calendar and by set passages from the four Gospels, and were followed (in the book's sparest form) by the seven penitential psalms, the litany of the saints, and the office of the dead."[25] Less spare versions of this book could include the alphabet and additional prayers and instruction on the seven deadly sins, the seven principal virtues, the seven works of bodily mercy, the seven works of ghostly mercy, the five wits, the four cardinal virtues, and the seven gifts of the Holy Ghost.[26] Interestingly, most primers were in Latin, which means that schoolchildren's first contact with religious texts was not through English, as Pecock evidently wished.

From Pecock's comments it seems that the *Donet*, as well as other books in his corpus, such as his books of reformed prayers, *The Book of Divine Office*, and *Enchiridion*, could replace texts used at the elementary level. It would be interesting to know with more certainty if Pecock envisioned a form of elementary education that reflected his own "religious preoccupations"[27]—in other words, if Pecock's disapproval of current forms of instruction on the Creed, the seven sins, the five wits, the works of charity, and the Ten Commandments would extend to a desire to reform the basic level of instruction in literacy, at which children were exposed to these elements of the faith. Pecock's efforts to ensure that the laity would understand rather than memorize doctrine, prayers, articles of belief, and rules for Christian behavior may have required a change in the syllabus used to teach literacy to young children. In any case, this passage on the need for all members of society to be properly educated, through formal education, in Pecock's seven matters sets him apart: while the writers of works like *A Myrour to Lewde Men and Wymmen* voice similar desires to write fruitful treatises that will help readers to understand "what is vertue and what is sinne," they do not provide instructions for the use of their works in a broader educational system including children, men and women of the laity, and clerics.[28]

Though Pecock's desire to have his works on the curriculum at schools and universities may seem radical, his interest in the endowment of schools and universities aligns him with his reform-minded contemporaries. In her study of education in fifteenth-century England, Clara McMahon describes the foundation "of at least seven new colleges at Cambridge and Oxford, a series of endowments made not only to the universities proper but to individual colleges, and a building program that was undertaken at the beginning of the century and successfully carried through regardless of barriers and financial upsets."[29] McMahon suggests that "institutions of higher learning were at least holding their ground, and in some instances advancing," helped by the efforts of numerous churchmen, including Richard Fleming, bishop of Lincoln, who "proposed to supply a perpetual succession of enemies to Wycliffe's doctrines by building a college for theologians," as well as Henry Chichele, archbishop of Canterbury and "steadfast patron of Oxford," who did "much in the way of foundations" and "conceived the idea of an academic foundation for the study and training of clerks for the increase of clergy in England."[30] The founding of colleges and the growth of education were also assisted by the "patronage and protection of Henry VI, who was keenly and profoundly interested in the furtherance of education."[31] Pecock is not alone, then, in considering the importance of founding colleges and universities in order to ensure a supply of well-qualified teachers and preachers for both laity and clergy.

Nor is Pecock unique in his inclusion of children, both male and female, in his scheme, his emphasis on the need for citizens to make provision for the education of these children, and his comments about the need to train both clerics and laymen in the seven matters so that they can provide instruction for these children. These concerns are in keeping with general trends in medieval education noted by Orme and Moran. For instance, Orme testifies that toward the end of the medieval period, both laymen and members of the religious orders taught in public, secular schools.[32] As well, Orme notes that the fifteenth century saw an unprecedented rise in endowed schools; previously, students had had to pay fees to the schoolmaster to acquire an education, but in the fifteenth century free schools funded by clergy or wealthy laymen were becoming more common.[33] R. N. Swanson points out that Henry Chichele, for example, created an establishment at Higham Ferrers that was "intended to provide free education for local children."[34] Pecock's interest in educating children, both boys and girls, is in keeping with fifteenth-century ideas about the need to educate more children in a public system. Moran writes that girls learned alongside boys in household schools, convents that admitted children of both sexes, and even some public elementary schools.[35] While it is hard to get a clear sense of whether girls were routinely included in the public, secular schools that were multiplying in the fifteenth century, Pecock's directions to send both sexes to school seems to support the notion that girls had the opportunity to receive elementary education.[36]

Pecock's educational scheme is therefore in line with other orthodox efforts to increase the quality and availability of education in the fifteenth century; it is also in line with Wycliffite interests in education. Pecock's ambition to provide formal schooling in his corpus for children, laity, and clerics may also point to his awareness that the only way to put a stop to the schools of Lollardy was to replace underground systems of religious instruction with formal, orthodox systems of education. Pecock's mission to eradicate heresy and convert the "yvel disposed men of the lay partie" can help us understand why he is so keen to see his books integrated in a structured program of education in both schools and universities. His vision of educating adults in his seven matters through books, informal teaching, or formal teaching in school or from the pulpit can be viewed as a calculated response to Lollard initiatives in lay education.[37] Pecock writes that he hopes to provide an alternative to Lollard religious instruction with the kinds of books that are made "profitably and dewly" for "Cristen mennes sufficient scoling" (*Reule*, 18). The right kinds of books—those that are made "groundly and fruitfully and formaly and treuly, unwaastly and saverosely into her necessarie scoling and leerning"—will "wowe the more multitude" and win "summe lovers" for God (19, 36). Pecock makes it clear that his motivation to write books like the *Reule* comes in part from his awareness of the dangers posed by the instruction provided in Lollard books and Lollard schools: he aims the *Reule* at those who dedicate themselves to Bible study and who believe that "al bisines which men don forto haunte scolis and forto leerne or to teche by writing, in eny other maner than by reding and studying in the bible" is "a deceit into which men ben led by the feend" (17). It is Pecock's duty to assure these avid Bible readers that study or schooling in his seven matters is not a "deceit into which men are led by the devil" but a more productive method of learning God's law. He writes books like the *Reule* in the hope that erring laymen will "caste aside her seid wlatsum bookis, yhe perilose bookis, untrewe bokis, un-sufficiently teching bokis, unformally, unschaply and unseemely tret-ing bokis, as thingis no lenger worthy to be had in haunt and in use" (19).[38] Convincing readers to cast these books aside will be no easy task: the Lollards view their books as "noble and worthy and profit-able bookis to alle cristen mennes leerning and rewling, and ben as riche jewelis to be dertheworthly biclippid, loved, and multiplied abrood of alle cristen peple" (18). Pecock observes in *The Book of Faith* that the erring members of the laity have their own books "in grete noumbre," showing us how important books are to the kinds of read-ers he hopes to win over (119).

Pecock's ideas about the need to instruct adults through the pro-vision of books in his seven matters and his suggestion that "greet let-trid men and leernid men" must be found and encouraged to write "profiitable bookis" indicate his awareness that readers could not be drawn away from their heretical books by just a few orthodox books; rather, what was needed was a corpus of books that would form a coherent and consistent educational system—a kind of curriculum for lay readers (*Reule*, 363). Indeed, Pecock recognizes what Anne Hud-son has revealed to us about the importance of books to the Lollard heresy: Hudson identifies reading in the vernacular as "the basic de-vice of Lollard education" and suggests that "the written word spoke louder and clearer than the heard word" for Lollards, who set a great deal of value and spent a great deal of time on their books.[39] She de-scribes how the Lollards ensured lay access to books for those who desired it through a system of group ownership: "Members of a group might contribute money to a book or books, and the lending of books was so commonplace that it implies that the ownership was probably communal." Such arrangements make it clear that "social insignifi-cance, and even poverty, was evidently . . . no bar to Lollard access to books."[40]

Though Pecock's books will provide content different from that of the books so beloved by the Lollards, Pecock's methods of instruc-tion will be similar to the Lollard project of education: Pecock has observed the power of dialogue, informal teaching, schools, preaching, and books to spread heretical beliefs, and he exploits this system in his own vision of orthodox education in his seven matters. For example, both Pecock and the Lollards recognize the value of informal teaching in "counceil" of a small number of people (*Reule*, 363). Both Anne Hudson and Rita Copeland emphasize the importance of dialogue and discussion in spreading Lollard beliefs.[41] As Hudson writes, "Discussion obviously formed, along with reading and preaching, the basic ingredient of Lollard education."[42] Conversations such as "Margery Baxter's frequent instructions to her neighbours, whether singly or in twos and threes, her communications with William White, and even her nocturnal instruction in the scriptures by her husband are none of them called 'schools,'" but they were important in the passage and development of ideas.[43] For example, Hudson's study of the development of beliefs about salvation among members of the Lollard community in Coventry (eight of which were accused of heresy in 1486) leads her to the conclusion that "it is possible to perceive how the discussion could have developed, and how intelligent, if unacademic, Lollards could progress from the conventional distrust of their sect in prayers for the dead and well-attested doubts about purgatory . . . to a much more advanced and unusual, albeit undeveloped, concept of salvation by faith alone."[44] Dialogue and discussion among members of heretical groups could lead to the development of more advanced and sophisticated concepts. Pecock recognizes the power of discussion in the spread and development of heretical beliefs and is prepared to use a more structured form of dialogue to correct Lollard views and reinforce orthodox beliefs: he wants instruction on his seven matters to take place "in eny counceil giving or in eny doute or questioun assoiling apart to oon or ii or fewe herers out of open congregacioun of peple" (*Reule*, 363), and he notes that informal discussion has been a useful tool in his own experience for correcting Lollards and pointing out their errors: "I have spoke oft time, and by long leiser, with the wittiest and kunningist men of thilk seid soort, contrarie to the chirche, and which han be holde as dukis amonge hem, and which han loved me for that y wolde paciently heere her evidencis, and her motives, without exprobacioun. And verrili noon of hem couthe make eny motive for her party so stronge as y my silf couthe have made therto" (*BF*, 202). Pecock invites members of the community to share their doubts or questions with him; this exchange of ideas between laymen and well-trained clerics like Pecock can be a strong force in correction by identifying and removing erroneous beliefs. Correcting the errors held by the lay folk for whom Pecock writes *The Book of Faith* will require, first, the publishing and multiplying of his books and others like them, and, second, "communicacioun" with readers of these books "by word and speche at diverse leisers" (*BF,* 114).

It is unclear, however, whether Pecock's vision of instruction in councils or small gatherings or even "open congregacioun of peple" resembles actual Lollard schools: Hudson describes these schools as communal events that happened in private places, "out of the public gaze"; often, passages from the Bible were read aloud or recited from memory and discussed by members of the group, which could be composed of neighbors, family members, and sometimes visiting preachers.[45] Hudson argues that Lollard schools can be differentiated from more informal discussion between members of the heretical sect because the schools "consisted in more formal, and usually group instruction." However, the group could be as small as seven people. It appears that demarcations between teacher and student were less clear in Lollard schools than in Pecock's vision of religious instruction: "Men and women who might at one time, or in some company, be learners might at other times, or in other company, be teachers."[46] Local laypeople—women included—could be the teachers, rather than formally trained clerics. Some Lollard communities seem to have flourished without the leadership of a trained cleric: Hudson notes that the group in Coventry seems to have lacked an "outside teacher who could have dominated them."[47] In Pecock's plans for the instruction of the laypeople, by contrast, whether the teaching is done "in chaier of scole or in pulpet of chirch or in eny counceil," there is a clear division between the pupils and their "greet lettrid" and "leernid" teachers, who are formally trained at endowed colleges and universities to instruct and "teche othere in the vii principal maters" (*Reule,* 363).

Pecock's sense of the need to instruct the laity, then, is not radical. He is drawing on Wycliffite traditions of schooling and following in the footsteps of the bishops who undertook an "incredibly ambitious programme" of religious instruction following the Fourth Lateran Council of 1215.[48] Indeed, his program can be understood as a new stage in an educational program that aimed to instruct the clergy in "fundamental theology and pastoral care," to ensure the laity's access to the whole of pastoral theology through frequent preaching and teaching, and to provide "the resultant training in self-analysis which was propaedeutic to confession and must have left an indelible imprint on Western consciousness."[49] It is important to acknowledge that Pecock is an outgrowth of this pastoral tradition, especially in his decision to make his seven matters the new basis for lay confession, and hence for training in self-analysis. Pecock's decision to cast aside the proven formulas of the instructional program, however, marks him as an innovator within this pastoral tradition. His sense that religious instruction should take the shape of progressive, formal, standardized, and systematic study in a single corpus of works based on his unique system is new. Members of the pious laity who owned religious manuals and contemplative treatises, like Cicely of York and Robert Thornton, may have devised individualized and highly structured spiritual routines for themselves and their families that incorporated reading, prayer, and meditation, but there was no universal, formal educational program in religion for members of the laity involving different pedagogical stages. Primers and pastoral manuals were perhaps the closest thing to a common program of religious instruction, but there was no standardized table of contents in primers until the middle of the sixteenth century, and pastoral manuals, though common, could be radically different from one another, rather than consistent and uniform.[50] Furthermore, these kinds of works lacked extensive instructions about the methods of use and frequent reminders of the need for progress to more advanced stages of knowledge. Pecock's insistence on the superior nature of his methods, combined with his efforts to provide a single consistent and unified syllabus for religious instruction and to get the learned clergy involved in filling out the learning process through "conseil" as well as public teaching, takes the educational impetus behind the creation of primers and pastoral manuals one step further, making this instruction programmatic and universal (*Reule*, 363).

Medieval views about the nature of education can throw light on the distinct aspects of Pecock's vision. Orme states that orthodox religious instruction was viewed and treated as a form of preparation for Christian life rather than a distinct, formal process of education. He writes,

Boys and girls, particularly those of the aristocracy, grew up in a society so permeated by clergy and religious activities that Christian belief and behaviour could reasonably be expected to grow naturally, rather than needing to be planted and tended artificially. . . . There was little or no idea of "coming of age" in religious terms, in the form of a first confession or first communion; there was no public instruction of children as such, no "Sunday schools," or texts specifically devised for children's use. Most of the religious education of the young must have occurred informally. Parents, godparents, and masters taught the Creed and the basic prayers, religious stories and the principles of morality. . . . Children were exposed to religious art, went into sacred buildings and watched their elders at their devotions. They learnt by experience what went on, and by example how they should behave.[51]

Orme argues that religious instruction was not viewed as a systematic, formal procedure in the way that Pecock seems to view it; instead, it was felt to be part of the general shaping or nurture of the whole individual. Learning about God did not take place separately from learning about life in general and did not receive the "special emphasis" that Pecock wants to give it.[52] The way that Orme compares the organic process of natural growth to a more artificial kind of planting and tending suggests that in the view of medieval thinkers, religious knowledge grows organically in the individual through a gentle process of nurture (parental guidance, participation in social rites and religious activities, exposure to religious art) rather than through a more active implantation of information. Religion was taught to children along with principles of self-discipline, good behavior, ceremonial actions, and good manners.[53] Knowledge about God and morality was acquired through general life experience rather than in a formal, or "artificial" manner. Orme suggests that the reason for this failure to distinguish education as a distinct, formal procedure was related to general views about education: "Most medieval thinkers and writers failed to distinguish . . . education as a process separate from human life in general."[54] He writes,

What separated the fourteenth- and fifteenth-century aristocracy from their Tudor and Stuart successors was not a lack of education but a lack of consciousness about it. This arose from the nature of medieval education, which was less distinct from life in general than it has since become. In the great household, the chief location of aristocratic upbringing, education was only one of many activities. Most of those who provided it . . . were not specially trained to do so, and had other duties and interests. . . . The evolution of a specialized literature of education was complementary to this process—education had to become a distinct process before it could stimulate a distinct genre of writing.[55]

Orme indicates that religious education was not separated from other aspects of a child's upbringing or singled out as a specific and distinct process of public instruction based on ideas of progress, "coming of age," and what Copeland would call "'duration,' the idea that real knowledge is produced through prolonged institutional mentoring that coincides with the years of biological development."[56] Marie Denley echoes Orme's suggestion that religious education was not seen as a separate process from the general formation of medieval children: "The more one considers what can be gleaned about the basic education of medieval children, the more apparent it becomes that it is a continuum in which the intellectual, the religious, the moral, the social, and the practical cannot be separated without doing violence to the beliefs of medieval educators. The formation of the virtuous Christian from the untutored child is the unifying aim."[57] The idea of treating religious education as a separate practice, which should be conducted in a formal and methodical way, would be foreign to those who mingled "precepts of Christian behaviour" with instruction "on how to be a good gatekeeper or butler."[58] According to Denley, the socialization of the child within the household, the social and moral grooming of the child, and elementary religious education were seen as one "holistic" process: children were "themselves programmed from an early age to see the content of their 'curriculum' as a continuum and not to separate, or to be surprised at the conjunction of, religious and practical educational matter."[59] Education prepared children for the roles they would assume in society, as Christian men and women, rather than training their rational faculties and setting out a course for intellectual progress. As Swanson points out, basic education, provided within the parish, was "closely linked to training for participation in church services";[60] for Pecock, however, basic education is not so much about training children to say prayers correctly and more about training both children and adults to think more rationally about doctrine and devotion.

Given these ideas about the nature of religious instruction, Pecock's sense that laypeople must be schooled properly in his seven matters seems like an entirely new stage in the tradition of instruction in pastoral theology beginning with Pecham's syllabus. Pecock thinks a great deal about the distinct process of education, and his works are characterized by his consciousness of education as such: rather than simply acting out of a desire to pass on religious knowledge to the laity, Pecock is constantly thinking about how his works will affect the learning process of the lay reader. Though moral instruction on sin and virtue may be "naturally" absorbed or memorized in childhood, the lay reader must go back to the basics, as it were, and relearn moral principles in a rational, systematic way to secure a stronger foundation for Christian belief and behavior. For Pecock, religious education must offer each believer the how and why of the faith, explaining the basis of moral principles, the reason behind Christian ceremony, the foundations of ceremonial actions, the principles of the basic prayers, and the nature of virtue and sin. This kind of teaching is quite a contrast to what Orme describes as a "natural" or organic process of religious education by which a layperson absorbs beliefs and moral directives from life experiences, from informal instruction, from participation in communal rituals and practices, or from the rote learning and memorization of doctrine facilitated by current forms of religious didactic writings.[61] Pecock may not go so far as to outline a plan for "prolonged institutional mentoring" in his corpus of educational works "coinciding with years of biological development,"[62] but to suggest that adults must set out deliberately and methodically to educate themselves in his seven matters and to study each day in his books is to imply that religious teaching must receive "special emphasis."[63]

Innovating a tradition of pastoral teaching, and extending the tradition of Lollard schooling, Pecock provides a kind of institutional response to Lollardy that differs greatly from other responses, namely, those of the Constitutions of Archbishop Arundel. If we keep in mind that Pecock played an important, authoritative role as a bishop of the church and that he viewed the religious education of the laity as one of the most important duties of the clergy, we can surmise that his production of sophisticated tools of religious instruction was intended to be, not an act of deliberate defiance to the Constitutions (legislation that I discussed in the introductory chapter), but rather an alternative to them. The most important of the Constitutions for this chapter is that which forbids the teaching of the rudiments of the faith in schools. Pecock's plan to educate the laity in his seven matters, which draw upon the truths of reason and faith, flies in the face of this legislation.

I would suggest that it is not entirely clear whether someone like Pecock would have felt that these ecclesiastical decrees would have applied to someone like him: at times it seems that he is being careful to obey them, yet at other times he does not seem to indicate any concern about the need to limit or restrict his discussion in light of them. For instance, in his *Reule*, Pecock refers readers to other books in his corpus for discussion of matters that we know were deemed dangerous by the Constitutions: he indicates that he will provide more elaborate treatments of the various truths of faith in his *Book of Faith* and refers readers interested in more detailed exposition of the sacraments to his *Bokis of Sacramentis* (309). He does discuss the sacraments, however, under the general topic of man's duty to God,[64] and he does list the truths of the faith, including truths about the nature of the Trinity (*Reule*, 71–99). He remarks that because "manie of the lay partie bileeven amiss in mater of the eukarist," he has written the *Book of Eukarist* to set these people straight (*Reule*, 96). Rather than indicating that this is a forbidden and dangerous subject, therefore, Pecock devotes an entire book (no longer in existence) to the topic of this sacrament. Moreover, he quotes the Bible throughout his discussion of the seven matters in the *Reule*, in both Latin and English. While all of this would seem to indicate that Pecock was acting in violation of the Constitutions, it is unclear whether he actually felt that he was breaking the rules. In the first part of the *Reule*, he anticipates objections to his treatment of the Trinity and begrudgingly accepts that this section may have to be omitted if some people deem this doctrine to be too difficult for lay readers; he then presents the most difficult discussion of the Trinity in Latin to avoid censure. But as I stated in chapter 1, Pecock bristles at the idea that lay readers cannot handle this kind of intellectual labor, declaring that "the lay peple muste nedis and schulen be drive to forto conceive herder and darker trouthis with harder and darker evidences in plees of lond, in plees of dette and of trespace, in rekeningis to be maad of receivers and rente gaderers in the account of an audit, yhe in bargeins making of greet marchaundisis and in rekeningis making thereupon, as a man schal soone wite if he take homlines with mercers of London" (93–94). Despite these objections, however, Pecock agrees to accept the judgment of others about which portions of his books should be left out when they are made available to the "comoun peple" (99). From what Pecock says about his willingness to censor parts of the *Reule* that do not receive institutional approval, it appears that Pecock thought that his teachings on the seven matters were perfectly legitimate, if a little too ambitious in certain places. I would argue that it is likely that Pecock, writing from a position of authority as a bishop, did not feel that the Constitutions were intended for someone like him and that he was more concerned to respond to a more general feeling among the highly learned clergy that certain truths about the Godhead, treated by theologians like Peter Lombard, were too dense for the common lay reader: in Pecock's view, such truths may "passen the undirstonding and the receivabilnes of the comoun peple and of clerkis being yonge biginners in scole or divinete and of clerkis not leernid moche in comoun philosophie, in metephisik, and in the highest party of divinite" (86). Such truths are not appropriate for readers—lay *or* clerical—who lack specialized training of higher studies at the university level. Pecock omits dense theological discussion because of his feeling that beginners must start with easier matters before they progress to more challenging theological problems; he seems confident, however, that lay readers could deal with these matters just as easily as clerics once they had reached a certain level of study. I would suggest that Pecock seems less concerned about the Constitutions, in this passage, and more concerned about how his works will be viewed by those who believe that providing elaborate discussions of the sophisticated and complex doctrine of the Trinity is inappropriate for readers—lay or clerical—who lack the necessary training. I would argue that Pecock is not acting in open defiance of ecclesiastical authorities; rather, he is a creative thinker who was highly motivated to come up with other solutions for promoting orthodoxy.

Indeed, Pecock's frequent addresses to the reader about the value of his books and his frequent instructions to his fellow clergymen and highly learned laymen about the need to provide all members of the laity with his books (or at least books like his) suggest that Pecock had more important matters on his mind than the Constitutions in his earnest efforts to find an effective method of combating heresy and fortifying orthodoxy. The way that he introduces the *Folewer*, by invoking God's help in creating a work that will bring the most profit to his readers, makes it clear that Pecock felt that he was doing God's work and that his "mission in the Church's fight against heresy" was divinely inspired.[65] He prays for divine assistance, addressing God as "grettest lover of men, and grettist desirer that thy peple schulden love togidere and leerne togedir the vii cheef maters of my writingis devisid for lay men, and that they schulde speke therin togidere into eche of hem otheris edifying" (*Folewer*, 8). Pecock's progressive plan for lay education comes from his notion that God himself wants his people to work together to learn to know, love, and serve God through Pecock's seven matters. And even though we find no traces of evidence that Pecock's scheme was put into practice, or that he had a direct influence on the thought of subsequent churchmen with interests in Christian pedagogy, the fact that six of Pecock's books survive and that multiple searches had to be performed to extract his books from his adherents tells us that others shared Pecock's notion that an educational system that cultivated the lay intellect was a divinely approved and potent means of stabilizing orthodoxy and rooting out heresy.

three

Theological Training
and the Mixed Life

In the previous chapter, I suggested that Reginald Pecock's vision of lay education for "alle cristen peple" (*Reule*, 13) constitutes both a massive transfer of *clergie*—of knowledge and learning—to a lay audience and an innovative approach to the religious instruction of the laity. Pecock's religious writings are part of the "extensive and consistent process of assimilation by the laity of techniques and materials of spiritual advancement," but they also offer readers a bold alternative to the majority of materials of spiritual advancement.[1] These books provide extensive and systematic theological training for the laity, covering a wide range of matter including the nature of the soul, the different kinds of grace, the nature of the Trinity, the rewards of heaven, and the best ways to earn God's forgiveness. Determined to share his system of the seven matters of religious knowledge with all members of society, Pecock even makes arrangements for his larger works to be condensed into shorter "extractis or out draughtis" (*Reule*, 86, 22) that presumably will be more accessible and affordable for a wider range of lay folk. Pecock's *Provoker*, for example, is "lasse compendiose" than the more ample *Witnessing of the iiii Tablis*, which is "peraventure, over costiose to pore men" (*Donet*, 177). The *Poore Mennis Myrrour*, an extract from his *Donet*, is of such "litil quantite that welnigh ech poor person maye by sum meene gete coost to have it as his owne" (*PMM*, 226). Pecock is not simply being charitable; he sounds like a stern schoolmaster when he says that after the "sufficient pupplisching" of the *Poore Mennis Myrrour*, no man will have "excusacioun" for not knowing Pecock's seven matters (*PMM*, 226).

In this chapter, I examine Pecock's ideas about the place that this theological training occupies in the lives of his lay readers. I suggest that Pecock views theological training in his corpus as the necessary foundation for the first stage of Christian life—a stage that is contemplative in nature and followed by active life in the world. I begin by studying a passage in the *Reule of Crysten Religioun* in which Pecock discusses the story of Mary and Martha, the sisters visited by Christ in the Gospel, who became in the Middle Ages the traditional symbols of contemplative and active lives.[2] Pecock's version of this story highlights his understanding of the contemplative life as both learning (training the intellect to know God and self) and devotional activities (training the heart and the will to turn toward God). What comes through in this story is Pecock's understanding of the mixed life as a life suitable for all Christians, a life that begins with contemplation, is fulfilled in action, and requires constant oscillation between the two. Once I have examined the passage on Mary and Martha, I look at other passages in which Pecock discusses the nature of contemplative life and its various practices. Throughout, I argue that Pecock's vision of lay religious education both situates his corpus in a tradition of Middle English works that sought to direct lay religious life through demanding practices of learning and devotion and redefines the concept of the mixed life. Pecock insists that theological training in his seven matters is the core of contemplative life and, further, that contemplative pursuits of learning, prayer, and meditation are the duty not just of monks and pious noblewomen but also of each individual Christian. In his mapping of the mixed life and in his establishment of ambitious requirements for those who lived it, we can see just how instrumental and pivotal his program of Christian education was intended to be in restructuring the lives of the Christian laity.

The story of Mary and Martha illustrates the best way to order the Christian life. Pecock uses this story to direct readers who are unsure about how best to serve God and whether they should start or finish with good works. For Pecock, Mary and Martha do not represent two exclusive choices of contemplation and action; rather, he argues that the Gospel draws a comparison between their two ways of life, both of which were a mixture of action and contemplation but were ordered differently. Pecock argues that Mary was superior because she followed the correct order in life, beginning with contemplation, defined as paying heed to God's laws and words, then fulfilling this learning and devotion in action: Mary was commended by Christ because she "bigan at the contemplatiif liif and at contemplacioun in heering of thy word to dispose hir and scharpe hir the bettir ayen the time sche schulde wirche outward werkis" (*Reule*, 490). Contemplation, defined here as listening attentively to God's word in a way that disposes Christians toward outward works, is an activity that generates love and goodwill toward God, as well as desire to serve him. It is not a moment of rapture. Mary was praised because she began with contemplative life, which Pecock defines as follows: "Contemplatiif liif is not ellis than the uss of inward leerning or remembring, the uss of inward preising, dispreising, worschiping, disworchiping, thanking, preying, and sacramenting" (468–69).

As a model of the mixed life that begins with contemplation and ends with action, therefore, Mary started with the primary activities of "inward deedis" of "resoun, of biholding, or considering" that helped her acquire knowledge, reflect on this knowledge, and generate "welwilling" to God from this knowledge (469). It is significant that Pecock defines Mary's contemplative activity at Christ's feet not as a kind of restful state of meditation on divine mysteries—a state that separated her from the human world—but as a kind of active attention in which she received instruction and knowledge about how to love and serve God. Mary "desirid in thilk time to heere and to leerne the trewe service of god and how sche mighte love him more and bettir serve him than sche dide afore" (491). Christ did not speak to Mary of heavenly mysteries, but "thou taughtist thy Fadris dewe service, how he schulde be loved and served" (492). Pecock emphasizes that Mary wished to gain knowledge and increase her devotion so that she could "scharpe hir the bettir ayen the time sche schulde wirche outward werkis" (490). Mary is defined as the Christian who begins with knowledge and love, both of which come to fruition in good works.

Christ praised her because she had the proper intent for her service to God—learning the true service and worship of God ensures the proper motivation for the active life.

Martha, on the other hand, did not have the proper foundation of contemplation before she engaged in active service to Christ. As a result, her service was flawed—"troublid" and "carkful"—because she lacked the proper intent (489).[3] In Pecock's version of the story, Martha was rebuked because she had given herself to active works without enough "inward contemplatiif bisines." Without the contemplative activity her sister practiced, Martha lacked what was needed to whet and sharpen a person "sufficiently to continue the outward actiif werkis forth in perseveraunce and to kepe him from these now seid defautis of solicitude, trouble, inpacience and unpure entent" (488–89). By neglecting the inward activities meant to shape the Christian's intent, Martha opened herself to the distraction of worldly concerns in her active duty in service to God. Though she started off on the wrong foot, however, Martha was not a lost cause; Pecock writes that Martha improved her situation after Christ's death, embracing contemplation and then fulfilling it in action: "Aftir thy deeth, Crist, whanne sche was more spiritual, sche uside the governaunce of Marie til bothe sche and Marie and also hir brothir weren made ful able by contemplacioun forto wirche into peple and for to converte him into the feith, as hir legende makith mencioun" (490). In Pecock's view, Mary and Martha ended up governing themselves ideally in a mixed life of contemplation and ministry, but the early stages of preparation for this life were slightly different. Mary was correct to begin by immersing herself in contemplation and then to proceed in the work of converting others to God. Pecock emphasizes that contemplation is the necessary stage before the activity of converting others to the faith; gaining knowledge and kindling devotion must precede active ministry.

Pecock's interpretation of Mary as a representative of the ideal form of mixed life rather than a representative of the purely solitary contemplative life has its roots in what Giles Constable describes as a strand of thought on the subject of active and contemplative lives that was prominent toward the end of the Middle Ages. Constable notes that Martha's active part tends to be valued more highly during the late medieval period. Martha begins to receive more praise for her active service, which is seen as more meritorious than contemplative withdrawal. As Martha is commended for her active service in the world, Mary begins to emulate her conduct, taking on some active works like penance and ministry.[4] Concerned with reforming not just the lives of lay Christians but also the monastic institutions, Pecock argues that contemplation must be combined with action at all levels of society. Monastic brethren should be occupied less in prayer and song and more in education and conversion (*Reule*, 419). The activities of the contemplative life—of prayer, meditation, and worship—must not be used alone; they must be understood as "meenal" virtues that "han a dewe ordre forto go bifore the thingis into whiche thei ben meenis" (*Donet*, 24). He warns, "No man schulde neither may allowably wirche and do and haunte meenal moral vertues as though they were pure and uttrist eendal moral vertues; and if eny man so do, he lesith the grace and the meede whiche therby ellis mighte be deserved" (*Reule*, 379–80). Pecock adds that too many Christians pursue the contemplative life as an end in itself, commenting that the notion that the spiritual practices of contemplative life, like prayer and meditation, are a goal in themselves is "holden for treuthe and is ful miche usid undir colour of greet religiosite and holy moral goodnes" (381). As he explains further, "It is not discrecioun, neither the good demeening of resoun— and therfore not vertuose governaunce, and not so meritorie neither to thee, god, plesaunt governaunce—to spende as it were al time in use of preising or preier and meditacioun, worschiping and sacramenting, and therby leve undoon the final werkis whiche ben othere vertues toward thee, and toward oure neighboris, and that for greet attendaunce to these meenis . . . right as a man oughte no lengir whette his knyf than it is at first maad sufficiently able to kutte therwith his mete" (390). A knife must be sharpened to cut meat; sharpening it further wastes time and effort. Similarly, the soul must be sharpened and whetted to carry out God's service; engaging further in contemplation does not make one holier or more religious. Pecock makes it clear that the singular pursuit of the contemplative life would be a kind of unfulfilled, half-empty Christian life. He integrates the lives seamlessly, showing that contemplation flows naturally and necessarily into action and erasing the boundary between the two types of life.

Pecock emphasizes the value of action, suggesting that contemplation should lead directly and naturally into an active life of good moral deeds in God's service. The way he commends active service in the world—for everyone—can be seen as a development within a textual tradition that fostered meaningful religious lives among ambitious lay readers. The writer of *Book to a Mother*, for example, offers spiritual direction not only to his widowed mother but also to a general Christian audience, showing models of conduct and piety that would inspire lay readers. One of these models is Mary: the story of Mary and Martha functions in this treatise as encouragement to pursue the contemplative life. Nicholas Watson points out that this author seems to indicate that "Martha will actually be damned unless she becomes Mary before death": "The widow and those who read with her find themselves in a world in which the only viable form of religious life is one of radical holiness, in which sin is remedied only by perfect living, not by mere obedience to the commandments. Following this logic—which in practice restricts its notionally universal audience to a group of like-mindedly austere readers—the *Book* asserts that the only remedy for sin is the rigorous imitation of Christ."[5]

In contrast to Watson, Nicole Rice argues that the *Book to a Mother* "does not privilege the contemplative life" but instead "insists upon an active form of *imitatio Christi* in the world." By establishing Christ in his teaching capacity as a model for the reader, Rice argues, the author of the *Book to a Mother* promotes the active work of learning and teaching instead of passive suffering.[6] The discussion of Mary and Martha in this treatise, however, complicates things, suggesting that Christ as model exists side by side with other models in a way that gives readers options in charting the devotional life. In the discussion of Mary and Martha in the *Book to a Mother*, for example, the writer associates the perfect life with Mary. Unlike Pecock, this writer separates Mary and Martha as two mutually exclusive choices, writing that "Crist undernome Martha for sche chese not the lightere and the best part, as Mary dide. Therfore, moder, be sory that thou hast taried so longe fro chesinge of the best part. For Crist seide to Martha that o thing is necessarie, that is, forte forsake alle thing for Cristes love. And bot a man chese the best part while he is in this world, he schal never come in hevene."[7] This writer suggests that the reader must flee worldly life before she can enter contemplative life and receive Christ's praise, as Mary did. Contemplation is defined here not in the way Pecock envisions but as a life set apart from the active world. This strict advice about the need to leave the active world behind and rise to higher spiritual things can be situated within a tradition of thinking on active and contemplative lives that emphasizes the superiority of contemplation and contrasts with Pecock's more overt notion that contemplation is a way to help Christians serve God better in the active world. Pecock's emphasis on the value of action and on the need even for monks to provide some kind of service through education suggests that he may be responding to texts like *Book to a Mother*, which encouraged withdrawal through the model of Mary while perhaps encouraging a more active life through the model of Christ. For Pecock, writing at least four decades later, there is less ambiguity and indeed less choice: there is no sense in Pecock's work that salvation depends on being able to escape the world in efforts to elevate the soul. For Pecock, it is essential that all Christians dedicate themselves to being productive, active participants in God's service. Pecock's refusal to see Mary and Martha as exclusive choices suggests a more general refusal to construct hierarchical levels for different practitioners of the religious life: if contemplation is not better or holier than action, then those who spend more time in contemplation—like monks and nuns—are not necessarily truer servants of God. The lay Christian can pursue just as meaningful a spiritual relationship with God by sharpening his intellect with knowledge of God, focusing his affect on generating love for God, and devoting himself to God's service by loving others in his community.

By instructing readers to follow Mary's example, proceeding from knowledge to love to active service to God, he reinforces his own model for the development of the individual. If the contemplative life is defined by Mary's occupations of learning about God's service and learning how to love him with greater devotion, then we can conclude that Pecock defines contemplation and action in general terms, as two stages in life: in the first stage we develop knowledge about God, we learn about his moral law, and we dispose ourselves properly by disciplining the will to desire God rather than worldly things; in the second stage we engage in active pursuits that are motivated by the purest intent to serve God. Pecock's spiritual path for Christian people, laid out in his *Reule* in the form of four tables, outlines the various stages of Mary's life; though he does not make the connection explicit, his commendation of Mary's more perfect life and his recommendations for progress through the four tables are essentially mirror images of each other. The four tables are Pecock's remodeling of the Ten Commandments, which Pecock feels do not sufficiently contain God's moral law. In short, the four tables teach Christians how they should behave in this world to guarantee their salvation. The first table establishes the foundation of Christian life by preparing the Christian and prompting him toward God's service: he must begin by learning about God and his service and then engage in activities of worship, praise, and prayer to provide the intellectual and emotional motivation to follow God's moral law in relation to God, self, and neighbor. The first table, therefore, in Pecock's view, is contemplative life: the activities of governing ourselves "leerningly, preisingly, dispreisingly, preiyngly, thankingly, worshipingly, disworschipingly, and sacramentingly" (*Donet*, 24). These activities constitute the soul's preparation for moral life: they help to sustain our obedience to God's moral laws, so that everything we do in relation to each other and ourselves, and to God himself, will be done with good intent. The second, third, and fourth tables teach us the commandments that must be fulfilled in God's service in relation to God, ourselves, and our neighbors. The second table provides information on the way we are supposed to behave in the fulfillment of God's commandments: for example, we should not tempt God, and we should use his goods and creatures according to his commands. The third table teaches us how we must govern our bodies and our minds; the fourth table teaches us how we must live within our communities. The first table prepares our mind, heart, and soul so that we are incited to serve God and follow the moral laws laid out in the other three tables.

Pecock's understanding of contemplative and active lives is therefore tied to his model of the first table and his concept that any kind of moral action must have the underpinnings of knowledge and love. The first stage of contemplative life, and hence the first stage of Christian life, is to live "leerningly": to acquire knowledge about God, his nature, his benefits, his punishments, and so on, as laid out in

Pecock's *Reule* as his seven matters. Obtaining this knowledge is not simply a requirement of a mixed life appropriate to a spiritual elite; rather, it is the most basic task of every Christian, "the first bisines at which a man schulde biginne to be thy servaunt" (*Reule*, 371). Each individual must receive a proper grounding in Pecock's seven matters to ensure a spiritually healthy Christian community: it is the business of each and every man: "forto wille, chese, and be bisie forto knowe, leerne, and kunne, and thanne aftir forto remembre, alle tho trouthis whos kunning and remembring schulen be meenis to us forto governe us in dedis of oure wil aftir resoun or feith, anentis god immediately, anentis us silf immediately, and anentis oure neighboris immediately" (*Donet*, 27). Acquiring knowledge—preferably from Pecock's corpus of works—is the first step in a Christian life that begins with contemplation and is fulfilled in action. The stage of learning is examined in more detail in chapter 5 of this book, on Pecock's concept of the book of reason. Pecock's emphasis that discipline is required to build the necessary foundation of knowledge for the contemplative life aligns him with authors of what Nicole Rice describes as "late Middle English prose spiritual guides . . . that propose to define and routinize religious life for lay readers wishing to move beyond catechism to explore the ordered practices and contemplative experience traditionally associated with life in religious orders." The map Pecock draws for lay readers trying to navigate the religious life points to lay study and structured devotional practices as the primary destination; contemplative experience of a more mystical sort, "traditionally associated with life in religious orders," is not as clearly marked.[8]

Once this knowledge of matters such as God's nature, his benefits, his punishments, and man's wickedness has been acquired, it must be considered and remembered through various devotional activities. The kinds of devotional activities that Pecock envisions for practitioners of the mixed life are treated more extensively in chapter 4 of this book. Devout prayer and meditation, for example, follow directly after knowledge acquisition: Pecock insists that the more intensely the mind dwells on and considers notions of God's goodness and mercy, the more intensely the heart will respond in desire, love, and a feeling of "welwilling" toward him, which according to Pecock "is to be clepid a loving toward God, and it is a conforming and an ooning of us to God" (*Reule*, 237). On a side note, it is interesting that Pecock's concept of "ooning," or union with God does not involve mystical marriage or union with God in a momentary flight of the soul in contemplation but is instead a practice of cultivating adoration of God in order to focus the intent so that the individual will want to serve him. Activities of prayer, praise, and worship are effective in calling knowledge of God into the mind, from its hidden recesses, so that the will can be properly directed; these activities focus the mind on the knowledge previously acquired about God's benefits, his punishments, human weakness, and the need for salvation, for the purpose of stimulating within the heart intense feelings of desire and love toward God that will motivate moral and virtuous action within the Christian community. If the individual neglects these practices, the "welwilling" he feels toward God will fade: each Christian must learn to sense when his desire and love for God have become "extinct or queint or maad so feint that they sufficen not to lede us ferther in outward worching" (*Reule*, 378). When the emotions are too weak to motivate good works, the believer must abandon worldly activities until he has cultivated deeper love for God: "Thane ech man in such wise undisposid oughte to renewe and to fortifie and strengthe ayen the same inward endewingis by the same proces" (*Reule*, 378). Pecock assigns to readers a high degree of self-control and discipline here, noting that each Christian must sense his own weaknesses and tendencies in order to regulate his spiritual life properly. Outward works can be continued only after the individual has gone back to the first step of acquiring and remembering knowledge of God, considering and concentrating on this knowledge through devotional activities and engendering feelings of love and desire for God that will motivate him to work properly in God's service. Pecock's model of the mixed life empowers the lay individual by requiring that he chart his own course, using Pecock's *Reule* as a guide.

As I mentioned above, it is immediately clear from Pecock's definition of "contemplatiif liif" as "not ellis than the uss of inward leerning or remembering, the uss of inward preising, dispreising, worschiping, disworchiping, thanking, preying, and sacramenting" (*Reule*, 468–69) that his model of the religious life does not point lay readers toward the kinds of goals that inspired the enclosed religious.[9] For Pecock, contemplative life includes a variety of activities that focus the mind and heart on God; it does not necessarily lead to what other writers conceive as contemplation itself—mystic experience. Contemplation is a difficult concept; it can be described differently in works written in the twelfth century for a monastic audience and works written in the fourteenth and fifteenth centuries for a lay audience by writers like Pecock. Vincent Gillespie notes that contemplation as mystic union with God, a pure vision of God, or marriage between the soul and God is customarily seen as the ultimate goal or final stage of the contemplative life.[10] The route to this goal can be described in different ways, but usually one must to do certain things like purge the soul from sin, focus the mind and desire on God, and pray for God's grace. For instance, the stage of contemplation follows reading, meditation, and prayer in twelfth-century treatises such as Guigo II's *Scala Claustralium*, which was translated into Middle English and entitled *A Ladder of Foure Runges by the Which Men Mowe Clyme to Heuene*. In this traditional model of the ladder by which believers climb from the earth into heaven, the individual begins by reading the Bible and meditating on its contents. After "lesson, meditacioun, [and] orison," the individual hopes to ascend to contemplation, which is described, characteristically in poetic language, as "a rising of the hert into God that tastith sumdele of hevenly swettnesse and savourith" and as a moment of mystic union between the contemplative lover and the divine spouse.[11] These stages are inseparable: reading, prayer, and meditation are not mutually exclusive activities but activities that naturally flow into each other.

Envisioning contemplative life not as mystical experience but as learning, devotion, and worship of God is characteristic, Gillespie explains, of religious works written toward the end of the Middle Ages for lay readers who lacked the formal and systematic training of their monastic peers. One of the changes Gillespie observes, as texts were "adapted, translated, and quarried to supply the needs of a wider clerical and lay audience," was the nature of the route to contemplation.[12] Studying the Bible and even reading itself were increasingly replaced by other activities more suitable to a wide audience. Guigo II may have felt that the "foure degrees be so bounde togedir" that each was inseparable from the others, meaning that contemplation could not be found without reading, meditation, and prayer, but for lay readers in the late fourteenth century in England, the structure and goal of this spiritual ascent were felt by some to be unrealistic.[13] Gillespie re-marks, "The monastic view of the ladder of contemplation clearly posits a level of individual literacy on the part of the monk . . . yet the new audiences of the fourteenth and fifteenth centuries in England cannot be assumed to have had the same kind of Latin literacy."[14] For lay readers in this period, Gillespie tells us, rumination on the Bible as the first stage of this ascent is replaced increasingly by imaginative meditation on images such as the body of Christ. Rather than reading actual books, the laity often meditated on their "reading" of the book of Christ's body, the book of the soul, and the book of the conscience. This meditative reading of internal books was not necessarily anti-intellectual, however, and it did not necessarily replace reading itself. Instead, it could supplement it: the laity's meditative "reading" of the book of conscience or the book of Christ could start from the reading of familiar prayers in a book of hours—prayers that offered, according to Sylvia Huot, the "occasion for a potentially endless review of reli-gious dogma, sacred history, and individual morality."[15] Huot argues that reading books of hours was "polytextual," stimulating the reader to produce "supplemental texts" through "intellectual and imaginative processes of memory and association, whereby a single text becomes a springboard for the recollection and reconsideration of others."[16]

Pecock's description of the contemplative life therefore fits within a tradition of works that sought to guide the laity in structuring the religious life. In these kinds of works, activities like reading and prayer—formerly stages en route to contemplation—are recom-mended as ways to increase devotion and encourage moral virtue. Indeed, an activity like reading may become a separate activity—to cultivate discipline—rather than one step in a seamless ascent to God, in a systematic practice that climaxes in contemplative prayer. The traditional understanding of the ascent to contemplation changed when the ascent stopped short of its final goal of sharing divine wis-dom or a divine embrace. Gillespie describes Richard Rolle's mystical understanding of the ascent toward contemplation in the following way: "Man's will is corrupt, it must be reformed through a rejection of carnal affections and an acceptance of the love of Christ, a yearning love of Christ will lead to a further kindling of love as a gift from God, this new kindled love will fix our intellects and the eye of our soul on the contemplation of God and will help us to achieve wisdom."[17] For many lay readers of the fifteenth century, however, reforming the will, accepting the love of Christ, and working to reciprocate this love was the furthest they would go along this spiritual journey. Gillespie's observations are a useful reminder that the way contemplation is understood in the monastic and mystical traditions, as the final stage of a structured ascent to God, is not necessarily the way it will be treated by writers like Pecock.

Indeed, in works directing the laity in the spiritual life that are roughly contemporary with Pecock's writings, opinions vary about the nature, boundaries, and limitations of contemplative life for those who lived in the world. The compiler of *Contemplations of the Dread and Love of God* suggests that there are limitations for the laity in their experience of contemplation. This work, written sometime between 1375 and 1425 and surviving in numerous fifteenth-century manuscripts (sixteen complete versions and twenty-two instances of various chapters occurring independently of the main text), aims its advice on ascending through various stages of love for God at members of the laity who cannot flee the world but want to have "as stable an herte and wil as some religious that sitteth in the cloistre."[18] The work recommends a kind of contemplative life for its active readers, inviting them to progress through stages of love—"ordeined love," "clene love," "stedefast love," and "parfit love"—in a scale of ascent that mirrors, but is several steps down from, the degrees of love through which proper contemplatives can ascend. Though there is a difference between the contemplative experiences of a monk and a layman, the layman is to strive for an experience as like the monk's as possible, seeing the contemplative experience of an enclosed person as a kind of ideal. The author warns that only he who flees the world will reach that stage in which "with his gostliche yen then he may see into the blisse of heuene. His yen than ben so lightnid and kiendlid with the gracious fier of Cristis love that he schal have a maner brenning love in his herte evermore lasting, and his thoght evir upward to God."[19] Though his lay readers cannot escape from the world into a monastic enclosure, they can pursue holiness by training the will to cleave to

God's, by withstanding temptations, by dedicating time to prayer, and by developing patience and perseverance. This kind of piety will ignite the will and desire "to come to that love whiche is most parfit; that is to sey, evirmore to see almighty God in his gloriouse Godhed, evermore with him to dwelle."[20] Through this pursuit of holiness, the lay reader may develop as stable a heart and will as a hermit or a nun, finding balance between the pull of worldly duties and the pull of the divine. The compiler warns, however, that desire for this more perfect love is not the same thing as experiencing it: "lordis and ladies" and "housbond-men and wives" can not "come to suche hie contemplatif lif" as those who have fled the world. The compiler suggests that it is impossible for the laity to ascend to the same heights of contemplation as the enclosed religious.

Other works present the opposite view. *The Abbey of the Holy Ghost* is a spiritual treatise intended for members of the laity who wish to engage in contemplation without fleeing the world. The treatise was translated into English in the late fourteenth century from a French original intended for a more exclusive audience of aristocratic laywomen, dating from before 1300. The English translation survives in twenty-four manuscripts, most dating from the fifteenth century.[21] The English writer addresses his intended audience in the prologue, saying, "Mi deore brethren and sustren, I seo wel that monie wolde ben in religion but they mowe not for povert or for age or for drede of heore kin or for bonde of mariage. And therfore, I make her a book of religion of herte that is of the abbeye of the Holi Gost."[22] The author invites readers to erect a metaphorical abbey within their hearts and offers a spiritual outlet for those who cannot abandon their duties in the world but wish to engage in meaningful and pious devotions. The structure of the abbey is likened to the foundation of the Christian life upon virtues such as mercy and patience; the government of the abbey by its sisters in daily life is compared to religious practices such as prayer and meditation and other virtues that should guide the layperson's life; the defense of the abbey by the warden, the Holy Ghost, is likened to the assistance of grace in the spiritual life as a defense against sin and the worldly forces that threaten to turn the believer from God. Readers must undertake a demanding spiritual regimen to first purge their souls (since union with God cannot occur in a sinful soul) and then nourish their souls with traditional practices like the sacraments, prayer, devotion, and meditation. By inwardly cultivating virtues, by ruling themselves with charity, wisdom, and meekness, by engaging in devotional practices whenever possible, and by praying for the assistance of grace from the Holy Ghost, the *Abbey*'s lay readers can aim for the highest stages of contemplation experienced by those in the enclosed life. In meditation, they ready themselves to experience rapturous union with God so that as his true servants they can be enflamed with the bliss of his love and can receive from him "the win of swete teres," as well as the "oile of cumfort that giveth savor and lighteth his knowleching and scheweth him of his privetes of hevene that he hideth and huleth from tho that folewen flessches desires and giveth hem to the wisdam of the world and al is fantasie."[23] This promise of the sight of the "privetees of hevene" that are hidden from those tied to the world by fleshly desires is surely a hint of the highest stage of contemplation that awaits the purest and most desirous souls. The *Abbey*'s editor, Peter Consacro, suggests that "its most distinguishing characteristic is its implied premise that the fullness of the Christian life is open to all men, regardless of their condition or state in life. The author's assumption is that the 'mixed life'—though he never uses the term—is not only possible but probable."[24] Consacro points out that what is remarkable about the treatise is the author's notion that his reader's pursuit of the contemplative life through meditation and prayer can result in the kind of divine, mystical union that was thought to be accessible only rarely to people living the active life in the world.

Though the *Abbey* offers a demanding regimen and high goals for lay readers, it does not invite lay readers to disentangle themselves completely from the world in the search for spiritual profit. Nicole Rice argues that the *Abbey* opens up the contemplative life to lay readers while "carefully discouraging the detachment from the world that actual cloistered life (at least in its ideal form) would entail." She notes that after inviting readers to experience the heights of contemplation, the *Abbey* "turns to the internalization and stabilization of contemplative joy, revising the practice of contemplation to promote spiritual stasis as itself potentially pleasurable."[25] Rather than giving themselves over to the rapture and ecstasy of contemplation, readers should internalize their "jubilacioun" by giving expression within their hearts to the pleasure they experience in prayer: their "songes of love-longinge" ravish their hearts, but as Rice points out, their outward silence demands control and self-restraint.[26] This work, then, treads a careful line between the project of encouraging lay ambition in the religious life and regulating it. This tenuous balance is one that we can observe as well in Pecock's directions for meditative reading, which I examine in the next chapter. We can also observe it in Pecock's definition of contemplation as learning, remembering, worshiping, sacramenting, and other activities of knowledge acquisition and devotion: Pecock encourages readers to adopt the spiritual regimen of the clergy without directing them upwards to the heights of rapture. The religious lifestyle of the pious layman can mirror that of the monk, but the focus is on a process that leads to good works and service rather than to a mystical encounter with God.

Rice includes the *Abbey* in a category of guides "that reimagine cloistered modes of religious discipline as textual frameworks for lay self-regulation in the world."[27] For Rice, spiritual guides that offer the cloister or other "monuments of professed religious life" as models for "redefining lay religious practice" are to be treated separately from a different category of spiritual guides, which "encourage priestly life and the Bible as model and rule for lay Christian conduct, encouraging their lay readers to imitate clerical modes of biblical study, preaching and pastoral care." The guides that use the cloister as model for lay religious discipline are more "cautious" in their "ideological strategies" than those "reformist" guides that "accommodate new forms of lay spiritual authority within the boundaries of ecclesiastical hierarchy."[28] Rice's construction of two categories of spiritual guides is helpful in pointing to what makes Pecock's approach different from the approach in *The Abbey of the Holy Ghost*: for Pecock, the emphasis is on lay study within the active life rather than penitential discipline. Encouraging his readers to become scholars in his corpus, Pecock asks them to model themselves after clerics like him, who train tirelessly in the disciplines of moral philosophy and logic so that they can understand God's truths. As I argue in chapter 5, lay readers can emulate clerics in important ways when studying the book of reason as part of the contemplative life. Interesting, Pecock does offer readers a rule to live by—his *Reule of Crysten Religioun*. As I argue throughout this book, however, this rule does not structure lay religious practice alone but provides a spiritual guide universal to all members of society, cleric and lay. Instead of asking lay readers to shape their lives after the model of the monastery, Pecock suggests that even those within the monastery must learn that his *Reule of Crysten Religioun* is a vital guide to the spiritual life.

Pecock's guide to the spiritual life has important resemblances to Walter Hilton's treatise on the mixed life, helping us to see the way Pecock's work springs from a tradition of thought on directing the laity in the religious life. Like Pecock, Hilton emphasizes a blend of action and contemplation and tends to focus on activities that stimulate love and goodwill toward God rather than mystic union. Hugh Kempster writes that Hilton's *Mixed Life*, written for a secular lord probably in the 1390s, is the first work that formally defines the mixed life as a possibility for members of the laity and that as such it "marks the beginnings of what was to become a radical redefining of the boundaries of the contemplative life in late-medieval England."[29] Hilton is the first writer to recommend the traditional model of alternation between action and contemplation, usually prescribed for bishops and prelates, to a lay reader.[30] For those who find themselves in a state of some prominence in the world, with tenants or a family to rule and direct, Hilton suggests that the responsibilities of active life can be balanced with the efforts to ascend to a higher form of contemplative life. The layman should indulge his pious desires for God by focusing the mind on God and by engaging in meditative prayer, but when duty calls, contemplation must be temporarily abandoned: "Leve of lightely thy devocioun, whethir it be in praiere or in meditacioun, and goo doo thy dette and thy service to thine evene-Cristene as redily as oure lord him silf badde thee doo so, and suffre mekeli for his love, withouten grucching if thou may."[31] Hilton demonstrates this practice of alternation by describing the layman's worship of Christ: he worships Christ's head and arrays it with "perre and precious stoones" when he focuses the mind on God and thinks of the Passion and his other works "bi devocioun and meditacioun."[32] He worships the rest of Christ's body, cleaning his feet and clothing his body, when he tends to his fellow Christians. If he neglects one part of Christ, his worship is flawed: his attempt to live a full, whole Christian life can be thwarted by too much attention to contemplative activities, "as for to be al day occupied in the meditacioun of his manhede."[33] Hilton's metaphor, like Pecock's interpretation of the ideal mixed life of Mary, suggests that the full, complete Christian life requires a balance of contemplative and active activities.

Hilton and Pecock also offer similar advice on alternating contemplative life with active duty in the world. Both assign great importance to activities that stir up flames of devotion for God and sustain goodwill toward him. Hilton's reader must build a fire of devotion to God in his soul: the little coal of desire for God, implanted in us at the beginning by God himself, is nourished by feeding the fire with sticks of "good werkes of actif liif."[34] The active works of charity and mercy stimulate the fire of desire for God, enabling the believer to engage in prayers and meditations in a more meaningful way. Good deeds will increase devotion and stimulate the contemplative life. With this metaphor, Hilton shows why it is not recommended for a secular lord to simply abandon worldly cares and indulge his pious desires: in a mixed life of alternation between action and contemplation, action gives rise to contemplation and helps to sustain it.

Hilton employs the same metaphor when elaborating on various ways of enriching the devotional life and cultivating pious love for God. He says that for those who are illiterate, good deeds of mercy are just as effective as various other methods of stimulating the fire of devotion, including reading the Bible:

> Thise stikkes aren of divers matir; sum are of oo tree and sume of anothir. A man that is lettered and hath undirstondinge of hooli writte, yif he have this fier of devocioun in his herte, it is good unto him for to gete him stikkes of hooli ensamples and seiynges of oure lord bi redinge in hooli writte, and norissch the fier with hem. Another man, unlettered, may not so redily have at his hand hooly writ ne dottoures seiynges, and forthi it nedeth unto him for to doo many goode deedes outewarde to his evene-Cristene, and kendele the fier of love with hem.[35]

Some participants in the mixed life will nourish the fire of devotion with knowledge; others can nourish the fire of devotion with good deeds. Hilton's version of the mixed life has room for different levels of practice, according to different degrees of Christians. A degree of flexibility is normal in the practice of the mixed life: certain spiritual practices may be helpful for the learned few but not for the unlettered. Each person is to obtain the kind of fuel for his spiritual fire that will kindle it most effectively according to his abilities.

It is important to note that Pecock's advice about sustaining the fire of desire for God and the feelings of "welwilling" toward God differs from Hilton's in one important aspect. Pecock is more insistent that all Christians must stoke the fire systematically, in a uniform way. All begin with knowledge and learning, especially in the seven matters that he feels are fundamental and that are available in cheap extracts for poor men. While Hilton feels that the illiterate layman can use sticks of active work to engender the same kind of devotional fire as those who can read the Bible, Pecock feels that everyone must start by reading his corpus of educational materials. He does admit that some individuals may find other ways to obtain the knowledge necessary for engendering love and desire, such as studying the Bible, reading other holy works, or listening to sermons (*Reule*, 371), but he is insistent that a thorough education in his seven matters, described in the *Reule*, is the best option. Pecock is more emphatic than Hilton on the necessity of this first stage of gaining the knowledge that will stir the mind in devotional practice, and he takes a more systematic approach in outlining the various necessary stages that will structure the reader's progress through the contemplative life.

Hilton's teaching is closer to Pecock's when it comes to establishing limitations for active people wishing to embrace contemplative ideals. The contemplative part of the layman's life is defined by Hilton as participation in devotional activities such as prayer and meditation— "goostli occupacions"—rather than a structured ascent to momentary rapture or union with the divine.[36] Unlike the author of the *Abbey*, Hilton does not feel that rapturous union follows directly and naturally from meditation on Christ's passion. In fact, throughout *Mixed Life*, Hilton treats the contemplative life as engagement in devotional activities normally reserved for members of the monastic community and ecclesiastical hierarchy, rather than defining it in a more mystical way as a brief glimpse of the divine. By defining contemplative life in this way, he, like Pecock, does not admit his lay reader to the revelatory kinds of experiences described in other treatises such as *The Ladder of Foure Runges* or *The Abbey of the Holy Ghost*. His concern is to set out recommendations for a way of life and to provide practical advice about combining devotional activities with work in the world, rather than to prepare readers for mystical union. This concern with stoking the fire of devotion rather than leading readers toward mystical union with God indicates some doubt on Hilton's part about the ability of laymen to ascend on their own to the highest reaches of contemplation: while he encourages his lay reader to engage in periods of meditation in which he fixes his mind on God, Hilton does not believe that the layman can easily ascend to "verry contemplation" while he lives in the world. The reader can only become "verry contemplatif" in this life if he is delivered from his worldly duties and made "free from chargees and bisinesses"; the man who cannot be freed from worldly occupations may become "verry contemplatif" only in the "blisse of heuene."[37] While he remains tied to his responsibilities in the world, the layman will not reach the highest degree of contemplation.

Hilton does open the door to the middle reaches of contemplation, a "litil tastinge of the swetenesse in the love of God," for lay folk who are helped by grace.[38] In his acknowledgment that God's grace can elevate any believer to mystical contemplation, Hilton subscribes to the general notion, identified by Marion Glasscoe, that the fruits of meditation are a gift given to the believer from God: "This actual process of coming alive which is at the heart of meditation is experienced not as a function of the effort of the will itself, but as a gift from God."[39] It is even more rare, but still possible, for a layman living the active life to be granted the experience of the highest degree of contemplation, or "brennande love in contemplacion."[40] In his *Scale of Perfection*, Hilton acknowledges that God grants this "special" gift of "illuminacion of undirstondinge in delites of lovinge" to the privileged few, without paying attention to their state of life.[41] Such comments establish clear limits for his lay readers, reminding them that the highest forms of contemplation are reserved for the recluse and those who receive God's special favor. Hilton recognizes the possibility that the layman can ascend to the ultimate stage in contemplative life, but on the whole he is more cautious than the writer of the *Abbey*: his emphasis on the importance of grace, his hesitance about the possibility of mystical experience for the lay contemplative, and his definition of contemplation as participation in devotional activities provide the lay reader with a conservative outlook—much like Pecock's—on the mixed life.

Though we can observe many similarities in their teachings on the mixed life, Hilton and Pecock's understandings of the mixed life also differ in important ways. For example, Pecock ties his readers more tightly to the world than Hilton does. Hilton wants to enable his lay reader to nourish his affection for God so that he may experience at least the first stages of that contemplative sweetness of the monastic life. Hilton's goal is to help his lay reader—a man who wishes to abandon the world for the peace and rest of contemplation—find a spiritual outlet for his pious desires and cultivate a more intense spiritual love for God. While Hilton insists on the need to alternate between contemplative and active pursuits, he still tends to suggest the superiority of contemplation, and he tends to define activities of prayer and meditation as experiences that allow his lay reader a temporary escape from the world. Pecock is more careful to define contemplation not as a pious indulgence but as necessary preparation for God's service. He seems to be more concerned than Hilton that allowing the laity to indulge in the contemplative devotions of the anchorhold may cause them to neglect their roles in their communities. Pecock does not want the contemplative life to provide relief and comfort for the ambitious, pious layman; rather, he wants the contemplative life to nurture the Christian community.

Pecock's understanding of the mixed life builds on and extends that of Hilton: rather than recommending a practice of alternation between the two lives for those lords and ladies in positions of power in society, Pecock suggests that the contemplative pursuits of prayer, meditation, worship, and learning are the very basis of every Christian's life. While Hilton states that the layman in the mixed life can alternate between periods of intense devotional prayer and meditation and activity in the world, interacting with neighbors and providing

charitable services to others around him, Pecock suggests that the av-
erage layman cannot properly perform charitable works in the community, interact productively with others, or work on destroying sin
within himself until he has spent a significant amount of time learning
about God's truths, worshiping and honoring God, praying to God,
praising God, and participating in those church rituals that remind
him of God's mercy, his benefits, and his goodness. Pecock's advice
goes one step further than Hilton's in several important ways—in its
application of Hilton's concept of the mixed life to all members of the
laity, its emphasis on a more methodical, organized progression from
contemplation to action, starting with knowledge of Pecock's works
and moving through various stages, and its emphasis on the value of
active life in service to God. By defining contemplation as the first
stage of Christian life, Pecock defines himself as an innovator in the
tradition of discussion on active, contemplative, and mixed lives.

Pecock's suggestions on the mixed life make an important, novel
contribution to a tradition of teaching that was becoming a hot topic
for laypeople in late medieval England. In this period, a number of
laypeople from the middle and upper classes looked for ways to "clothe
their active lives in contemplation."[42] In a brief survey of fifteenth-
century lay piety, Hugh Kempster notes a growth of interest and participation in the mixed life, finding evidence of lay ownership of
mystical and contemplative texts in the fifteenth century and citing as
an example various common-profit manuscripts that "demonstrate a
sophisticated taste in contemplative literature among a small group of
London merchants early in the fifteenth century."[43] Research on book
ownership and bequests in wills shows that "in the first half of the fifteenth century there is some evidence that lay people who sought to
read, buy, borrow or bequeath books on this topic formed a distinct
class of readers, a spiritual aristocracy whose lay state did not bar them
from mounting the ladder of perfection."[44] Books that help those in
the world to cross over the boundary of the anchorhold in their pious
devotions find a new lease on life in the fifteenth century: these include Hilton's *Scale of Perfection* and his *Mixed Life*, Love's *Mirror*, the
anonymous *Contemplations of the Dread and Love of God*, *The Abbey of
the Holy Ghost*, *Pore Caitiff*, *Gracia Dei*, *The Seven Poyntes of Trewe
Wisdom*, St. Edmund's *Mirror*, and Guigo II's *Ladder of Foure Ronges*.

Figures that have become iconic in studies of fifteenth-century piety, such as Cicely, Duchess of York, Margery Kempe, and Robert Thornton, all sought in their individual ways to live a kind of mixed life in which their worldly duties and pursuits could be combined with internal devotions and spiritual practices that corresponded to those of the monastery or enclosure. Cicely, Duchess of York and mother to Edward IV and Richard III, led a life of extremely disciplined piety, structuring her day around spiritual practices of masses, reading, and prayer, without neglecting charitable work and the worldly duties of her station.[45] Margery Kempe's book documents her struggle to find the right balance between her role as mother, wife, and worldly creature and her role as one of God's chosen souls, graced with divine visits and conversations. Robert Thornton, the scribe of two domestic volumes dating from the mid–fifteenth century, found time during his busy life as a landholder and tax collector to copy a wide range of devotional materials that range from simple prayers to more complex contemplative works of figures such as Rolle. His meticulous efforts to collect and record a number of contemplative spiritual writings show "deep concern for his own moral and spiritual welfare and that of his family" as well as a belief, shared by other pious laymen, "in the possibility of transcending these limitations of fallen man's ability to 'knawe God Almightin' and of enjoying at least a glimpse of 'that blisse that never mare blinnes.'"[46] What these three people had in common was a desire to extend their spiritual lives beyond the basic activities of charitable work in God's service; they wanted to find a middle way between active life in the world and the more peaceful, spiritual world of the religious recluses who seemed to have a better chance of seeing God.

What Pecock provides for people like Margery, Cecily of York, and Robert Thornton is innovative: viewed in the context of the contemplative reading material that served as the "gateway and the guides by which English laypeople were able to embark on the intense spiritual journey that characterizes the true contemplative," his writings offer a more coherent and systematic spiritual program that is rooted in theological training.[47] Furthermore, for Pecock, the mixed life is not simply an alternative option for certain members of the laity—Carey's "spiritual aristocracy"—who wish to extend the bounds of active life beyond charitable works and cultivate a more meaningful relationship with God.[48] For Pecock, the active life of every member of the Christian community must be grounded first of all in this meaningful relationship with God: Pecock's notion of how action and contemplation work in successive stages in the life of each individual allows him to develop the concept of the mixed life and suggest that it is not simply the particularly pious laity who must engage regularly in practices that require discipline and devotion and that cultivate knowledge and love for God. It is clear that Pecock intends his corpus for a wide range of lay readers, since he goes to great lengths to make his books available in cheaper forms to poor members of the community; he informs readers that books like the *Reule* teach "al what *ech cristen persoone* owith to do and to suffer by bidding of god forto be a trewe cristen liver and the servaunt of god" (*Reule*, 13; emphasis added).[49] Pecock's instructions on the best kind of Christian life, a mixture of contemplation and action, are intended therefore for a broad audience of lay people.

Most notable about Pecock's contributions to discussions on the mixed, contemplative, and active lives are his assertion that everyone living in the world needs the proper foundation of a contemplative life and his efforts to provide a systematic program for ensuring this. It is not sufficient for a merchant in London to do the occasional good work and give alms to his fellow citizen. It is not sufficient to perform the works of bodily and spiritual mercy. It is not sufficient to perform active deeds "for worldly curtesie and worldly love and favour and civile freendschip such as oon hethen man hath to an other of his kin or hise wel biloved freendis" (*Reule*, 491). These kinds of works, and all worldly deeds, must be performed with the correct intentions: God must be "entendid and purposed principaly or hoolly in every moral vertuose occupacioun" (489). Those living in the world must ensure that their every action stems from pure and holy intent, which is generated from systematic training in Pecock's program. Everyone must begin at the same place, by acquiring knowledge of God and his moral law, by reflecting and meditating on this knowledge until love, desire, and "welwilling" toward God is produced, and by bringing this knowledge to fruition in everyday life in the care of the household, interactions with neighbors, personal relationships, and business occupations. This aspect of Pecock's teaching grows from the tradition of prose instruction on the religious life, with its emphasis on balancing ambitious spiritual goals and rigorous discipline with life in the world: Pecock develops this strand of thought about the need to prevent the laity from separating themselves fully from the world, and he makes it more overt. For people like Cecily of York and Robert Thornton, Pecock provides concrete instructions for a sophisticated spiritual regimen and offers careful reminders of the importance of well-intended active works. For other members of the community who may have been less inclined to seek spiritual perfection and more concerned about worldly winning, Pecock offers cautionary advice on the importance of following Mary's example rather than Martha's and dedicating time and effort to "whetting" and "sharpening" oneself in "inward contemplatiif bisines" (488–89). In his recommendations for integrating contemplation into the active life, Pecock demanded a lot from his readers. Pecock's project to reform the active life in this way can only be described as ambitious: each of his lay readers must learn how to become a "worcher to serve God in active liif" by taking Pecock's corpus of books "into use of ful bisy, ech day studying, leerning and comuning and afterward therupon remembring, and if not in ech day, yitt in holy daies, and that as bisily as peple ben in werk daies y-occupied aboute worldis winning" (13).

f o u r

Ritual Reading and Meditative Reading

In the last chapter, I discussed Pecock's sense of the way contemplation, as he defines it, is at the core of every moral action and is therefore the foundation for active life in the world. In this chapter, I examine some of the sophisticated and demanding spiritual practices—namely, forms of "preising and of preiyng devoutely" (*Donet*, 202)—that are to be used either "in placis of cumpanie" or as part of a private meditation practice, in "a secrete and privey place, partles of noise and trouble of the peple" (*Donet*, 207). First, I consider Pecock's instructions for ritual reading, forms of praise and prayer that are spoken aloud, "by voice, or by speche and noise of mouthe, to god" (*Donet*, 207). Then I examine Pecock's directions for meditation, a silent practice, following reading, that is superior to praise and prayer spoken aloud (*Donet*, 208). Because prayer, worship, and meditation are not discussed, typically, in scholarly literature on Pecock, the first task of this chapter is to familiarize the reader with his treatment of these subjects. The second task of this chapter is to show that Pecock's treatment of these subjects constitutes an ambitious effort to reform current devotional practices: Pecock's books, and the knowledge they provide, constitute the essential resources for devotional practices that can intensify the spiritual lives of his readers.

Pecock's reform of ritual reading focuses on the most familiar prayer, the Pater Noster. Pecock presents three forms of praying the

Pater Noster, by words spoken aloud, to God. The first form is "called in Latin 'Pater Noster,'" and the individual is to recite this prayer without "eny setting therto of othire wordis." The second form is to read the Pater Noster "with setting to of othire wordis and othire processis." The third approach is to pray "in foormes dividid by holy mennis laboure in othire wordis than is the Pater Noster, though they ben not contrarie to the sentence of the Pater Noster, and they asken the same thingis which asken the parties of the Pater Noster, though in othire maner wordis" (*Donet*, 204).

Having identified these three forms, Pecock directs readers to resources for each. Unfortunately for modern scholars, these resources do not exist today. The first form of lay prayer—reciting the Pater Noster on its own—is more effective when the reader has read Pecock's exposition of this prayer in a part of the *Reule* that is missing; in the *Donet* he tells us that the seventh treatise of the *Reule* contains "exposicioun and undirstonding" of this prayer that can help readers comprehend the doctrine of each petition (204). We know that the *Reule* is written in English, so we can assume that the seventh treatise would have been especially helpful for lay readers who lacked Latin learning and wanted fuller understanding of the Lord's Prayer. Pecock's efforts to provide commentary on the Lord's Prayer roots him in a tradition of pastoral theology: Maurice Hussey notes that the prayer's "extreme adaptability" made it a popular vehicle for "almost the whole religious training that the laity were given or needed to assimilate."[1] It is impossible for us to know whether Pecock used the petitions of the Pater Noster to frame his teaching of the seven matters; he does tell us in the opening of the *Reule* that the four things necessary for good living (knowledge, love, good works, and grace) receive expanded treatment in his exposition of the Pater Noster, constituting the petitions of this prayer. Readers pray for knowledge in the "firste boone," for love in the second petition, for good works in the third petition, and for various forms of grace in the fourth, fifth, sixth, and seventh petitions (*Reule*, 8). This exposition is "light and cleer to undirstonde and esy to bere in minde whilis the preier is in seiyng," and in Pecock's experience he has never found such a good "and profitable" exposition "neither in writing, neither in heering or preching, notwithstanding that manie of hem I have received into my beholding"

(8). The discussion of the material in the missing seventh treatise of *The Reule* therefore offers tantalizing hints about his approach to worship. We cannot read Pecock's English glosses of the Pater Noster, but apparently they "berith the price," and are "so riche, so swete, and so preciose" that his reader "schalt desire aftir noon othire" (*Donet*, 204). I find it particularly noteworthy that it is not the Latin words of the Pater Noster itself that are cherished here but Pecock's English translations, glosses, and interpretations.

The second and third forms of prayer require different resources: two additional works that do not exist today. The second form of prayer, the expanded Pater Noster, mingles petitions with other words. Readers interested in this extended Pater Noster, containing "doubling and trebling of peticioun," should read either Pecock's *Book of Divine Office*, "in the first evensong for Friday," or his *Enchiridion* (*Donet*, 204). The *Divine Office* is also the resource for the third form of prayer: Pecock tells readers to look in this book for "rubrisch sett afore in this maner, 'Preiers for evensong,' or in this wise, 'Preiers for matins'" (*Donet*, 205). Neither the *Divine Office* nor the *Enchiridion* (also known as Pecock's "*Manuel*") survives, but both are cited frequently throughout Pecock's corpus: they appear to be books of reformed prayers (*Donet*, 204). Pecock has renewed the practice of worship and ritual reading through the addition of "sett obsecratiif preisingis and also manie diverse argumentaciouns, allegaciouns and suasiouns—as it is ensaumplid thorugh the preiyng party of the book clepid '*Divine Office*' and in the book clepid '*Enchiridioun*'" (*Reule*, 404). Prayers in these two books are distinguished from other forms because they are shaped from Pecock's teaching, in his seven matters, on God's "nobiltees, of thy benefetis and of thy lawis" (*Reule*, 416). The *Divine Office* is a book of liturgy, to be used, for example, "in evensong of the Friday" (*Reule*, 8), in "service of Trinity Sunday" (*Donet*, 85), in "the service or office of Palme Sundaie week" (*Donet*, 89), and as a source for prayers "assigned for Thursdaie to alle seintis" (*Donet*, 93). The one thing we can be certain of was their importance within Pecock's system of teaching: though we can only wonder what *The Book of Divine Office* contained, we are promised prayers that are "bettir, swettir, fairer or devouter" than any others his readers may find

(*Donet*, 205). We cannot access the extended Pater Noster in the *Enchiridion*, but apparently it is a resource worthier than "silver or golde" (*Donet*, 205).

The language and the relationship between these two lost books are somewhat difficult to gauge. It is not completely clear whether the *Divine Office* is written in Latin or English, and therefore it is not completely clear how far Pecock's liturgical reforms go. Much of what follows is speculation based on what Pecock tells us about these missing books in his *Reule* and *Donet*. The English title of the *Divine Office* is not particularly helpful as an argument that the book is written in the vernacular, since Pecock gives other Latin books English titles, like *The Book of Questiouns* (*Donet*, 181). Pecock does indicate that the *Divine Office* is a resource of prayers for all Christian men, which could lead to the assumption that it is written in the vernacular. For example, when he justifies his use of English to treat the Godhead, in the first treatise of the *Reule*, Pecock mentions that though "hardir doctrines" can be found in the writings of doctors like the Lombard, his teaching is "scole ynough" for men and clergy outside of the theology faculty: the treatment of the Godhead in the vernacular *Reule* provides a common resource for both laity and clergy (*Reule*, 86). He continues on to say that "ferthermore to alle men as for spechis to be had to God upon hise worthinesses and upon the persoonis as it spedith to a man whilis he yeveth him to the officis of devout preising and preyng God forto gendre therby devout loves and desires, servith ful wel as it what is writun in the '*Book of Divine Office*' and in his extractis or out draughtis and in '*The Enchiridion*'" (*Reule*, 87). This reference could imply either that the *Enchiridion* is an extract of the *Book of Divine Office* or that it is written in addition to both the *Divine Office* and the extracts of the *Divine Office*. The context would seem to indicate that these books are in English, since Pecock says that they are references for "alle men" and since he is in the midst of defending his "deliveraunce of tho trouthis to the lay peple in her modir langage" (*Reule*, 87). However, it is also possible that Pecock is intending to reach this audience of "alle men" by providing the *Divine Office* for the "clerkis" in his audience and the *Enchiridion* for the "comoun peple" (*Reule*, 86).

The question of language arises again when Pecock refers to these missing two books in the context of a discussion on increasing understanding among both "unlettrid men" who read the Psalter or the Pater Noster in Latin and clerks who read "derke psalmes and othere derk chapitris, responses, and lessouns" of the liturgy (*Reule*, 401). All Christian souls, says Pecock, must be encouraged to understand what they pray through the reform of "oolde formes of preying," a process Pecock has begun "in thy newe book, Lord, y-callid the '*Book of Divine Office*' and '*The Enchiridion*' for unlettrid men in Latin" (*Reule*, 403). Here we have several choices: we can interpret the *Enchiridion* to be an English version of the Latin *Divine Office;* or a shorter book of extracts, in English, of the English *Divine Office;* or a companion book to the *Divine Office*, both of which are written for men who do not know Latin. It is worthy of note that the *Divine Office* and *The Enchiridion* are usually paired in references throughout Pecock's corpus, indicating that they could be versions of the same book, as the reference above to "thy newe book" would seem to substantiate (*Reule*, 403). If the *Enchiridion* is an extract of the *Divine Office*, then it makes sense that both would contain the same prayers; Pecock says, "I settide forth a schrift in '*The Book of Divine Office*' in Fridaies matins, and in his gretter extract or outdraught" (*Folewer*, 118). Both are mentioned together in a list of "purtenauncis" that must be "weel over studied and seen and cleerly comprehended" by all Christians along with *The Reule of Crysten Religioun* (*Reule*, 9).

In my opinion, it is most likely that the first missing book, the *Divine Office*, is a Latin book of Pecock's reformed liturgy, intended for the clerics, monks, and prelates in his audience, and that the second lost book, the *Enchiridion*, is a sort of book of hours, meant to facilitate access to some of the Latin prayers of the liturgy for readers who do not know Latin, probably through vernacular expositions of Latin prayers. It is probable that the *Enchiridion* would thus contain both the Latin prayers and Pecock's vernacular expositions. I am convinced that their continual pairing is important. It shows us that they are different versions of the same basic book. Because Pecock does not mention the *Enchiridion* when referring readers to particular liturgical occasions, like the services for Trinity Sunday, Palm Sunday, and various saints' days, I believe that the *Enchiridion* is a shorter book of extracted prayers rather than an exact translation in English of the Latin *Divine Office*. This makes more sense to me than the idea that Pecock has translated his reformed liturgy into English. If this were the case, why would he make a distinction between the different forms of prayer for laypeople and clergy when he is discussing the need for all Christians to understand prayer properly? He says that clear understanding should be the goal for both "unlettrid men . . . whanne they reden her Sauter or her Pater Noster in Latin" and "clerkis . . . in seiyng of her Latin Divine Office whanne they reden derke psalmes and othere derk chapitris, responses and lessouns" (*Reule*, 401). Though Pecock does not take his reforms to the next step, by translating the Divine Office into English, he does bring clergy and laity on to common ground in a fascinating way in his discussion of the need for clear understanding in prayer. Though the clergy and laity pray in different forms, their method should be the same: all Christians need proper understanding, and therefore all Christians work in the same way when lifting their voices up to God.

For example, when Pecock's reader recites the Pater Noster "by voice, or by speche and noise of mouthe to God," he must, above all, focus his "undirstonding" and "affeccioun" on the words (*Donet*, 207). When he recites or reads the prayers that are contained in Pecock's books, the individual must not run "swiftly" over the words, mumbling them incoherently; instead, he must speak slowly, and "wrastlist with hem" in the understanding and in the will or affect (*Donet*, 205). When Pecock offers detailed instruction on prayer, referring to "the maters which thou redist" and "the reding of hem" under the general subject of "preier to be maad by voice, or by speche and noise of mouthe, to God," I assume he is envisioning readers who will read aloud rather than silently (he treats silent prayers in a subsequent passage). During this oral reading of prayer, Pecock advises, "thou muste holde thin undirstonding and thin affect or wil coplid stifly to the maters which thou redist, and thou schalt sett these bothe now seid powers, undirstonding and wil, into her fervent wirching aboute the maters which thou redist" (*Donet*, 206). Focus and comprehension are vital.

Pecock stresses that understanding prayer is more important than saying the words aloud. It is better to "seie oonis wel the preier clepid in Latin Pater Noster, with suche a labour as is now spokun off

thorugh a certein time, than forto seie an hundrid rabbischly and renningly thorugh the same time" (*Donet*, 205). He warns that the Latin
words have no charm of their own and that only a rude, lewd man
would believe that it were possible for God to be "charmed, con-
streined and drawen by vertu of the wordis, which vertu the wordis
schulde have by her sown, as it wolde seeme the moost party of alle
the peple ffeelith. And sothely this is not fer from wicchecraft" (206).
Words "swiftly spokun" in a language "not understonde" do not constitute magic; superstitious belief in the incantatory power of the
sound of the words themselves is sheer folly (206). Here Pecock opposes the notion that the sound and "vertu" of the Latin language
make Latin prayer more powerful and meaningful to God than
English. The language of ritual is meaningful only when the ritual is
properly understood. The question that this passage provokes, however, is how understanding is facilitated: How can readers literate only
in the vernacular pray meaningfully in Latin?

Pecock's solution to this problem brings laity and clergy on to
common ground by raising an issue of concern common to both. The
problem of misunderstanding is not limited to laypeople without
Latin. The clergy experience the same problem during the Divine
Office when their minds cannot keep up with the speed of the service.
Pecock offers advice that is applicable to both clergy and laity, suggesting strategies for three kinds of reader: the first speaks or reads "in
a langage which he undirstondith not in the proper significaciouns of
the wordis"; the second understands the language but reads so fast
"that his minde may not hold cours with his tunge"; and the third must
use an assigned prayer that does not run on relevant matters—a prayer
that "makith not mencioun of tho pointis whiche he desirith and for
which he preieth, as it fallith ful ofte whanne we preien by psalmes the
Sauter" (*Reule*, 400). The first reader could be a layman praying his
Pater Noster in Latin; the second could be a clergyman participating
in the Latin Divine Office; the third could be either, reciting psalms in
a situation of public worship that are chosen because they are meaningful for a particular feast day or service and not because they have
individual meaning for the participants or observers.

In each case, the trick is to find other ways to focus the intellect
and affect on the subject of the prayer. It is possible to make prayer

effective by focusing the attention on other things, such as the various "laudis and preisingis" of God and the various benefits of God listed in the first two treatises of Pecock's *Reule* (*Reule*, 400). Pecock suggests that the person praying should "thinke in general upon al maner good to be yoven or upon al maner yvel to be avoided or upon alle thilke special boonis for which he laborith" (400). If the person praying is able to focus on matters from Pecock's *Reule*, rather than the prayer text itself, "he schal not laboure in idil neither lacke his avail," because his desire and mental concentration will be fervent even if the "wordis red or spoken maken no mencioun in her propre significaciouns upon tho desirid pointis and purposis" (400–401). As this individual recites the formal prayer of various texts in the Psalter, for example, his desire and his thinking on other matters will speed his prayer; indeed, the intensity of his desire can actually change the meaning of the words he recites so that God hears his mental prayer:

> This man in this present caas ordeineth tho wordis whiche he redith and spekith to signifie to him the asking that al good be yoven and that al yvel be awey removed and awey driven or ellis the asking of the special desirid thingis whiche he thinkith upon whilis he redith the seid formes of wordis whiche he undirstondith not in her proper significaciouns, and therfore this reding or speking is to him a verry preier and of this same preier he hath the cleer undirstonding, forwhy he hath the cleer undirstonding which he him silf at his owne volunte makith and geveth to tho wordis red and spoken. (401)

Through concentrated, focused reflection on other matters, an individual who does not understand or connect with the words he is saying can change the meaning of these prayers so that they represent his inner devout reflections.

Pecock's instructions for meaningful prayer here are intended both for clerks and laymen. He says that thinking on "worthy and digne trouthis" in these kinds of situations is a way of focusing the intellect and affect on the prayer, making it meaningful: "and in this wise ben unlettrid men holpen whanne they reden her Sauter or her Pater Noster in Latin, and clerkis ben holpen in seiyng of her Latin

Divine Office whanne they reden derke psalmes and othere derk chapitris, responses and lessouns, and whilis for speed to accorde with the qweer and to do othere good servicis they muste rede so faste that her mind and undirstonding may not felouschipe with her tunge" (401). Clerics and laymen find themselves in the same boat when their comprehension of prayer is hampered in some way, by the difficulty of the language, the density of the passage, or the pace of the liturgical process. Though their challenges are different, the solutions are the same: both must find ways to focus on other matters in a way that generates "cleer undirstonding" (401).

This solution, however, is not ideal, for either group. While Pecock's comments about the importance of intent suggest that a pious mind-set and devout inner reflection can make oral prayer effective and meaningful, he also makes it clear that this elementary manner of prayer, which depends on devout intent rather than comprehension of the prayer text, is a stepping-stone to proper forms. Indeed, those "Cristen soulis" who do not progress beyond this basic manner of prayer, which he describes as such "lowe and so ruide maner of preying," are reprimanded for not coming to "the worthier" manner of prayer (402). The movement from clearly defined "unlettrid laymen" and "clerkis" to the broad category of Christian souls is interesting, first of all, because it blurs the boundary between these groups and suggests that everyone must work toward the same goals, no matter what forms he is using (401). The distinction is dropped, enabling the reader to envision both laymen and clergy working in the same way as they communicate with God. The lack of progress from such a "fful ruide and ful boistose and ful unfitting" manner of prayer to meaningful prayer rooted in clear understanding is partly the fault of negligent bishops who do not take the time to write books like Pecock's and partly the fault of people who do not challenge themselves to learn a better method (401). Pecock actually scorns the first level of prayer, saying:

> Suche maner of asking and preiyng . . . is liik to the maner of asking and preiyng which yong unkunning babis maken as whanne they schulde aske and seie, "modir, geve me drinke," they seien, "brom, brom." And in stide of that they schulde seie, "geve me breede," they cryen, "pa, pa." And summe othere eldre whanne

they desiren and asken to be leid in bed to slepe, they seie, "lete the cat winke," or sum othere inpertinent resoun by which nevertheles they entenden her purpos; and therfore how ruide and boistose this maner of preising and of preiyng is in reward of the othere . . . namely to resonable soulis whiche mowe leerne thilk better and it use—is open ynough to se. (402)

Pecock's comparison between babies and reasonable souls who use the first level of prayer resembles other comparisons made between meek children and the laity that stress the weak intellectual capacity of the laity and their need for less demanding spiritual tasks. Nicholas Love, for example, defines the laity as "simple creatures the whiche as childrin haven nede to be fedde with milke of lighte doctrine and not with sadde mete of grete clargye and of hie contemplacion."[2] However, Pecock indicates that just as babies must grow into responsible adults, his readers—both clerics and lay folk—must leave their spiritual infancy behind: for Pecock, all reasonable souls are capable of a higher form of prayer. Pecock's God is of an intellectual nature and expects more than baby talk from his supplicants. He says that a mother will have compassion for the "unkunning and the unpower of her babis to preie in fairer and more reverent forme" while they are young, but "sche wole not so allowe suche ruide and uncomely askingis and preiyngis of her elder children whiche mowe leerne, kunne and use to aske of her modir alle thingis in faire honest forme and reverent maner, but sche ellis blame hem, rebuke hem and punische hem" (*Reule*, 402). Children must learn to ask properly for the things they desire; lay readers and clerics who struggle to understand the Pater Noster in Latin or the Latin Divine Office must learn a higher form of prayer rooted in intellectual understanding. Pecock indicates that God will not turn away those who are forced to use the first, rude form of prayer, but there may be severe consequences for those who content themselves with this rude form despite being capable of using "wordis and sentences cleerly undirstonden" in their prayers (402).

Pecock's scorn for those who do not ascend to the level of prayer that is appropriate for their intellectual capacity is noteworthy; his comparison between babies and people who engage in the first level of prayer is meant to prod readers to leave this sort of prayer behind rather than designating in a more neutral way the kinds of activities suitable for beginners and more advanced people. For others who use the metaphors of milk and bread to explain the different kinds of devotional activities and reading material suited to souls at different stages, those who receive milk are not treated pejoratively, in the way that Pecock treats people who are too lazy to use their intellects. For example, when Bernard of Clairvaux claims that some souls must receive milk before they are ready for the more complex nourishment of the Song of Songs, he speaks matter-of-factly about the two different states without subtly denigrating one and indicating its inferiority.[3] Pecock calls his readers babies not because he wishes to describe the elementary stage of their development but because he expects all of his readers—lay and clerical alike—to learn to exercise their reason and will, leaving infancy behind.

Pecock blurs the lay and clerical worlds in this call for all Christian souls to work harder at prayer, making it clear that there is no inherent difference between clergy and laity in terms of their ability to progress to more meaningful practices. Though each is working with a different form of prayer, the goal of clear understanding is universal. By bringing together instruction for those involved in celebrating the liturgy with those working on comprehending their Pater Noster, Pecock helps us see how liturgy could be, as Clifford Flanigan, Kathleen Ashley, and Pamela Sheingorn demonstrate, "the arena of intense communication of cultural values and negotiation of power within social formations at given historical moments."[4] Pecock's decision to enfold liturgical practice and lay devotions together in his instructions on clear understanding helps to bring together "'official' liturgical practice" with "what might be considered para-liturgical or even non-liturgical activities" in a way that helps to "undermine the privileged status of the Latin liturgy controlled by the monks and to authorize lay and vernacular 'liturgies.'"[5] Though I would not go so far as to say that he "explodes" the distinction between official liturgical activities and the paraliturgical, I would argue that treating liturgical understanding as the same intellectual process for clerics and laymen shows that ritual practices, or instructions for them, can "teach us about ideology and the uses of power within specific social formations that existed at given moments in medieval history."[6] In Pecock's system, both cleric and layman are taught a similar practice with similar goals, though they are praying with different forms: hierarchic divisions are not effaced, but they are somewhat fluid.

It is vital in Pecock's view that other "prelatis in the chirche" join him on his mission to reform "by light and esy labour manie oolde formes of preiyng and preising hard and derk to be undirstonde" (*Reule*, 402). This reform is described as a form of renewal that will foster "cleerist and swettist and devoutist maner of preising and preiyng" (402). Though we have no access to the new forms of prayer in Pecock's missing books, we can gather some sense of what it meant to him to foster clear understanding. For example, he remarks that the original desire of the church "in making the divine office in Latin intendid and meened that ministris therof schulde make her attendaunce and her affecciouns answering to the lettir" but that in reality "so derke, so looce, so difforme and so unhanging office" is now "rad and seid and into so greet haunte and quantite" that the church's original desire for meaningful prayer is no longer fulfilled (406). A reformed Divine Office would have clearer divisions and distinctions between texts used for praising and texts used for prayer, because the current mixed forms are "unstabil and so not firme neither strong neither fers, intense or highe in his kinde" (406). The activities of praise and prayer will be most effective and devout if these divisions are made and psalms, hymns, and "proses or versis" suitable for each activity are gathered together and kept separate (406). Furthermore, it may be helpful to "cleer the derk processis" of various liturgical texts "by exposicioun of hem mengid with hem" (407). Pecock emphasizes that the main problem with forms currently in use is that they do not facilitate clear understanding. The affective potential of hymns, psalms, and formal prayers cannot be realized in their current state because they "renne upon so derke lettre to undirstonde and upon so bare and boistose maters as to the litteral undirstonding" (416).

Pecock's lost forms of prayers, which run upon "cleer to be undirstonde and upon worthy and digne maters of thy nobiltees, of thy benefetis and of thy lawis," would make the occupations of praise and prayer in monastic houses "miche higher and plesauntir" (416). These worthy matters are, of course, Pecock's seven matters, which we know are accessible, in the vernacular, in his *Reule of Crysten Religioun*. The parts of the *Reule* that teach the nature of God and his benefits, such as Christ's moral life on earth, the Trinity, and the Redemption, generate material for praising God "by rehercels of doctrine and of cleer knowing upon Goddis worthinessis and dignities and goodnessis"; readers need not have "a fairer, fruitfuller, a devouter foorme to preise God therby" (*Donet*, 203). Pecock's *Reule* is an ideal template for praising God and declaring his great worthiness. It is tempting to speculate, from our understanding of the *Reule*'s teaching on the seven matters, about the possible character of Pecock's reformed liturgical rites. What sort of community would these rites "validate" and give voice to? In her work on the Brigittine Divine Office, Katherine Zieman argues that the "distinctive Brigittine rite" gave a unique voice to the Brigittine community and "validated the women's community in particular."[7] For example, Birgitta's emphasis on "wisdom" as opposed to "knowledge or letteredness as the goal of learning" suggests a way for the Brigittine sisters to consider themselves "true scholars."[8] It is dangerous to speculate too much about the contents of missing books, but I imagine that the voice of prayer and praise in Pecock's reformed liturgical rites would validate the textual community enfolded in Pecock's *Reule* in important ways by enabling the members of that community to engage in a rational dialogue with God based on common knowledge of the book of reason. For example, it is important to note that Pecock's reform of prayer focuses on making it more rational: he says that he will educate readers in "preier wel devised and maad by obsecracioms and by laudis or preisingis, including in hem setis and placis of strong argumentacioun" (*Reule*, 387).[9] He explains that rational prayer is a form of argumentation, requiring the construction of various points and persuasions. It is better to ask God for things with specific requests and arguments than to ask for them "nakidly without therto setting of cleere redy manie and diverse preisingis, making obsecracioun, and without therto setting of manie cleere and redy qwik argumentis and suasions" (404). Asking for things "in her specialtees with suche manie therto sett obsecratiif preisingis and also manie diverse argumentacioums, allegacioums and suasioums" (404) roots the prayer firmly in the faculty of understanding, or intellect. For Pecock, prayer is more firm, fierce, strong, intense, and "highe in his kinde" when it is motivated by rational consideration of the kinds of boons asked for by the person praying (406). A firm rational basis of understanding will motivate the will to greater desire and devotion: "Oure desiir schal be more rerid up upon the thingis askid and we more fervently and devoutly schulen be turned to [God]" when we have deeply and rationally considered the points and matters of our prayer (403). This emphasis on argument in prayer is important when we reflect on what character Pecock's reformed liturgy may have had. His notion that prayer is a kind of devout conversation with God in which Christians must declare their desires in an informed, reasonable way rather than in a heedless, impassioned overflow of emotion illustrates his sense of reason as the preeminent human characteristic. Such rational prayers validate and give voice to a community whose members are bound together by common modes of discussing, debating, sharing, and acquiring knowledge. Pecock's approach to conversation with God encourages members of his textual community to develop a scholarly identity as they engage in devotions. When they lift up their voices in praise of God, they speak together as students of Pecock's philosophical theology; as I argued in chapter 1, the communal voice of praise and prayer that we hear throughout the *Reule* can integrate cleric and layman. It is likely, given Pecock's critique of older forms, that his revised liturgy, based on the doctrine of the *Reule*, would be fairly accessible for readers versed in the *Reule*'s contents. In other words, the reformed liturgy would be likely to act as a bridge between clerical and lay religious culture.

If I am correct in thinking that the lost *Divine Office* is a Latin book of reformed liturgy and the lost *Enchiridion* a book of extracts from the former, then we can assume either that lay readers would have access to such fruitful, devout, reformed prayers in English or that they would have had copies of the Latin prayers surrounded by English commentary, paraphrase, or exposition, all of which would intensify their private and public devotions. Pecock's effort to reform prayer and the Divine Office itself brings him into a larger discussion in late medieval England about the role of Latin and the vernacular in worship. He does not, I argue, offer lay or clerical readers a translation of the entire Divine Office. He does, however, reshape the Latin Divine Office to enable clerics to understand the liturgy better, and he does reshape lay people's experience of the liturgy by providing them with a version of a book of hours. If we assume that the lost *Enchiridion* is a kind of book of hours, then, we can place Pecock firmly within his fifteenth-century moment, a time in which the popularity and circulation of primers was on the rise. Eamon Duffy describes the book of hours as "a book designed for lay people seeking to imitate clerical prayer . . . designed originally for the aristocratic and wealthy, which moved decisively down-market and became in the end a book equally available to minor country gentry and strong farmers, to city shopkeepers and merchants."[10] Mary Erler states that the book of hours or primer "assumed an extraordinary centrality in popular culture," crossing boundaries of class as well as "lines separating orthodoxy and heterodoxy."[11] Erler describes the book's contents as follows: "The book's core was the hours of the Virgin; these were preceded by a calendar and by set passages from the four Gospels, and were followed (in the book's sparest form) by the seven penitential psalms, the litany of the saints, and the office of the dead."[12] Some people owned luxurious books of hours while others owned "humbler" copies.[13]

Whether beautiful or not, books of hours were valuable spiritual possessions because they intensified devotion and understanding during worship. Paul Saenger writes that the vernacular was used in some books of hours to provide rubrics and other aids for understanding the texts used in the Mass, which were written in Latin and "obtained force through pronunciation."[14] Increasingly, though, in the second half of the fourteenth century, "translations of these Latin prayers and a great variety of original vernacular prayers were similarly incorporated into books of hours or circulated separately in small prayer books." These translations "dramatically affected the relationship between the celebrants and the laity in the performance of the public ceremonies of the Church, particularly the Mass." The lay observers could read along, silently, in their vernacular prayer books, synchronizing their silent prayers "with the oral prayers of the celebrants of the Mass."[15] It seems clear from Pecock's instructions on prayer that his *Enchiridion* is written with this process in mind, as a way of heightening the spiritual experience of lay observers during liturgical ceremonies. This shows him to be a man of his time, in line with trends in using the vernacular to stimulate devotion among the laity. His particular approach of providing prayers modeled on his seven matters and including arguments and rational "suasions" was one among many, "invariably different" forms of prayer books. Because books of hours were above all personal and idiosyncratic, a "great variety of separately programmed religious experiences" flourished within the category of a "single uniform Roman mass."[16] Duffy writes that though books of hours promoted lay interiority, "the personalizing of religion," interiority is "by no means to be equated with individualism."[17] For Duffy, books of hours served to connect "the lay devotee more closely to the institution by encouraging him or her to participate in its formal worship."[18] I would suggest that Pecock's approach promotes this connection, fostering interiority without providing opportunity for a high degree of individualism. I suggest this because of Pecock's overt attempt to differentiate his forms from others, calling them sweeter, more fruitful, and more valuable than others he has witnessed; as usual, Pecock recommends his approach as a standard, in a way that shows resistance to this great variety and an effort to contain it within his eminently rational program.

Pecock's sense of the urgent need to reform the Divine Office to increase understanding among its celebrants also shows his affinities with other reform-minded churchmen like the author of the *Myroure of Oure Ladye* (written sometime after 1420), a translation of and commentary on the Divine Office for the Brigittines at Syon. This writer justifies his translation of the Divine Office very carefully, showing how much caution was required in approaching this sensitive question. As I mentioned in the first chapter, there were strong connections between the monks at Syon and citizens of London, so there must have been some knowledge and interest among the London laity with what was happening at Syon. The decision to reform the nuns' Divine Office did not happen in a vacuum, therefore, but would have reverberated through lay society. According to the author, the nuns at Syon have dedicated their lives to the praise of Mary, but to praise her properly they need a firm understanding of Mary's "excellent highness and worthiness," which are both expressed "in al youre holy service." The problem is that the nuns' "inward understanding" of Mary is hampered by their inability to comprehend "the meaning" of the matters they "singe and rede." A translation of the Divine Office will provide the nuns with "gostly comforte and profite," enabling them to praise Mary more devoutly.[19] The author takes care to arrange his text so that readers will be able to distinguish between the Latin, the "bare englisshe of the Latin," and the additions that are "putte therto for to expounde it."[20] Clear directions on using the translation are provided, which ensure that the Latin will not be neglected: the sisters may read the English "while the Latin is read" when they say "theire matins or redde their legende," but in other situations, says the author, "I wolde not counsel them to leve the heringe of the Latin for entendaunce of the Englisshe."[21] The author maintains a clear hierarchy, both in the structure of the Divine Office and on the material page, between the use of the more authoritative Latin and the application of the more serviceable English. To allay any remaining anxiety about his English translations of scripture, particularly during a time when "it is forboden under paine of cursing, that no man shulde have ne drawe eny text of holy scripture in to Englisshe without license of the bishop diocesan," the author confirms that he has obtained "lisence of oure bishop to drawe suche thinges in to Englisshe."[22] This author's reference to Arundel's Constitutions indicates that he must have felt strongly enough about the need for the translation at Syon to bring before the authorities the argument that his work constituted a special case.

Like Pecock then, the author of the *Myroure*, who is writing about the same time, connects clear understanding with meaningful devotion; unlike Pecock, the author of the *Myroure* "confronts head on the role of the vernacular in orthodox worship."[23] For Jennifer Bryan, translating the Divine Service for the Brigittines registers "growing discontent with the almost wholly externalized experience of the Latin liturgy."[24] Both Pecock and the author of the *Myroure* have thought hard about ways to facilitate that crucial connection between what is read and what is understood in the performance of the liturgy. These authors show different degrees of caution as they justify reform, with Pecock making changes to the Latin Office rather than offering a translation and the *Myroure* author reinforcing the authority of the Latin text, policing the way the translation is used, and limiting his audience to the women enclosed at Syon. Elizabeth Schirmer argues that the *Myroure* demonstrates a tension "between empowering the women of Syon as readers and containing and controlling their read-

erly agency."[25] On one hand, the author offers the sisters "unprecedented agency as readers," placing the nuns in a more "cleric-like relation to their liturgical texts."[26] On the other hand, the *Myroure's*
instructions for liturgical reading limit that reading experience by locating "the sisters' spiritual progress precisely in the act of reading
itself" rather than teaching them that reading is the first step "on a
ladder to higher spiritual activities" like contemplation.[27] For Zieman,
this constitutes an odd balance between inviting and limiting readerly
agency at Syon.

   The problem of what to do about nuns who do not adequately
comprehend Latin was not new to fifteenth-century England. An odd
balance between a sense of the need for English translations and a
sense that Latin is more spiritually authoritative is evident in *The
Chastising of God's Children*, a work that is dated by its editors to circa
1382, that survives in fourteen copies (not all complete), and that
achieved wide circulation in the fifteenth century, not only among
nuns but also among lay readers. Schirmer notes that *The Chastising*
was written for the nuns at Barking Abbey, a "wealthy and prestigious
institution" that was a "more venerable and in many ways more traditional women's institution than Syon."[28] The writer of this work acknowledges that English translations of the liturgy are controversial
and that "many men repreven it to have the matins or the sautir or the
gospels or the Bible in Englisshe, because they mowe nat be translated
into vulgare, word by word as it stondith, withoute grete circumlocucioun, aftir the feelynge of the first writers, the whiche translatid that
into Latin by teching of the holy goost." This author is less worried,
however, about the dangers of "circumlocucioun" and more worried
about the possibility that English will replace Latin: "But utterly to
usen hem in Englisshe and leve the Latin, I holde it nat commend-
able." Those who are bound to say "her sautir or her matins of oure
lady" in penance must use the Latin words without any English
glosses.[29] Here the Latin seems to play a formal role, as the proper
form of prayer, while the English simply serves as a means of stirring
devotion, presumably through increased understanding. By arguing
that the English forms of prayer do not qualify as proper penance, this
writer approaches the notion that worries Pecock, that the Latin words
have virtues and spiritual properties that the vernacular lacks.

These authors all agree that the vernacular facilitates understanding, but they are careful to prevent it from becoming an equal player in the Divine Office. Each takes a slightly different position along a spectrum of ideas about the power of intent, or a pious mind-set, in late medieval discussion of prayer. Paul Saenger notes that some theologians believed that "the *attention mentale et cordiale* for reading hours and other verbal prayers need only be the actual or habitual desire for God."[30] This concept was applied by some theologians to members of the laity who possessed only phonetic literacy (the ability to decode texts syllable by syllable and pronounce them orally) in their reading of Latin prayer books. For the author of *The Chastising of God's Children*, the nuns' intent can be pious despite a total lack of understanding. As Schirmer points out, this author explains that a sister's "fervent desire" for God and the "vertue of the wordis"—not her understanding of their meaning—make her devotions more "acceptable to God."[31] More than five decades after *The Chastising* was written, ideas have changed. The writer of the *Myroure* is not content to interpret intent as habitual desire to serve God; instead, the nuns' intent comes from their understanding of the Divine Office, and their spiritual rewards go hand in hand with their attention to study. Finally, for Pecock, pious intent is connected intimately with comprehension of the words of prayer. Failing that, readers must at least gain an elementary knowledge of his seven matters so that they can focus their minds on doctrine that is clearly understood. Pecock's strident remarks about the need to renew old forms of prayer and his position on prayer as an intellectual conversation between a believer and a God who is not charmed by Latin demonstrate that reforming devotional practices is just as important as his project to reform the teaching of doctrine in his textual community.

The need to focus the intellect on the matter of praise and prayer is even more essential and intense during the devotional practice that I examine in the rest of this chapter, the far more demanding and rigorous practice Pecock outlines, of "preising and preier in meditacioun and bithenking" (*Donet*, 207). This activity of "inwarde speche in thin undirstonding to God," when conducted in a "secrete and privey place, partles of noise and trouble of the peple," actually can be more effective than prayer and praise conducted "in placis of cumpanie"

(207). This meditative experience is best conducted in "time of the night, namelich aftir thy first sleepe, or eerliche in the morowe, fer before that the peple risith" (207). At these times, Pecock tells his readers, "thy undirstonding and thy wil or affeccioun and thine othire lower wittis and her appetitis ben more naked than in othire times from alle maner of worldly thingis" (207). Attention on the matters of praise and prayer is essential: the intellect and will must not be "sluggy, unquike and hevy" but focused (208). The challenging practice of meditation is designed for, and essential for, all Christians; unfortunately, however, it is neglected (along with oral prayer and praise) both by those in "private religiouns" and by those "oute of private religiouns" (214). The labor of meditation, however, is so important that it should occupy "eche man and womman, or eny man and womman" who is not prevented by infirmity (214). Pecock emphasizes that the devotional practices he outlines are for all: "My meening is that eche man and womman schulde in the morewtide, or in the night time before the morewtide, take a sawly [satisfactory portion] of these occupaciouns, and in the eventide eftsoones" (214). This requires a lot of his readers: like those in the enclosure, they are to be vigilant, staying up late and awakening early to find a private space to meditate on God.

The practice, or "craft and laboure of meditacioun," is highly structured, beginning with reading and ending with prayer (213). The process must be followed "reulily, ordinatly, by rewe and in cours" (213). The reading of Pecock's books is followed by deep reflection on various possible topics, which engenders both intellectual understanding and affection in the will. The practice concludes with the private recitation of a prayer in which the believer praises and worships God. This practice brings together all the facets of contemplative life that Pecock outlines when he says that "contemplatiif liif is not ellis but exercise in these deedis before rehercid," namely, "kunning, loving, wel willing, preising, worshiping, asking and desiring" (*Reule*, 475). The goal of this practice is the stimulation of affective desire and love for God: as Marion Glasscoe suggests in her definition of meditation, "It can safely be said that by the fourteenth century the term *meditation* had come to denote a willed mental concentration on aspects of the faith, either as formulated in Scripture, or prayer, or other devotional writing, hymns for example, which brings a quickening of love and understanding."[32] This means that we must be careful to distinguish between the specialized monastic practice of *lectio divina* and practices of meditative reading adopted by the laity of late medieval England. Though meditative reading has its roots in *lectio divina*, it is a more flexible and wide-ranging practice. As Vincent Gillespie points out, Anselm's definition of monastic reading is "closely bound up with the processes of meditation on the words of Sacred Scripture," while meditative reading among the laity in late medieval England may not even involve the Bible.[33] Benedicta Ward says that "for Anselm and his predecessors" reading, meditation, and prayer were "different aspects of the same thing, not separate exercises in their own right."[34] Through the practice of *lectio divina* the Bible becomes part of the monk's very self as he ingests the text, assimilates it, and brings it forth through prayer. Lay believers, on the other hand, can meditate on any kind of text, internal or external, that concerns the divine; Pecock's readers must concentrate on the matters of his books, which best stimulate the intellect and the affect.

It is important to note, in our examination of Pecock's program for meditative reading, that to successfully achieve this quickening of love and understanding, the supplicant should be an advanced reader of Pecock's works: the seven matters of the *Reule* are to be fully understood and integrated into the mind, since they form the basis in the supplicant's mind for meditative thinking. Pecock writes, "Thou muste kunne the treuthis of the vii seid maters whereupon rennith 'the book of cristen religioun'; and thou muste kunne remember thee ipon hem parfiytly and currauntly, and that withoute eny biholding upon a book to be maad therfore" (*Donet*, 207).[35] Pecock instructs those who wish to engage in this meditative activity to master his *Reule* so that their meditation will proceed from total comprehension and absorption of its contents; however, he concedes that it is permissible to lead oneself through the various topics for meditation with the help of a kind of crib sheet, or else "a schort pointing of hem in a papir leef, sumwhat aftir the maner in which they ben pointid in the first party of this present book" (207). This list of topics to be covered in meditation helps to direct the process by calling the mind back to the stores of knowledge gained from reading Pecock's books; this keeps the person's mind from wandering. It is important to note that Pecock's "papir leef" summarizing the contents of his books is much different from the paper icons recommended for use by the unlettered laity in meditation. For those who could not read, preachers could advise the use of a cheap kind of text, on which was pictured a key moment in the story of salvation, such as Mary's visit with Elizabeth. Margaret Aston comments that "this kind of text was a sort of halfway house between church image and illustrated text: a paper icon. It was expected simultaneously to teach the unlettered believer . . . and to be venerated by him or her."[36] In the context of these instructions for meditation on his seven matters, Pecock suggests that an image will not suffice; the "papir leef" assumes a high level of literacy and comprehension and the individual's ability to thoroughly digest the contents of his books.

Pecock's effort to secure a place for his works in the exercise of meditative reading may well be an attempt to provide an alternative practice to the Lollard rumination on the biblical text itself. For Pecock, lay meditation on the biblical text could lead to many errors because of its mystical and difficult passages. Reacting against the Lollards and attempting to reinforce orthodox doctrine, Pecock may be taking a step back by providing what he feels to be an alternative, safer, and more fruitful source for contemplative reading. The challenging nature of the source that he does provide, however, is noteworthy: he provides sophisticated books of doctrine as the food for this affective practice of meditation. The reader must master the *Reule* before he can proceed to the stage of meditation, and this requires long study in the book of reason, in matters such as Pecock's explication of the philosophical foundations of God's moral law.[37]

In his provision of instructions for meditation that do not require the use of the Bible, Pecock reaches for models such as the *Speculum ecclesie* by Saint Edmund of Abingdon, archbishop of Canterbury from 1234 to 1240.[38] This work, addressed to an audience of enclosed religious, circulated in Anglo-Norman, English, and Latin. The editor of the Latin text, Helen Forshaw, tells us that English translations of this work of Victorine spirituality were popular during Pecock's lifetime: "In a final burst of popularity in the fifteenth century both Latin and French texts were translated many times into English."[39] The English version located in Robert Thornton's 1440 household miscellany of spiritual works opens, like Pecock's *Reule*, by emphasizing the important of both "knaweynge and lufe," charging the reader with the task of developing self-knowledge, knowledge of God, and love of God.[40] Like Pecock's corpus, the *Mirror* is a work of both doctrine and devotion, offering education in the basics of the faith as well as incitement to move closer to God. The reader of Edmund's *Mirror* can learn about himself and God through "thre manere of contemplacion."[41] Contemplation here does not have a "restricted meaning" but is used "interchangeably" along with meditation to describe "a number of spiritual exercises—meditative reading, prayerful reflection, the interior prayer of devotion, the set meditation on a theme or event in Christ's life, and the forms of prayer which later writers would call acquired and infused contemplation."[42] Describing contemplation, then, Edmund says: "The firste es in creaturs, the tother es in haly scripture, the thirde es in Gode himselfe in His nature."[43] The first kind of meditation focuses on God's creation, which reminds the reader of God's greatness and wisdom. The second does not actually require Bible reading and instead focuses on anything "wreten" that "may availe the till edificacioun," such as the petitions of the Pater Noster.[44] Edmund's advice to say the Pater Noster just once "with gude devocion" rather than a thousand times "withoutten devocion" may well be a source for Pecock's own emphasis, discussed above, on saying one Pater Noster with the proper intent rather than saying "an hundrid rabbischly and renningly thorugh the same time" (*Donet*, 205).[45] The third type of meditation in Edmund's *Mirror* focuses on God himself, inviting the reader to come to deeper knowing of God by envisioning the events of the Passion and reflecting on the persons of the Trinity. There are important differences between the programs for meditation outlined by Edmund and Pecock. For example, Edmund encourages readers who cannot read the Bible to meditate instead on groupings such as the seven deadly sins, the seven virtues, the Ten Commandments, and the twelve articles of the Creed. Pecock's readers are to focus on his seven matters, and not on these forms, his disapproval of which I discuss in the next chapter. However, the many resemblances between these programs for meditation illustrate that Pecock's teaching on the devotional life develops from a tradition of thought about meditative reading that proved popular among his fifteenth-century audience. Furthermore, these resemblances reflect Pecock's larger project of providing firm rational foundations for contemporary practices in a standard, uniform corpus of spiritual instruction that would steady and streamline the currents of lay devotional life.

In his instructions on matters to consider during meditation, Pecock provides a variety of possible options.[46] For example, on one day the individual can "bithenk" first on the nature of God and his benefits, to inspire feelings of gratitude and love, and then proceed to the subject of the fifth matter of the *Reule*—our natural wretchedness—to inspire feelings of unworthiness (*Donet*, 208). This meditation will motivate shame for past sins and conclude with both a personal, spontaneous prayer beseeching God "that thou schalt offende him no more, and that thou schalt have alle the vertues contrarie to thy sinnis and to alle sinnis" and a Pater Noster (209). On another day, the course of meditation could run over other numerous benefits given by God; on yet another day the subject for meditation could be God's law or God's punishments in hell. In each case, the person meditating must fall into the fifth and sixth matters, which remind man of his guilt, sins, and wretchedness, before ending with a prayer beseeching God's forgiveness, his help, and salvation, followed by a Pater Noster.

The subject matter that Pecock recommends as food for thought in meditation, such as the benefits and gifts of God, the punishments of God that await the sinful in hell, and the wretchedness and wickedness of man, is similar to that recommended in Edmund of Abingdon's *Mirror*. When the reader rises from bed in the morning or at midnight, he is to think first about the thousands of people "in perill of saule, that es to say, in dedly sin." He then turns to consider that Christ has delivered him "of all thise illes . . . withoutten thy deserte." Keeping his thoughts on the "gret gude" Christ has done for him alone, he must lift up his hands and thank the Lord for these individual benefits, saying: "My Lorde Ihesu Criste! Grace I yelde, and thanke the, that me, thine unworthy servaunde, thou hase kepid covered and vesete in this night (or in this day) hale, safe, and wemles unto this tim thou hase made to come, and for all other gudes and benefetis that thou hase geffin me, anely thurghe thy gudnes and thy pete, thou that liffes and regnes endless. Amen."[47] The program for meditation resembles Pecock's in the progression from thoughts about unworthiness and sin, to thoughts of gratitude for God's deliverance and protection, to prayer thanking God for the gift of benefits. This common method is also recommended in the eighteen religious articles contained in the late fifteenth-century MS Bodley 789. In his study of this manuscript, John Hirsh explores the way the arrangement of these eighteen articles guides the reader through a carefully structured system of thought designed to provoke sorrow for sins and dedication to virtue.[48] Hirsh shows how the contents are arranged to initially place the believer in a "timeless frame of mind" and to make him think on his sinful state.[49] Once he has contemplated his particular wretchedness, he proceeds to a meditation on Christ's passion, which makes him aware of his guilt and involvement in it, as well as God's great mercy; his attention is then directed to his personal salvation and that of the Christian community; once he is intent on being saved, he turns to contemplation of those "forces that would pull him back to sin," such as the deadly sins.[50] According to Hirsh, the items in the manuscript are strategically ordered to allow for an effective progression of thought in the supplicant that leads him away from sin and toward virtue.[51]

In the *Mirror*, Edmund recommends a structured progression of thought that enables the soul to ascend through degrees of "thoghte of Godde in gret likinge in saule."[52] Edmund's three degrees of meditation lead readers progressively through a hierarchy of knowledge of God. In the first kind of meditation, readers reflect on what the created world tells them about God; in the second kind, readers consider the knowledge about God offered in scripture; in the third, they meditate on what Christ's life on earth reveals about God and finally on what the doctrine of the Trinity reveals about God. Readers are warned that order must be observed: it is important, for example, that the reader meditate on God's manhood before contemplating his divinity. The reader is given "matire and manere for to thinke of Goddis manhede," and it is only "eftirwarde" that he should turn to contemplate him "in His heghe Godhede."[53] The formation of the soul depends on the proper sequence of meditation, ascending from lower to higher as the individual develops understanding of self and God.

Pecock's program for meditation, on the other hand, can proceed in various ways through the seven matters in his *Reule of Crysten Religioun*. For example, reflection on God's triune nature might precede rather than follow reflection on the wretchedness of the self. Furthermore, instead of separating what we know about God from reason and what we know about God from revelation, and moving in vertical steps from one to the other, Pecock mixes sources of knowledge together in his categories of God's benefits, God's punishments, God's moral law, and God's nature. This implies, then, that Pecock's instructions for meditation do not have the same purpose as Edmund's *Mirror*, of leading believers through various hierarchical forms of knowing God. The goal for Pecock's reader is not to ascend progressively to more meaningful ways of knowing God but instead to gather together all of this knowledge from diverse sources in order to train the will on God or to "gendre affecciouns" for God (*Donet*, 211). Consideration of the seven matters will stir various affections, including "love, drede, desiir, sorewe, repentaunce, shame, gladness" (*Reule*, 12). Of course, it is also important for Edmund's reader to generate "sekire devocion" through meditation,[54] but the focus in the *Mirror* is on understanding God in ever more meaningful ways. Pecock's readers are on a path to self-improvement and reform, while Edmund's readers journey toward enlightenment.

Pecock's system is more flexible than that of the *Mirror*. While meditation on Christ's passion forms an important part of the third degree of contemplation in Edmund's *Mirror*, Pecock has room for this kind of meditation in a more user-oriented system. He includes the Passion under the many benefits offered us by the Lord. His lists of things like the benefits and punishments of God, provided in the *Reule*, would presumably provide readers with a certain amount of choice for their meditations: whether they chose to focus on the benefits of the Passion, grace, or the Redemption, would be their decision.[55] However, Pecock insists that the subject matter must change frequently so that all of God's benefits are covered over a certain period of time. Though Pecock's *Reule* provides the subject matter for most of these meditative experiences, he does have room for more individualistic piety: he says that on certain days, once the person has meditated long on God's general benefits, he can think on the special gifts God has given to him, the "singuler benefetis of god which he hath yovun to thee and to noon other" (*Donet*, 210). This more personal meditation should bring the supplicant into strong feelings of guilt for any sins committed by him against such a generous and loving God. Furthermore, when contemplating the wretchedness of the world, one can either use the subject matter provided in Pecock's sixth treatise or use the matter of personal experience: "Thou maist gadere into thy minde by thin experience takun thereupon" (211). Memory and the knowledge of the self are therefore key sources for more personal, individualistic meditation. Yet another method of contemplating the wretchedness of the world is "by reding in stories and cronicles gaderid of thee and to thee for this purpos" (211). Pecock therefore envisions a certain level of flexibility in the experience of meditation: the intense "bithenking" that characterizes this experience can be derived from numerous sources, such as personal experience and the stories of other people's lives. At the same time as he carefully circumscribes his readers' activities by setting them on a path to self-improvement rather than enlightenment, Pecock allows for a certain degree of individuality and autonomy in a form of meditation that is pertinent to the supplicant's interests.

Another noteworthy difference between the approaches in the *Mirror* and the eighteen articles in Bodley 789, on one hand, and Pecock's books, on the other hand, is that Pecock explicitly directs the reader to take care when directing himself through various thought processes. He insists that meditation must be made "reulily, ordinatly, by rewe and in cours, as the pointis of maters in her processe and kinde liggen, that he make not hise meditaciouns by fals heedis and feinid pointis in stede of trouthis, and lest he make his meditacioun startling, heedling, tumbling or reeling, and therby bring not forth the ful availe of good affecciouns, which might ellis be foorth broughte, if the meditacioun were wel reulid" (*Donet*, 213). Pecock insists that the supplicant should try to keep his mind fixed on one matter at a time, keeping separate his petitions and requests in prayer from his meditations. He writes, "Nevertheles, sone, I wote wel that thou schalt stertmele and by litil whilis menge these maters to gider, wille thou, nille thou. And thou schalt menge schort preiers soone aftir that thou hast bigunne thi preisingis, and so aftir whilis thou schrivist thee, where ayens I wole not be. But yitt, not withstonding this menging which schal so bifalle for habundaunce of consideraciouns and of affecciouns, I wole that thou make thy cours to kepe thi seid foorme fro mater into mater, as it may be kept with the seid schort among mengingis of preiers" (211).[56] Pecock admits that at times the structure of meditation will fall away and the mingling of thoughts and prayer will occur because of the level of intensity and emotion, but he insists that the supplicant should make an effort to rein in his passions and curb this tendency for more disordered, widely ranging reflection. Pecock acknowledges that the experience of meditative prayer will be naturally spontaneous, to a certain degree, but he makes it clear that the mind must be focused and ordered.

This intense reflection on matters read and remembered leads directly to prayer. Once the meditation has ranged through various subjects covered by Pecock's books, such as God's benefits, God's punishments, man's wretchedness, and God's moral law, and the emotional state has been quickened, it is natural to turn to God in prayer and ask forgiveness for sins. The supplicant is to finish with prayers for God's forgiveness, prayers for further help and salvation, and a Pater Noster. The experience of meditation concludes when the reason and will are trained on the truths contained in the Pater Noster, in a passionate prayer to God: the individual strives to see "cleerly the trouthis" of the Pater Noster with "resoun" and to gender "affecciouns of desire" in the will (*Donet*, 209). Though Pecock does not furnish his text with examples of the prayers that are to be used in meditative practice, it is probably safe to assume that his comments about the need for rational understanding and logical argumentation in prayer, treated above, would apply even more to meditation.

What kind of knowledge or sight of God does this practice make possible? In Edmund's *Mirror*, the third kind of contemplation, on God in his humanity and divinity, leads the reader to lift himself "aboven himself" and to "paine him for to luke one his Godd in his awen kinde."[57] The goal is to see God in his divinity, as he is rather than as we imagine him. Once the reader has struggled to leave "bodily imaginacion" behind in meditation on the greatness of the soul, in its ability to comprehend in a single thought "heven and erthe and all that in thaim are," he sees how "grete and nobill" God is for creating such a soul; he can then understand that God is "aboven all thinge, all thinge governande, benethe all thinge, berande all thinge, within all thinge, fulfillande all, withoutten all thing, abowte gangande all."[58] Pecock does not go so far in leading readers toward this contemplative understanding of God, but he does imagine that his readers might be graced with knowledge that "God wole sende and caste to into thy minde whilis thou schalt be in thi laboure of bithenking" (*Donet*, 210). The individual should think on one truth and then another, "with manie othire ful swete pointis of trouthe which wolen falle into thy minde with hem" (208). Pecock seems to be suggesting that at the same time as the supplicant is striving to fill his mind with divine truths, God may pass down other divine truths to him for further meditation that are perhaps sweeter than what can be found in Pecock's *Reule*. This reference to the reception of thoughts from God during meditation corresponds to the general understanding among fourteenth-century writers that "the fruits of meditation" were a divine gift.[59] Pecock further illuminates the nature of this divine gift in his conclusion to his passage on meditative prayer, with the following directions for what to do with these sweet truths that fall from divine grace into the supplicant's mind: "Thus moche is ynough to thee, my sone, for use of meditacioun, with alle the othire consideraciouns which God wole yeve to thee whilis thou laborist therinne—which consideraciouns thou schalt not recchelesly forgete, but point hem in a papir, and tho same reherce in anothir daie journey, with the standerdis of the seid 'book of cristen religioun,' til God wole yeve to thee newe with the same standerdis" (*Donet*, 211–12). Pecock does not elaborate on exactly what he means by these sweet truths that fall from above into the mind of the person meditating, other than to indicate that they should be formally recorded so that they may be integrated into subsequent meditative experiences. The thoughts and considerations that God sends into the mind should be integrated "with the standerdis" of Pecock's *Reule*: if God should send thoughts of man's wretchedness, for instance, the person meditating should group these with Pecock's section on man's wretchedness to extend his meditative practice. This means, therefore, that both God and the individual believer participate in the meditation: the benefits of meditation are both earned and given.

Other than indicating that they are sweet and worthy of consideration, however, Pecock does not suggest that the reception of these points for further meditation leads the reader into an altered state, an experience described by contemplative treatises current in the fifteenth century, like the *Ladder of Foure Ronges*. *A Ladder of Foure Ronges* is a translation of the twelfth-century *Scala claustralium*, by Guigo II. While the original letter on the contemplative life was intended to lead twelfth-century monks toward "contemplative union," its English translation introduced changes making it "more suitable," according to Colledge and Walsh, "for devotional reading."[60] The *Ladder*'s description of "the swettnes & liking of contemplacion" as a "swete hevenly dewing, that the sowle drinkith in liking & in joye," contrasts sharply with Pecock's notion of "sweet points of truth." In the perfect contemplation portrayed in the *Ladder*, the soul is "enflaumid & so ravished in desire" to see God.[61] This description of the ravishing of the soul, which is achieved in the culmination of contemplative prayer, is absent from Pecock's description of the soul's reception of knowledge from God, sent as material for further reflection. Indeed, Pecock is quite cautious about the subject of rapture. For Pecock, God acts as a kind of teacher rather than a divine lover when he communicates to the person praying; this notion of the interaction between God and believer differs greatly from the description of the unitive phase of prayer in contemplative treatises like *A Pistle of Preier*, extant in four late fourteenth- and early fifteenth-century manuscripts. In the *Pistle*, the writer describes prayer as the activity of engendering in the affection two emotions, dread and hope. Focusing on these feelings and thinking "hertly" on them produces in the believer a reverent affection for God. Through this reverent affection, which is characterized by love of God in himself and without any "mene," the believer ascends into union with God, a "oonheed" of "mariage mad bitwix God and the soule."[62] The believer and God are knit together into one, momentarily, through the believer's "love and acordaunce of wile."[63] While the writer of the *Pistle* views prayer as the process that leads to this divine union, through a focus on certain thoughts and emotions, Pecock has no room for a marriage of the soul and God in prayer. Pecock does describe one of the goals of prayer as a stirring of desire and love for God, but he does not elaborate on whether the love produced through prayer enables the believer to participate in this kind of unitive experience. For Pecock, therefore, the ladder of ascent through reading, meditation, and prayer is not likely to result in mystic union.

Interestingly, Pecock does not give advice on how to determine whether these thoughts, received during meditation, are from a divine source or a more suspect source; he merely states that his reader may receive insights from God that will provide new food for thought. He seems to suggest that a properly structured, directed inward meditation, guided by the progression of matters in his *Reule*, will prevent his reader from the dangerous experience of wandering thoughts: if he has studiously mastered the *Reule*, he will "wisely, treuly, surely, coursely, and rewlily him silf forth lede and continue" (*Reule*, 11). Without this kind of mastery, however, he will "ramble and wandre, seching him silf now in oon kinde, now in an other kinde, of contemplable maters"; he will experience "wandring contemplacioun" rather than "stable contemplacioun renning longe time upon trouthis of the same kinde of contemplable mater" (11). Note here that Pecock uses *contemplation* and *meditation* interchangeably instead of using *contemplation* to describe union with God. Pecock is certain that those who have not labored extensively and intensively to understand the *Reule* will run into problems: "He schal take falseheedis in stide of trouthis and wamble in lesingis of his owne invencicuns renning into his minde, weening to him that they ben hevenly apperingis, as is had ofte here upon ful sure experience" (12). With this statement, Pecock shows a desire to restrain and structure the meditative experience into logical rather than spontaneous progressions of thought to prevent people's misinterpretations of their "owne invencicuns" as divine truths (12). If the contemplative is able to keep his mind only on those matters "tretid openly and surely" in the *Reule*, which truths are "weel tried withoute eny dout of lesing or falseheede," then the meditation will be stable, secure, and fruitful (12). Any lay reader who has mastered these subjects through Pecock's treatment of them will not be in danger of contemplating falsehoods instead of truths. Such a reader can be confident that the inward thoughts that spring to mind as he proceeds through the various stages of meditation are inspired by God and can be trusted as a credible source for illumination.

For Pecock, any lay reader willing to submit himself to the intellectual labor of studying Pecock's *Reule* and wrestling with its divine truths can master the subsequent stages of meditation and prayer. A person can achieve perfection in these activities, in Pecock's view, "if his heed be strong and hool, not sicke or litil sick, and but his minde be stable to procede ordinatly from oon point of trouthe into anothir, and that he may holde his minde upon trouthe as long as nede is, til deepe affeccioun be gendrid thereupon in the wil" (*Donet*, 212). Pecock emphasizes long hours of study and effort as the way to master meditative or contemplative prayer, suggesting that this goal is well within reach for readers committed to the task. This experience is therefore within reach of ordinary people who can read in the vernacular: basically, every reader of Pecock's *Reule* can train the mind for meditation.

For Pecock, any lay reader who devotes himself to these practices can succeed in acquiring deeper knowledge of God, developing deeper devotion to God, and praising and worshiping God with insight and passion. Pecock also notes, however, that God himself may choose to instill knowledge in the believer, awaken his desire, inspire him to more devout forms of worship and praise, and stir his love and emotion. God may bring to the individual that "quickening of love and understanding" that Glasscoe defines as the fruit of meditation.[64] It is noteworthy that Pecock suggests that these fruits of meditation, thought to be a gift of God, can also be plucked through the labor of the intellect and will. Pecock says that the fruits of contemplative life "may be yoven to us from above into resoun and wil by infusioun, fforwhy kunning, loving, wel willing, preising, worschiping, asking and desiring may be had in us by oure naturals therto moving, and also may be had in us by supernatural gift from thee, God, descending" (*Reule*, 475). God may move the passive individual in prayer, praise, and worship, inflaming his emotions and heightening his understanding, but the individual can produce increased yearning and understanding on his own.

What does Pecock mean when he talks about the supernatural gift of contemplation? He acknowledges the possibility that God can

infuse the believer with knowledge and emotion, granting him illumination, when he says, "God maist make and hilde contemplaciouns of
ech of the iii maners bifore seid into men though they not laboure
forto so gete the same contemplaciouns" (*Reule*, 475). It is possible
(though very rare, in Pecock's view) for a man to passively receive this
contemplation without earning it or striving toward it. This kind of
divine gift is "purist contemplatiif liif in this world by rapte, which
is not in mannis power to take and have, neither it stondith in mannis
worching but more in suffring thy worching, lord, to be doon into
him" (437). Pecock does not deny the possibility of inspired contemplation, whereby the individual is granted knowledge and infused with
emotion, but he carefully circumscribes its definition. He emphasizes
that the experience of receiving this gift from God as opposed to
striving on our own to acquire knowledge, increase devotion, praise
God, and worship him with passion, is different only in terms of the
source: God can perform a supernatural act by inspiring our minds,
but our minds do not perform a supernatural act when they meditate
on the knowledge he provides. The reception of revealed truth and
pure emotions does not transform the mind, give it different abilities,
or transport us into a new reality. Pecock says that when contemplation is performed by God, "above kinde," it "sufficith not ferther into
eny effecte than it schulde suffice if it hadde be maad by hise natural
and kindely causis and in the comoun and woned cours of kinde"
(476). Though God's inspiration, or the act of ravishing the believer
into contemplation, is a supernatural act, once it is set into being, the
working of it does not surpass the capacities of the individual's intellect or will. When the "wirching" of contemplation is "above nature
and kinde," the contemplation "in him silf" is made: "not higher than
into a kinde and into the same kinde and into the same qualitees into
which he schulde have be brought forth and maad if natural and
kindely causis mighty to make such a contemplacioun and of the same
qualitees hadde be applied to worche forto make contemplacioun"
(476). Though the source is "above kind," the way that it functions is
natural. Pecock compares the "inhilding" of contemplation from God
to the ability of God to create a fire that is hotter than any natural
fire, or wine that is higher in quality than a naturally occurring wine;
though these are both made by miracle, they are still fire and wine,

and they "mowe not worche ferther or more than they mighte if they mighte have be maad by kinde" and they do not "have eny power or worching which he schulde not have if he had be maad by kinde" (477). Pecock indicates that the power or working attained by the intellect and will simply by striving on their own in meditation is the same as that attained by the intellect and will when they are passively illuminated by a divine source. Pecock is careful to show that the mind of an inspired contemplative will not be given the power by God to work beyond its natural powers; though inspired knowledge may be "hilden into us by miracle above kinde, if kinde mighte make the same contemplacioun in height, thilk same contemplacioun schal mowe no more do than he mighte do if he were maad by comoun uss of kinde withoute miracle" (477).

This distinction between inspired and ordinary contemplation makes the highest kind of contemplation accessible to any person who labors sufficiently in this activity; it also removes some of the mystique and allure of the experience described in treatises such as the *Ladder*. Pecock indicates, moreover, that even people who are treated to divine revelation by God must be able to account for their experiences rationally. He says that often the Lord stirs and moves people with his "special gracis" to pursue "ful singular weies of conversacioun miche diverse from the woned good weies of other vertuose livers" (*Reule*, 445). When God directs individuals on these alternate paths, he also teaches and informs them, through his special grace, "why and wherfore tho singuler weies ben to hem good and to thy plesaunce and to her profite" (445). This teaching enables these individuals to "stiren and ministren evidencis and skilis into her party that into the contraries of tho parties ben not so strong evidencis" (445). God gives these people the power to defend their chosen paths through the evidence of "lawe of kinde": "though thou so ofte endorme and stire by thy special gracis yoven above kinde, yit the enformacioun which the persoon so gracid takith therby is not but a science or an opinioun withinne the boondis of lawe of kinde, and it is not feith" (445). Pecock argues that visionary knowledge, provided by God as he personally directs the spiritual development of a chosen soul, is not a kind of extravagant faith that stretches our understanding and extends the limits of what we know but a kind of science that accords with the laws of nature. Part of the gift of divine illumination is the ability to make others understand why a chosen form of life or experience is acceptable to God. This emphasis on the need for contemplatives to marshal evidences and reasons in order to back up their arguments shows Pecock's concern that anyone laying claim to a singular kind of faith must be able to justify his or her practices; this curious blend of mystic illumination and rational explanations for these experiences provides an apt illustration of Pecock's desire to assign limits and boundaries to contemplation.

Pecock also brings contemplation within reach of his readers by defining it as a kind of exercise that has a practical purpose. The goal of meditative prayer is not the acquisition of divine knowledge, a glimpse of the divine, or momentary union with God; rather, the practice of contemplative prayer is grounded in the here and now and is a method of combating sin and vice. Pecock reminds readers: "We schule finde noon hour of the day in which schal not be ministrid to us sum mater of these bateils, that is to seie to fighte ayens pride, and forto have practik and uss of mekenes, to kepe us from wrathe and to gete mildenes, to kepe us from envie and to have benevolence and welwilling, to kepe us from slouthe and to haue the uss of doughtines" (*Reule*, 391). Meditation is a means to help us to fight against temptation and strive for virtue. Pecock says that the affections produced during meditative prayer "wolen arme and strengthe and chere a man forto stonde as a giaunt ayens temptaciouns, to not over deintily apprise eny thing a this side God, forto not over moche cherisch him silf and pampre his fleisch" (*Donet*, 213). Those who neglect the practice of meditation will find that "ful hard schal be a mannis batail ayens sinne to stonde, and into hard werkis of vertu to be into the eende doughti and strong" (213). The "craft and laboure of meditacioun" are designed to bring forth certain affections or dispositions that enable the believer to live a virtuous life and perform moral acts (213). The "dewe and according purpos or eende" of meditation may be the stirring of love, dread, desire, sorrow, repentance, shame, or gladness, which in turn lead to virtue and moral behavior (*Reule*, 10). We should engage in devotional practices like meditation not from a desire for divine ecstasy but with the knowledge that moral deeds are ultimately more valuable than prayer itself: "Ech man schulde rather worche alle maner moral virtues to paie satisfaccioun or provocacioun into mercy and foryevenes of sinnes and to gete or deserve grace and glorie for him silf or for othere, than forto for long preiyng to be made for the same to leve suche othere moral vertues deedis undoon" (*Reule*, 408). The emphasis on the emotional and moral ends of meditation shows that Pecock belongs in that tradition of writers who are remarkable "for their deep but restrained piety; they are concerned with the affections and morals, but they do not touch on the states of mysticism."[65]

Pecock's attempts to make this practice of meditation accessible, through the use of his books, to all members of society make it clear that he feels it necessary to answer the growing need of the laity for stimulating activities of personal devotion. Pecock instructs lay folk, "torn between the conflicting claims of their responsibilities and their spiritual desire, that living the mixed life of both contemplation and action is not about performing charitable services every now and then";[66] rather, the way Christians treat themselves, the way they behave toward others, and the way they conduct their lives should emanate from this intense, inward devotionalism. Using his books for reading, meditation, prayer, and contemplation, Pecock's lay readers can develop richly pious lives that balance the intellectual and spiritual discipline of the cloister within the tumult of the world. Though he is ambitious in his restructuring of lay devotion, Pecock is careful to insist that this inner cultivation of love and desire for God must not be seen as a break or a respite from the world. Pecock's efforts to direct the tide of devotionalism to the welfare of the Christian community may relate to his involvement with members of London's merchant community, who were the kinds of keen owners of contemplative material such as *The Abbey of the Holy Ghost*.[67] As more people expressed an interest in the mixed life, engaged in more personal, private religious practices, and invested in the kind of material that promised them a sight of the divine, Pecock felt it was necessary to foster, yet anchor this piety more firmly in the world through the model of a more fully integrated Christian life of contemplation and action.

In his provisions for the practice of meditation, Pecock offers lay readers the framework and resources for a sophisticated mixed life that involves intellectual training and ambitious devotional practices. Meditation requires a stable mind and the fervent working of the

intellect and the will; prayer requires the power of strong argumentation. There is no room in this system for superstition, for laxity, for
the tendency to "wamble" and misinterpret "invenciouns" for "hevenly
apperings," or for the misunderstanding of important doctrinal points
obscured by devout speeches (*Reule*, 12). Pecock helps readers to cultivate meaningful inward lives of piety through his insistence that devotion is fruitless without the moving of the will upon things known and
understood. Pecock's books anchor the foundations of piety on the
stable ground of "plein trouthe" (*Reule*, 214) and "cleer knowing" of
doctrine (*Donet*, 203).

Scholars who have focused on Pecock's polemical works or his
strategies for countering heresy rarely consider his interest in fostering the devotional lives of his readers. Studying his approach to ritual
reading and meditative reading reminds us of the comprehensive nature of his vision: Pecock himself indicates that his purpose in producing the *Reule of Crysten Religioun*, for example, is twofold: "Oon is
forto geve the peple instruccioun or doctrine, namelich upon the seid
vii maters moost necessarie to be leerned, an other cause is forto stire
and bring the peple into love and into devotioun anentis God"
(*Reule*, 19). This comment reveals that Pecock wishes to engage with
the intellect and will of his readers, providing them with knowledge
of the doctrines and laws of the church and showing them how they
can produce from this knowledge "a profound yearning to embrace
God through those same laws."[68] Pecock recognizes and addresses a
common problem that troubled theologians and writers of the Middle
Ages, which Vincent Gillespie describes in the following way: "Although it could be assumed that most Christians knew what was required of them in terms of moral rectitude and spiritual orientation,
just as they would know wine if they saw it in a glass, the problem was
bridging the gap that existed in fallen man between perceiving the
true and embracing the good. . . . Theoretically, once the intellect has
verified the data by reference to what it knows of the true, the *affectus*
yearns toward the good or away from the bad. Or so it would be if a
man was not a fallen creature."[69] Pecock offers readers training in theology and moral philosophy that helps the intellect to distinguish
what is true; he offers readers direction in devotional practices that
will produce this yearning for the good. A better understanding of

Pecock's instructions for the devotional life shows that Pecock's corpus as a whole is not fundamentally at odds with the devotional currents of his time; rather, he is determined to steady this devotional current by balancing an emphasis on affective practices that stir love for God with an emphasis on intellectual inquiry into the why and wherefore of the Christian faith.

five

The Book of Reason

I suggested in the previous chapter that Pecock's books provide a source for devotional practices, an abundant resource of truths upon which an individual reader can meditate in a way that engenders love and desire for God. Studying the way that Pecock's books develop spiritual practices of prayer and meditation among the laity brings me to the conclusion that his books propose changes to ways of organizing religion in his imagined textual community. In this chapter, I study the impact of his books on the practices that generate belief—processes of knowledge acquisition—among the laity. Pecock's project of vernacular theology adapts modes of cognition and learning from the university environment to revitalize modes of understanding religion in his textual community.

The focus of this chapter is the role of the book of reason in Pecock's imagined textual community. As I pointed out in the introduction, the book of reason is one of Pecock's sources for his teaching in *The Reule of Crysten Religioun*, *The Donet*, and *The Folewer*. He also marshals arguments from the book of reason in his *Repressor to Overmuch Blaming of the Clergy* and his *Book of Faith*. Basically, the book of reason is our primary source for knowledge of God's moral law. Pecock calls this book "the largist book of autorite that ever god made, which is the doom of resoun" (*Folewer*, 9–10). Pecock defines the "doom of resoun" as "moral lawe of kinde and moral lawe of God," or "the book of lawe of kinde in mennis soulis, prentid into the image of God" (*Repressor*, 18). In its original form, this text is not actually a material book—it is written by the finger of God on each man's soul. Its value surpasses that of all other manmade books: it is an "inward book or inward writing of resounis doom passing all outward bookis in profite to men for to serve God" (*Repressor*, 31). In terms of its teaching on the articles of natural law, this book's value surpasses even that of the Bible. The book of reason contains those truths about ethics and human conduct that we can determine with the use of our rational faculty. We do not need God's direct aid in acquiring knowledge about the nature of man's soul, the uses of the five wits, the nature of a virtuous deed, the varying degrees of sin, the goodness of God, the need for each person to love and serve his neighbor, and the uses of pilgrimages and images in worship. Our power of judgment allows us to deduce general truths about God's natural law by observing certain aspects of our nature, our tendencies, and our surroundings. The book of reason teaches the truths of moral philosophy, which were discovered by ancients like Aristotle.

What does it mean to read the book of reason, to see the contents of this inner book? Pecock tells us about the nature of this reading experience when he distinguishes his own books from the book of reason itself. Books like Pecock's, which inscribe the truths of the inner book of reason, present moral truths that an individual actually can learn on his own by cultivating his rational faculties to recognize the moral law that God has set out for man. Essentially, reading the book of reason means using the intellect to decipher the moral law that God wrote for mankind. This is difficult, however, because mankind has been at a natural cognitive disadvantage since the Fall. Had Adam and Eve not sinned, the eye of reason would not have become bleary: "if man had not falle into derking of resoun by fal fro innocencie into sinne in paradise wherby he muste have now labour to encerche and finde the trouthis of thy lawe, but that he mighte have redy remembrance of alle of hise pointis in lawe of resoun and kinde as he schulde have had if he hadde continued in innocencie fro sinne, ther schulde no bokis or tables written have be yoven to man upon the iii kinde of maters, for therto schulde have be no neede" (*Reule*, 463). Before the Fall, mankind had clarity of vision and ready remembrance of God's law without the need of external aids like books. In paradise, man read the book of reason in its original form, seeing the truths of God's moral law clearly.

After the fall of Adam and Eve, however, it became necessary to write down the truths of reason because man had lost the ability to see them simply with the innate powers of reason. Man's reason has become so darkened that he can see the moral law of nature only with great difficulty: he must read texts rather than simply opening his eyes to the truth set out before him. For those who have forgotten God's moral law, Pecock provides books that transmit the book of reason in textual form; such tools are sorely needed among lay readers because the book of reason could generate, through the "labour and studying of clerkis," "mo conclusiouns and treuthis and governauncis of lawe of kinde and of Goddis moral lawe and service than mighten be writen in so manie bokis whiche schulden fille the greet chirche of Seint Poul in Londoun" (*Repressor*, 31–32). Without these textual resources, God's moral law will remain obscured. Man's need for texts is the result of his fallen nature: returning to his original blessed state would require the gradual illumination of the eye of reason to the point where God's truths could be seen with ease.

Pecock's books, however, are not merely alternative sources for the book of reason itself. Certainly they are storehouses of religious and moral knowledge that comprise everything a Christian needs to know. They do function as repositories of truth, containing all the "conclusions and treuthis and governauncis of lawe of kinde and of Goddis moral lawe and service" for those who do not have the capacity to see God's moral law without textual aids (*Repressor*, 31). But they also train readers to grasp the grounds and fundamental principles of these truths rather than to passively accept them (31). Pecock's books start readers on their path back to God by teaching readers to open their eyes to the book of reason. This requires the knowledge of principles of logic, fundamental philosophical principles, and tools like the syllogism (40). Pecock's primary task is to help clear away the darkness in man's reason by providing light in the form of skills and strategies of rational inquiry. His books offer training, skills, and strategies to readers who wish to learn God's moral law with the rational faculty.

At the core of Pecock's thinking about the book of reason is the idea that God gives to man the power of reason—the ability to observe, rationalize, and form proofs, demonstrations, and arguments—so that he can investigate and determine for himself the moral law of nature. Man is meant to labor in an extensive search for the truths of reason: he must use his intellect to perceive, examine, and follow the truths that God intended as a rule for life. For Pecock, the ideal Christian community is gathered around the book of reason, with each member engaged in the pursuit of moral knowledge. Because the truth is "out there"—so to speak—rather than preserved in a special, revelatory text, the practices that govern this textual community are cognitive rather than interpretive: mental activities in observing, reasoning, examining, and contemplating moral or philosophical ideas are of more use than exegetical strategies. Of course, in this textual community, books serve as important aids by recalling to us the general truths that we need to examine and that have become difficult for us to see clearly. While books of moral philosophy help with the study of God's moral law, there is no one definitive, unique text at the center of this moral community whose function is to register the most important sacred knowledge in a direct, revelatory way. Instead, the locus of study is the very soul itself, on which is imprinted the natural law of God. In other words, Pecock visualizes a community of thinkers—philosophers, even—puzzling through moral dilemmas and questions about the best way of living the Christian life, with sharply honed faculties of perception and reflection, rather than a community of readers engaged in interpreting one key text with a similar goal.[1]

This task of training readers to perceive the truths of God's law has serious implications for the issue of textual community. I am interested in the way that Pecock's books provide a kind of education in ways of structuring thought processes to enable the truth to emerge more clearly as well as to provide a common ground for discourse among members of the textual community. One of Pecock's most important tasks is to help his lay readers to develop the "tools for mapping out reality and structuring their thought" and the ways of thinking of the learned world.[2] As Anneke Mulder-Bakker writes, "Trained in logic and rational discourse, the world of learning structured its thought accordingly. . . . Outside the stronghold of the learned, people thought along different lines and envisaged their world in different ways."[3] Pecock asks his reader to enter the stronghold of the learned by thinking along the lines of logical discourse. He creates a common ground within the textual community by getting everyone thinking along the same lines.

It is important to note that Pecock's teaching of God's natural law, together with his instruction on faith, proposes major changes for the way that religion is thought about and discussed in the textual community. It is clear that he wants the matter of his books to be on the minds and lips of Christians everywhere, influencing the way that people think and talk about moral life and Christian faith. Pecock's books are to be the source of "comuning" in various settings, from the household to the larger community (*Reule*, 13). In his *Book of Faith* he states that the correction of particular members of the laity depends first on the publication and dissemination of his books "to tho personis" and second on the "communicacioun" that shall be had "with tho personnis" by "word and speche at diverse leisers." By providing the sustenance for discussion about the matters of his *Book of Faith*, Pecock hopes to bring back to God his sons and daughters "fro lengthe and breed of erring, and of untrewe wide wandring" (*BF*, 114). His seven matters in the *Reule* are to be "taken of alle thy cristen peple into use of ful bisy, ech day studying, leerning and comuning and afterward thereupon remembring" (*Reule*, 13). Books like his, that contain truths of reason and faith, should be like children who play "at every mannis lappe" (33). The image of his books as children playing in the laps of men helps us to understand the way his books are to be treasured and intimately embraced by readers. These books also provide fodder for discussion at the dinner table: the universal truths, who inspire the creation of the *Reule*, complain that "no man of us or of oure children in eny feeste or cumpenie or honest congregacioun can talke or mensioun make" (33). The truths of reason and faith worry that less profitable books are the source of reflection and conversation when they complain, "With hem every man him silf cheerith, and with hem every man ech other in talking occupieth" (33). Presumably, once Pecock gives the universal truths textual form, they will be able to cheer men and be the subject of friendly discussions. The seven companies of truths tell Pecock that they provide "stuff enough," "with which stuf thou schalt sufficiently reule thy liif religiosely, teche and counseile al othere to live cristenly, preche booth leerningly and devoutly, commune and talke in alle compenies and with alle persoonis plesauntly and fruitfully" (34). The truths contained in Pecock's books will be the subject of "talking about the things of God" in all kinds of pleasant, fruitful conversations. God himself desires that men should "love togidere and leerne togedir the vii cheef maters of my writingis devisid for lay men, and that they schulde speke therin togidere into eche of hem otheris edifying." The matters of Pecock's books will provide the source for "good acqueintaunce and felawlik comunicacioun" among all members of the textual community (*Folewer*, 8).

Comments like these throughout Pecock's corpus indicate that by providing the "stuf" of "comunicacioun" among men "in eny feeste or cumpenye" Pecock's books will revive the "talking about the things of God" among members of the textual community by focusing conversation on the matters of God's nature, God's benefits, God's punishments, God's moral law, man's wretchedness, man's wickedness, and remedies for these.[4] One wonders if Pecock's texts would be the kind of thing read at the dinner table by men like the recipient of the fifteenth-century text *Instructions for a Devout and Literate Layman*, edited by William Pantin. In this text, the reader is advised, "Let the book be brought to the table as readily as the bread. And lest the tongue speak vain or hurtful things, let there be reading, now by one, now by another, and by your children as soon as they can read."[5] Given the prevalence of anecdotes, fables, and stories in the sermon literature of late medieval England, such as Mirk's *Festial*, however, it may have been more likely that talk regarding matters of faith and doctrine at the dinner table and among friends involved stories of miracles, relics, and saints, rather than discussions of the nature of man's soul, the nature of our "soverein good and oure uttirrist natural reste" (*Reule*, 41), and the difference between "eendal" and "meenal" virtues (*Folewer*, 175–76). It is clear, however, that the kinds of things that were commonly the subject of conversation in men's homes and communities did not sit well with Pecock, given his efforts to make his own books the subject of "comuning." Pecock's efforts to reshape the parameters of religious discourse in the textual community, to change the fabric of everyday conversation about matters of Christian belief, and to revitalize the "talking about the things of God," necessitate a return to the very first truths, inscribed by God on man's soul, as a model for belief and behavior. Redirecting people back to this original source of truth and away from scripture is one way to prevent the spread of error, of "untrewe opiniouns feined and forgid by enviosite withoute ground of sufficient resoun or holy scripture" through informal "talking about the things of God" (*Reule*, 33). Changing the way that belief is engendered in the religious community first requires a change of reading material.

This chapter proceeds in the following way: the discussion centers, first, on the design of Pecock's corpus: second, on the function of the syllogism; third, on the use of analogy as a practical strategy to equip lay readers with the ability to analyze questions of moral doctrine; and fourth, on Pecock's ideas about the best strategies for Christian pedagogy. The way that Pecock sets his corpus apart from other available didactic material highlights the necessity of transforming modes of thought and understanding in the textual community, particularly in light of Pecock's notion that the most profitable, productive works of religious instruction are those that fertilize the lay intellect and stimulate its growth, rather than simply passing on knowledge.

As I pointed out in chapter 2, the construction of Pecock's corpus, as a whole, is geared to intellectual training. His books take readers through various cognitive stages in their apprehension of God's moral law, gradually leading the lay intellect from "derking of resoun" to clarity of vision (*Reule*, 463). In the *Folewer to the Donet*, Pecock discusses his use of different teaching strategies in the *Donet*, *The Reule of Crysten Religioun*, and *The Folewer to the Donet*. These books represent three different approaches to the teaching of the same religious truths: Pecock teaches the same things in all three books, but his manner of teaching the same content changes as he amplifies, extends, and modifies his instruction. This approach to writing vernacular books of religious instruction is unique in late medieval England: writers of didactic treatises sometimes address the same topics that Pecock addresses, but I cannot find another example of a writer assembling a set of instructional manuals that are meant to form a sequence, in which the same material is taught in progressive stages.

Beginners start with Pecock's *Donet* because they profit most from teaching that provides the "summes" and her "instiwes" of doctrine, "in such schort breef manner, without ministring to hem whies and causis of the treuthis to hem ministrid" (*Folewer*, 13). This method of presenting truths to be believed, without elaborating the grounds of these truths, is used with beginners in faculties of logic and civil law, as "leernid men in these faculties" will acknowledge (13). The *Donet* presents truths in a ready-made form for those who are not equipped to probe the rational foundations of truths about man's service to God and human conduct. The reader then moves from a focus on the content of truths to basic, underlying principles of philosophy and logic that allow readers to analyze these truths; when readers progress to the *Reule*, they see the "skile and fondement of these profis" (*Reule*, 39). The *Folewer* is more advanced still: matters that are taught "biginningly" in the *Donet* are "taught therwith eendingly and fully" in the *Folewer* (*Folewer*, 4). In the first part of the *Folewer* "schal be yovun larger doctrine of the groundis of moralte and of moral virtues than is yovun in the biginning of 'the donet'" (4–5).

Though the *Donet* is an easy book, readers are not to linger too long with it in the beginning stages. They must face the intellectual challenges presented by the other books. In the same way, the reader who finds the content of any book too difficult should "overleap" it but return to it after "feeding" himself on other matters (*Folewer*, 30).[6] Those who abandon an intellectual challenge entirely, however, at the first sign of difficulty, are cowardly. Pecock says, "It is ful profitable ech man forto use him and aqueinte him with sumwhat to him hard and derk maters, and forto not be over mich coward to leve of the leerning of a mater or of a book for hardnes to his witt in the biginning; ffor certis his witt schal therby take in maner now seid a greet upreising" (15). If readers who back away from intellectual challenge are cowards, then we can be certain that the training of the intellect— the "upreising" of the wit—is a major priority for Pecock's readers.

Pecock emphasizes the need for readers to work hard to ascend in comprehension of more difficult matters when he describes his corpus of works as a painting whose colors are gradually built up, level by level:

> Even as a peintoure puttith upon and aboute a graved or corven image firste a white coloure forto be a ground that thereupon he sette the ii coloure, and aftirward upon hem boothe he settith the iii colour into the parfiit bewteful ourning, and the ii coloure may not wel and profitably be received of the image but if the first colour be bifore received . . . so it is that the kunning of the "donet of keye of cristen religioun" is to a mannis soule a simple or a sengle and rude fundament wherupon cometh the kunning of this present book, "cristen religioun" in hise ii parties, and thanne aftir comith . . . other bookis therto felawschipid as an higher and a fairer array of the soule. (*Reule*, 367)[7]

Each text in succession lays the ground for the next; progression requires a higher order of thinking. The *Reule* is superior to the *Donet* because it treats matters not in a "schort and a general fundamental maner" but in a "larger and clerer and dilectabler maner" (*Reule*, 367). By describing the different stages of training in his corpus as the different layers of paint in a work of art, Pecock stresses that each pedagogical stage leads organically and necessarily into the next: changes in modes of thought and understanding are required. Readers do not simply acquire knowledge by reading his books; a primary use or function of Pecock's books is to train readers gradually to think in more sophisticated ways. Readers must build on what they have already learned; once they have developed a sufficient foundation, they are given a new perspective on the knowledge that they have acquired. Pecock suggests that it is impossible to simply inscribe knowledge on a blank mind: learning occurs when we revisit and transform what we already know. The reader's continually changing perspective on truth constitutes the labor that each man must undergo in reading God's moral law in the book of reason.

One of the most important functions of Pecock's corpus is to provide training that builds on man's natural rational powers, helping readers to combat the "insufficience and the infirmite, the lownes and the derkenes of oure natural resoun." Though the fall of Adam and

Eve made the reason weak, God has given man a "natural gifte of light in oure resoun" by which we can "stiye up to have probably and likely ynough al the knowing which is necessarie to us" (*Reule*, 71). This natural light is a tendency toward logical thinking, an ability to "combine to gidere . . . affirmaciouns and negaciouns or affermingis and denyingis in such maner that out of two of hem knowun for trewe he may drive forth the thridde affirmacioun or negacioun as for open to be knowun trouthe there that it was afore to him unknowun for trewe." This syllogistic construction of proofs or arguments, this "combining to gidere," is called "argumentacioun, arguing or discurse." The knitting together of affirmations and negations "in forme of an argument" allows an individual to "drive out, prove and conclude" certain truths about the nature of the soul and of God, which cannot be known "by eny outward or inward sensitive witt" (38). The ability to affirm, deny, prove, and conclude, "namelich in thingis not sensible," distinguishes man from beasts, who can reason only about sensible things (39).

Education in syllogistic thought is an important way in which Pecock's books make the truths of God's law more visible to readers. This education in methods of logical thinking hones the reasoning powers that man has by nature and takes them to another level of sophistication. Though he assigns to each man a natural tendency to abstract higher truths from visible truths, Pecock cautions that this innate power of reasoning "by labour of kindely witt" has its limits, especially in the contemplation of abstract and difficult truths (*Repressor*, 132). Pecock discusses the need for each person to develop more structured ways of logical thinking so that abstracting higher principles from everyday observation will become more natural. What the laypeople need is proper training in logical modes of thought, which help them to hone this power to conclude, affirm, and deny through argumentation and syllogistic thinking. At the beginning of the *Repressor*, he writes that he intends someday to provide, on the behalf of his lay readers, a "schort compendiose logik" that will be precious to them, and he exclaims, "Wolde God it were leerned of al the comon peple in her modiris langage, for thanne they schulden therby be putt fro miche ruidnes and boistosenes which they han now in resoning; and thanne they schulden soon knowe and perceve whanne a skile and an argument bindith and whanne he not bindith" (9). Though he does not have time at the moment to provide this book of logic, Pecock believes that it is essential to submit readers to a kind of training in modes of rational inquiry. Training lay readers in the principles of logic would help them to acquire skills in the kind of structured thinking that lends itself to knowing truth with certainty. Readers trained in logical methods like the syllogism would be able to see both truths that are revealed "openly in light of oure natural resoun" (*Reule*, 84) and the "whies and causis" (*Folewer*, 13) of more complex truths.

God's gift of the syllogism ensures that its practitioners "schal nevere be deceived" in their inquiry for truth. Pecock says that the reason why men are deceived in their processes of reasoning is "her hastines, that they wole juge by schorte argumentis, eer tho argumentis ben reduced into formes of syllogism." The individual who develops skills in syllogistic reasoning "schal nevere be bigilid aboute maters of resoning," "Forwhy ther is noon conclusioun or trouthe in the world, (except tho which ben open by experience of sensitiif witt or at fulle plein in resoun, whiche ben clepid groundis and foundamentis to alle the othere treuthis and conclusiouns in philsophie, and aboute which no man schal erre, by cause they ben so openly trewe) but that into proof of it may be had a sillogisme weel reulid." Truths that are evident "by experience of sensitiif witt" are open to all men, but more complex, abstract truths require the methical, logical workings of the syllogism: truths that are less evident must be tested and proven with certainty (*Repressor*, 76).

The syllogism is a tool for deciphering God's truth, offering a way out of the darkness to which Adam and Eve's sin condemned us, as "oure next and best and surest reuler or reule anentis alle resonable treuthis" (*Repressor*, 75). Pecock writes, "The power of resoun in him silf is not ordeined of God to be oure next and best and surest reuler or reule anentis alle reasonable treuthis, but the doom of reson is ordeined to so be; and yit not ech doom of resoun, but thilk doom of resoun which is a formal complete argument clepid a sillogisme in resoun" (75). God has given to us the power of reasoning, which admittedly can stumble and fail, in the same way that he has given to us feet to guide our movement, even though our feet might falter. God may be excused for giving man a power of reasoning that may fail, however, because he has also given man an effective means of preventing stumbling: God has given to man the syllogism, which is infallible. This formal mode of reasoning, through rules of logic, will help to direct man's natural reason so that he arrives at truth more effectively. Great labor of study "by avisingis and by counseil taking and by leernyng long time in scolis" can train our power of reason, but the use of the syllogism, given to us by God so that we may see his meaning more clearly, will be the simplest and most evident guide for readers who have not had this training (75). Through the gift of our rational power, and the doom of reason, God imprints on our minds the ability to find his truths; Pecock's education in the working of rational argumentation opens readers' minds and begins to hone this ability.

How does Pecock train readers to hone their rational faculty? In the *Repressor*, he teaches rational modes of thought by asking readers to proceed, in syllogistic fashion, from acceptance of basic premises, or truths that are "open by experience of sensitiif witt or at fulle pleine in resoun," to acceptance of the conclusions he derives by putting these more open truths together. The truths that are evident—which Pecock often establishes through the use of analogies—become the "groundis and foundamentis" to the other truths and conclusions that Pecock presents (76). Once he has gained readers' consent to his first principles, he combines these affirmations together to draw forth a third affirmation, or conclusion. Analogies to common experience, everyday life, community events, and shared knowledge form a starting point, therefore, for the training of the lay intellect.

Through his many analogies in the *Repressor*, Pecock asks lay readers to begin by analyzing their experience and applying logical thought processes to concrete events in order to derive basic principles and conclusions from them. For example, in the introduction to his arguments about heretical doctrine in the *Repressor*, Pecock provides various examples of the concept of grounding. He needs his readers to accept his definition of this term as an acceptable truth so that he can employ it as a premise in his syllogism: once the reader agrees to his definition of the term, Pecock can argue that it is not in the nature of the Bible to ground any governance of God's law. To accomplish this, Pecock provides not one but three analogies that draw on common experience and observation. The first reference is to the Midsummer Eve custom of bringing tree branches and flowers from the woods into the city of London with the aid of carts; the second reference is to the activity of bringing fish in baskets from the sea into London; the third reference is to the activity of preaching a sermon based on knowledge that is located and learned in a certain library book (28–32). With each illustration of the definition of grounding, Pecock establishes that a book that grounds God's moral law must be the ultimate source rather than the vessel used to carry or express various moral governances or virtues. The carts carrying the flowers, the baskets carrying the fish, and the sermon conveying the book's points are not the final sources respectively for the flowers, fish, and ideas. In the same way, the Bible cannot be the ultimate source for moral truths that God wrote before Christ descended to earth: "All the trouthis of lawe of kinde whiche Crist and hise Apostlis taughten and wroten weren bifore her teching and writing, and weren writen bifore in thilk solempnest inward book or inward writing of resounis doom passing alle outward bookis in profite to men" (31). Refuting the argument that every aspect of God's moral law is pro-vided by the Bible, Pecock argues: "Every thing groundid hangeth and is dependent of his ground, so that he may not be withoute his ground; but so it is, that al the leerning and kunning which Holi Scripture yeveth upon eny of the seid governauncis, vertues, deedis, or treuthis . . . hangeth not of Holi Scripture," so holy scripture can-not be said to ground moral law: "wherfore needis folewith that Scripture is not ground to eny oon such seid vertu, gouernaunce, deede, or trouthe" (17–18).

Pecock's analogies are important because they help to establish the first necessary premise of this syllogism: that something that grounds a moral truth or governance is its ultimate source and pro-vides all knowledge relating to it. As Anthony Kenny and Jan Pinborg point out, in their description of demonstrative argument, the syllo-gism is a tool of argument that relies on a gradual buildup of proofs from accepted principles: "Demonstrative science is a system of proofs deducing conclusions by ordered steps from first principles."[8] The demonstrative syllogism employed so frequently by Pecock garners the reader's assent by establishing first principles and leading to logical conclusions. However, Kenny and Pinborg note that this ideal of starting an argument from first principles is not necessarily the common practice: "The arguments adduced in a disputation have an almost fortuitous character and are certainly not always demonstrative. Their aim is principally to persuade the opponent, and because of that aim it is not necessary to start every argument from first principles. One can instead begin with commonly accepted presuppositions."[9] Pecock's arguments work precisely in this way, by starting with commonly accepted presuppositions; Pecock obtains his reader's acceptance of his presuppositions by putting forward analogies that demonstrate the truth of his first principles. In the case of the concept of grounding, Pecock must get the reader to accept the truth and validity of his necessary premises, which form the basis of his demonstrative syllogism; he does this by asking the reader to refer to everyday observations and common experience. Pecock therefore trains his readers to take part in syllogistic reasoning, and to follow the logic of his arguments, by starting with well-known maxims, observable truth, and common assumptions; these provide the vehicle that transports the reader's mind to a more rational level, understanding the philosophical basis of Pecock's conclusions. For a syllogism to produce knowledge, the premises must be "true" and "necessary":[10] Pecock asks readers to make the transition from reflecting on commonly observed truths in everyday life to philosophical premises such as the nature of "grounding."

Pecock's use of analogies require his reader's participation in the logical reasoning of his syllogism; he ensures that basic premises are understood before he goes on to his conclusions. The job of a demonstrative syllogism is to "manifest the truth or necessity of its reasoned fact to a particular person," but Pecock cannot begin this demonstration of his conclusions if his readers cannot fathom his premises.[11] In his argument against the heretical notion that the Bible alone grounds the whole of God's moral law, Pecock employs analogies to bring his readers on to the same level of agreement about basic premises. This grasp of first principles—of propositions that are necessary and evidently known—may come easily to a cleric trained in moral philosophy; Pecock finds a strategic way to make them evident so that lay readers can perform the same kind of logical analysis as clerks. Pecock follows the logical course recommended in Ockham's description of the demonstrative syllogism, by which "first we learn contingent truths about what is the case by experience, then we transform them into correlative necessary truths about what must be possible."[12] This movement from easily observable truths to higher principles constitutes gradual training in the book of reason: each step of the syllogism lights the way back to God by illuminating the eye of reason.

The analogies that Pecock uses to illustrate his first principles are pervasive and colorful: he likens the way a man bows to a knight to the way people worship images; he compares the rents paid to maintain London Bridge to the endowment of the clergy; he makes a connection between the habits that monks wear to distinguish themselves and the clothes women wear to display their difference from men (*Repressor*, 338, 545). Pecock takes up controversial subjects in this same methodical way, by drawing readers to contemplate philosophical truths through their observations of common experience and natural phenomena. For example, in his defense of the religious orders and their conflicting opinions on the best way to structure the enclosed life (conflicting opinions that came under attack by the Lollards), he compares the variety of religious orders with the variety of inns for travelers in London. He addresses the question of why such diversity of religious orders exists in the church in the following way:

> I ask of thee, "Why in a town which is a thorugh faar toward Londoun ben so manie ostries clepid innes forto logge gistis, though in fewer of hem alle gestis mighten be loggid? Is not this the cause, for that by the mo diversitees whiche schulen be had in the more multitude of innes the peple schal be the more provokid and stirid for to logge hem in tho innes, than if ther were fewer innes?" Thou muste needis seie, yhis. Forwhy what point in chaumbring, stabiling, gardeins, beddis, servicis of the ostiler, (and so in othere thingis) plesith oon gist, plesith not an other; and what point in these thingis offendith oon, plesith weel an other. (521–22)

This reflection on the various inns around London leads directly to a reflection on the great diversity in man's "affectis and passiouns" and the corresponding need to satisfy the different inclinations of men by providing numerous choices in the religious life (522). Pecock asks readers to follow through to his logical conclusions, abstracting from this observation of common life philosophical conclusions about the nature of man, the nature of the passions, and corresponding principles for ordering the lives of the enclosed religious to accommodate the different inclinations of men. In the passages where Pecock uses analogies such as this to help the reader dig down to the basic philosophical foundations of an issue, he leads the reader through a rational analysis of a difficult and abstract problem and demonstrates how the reader might structure his own mode of thought to puzzle through such problems independently.

Pecock continues to defend the religious orders in the same way by showing readers to abstract philosophical principles about the life of the enclosure from observations of common truths and natural phenomena. In response to the Lollard accusation that God never outlined specific rules for the enclosed religious in the Bible and therefore would not approve of the various ways in which they claim to be carrying out his service, Pecock again appeals to logical principles that can be abstracted from observations of the nature of man. He defends the power of each order to make choices regarding the best way to carry out God's commands, despite the lack of these commands in the Bible itself, arguing that God indirectly justified the creation of religious orders by giving man certain mental and physical powers to create the orders for himself. The hinge of this argument is the difference between God's mediate and immediate actions: though he can work directly through us, giving us specific commands to carry out, he can also work indirectly by blessing us with faculties that he intends us to use as we see fit. Pecock reduces his conclusion, that the religious orders are justified, to its grounds by defining the difference between mediate and immediate actions and by demonstrating the nature of a mediate deed in the following way: "If thou gavest to thy man hors and sadil, armour and spere, and schuldist bidde him ride into a certein feelde, and take to him a prisoner worthy in raunsum of an hundrid pound; and if her with thou mightist and schuldist like verily geve to him his boldenes, his strengthe, his inward and outward wittis, and his resoun and wil forto reule him in the taking of this prisoner; thou woldist seie that thou gavest to him this prisoner; for this that thou gavest to him alle the meenys by which and with which he schulde take this prisoner." In the same way, God gives inward and outer wits, as means, for men to figure out or "knowe by hem silf sufficiently" that the religious orders are spiritually profitable for those within them (*Repressor*, 520). By giving man certain powers in the inward and outer wits, God approves of man's use of these powers to determine for himself the most appropriate way to govern himself. Once the reader understands, through this analogy, the concept of a mediate deed, he can apply this concept to other matters so that he may draw different conclusions about the justification of the religious orders. Despite the lack of explicit divine commands regarding the enclosed religious orders, it is indeed possible, through Pecock's order of logic, for God to establish the religious orders "mediately." Pecock implies that his readers do not actually need to read the biblical text to know what God intended: by analyzing the nature of the gifts that God has given to man, such as the inward and outward wits, the reason, and the will, man can find out for himself the most appropriate ways of using these gifts in God's service.

Pecock's reader must not be too hasty to judge the enclosed religious for the lack of consistency among the four orders, for the lack of explicit legislation regarding their way of life, and for the vices and problems that can be attributed to the free will of various monks who fell into error; rather, each man must "abide" until he has assessed the problem with syllogistic logic, beginning with general principles about the nature of man and the nature of evil and putting these together to form more abstract conclusions and truths (*Repressor*, 76). Assigning readers this kind of task is daring, especially at a time when Lollards are marshaling arguments from the Bible to prove that the enclosed religious are new sects, unapproved by Christ. Though this attack on the contemporary structure of religious practice within the church is a highly controversial topic, and one that some viewed to be inappropriate for lay minds to puzzle over, Pecock redirects the line of thinking rather than redirecting thought itself away from the issue. In Pecock's view, thinking about this kind of issue is not problematic or dangerous for his readers as long as they avoid hastiness in their weighing of the logic of the matter. Everyone who possesses a rational intellect has the ability to study the world around him and to abstract from this power of observation deeper, philosophical truths that must govern practices and beliefs in the religious community.

It is important to understand the significance and function, in Pecock's works, of these analogies to inns of London and knights in battle, particularly when we consider how common these devices are in works of religious instruction. Figures like the analogy, which help a reader better understand a particular concept, are widespread in medieval works aimed at both lay and clerical audiences. For instance, Roy M. Haines describes a fifteenth-century text written in Latin for a clerical audience that calls upon "a wealth of contemporary metaphor and apt proverbial phrase."[13] Haines describes the preacher's use of a particularly "pointed analogy"—that which likens the domestic swan to contemporary magnates—in his advice to clerics about how to behave in the company of the upper class: "It enjoys having its back stroked, says the preacher, but touch the front of its neck and it ruffles its feathers—just like the magnates. Speak to them of their virtues, commend their life and deeds, look up to them and make much of them, and you will be held dear; but touch their gorge with talk of vices, take them to task for their evil life, tell them the truth, and they will knit their brows. There will be a rebuke for your labour and you will be sent packing without a drink."[14] Siegfried Wenzel cautions that although the clerical world is usually associated with a higher form of learning, stylistic devices such as the analogy are not unique to works aimed at instructing lay audiences. He writes that it is dangerous to infer a sermon's audience from the presence of "stylistic elements that one would consider 'popular'—not in the sense of being successful and having a wide appeal but rather of stemming from and relating to the lore, language, beliefs, and tastes of the common people, whoever those might have been." Wenzel suggests that elements of the sermon, such as "vernacular verses of different kinds . . . well-known exempla, and moralized 'scientific lore,'" as well as "similes and narratives from everyday experience, can indeed be found in many sermons of our period that have been preserved in English or in Latin." Wenzel cautions that "to infer from their presence a lay audience is a very slippery procedure."[15] He demonstrates his point by describing two contrasting sermons: one written for the laity, using the exemplum of Christ the Lover-Knight, and the other written for the clergy, using an exemplum that seems more popular and intended for a common audience. Stylistic devices referring readers to well-known examples from everyday life pervade works aimed at audiences of all kinds: Pecock's use of the analogy corresponds with the methods of numerous writers who used the fabric of daily life to illustrate their points.

Pecock's analogies work in the same way as Wenzel describes, explaining concepts by drawing upon common observations and everyday experience. However, it is important to understand that Pecock's practice of using common lore and experience to demonstrate truth is not designed to make these truths more memorable, to make them more appealing to readers, or to engage with his readers' emotions. With his analogies, Pecock points out fundamental connections between the principles that operate in human relationships and human experiences and the higher principles of moral philosophy. In Pecock's *Repressor*, the analogy is not a literary, figurative device but rather the expression of an earthly truth that leads readers to perceive a higher truth. Interestingly, Pecock likens his use of this kind of demonstration to Christ's teaching: "Lord, thou techist in thi gospel rewlis that we schulen leerne and deeme bitwixe us and thee, that is to seie leerne and deeme how we schulen bere us toward thee and how thou wolt bere thee toward us by parablis or liiknessis bitwixe kingis or housholders and her children or meyne in this world, ffor as miche as alle resonable trouthis founden amonge creaturis ben not suche trouthis save for that they comen out from liik to hem in thy Godhede, the everlasting trouthis" (*Reule*, 151). In his many parables, Jesus himself set the example for ascending in the contemplation of spiritual truths through earthly likenesses and sensible things, showing that all reasonable principles that we can derive from watching the behavior of natural and social beings on earth reflect the logic of God's plan for how Christians should order their lives. Watching the behavior of a "resonable temporal lord" can help us to understand what kind of service God wants from us, since God bears himself toward us "alwey aftir resoun," as Jesus indicated "ful faire by parablis in the gospel ofte times" (*Reule*, 409). Things that are evident and open to natural reason, such as the respect that is owed to a secular lord, can teach us about the way we must behave toward God.

Pecock's interpretation of the way Christ's parables point out reasonable truths that are connected to divine truths corresponds to that medieval habit of thought in which the earthly world is viewed in terms of its resemblance or connection to the divine world. While using an analogy to communicate a particular concept may appeal to a reader's affect or aid in convincing him through rhetorical means, explaining abstract ideas through analogy fundamentally works from the notion that God has organized earthly reality as an integrated whole, so that our minds can make connections between the sensible world and the eternal world. This habit of thinking in analogies and relating one observable truth to another more abstract one displays Pecock's leanings toward an Aristotelian view of knowledge, in which we come to know invisible, theoretical, spiritual truths through visible, tangible, earth-bound realities. This Aristotelian "theory of knowledge" is typified by Aquinas's notion that "all human understanding depends on sense impressions or *phantasmata*."[16] As Ruth Harvey writes, "Aquinas rejected the Platonic belief in externally existing universal ideas which the human intellect may glimpse in acts of contemplation without recourse to the evidence of the senses."[17] According to both Aquinas and Pecock, the way that we decipher God's moral laws is through our observations of natural phenomena, which provide us with hints of deeper realities. Harvey notes that according to this theory of knowledge, "in this present life, man can know God and immaterial beings only through the evidence of his senses: he starts with his experiences of the outside world, and learns, by deduction and comparison, how to arrive at some dim conception of the divine and immaterial."[18] As Sheila Delany points out, the analogical habit of thinking of moving from the better known to the less known is derived from the archaic notion that "transcendent reality provides models which the phenomenal world imitates" and that "the world itself thus participates in a cosmic analogy with supraterrestrial reality."[19] Delany examines the development of this way of understanding the connection between the earthly world and the divine in the thought of Plato and Aristotle, and she quotes Bonaventure's expression of this phenomenon as follows: "All creatures of this sensible world . . . are shadows, echoes, and pictures, the traces, simulacra, and reflection of that First Principle. . . . They are signs divinely bestowed which, I say, are exemplars or rather exemplifications set before our yet untrained minds, limited to sensible things, so that through the sensibles which they see they may be carried forward to the intelligibles which they do not see, as if by signs to the signified."[20] This habit of thought of moving from the better to the less known is popular with scholastic thinkers and shows Pecock's affinity with them. In his study of the structure and method of scholastic thought, Philipp W. Rosemann writes that "the possibility of illustrating a point made about angels by means of an example taken from the human realm depends upon an important conviction shared by all the Scholastics, namely, that all levels of being are held together by a basic similarity, by an all-embracing structural analogy. According to this view, no being can be totally exterior to any other being, as everything bears some traces of the cosmos, the all-pervading order."[21] What is important about Pecock's understanding of Christ's parables is his notion of this all-pervading order—this innate connection between the principles that dictate the expression of "reasonable truths" in the human realm and the principles of divine truths. Comparing the activities of an earthly ruler to the activities of God is not arbitrary but a way of conceiving of sensible reality as part of an intricate system; we are invited to see the reflection of the divine world in the mundane realities around us. Pecock's understanding of the way Christ's parables function helps us to comprehend the way he understands his own texts to be working on the reader's intellect, by starting with reasonable truths that are self-evident and proceeding to more abstract, yet still reasonable truths.

The idea that readers progress from observable truths to more complex truths in their reflection on controversial issues like the use of the Bible in grounding God's moral law and the founding of the religious orders as well as in less controversial, everyday decisions about the best way to serve God tells us a great deal about the way that particular habits of thought and particular structures of belief are engendered in Pecock's imagined textual community. Just as scholastic thinkers like Aquinas ascended from knowledge of the mundane to more profound reflections on divine reality, Pecock's readers are to develop modes of understanding that depend on seeing the world as a text that can be read by all. What lay readers need is eyes to see God's truths in the world and the structure of logical thought, of syllogistic thinking, that will guide them safely through the stages of abstracting grounds and principles from observable reality and finally putting these principles together to form conclusions. All have access to what Rosemann calls "the text of creation," which was just as important to "Scholastic masters so obsessed with their texts" of established *auctores*. In his discussion of scholastic intellectual practices, Rosemann writes about the medieval belief that "unfortunately, human beings have lost the ability to read the text of creation properly. This is a result of the Fall. Instead of tracing the signifiers of creation back to what they signify—God—we have acquired the habit of taking them at face value, for what they are in themselves. Consequently, the book of the world has 'died' for us, its text being tragically 'effaced' *(deletus)*."[22] This book of the world resembles Pecock's book of reason, but for Pecock it is imperative that we learn how to read it once more so that we can decipher God's moral law. For Pecock, there are different stages for apprehending truth on a kind of rational continuum: the lay reader starts with experiential knowledge of visible facts and learns to abstract from this knowledge fundamental principles that can be used to see the truth of a conclusion about the moral life with sharper perception. The analogy is an important tool in the sequence of rational thought, rather than fundamentally opposed to higher practices of logical thinking. In the introduction to *Seeing and Knowing*, Anneke Mulder-Bakker suggests that the analogy or the exemplum was seen to be fundamentally different from the way that the clerical, learned world mapped out reality and structured its thought, through logic and rational discourse. She says, "The discursive or abstract argument was the prerogative of schooled theologians; the short story and the exemplum, or a collection of exempla, were the popular genres of the *illiterati*."[23] But Pecock's application of the analogy to abstract argument would suggest that the analogy has an important role to play in bridging the divide between the lay world and the "stronghold of the learned": the analogy helps the lay reader to understand the philosophical foundations of a conclusion so that its truth can be examined and tested.[24]

In the final pages of this chapter, I argue that Pecock's corpus is characterized by an underlying imperative of changing the way that belief is formed and religion understood in the textual community.

When he talks about the spread of Lollard error, the variety of belief in all parts of England, the dominance of superstition, and the prevalence of misunderstanding among the members of the lay party, Pecock witnesses the problematic nature of current systems of generating and forming belief in the religious community. The problem lies with the way that thought is influenced and structured by works that purport to instruct the laity in orthodox doctrine but do not operate by the same principles as Pecock's works.

Pecock himself points out the major difference between how modes of understanding and structures of belief are shaped by his own corpus and how they are shaped by other works of religious instruction that open the door to error, superstition, and misunderstanding. In his *Repressor*, Pecock describes how all truths in the law of kind are naturally connected, growing out of each other in a kind of forest or garden, in the same way that seeds grow into plants, which grow into trees with branches and boughs:

> The maters and conclusiouns and trouthis of lawe of kinde . . . leggith ful fair abrood sprad growing in his owne space, the feeld of mannis soule. And there oon treuthe cometh out of an other treuthe, and he of the iii, and the iii out of the iiii, and into time it bicome unto openest trouthis of alle othere in thilke faculte of moral philsophie, and to the principles and groundis of alle othere trouthis in the same faculte (euen as the sprai cometh out of the braunche, the braunche out of the bough, the bough out of the schaft, and the schaft out of the roote). (29)

According to this model, a truth that is evident to a person's natural intellect, such as the need for a variety of inns around London, grows into the philosophical truth about man's nature; this truth becomes Pecock's premise and is connected with another so that the two can produce a final truth. Truths grow out of each other, starting with basic roots and flowering into boughs, creating an organic system that is continually regenerating. Teaching readers how truths are connected, and teaching them methods of making these connections, is extremely important. Writers must cultivate the field of the soul so that the "maters and conclusiouns and trouthis of lawe of kinde" can grow freely (29).

Pecock describes himself as a gardener in the field of truth located in man's soul. He plants and prunes truths and uproots untruths in this generative space, causing some truths to produce others and ensuring that the weeds of heretical conclusions are "unrootid and uppluckid, and sufficiently rebuked and proved for untrewe" (*Repressor*, 51). Pecock views himself as a gardener or forester in the "forest of lawe of kinde which God plaunteth in mannis soule whanne he makith him to his image and likenes" (29). In this forest are grounded the "seid treuthis and conclusiouns of lawe of kinde," and it is Pecock's job to take these "treuthis and conclusiouns" and set them "into open knowing of the finder and of othere men though not without labour and studie thorugh manie yeeris" (29).

As a clerk of moral philosophy, therefore, Pecock's job is to cultivate this field of knowledge and to make it fruitful for other "citeseins in London" by providing books of moral philosophy that bring God's moral law of nature into "open knowing" of each reader (*Repressor*, 29). Pecock does this in two ways. His books record and witness the truths of moral philosophy as a kind of vast encyclopedic resource, condensing everything that each individual needs to know. In this sense, Pecock's own labor and study are most important: lay readers profit from the work that Pecock has done in perceiving the reflecting on the truths of God's moral law. Pecock's books, however, are more than vessels of knowledge, passing on ideas. If his books were meant simply to act as storehouses of information, he would not need to spend so much time breaking down his own points into basic philosophical foundations. As an agent that causes growth in the soul of his reader, Pecock makes the lay intellect fertile and encourages his readers to engage in the kind of labor and study that can make their own sight of the truths of God's moral law sharper. The field of knowledge in the reader's soul is constantly generating higher truths as Pecock cultivates and harvests it through his activity of planting, pruning, and nurturing. What is important about this metaphor is the idea that the field becomes self-generating: the truths of the law of nature must flourish on their own once they are planted. Pecock's job is not to think for his readers but to give them the resources they need to think for themselves. Pecock's systematic approach to religious instruction, through careful analysis of conclusions and truths, shows that one cannot implant belief in readers without first preparing the soil of the intellect, without fertilizing the garden so that truths can grow up and flourish. If belief is to be properly engendered, if readers are to know truths with certainty, they must understand the logical structures and philosophical bases of the truths of God's moral law.

For Pecock, a vernacular work of instruction functions best by showing readers how certain truths are connected to others: for instance, before he can explain the aspects of specific virtues, he must provide a rational treatment of the nature of virtue itself, considering the philosophical basis of the concept before treating individual subjects like mercy or charity. Before Pecock can teach the moral laws of his four tables, he must teach readers the foundations on which these truths lie. For example, the reader must learn first the "openest treuthis" that "al good is to be lovid; al yvel is to be fled and forsaken; More good is more to be lovid; Ech hool body is grettir than is his party; and so of alle othere liik." These truths are so open to the faculty of reason that they cannot be proved by other more clear and more open truths: for this reason they are called "'principlis' or 'big-inningis' or 'heedis' or 'provers' of othire treuthis" (*Folewer*, 50). As I will explore in more detail elsewhere, this method of teaching moral law, by inculcating first principles and deriving more specific laws from them, is the method of Aquinas's *Summa theologiae*.[25] Pecock and Aquinas both organize their moral teaching in a way that demands the intellectual participation of readers: once readers understand first principles, they learn to apply these principles to work out more specific rules of conduct.

This system for generating belief, however, is not common in works that are aimed at lay readers, which tend to obscure rather than expose the rational, philosophical foundations of moral truth. In his review of contemporary teaching on the seven deadly sins, Pecock defines certain teaching as false, "forgid and feined" in the way that it grows not out of an organic system of truths but out of a mystical understanding of a certain biblical image, or out of figurative language that could lead to various interpretations (*Donet*, 115). Teaching on moral behavior should start from the philosophical principles of man's nature and the nature of vice and virtue, rather than from a striking image. Pecock criticizes allegorical works that treat familiar subjects such as the seven gifts of the Holy Ghost and the seven deadly sins in the following way:

> It might seeme that moche of her such seid bisines aboute the seid vii giftis of God is not but vanite and feinid curiosite; fforwhy what ever treting, afferming, or holding, not being historial or cronical, which is not grounded in resoun or revelacioun maad to us by scripture, or in othire surely and certeinly or probabily had revelacioun from God, is not but feined thing and vanite. . . . Wherfore it might seeme that suche teching is forgid, feinid and vein curiosite, difficulting, harding and derking Godis lawe more than it is derke in it silf, and traveiling and troubling mennis wittis with birthen which is not necessarie, and therby letting mennis wittis to attende into profitable and necessary thingis. (*Donet*, 115)

For example, Pecock argues that certain writers or preachers are so intent on making their teaching on the seven deadly sins fit with their allegorical interpretation of the Seven-Headed Beast of the Apocalypse that they refuse to consider rational arguments about the complex nature of sloth. Pecock explains that sloth can be considered, at times, as a "specialist moral vice" but at other times as a general moral vice; this point is overlooked by those preachers who are less interested in educating the readers about the nature of vice itself and more interested in making their teaching exciting, by aligning their explanation of the seven sins with "a moral undirstonding or an allegorie or an anagogie of holi scripture" (*Donet*, 106–7). In the effort to interpret the Seven-Headed Beast from Revelation in a particularly memorable way, these preachers obscure the fact that sloth has a particular nature that sets it apart from the other deadly sins: "Slouthe is noon special vice to be noumbrid with pride, envie, wrathe, glotonie, and leccherie" (106). This kind of teaching therefore does not provide a full, comprehensive treatment of each sin, grounding it in philosophical principles. Pecock states, "If in divinite were no strenger groundis forto holde therby thingis to be trewe than ben mistik conceitis takun

by holy scripture, as ben tropologies, allegories, and anagogies, divinite were a simple and an unsure faculte" (107). An interpretation of a
biblical figure does not provide as firm a basis for moral teaching as
rational discourse on sin's various properties. Such a discourse on a
topic like sin or a virtue or moral governance would consider "alle the
causis and motives and ententis, meenis, helpis, and lettis, and manie
othere circumstauncis of the same governaunce" (*Repressor*, 106), helping the reader to understand the complex nature of sin and providing
a proper grounding for the topic.

Presumably, then, Pecock would disapprove of a work that conveys *pastoralia* in an extended allegory, such as *Jacob's Well*, a fifteenth-
century vernacular text of sermons aimed at teaching a lay audience
about leaving a life of sin and starting a life of virtue.[26] In this text, the
figure of the well, rather than philosophical principles, is the starting
point for an explanation of vice and virtue. In this work, therefore, the
figurative description is primary, so that it becomes more important to
fit each aspect of pastoral teaching into the extended allegory. The aspects of teaching on the sins and the works of mercy, for example, are
made to match the grime of the well and the cleansing waters that can
purge it. The danger of such a teaching method, in Pecock's view, is
that important points may be glossed over because the knowledge is
assembled together in a way that serves a more aesthetic or affective
goal. In the late fourteenth-century devotional work *Book to a Mother*,
the author likens the world to a desert that contains "litel good comfort" and many dangers, including "breres, thornes and nettles, and
mony wilde bestis."[27] The writer warns that in such a dangerous world
the reader is surrounded by snares and perils: "breres, caching
thoughtes of coueitise; thornes, orible othes prikinge soules; netlis,
unclene wordis of brenninge lecherie, bitinge here neighbores with
here yvele ensamples. Also monie wilde bestis: proude men, fers as li-
ones; with diverse vices icolored as liberdus; irous and enviouse as
houndes; folowinge here lustes of lecherie as dulle asses; kuttinge here
throtes with diverse gyses as madde apes."[28] While one remains in this
desert, one must escape and avoid the threats of deadly sin. Though
this description of the sins may be convincing, memorable, and appealing to the reader, in Pecock's view it would never be an appropriate
basis for comprehensive instruction on the seven deadly sins. The kind

of teaching that gathers knowledge in the service of a striking image is didactic in the rememorative sense because it requires the use of the imaginative faculty to facilitate memorization rather than intellectual comprehension. When the reader of *Jacob's Well* approaches this text as an educational tool, he will acquire images of sin and virtue that will remain in his memory, but he will not comprehend the fundamental principles of the nature of sin, the nature of virtue, and the nature of man's soul.

Pecock is also deeply critical of popular works of *pastoralia* that do not foster the flourishing of truth in the reader's soul.[29] Commentaries on the Ten Commandments, for example, are especially "famose, . . . apprised and sett by clerkis and of the lay partie," but they contain neither the whole teaching of God's moral law nor any information about the philosophical principles of this teaching (*Donet*, 102). Because the Ten Commandments provide insufficient doctrine and teaching to Christians, preachers and teachers hang "about the same foorme of x comaundementis suche lose gibilettis as ben the teching of vii deedly sinnes, the teching of v wittis, the teching of vii merciful werkis, and othire mo" (146).[30] Still, despite all of this patching together of these pieces of teaching, "whanne alle these schulen be throwe to gider into heepe, for to make of hem an hool sufficient foorme of leernyng, remembering, and reporting upon goddis comaundmentis, this heepe schal not conteine alle the virtues of goddis lawe" (147). This teaching will never be ample enough, and it will never be as logically sound as Pecock's own methods, which provide rational analysis of every aspect of God's moral law: "Al it schal be oute of cours, of joint, and oute of lith, oute of ordre, and oute of dewe processe to gider clumprid, that it schal never serve to teche, to leerne, and to remember and to reporte so fair and so esily and so profitably as schal therto serve the foorme of the iiii seid tablis" (147). The kind of teaching that does not lead the reader from one truth to the next truth that naturally grows from it is disordered, hung together, patched, clumped and thrown together in a disorganized heap rather than functioning as an organic system stimulating the growth of truth in the reader's soul. Pecock emphasizes the lack of the generative power of works like these with the image of "lose gibilettis" hung around the Ten Commandments: the entrails of a dead body are appended to another body in a way that will never produce life. Pecock's assembly of organic truths, on the other hand, helps to propagate anew; each truth comes together to create a new one in his syllogistic arguments and in his carefully ordered didactic works.

In Pecock's view, popular works of *pastoralia* provide a ready-made approach to moral education that may be memorable and interesting but does not encourage readers to develop the cognitive skills to see and examine the foundations of these conclusions for themselves. These works will never teach the layman to develop sharper sight in the perception and examination of religious truths because they fail to resolve moral doctrine into its philosophical foundations, equipping the reader with more sophisticated ways of analyzing conclusions or the tools to "answere and assoile alle the harde scruplouse doutis and questions" about them (*Repressor,* 16). From what remains of Pecock's works, it appears that his wish was to reform the genre of didactic literature so that when readers approached works like *Book to a Mother,* with its colorful description of the seven deadly sins, they would have profited already from a firm grounding in the philosophical foundations of this topic. The first step in religious education is to hone the reader's intellect and to make that bountiful garden of truths in the reader's soul healthy and fecund. This garden must be cultivated and made self-sustaining before the reader can be introduced to works that manipulate the moral truths in figurative ways to delight, frighten, and move the reader.

The most important thing Pecock wishes to impart to his lay reader is the need to develop reading practices that will ensure that the garden of truths in his soul never becomes overrun with neglect: whether he is reading Pecock's work or another book, the reader must resolve an author's conclusions or ideas into its grounds in the same way that clerks must analyze the rational principles of complex theological works. Pecock states, "The ruide and simple leving to thy scripture and to doctouris seyingis, without resolving of it into ferther groundis out of whom her writingis and seyingis comen forth, hath holde men, and dooth holde so yit, into greet derkenes and blindnes where and whanne they wenen to se broode, and so to be ful bonde, boistose and thrall, unmanly unnaturaly unclerkely unleernedly, where it were more convenient and more good to be in other wise governed"

(*Reule*, 465). Men, whether of the laity or the clergy, are held in darkness when they do not subject that which they read or hear to careful logical analysis, testing the ideas conveyed in the work with tools such as the syllogism. Pecock implies here that man has an important role to play in illuminating that darkness as much as possible, in retraining the eye of reason to see with clear vision. We can opt to do things that mire us further in this darkness, like cleaving to authoritative, established texts rather than testing truth for ourselves, but we can opt to find a way out of the darkness. Certainty can be acquired only by "resolving of tho writingis into the groundis and principles of the faculte to which thei perteinen" (*Folewer*, 68). In the *Repressor*, Pecock cautions readers that they must get into the habit of studying the grounds and principles of truths before they believe conclusions: "Right weel waar oughte reders be, whanne thei redden in oold mennis writingis, that they cleve not over soone therto, into time they han reduced, resolved, and broughte the conclusiouns whiche thei there redden, in to the propre principlis and groundis of tho conclusiouns, of whiche and by whiche principlis and groundis tho same conclusiouns muste take her trouthis, if tho conclusiouns eny trouthe have in hem" (*Repressor*, 410). Whether men are reading the Bible, ancient theological texts, or Pecock's vernacular works, they will be bound in darkness if they do not expose the conclusions drawn in these texts to rational analysis. Pecock describes this kind of analysis, saying: "Ech conclusioun taketh his trouthe of and fro and by his ground and principil, fro and out of which he descendith in formal argument, though no writer in the world hadde ever ther of write eny word, or schulde in time to come write eny word. . . . Ech conclusion, in to whos finding and leerning mannis resoun . . . may come to, is to be founde grounded in philsophie, and in therof principlis so open that no resoun may ayens hem seie nay" (*Repressor*, 411). Any conclusion, whether expressed in written or oral form, must be taken apart and reduced to its philosophical grounds, rather than passively accepted and believed. Pecock trains readers in this process by structuring his analogies to show readers how they can resolve arguments into their philosophical principles. This kind of rational analysis is essential for those who wish to distinguish themselves from those who know God's moral governances as "unsure trowers and not proving knowers" (*Folewer*, 68). This kind of rational analysis does not necessarily require books: Pecock states that whether or not a conclusion is written down by an author, the conclusion is arrived at in the same way, from the ascension or combination of various grounds and principles.

The kind of intellectual training that enables readers to have certain knowledge of God's moral law can have a significant impact on the development of particular modes of thought and particular group experiences in the community. Pecock's books provide the tools that readers require for the development of a common intellectual framework: he instructs readers in common rules of discourse, and he invites readers to adopt a common vocabulary. He notes the importance, for example, of having a common ground for discussion of religious matters when he writes of the need for his readers to have "enformacioun of the terms or wordis" that are used in discussions about God's moral law. Once the "signifying of the wordis ben to hem knowun," readers can apply their wit with greater zeal to the matters that Pecock treats in his books (*Reule*, 21). Pecock's habit of providing multiple definitions for terms and for using many words when few will do to explain concepts helps his lay readers to develop a common vocabulary that will influence the "talking about the things of God." In the same way, the training in principles of moral philosophy and in the terminology of logic that his books offer creates a common ground of understanding for discussion and debate. What brings readers together as a group is their common approach to the matter of religious truth. The kinds of discussions that members of this textual community will have about the moral law of God operate by accepted rules of discourse: members of the group must agree on what constitutes certain knowledge before they can come to a consensus about the truths of God's law. For example, after outlining the terms and concepts that he will use in subsequent arguments, Pecock notes that those who do not understand or agree with these terms cannot participate in the conversation: "Al this is so open to be grauntid, that who ever denyeth eny point of it, he is unable to be admittid and to be received into eny enquiraunce or communaunce forto finde, leerne, and knowe treuthis, so that the significacioun of these wordis be maad open to him, that he understonde what the wordis meenen" (*Repressor*, 133–34). Controversial matters cannot be discussed until there is agreement on the terms and premises that will structure the discussion. Through Pecock's instruction in principles of logic and rational argumentation, readers learn not only to see truth with certainty but also to see truth in the same way. Laymen and cleric share the same modes of thought and the same frames of reference, which bring them together in a way that transcends professional allegiances or previous experiences. Members of the laity who devote time and energy to learning new modes of thinking through their study of Pecock's books undergo processes of initiation and conversion that transform them into "scolers" in "divinite" (*Folewer*, 13).[31] Despite the variety in their backgrounds, occupations, prejudices, and preoccupations, Pecock's readers are united by their common acceptance of certain boundaries, paradigms, and rules for discussion and debate.

In Pecock's textual community, the book of reason is the ultimate authority in these matters, and the book of reason is controlled, to some degree, by the clergy because they—or Pecock—determine the ways of reading it. Though Pecock's notion that all men possess innate powers of reason and that all men can learn to decipher God's law in the book of reason creates the possibility for all men to come together as equals to puzzle over decisions about norms and rules for behavior, it is the learned clergy who possess the highest skills for reading the book of reason, and it is the learned clergy who will instruct laymen in ways of arriving at the right interpretations of the book of reason. Pecock himself witnesses the power of learned clergymen to constrain agreement to the correct interpretation of the book of reason when he tells us about the times he has corrected Lollards and pointed out their errors: "I have spoke oft time, and by long leiser, with the wittiest and kunnyngist men of thilk seid soort, contrarie to the chirche, and which han be holde as dukis amonge hem, and which han loved me for that y wolde paciently heere her evidencis, and her motives, without exprobacioun. And verrily noon of hem couthe make eny motive for her party so stronge as y my silf couthe have made therto" (*BF*, 202). Though other members of the textual community are welcome to voice doubts or questions in an open exchange between clergy and laity, Pecock's training in moral philosophy and in logic enables him to convince these "wittiest and kunningist" men of their error. Pecock's notion that the learned clergy are the most skilled interpreters of the book of reason and that control of this book rests in their hands is an important strategy for reinforcing the authority of the clergy once he has begun to break down absolute boundaries between these two groups, as I suggest in chapter 7 on lay-cleric relations.

I have suggested in this chapter that for Pecock the most important task of vernacular theology is to train readers gradually to open their eyes to a book that is inscribed on their souls by God himself. We must develop reasoning processes that allow us to arrive at basic truths that apply universally, in each situation: these are general principles of how the world works. They help us understand how to behave in particular situations, such as how to respond to a wicked neighbor, how to treat one's spouse, or how to structure life in a monastery. The answers to all the questions about God's moral law are written on the soul, and we were once able to know these instantly, with clear perception. To come to these answers in our fallen state, we must learn new ways of reading this inner book. Our labor consists, therefore, in developing systematic ways of seeking for the truths that are now partially concealed from us. The tools that can help us in this task are the faculty of reason, the syllogism, and the signs in the mundane world that point us to higher realities. Pecock's books teach readers, essentially, to adopt philosophy as a way of life by cultivating intellectual practices that constitute our best—and only—way of reading the moral law of God in our fallen state.

s i x

The Bible

Throughout his entire corpus, Pecock makes it clear that much of his labor is intended as a corrective to the Lollard textual community. He identifies two major problems with the way that these members of the "lay partie" approach and use the Bible (*Reule*, 19). The first problem is their understanding of the nature of the Bible as the singular source of knowledge and exclusive authority on Christian belief and behavior; the second problem is their determination to read this text for themselves. These people believe that the Bible is superior to all other sources of knowledge, including other books written by the clergy: "Oon is of hem whiche holden hem silf so stifly and so singulerly, foolily and oonly to the use of the Bible in her modiris langage, and namely to therof the Newe Testament, that they trowen, seien, and holden bothe prively and as fer openly as they daren, alle othere bookis writun or in Latin or in the comoun peplis langage to be writun into waast" (*Reule*, 17). Those who view the Bible alone as the basis for all beliefs and behavior "wole have alle treuthis of mennis moral conversacioun there groundid" (*Repressor*, 86). By insisting that all aspects of moral law must be located in the biblical text in order to be deemed valid, these people cast doubt on every ordinance, law, tradition, and custom that is not revealed in the Bible. These "Bible men" present, in Pecock's view, a serious threat to orthodoxy: their strict adherence to *sola scriptura* leads them into all sorts of error and prevents them from opening their minds to other interpretations of biblical truths (*Repressor*, 86).[1]

In Lollard writings, the adherence to *sola scriptura* appears in the form of a clear distinction between God's law and men's law. A Wycliffite sermon on Luke 6, on the subject of martyrs, asserts that scripture is a higher authority than the traditions of men: "Certus, as tradicions maade biside Godis lawe, of prestis and of scribis and of Pharisees, blindedon hem in Godis lawe, and made it dispuisud, so it is now of Godis lawe by newe mennis lawes, as decretallis and decrees. . . . But remedie ayenus this is used of money men, to despuison alle these lawes whon they ben aleghgede, and seyn unto men that aleghgen hem, that falsehede is more suspecte for witnesse of suche lawis, sith Godis lawe telluth alle trewthe that is needful to men."[2] The decrees of the church are not as valid as the ruling of the Bible itself. The writer recommends caution when submitting to the laws and doctrine that the ecclesiastical hierarchy creates for Christians to follow and believe: rather than doing "worschipe" to these rules of men, the faithful should follow God's law alone.[3] In the Lollard sermon *Vae Octuplex*, the author echoes this notion of the superiority of the divine truth of the Bible: "Trewthe of the gospel is cristen mennis bileve, and by that schulden men stonden, bothe knightus and other, and other thingus chargen lasse, al yif they ben trewe; for not eche trewthe is evene for to charge, but trewthe that God himself seith and techeth in the gospel, that schulde men worschipon and taken as bileve. And othur lawe of mennis finding schulden men luytul telle by."[4] Even if other sources such as church teachings are true, laws of "mennis finding" are less authoritative, less binding, and less worthy than the truth of the Gospel. As Anne Hudson suggests, the tendency to elevate scripture with this emphasis on *sola scriptura* is a "reasonable summary" of the attitudes of Wyclif's followers.[5] Pecock's description of the heretical cleaving to scripture alone, in his picture of the "Bible men" of his day who will not listen to the arguments of their clerical superiors or the interpretations of the church, shows the extent to which *sola scriptura* has become a central concern for the followers of Wyclif.

Pecock also takes issue with the tendency of some Lollards to prefer their own interpretations of the Bible to the expositions of the church. He worries about the dismissal of clerical authority over the interpretation of scripture by the many members of the "lay peple whiche cleven and attenden over unreulily to the Bible" and who have decided that they "wolen fecche and leerne her feith at the Bible of Holy Scripture, in the maner as it schal happe hem to undirstonde it" (*BF*, 110). These people "protesten and knowlechen that they wolen not fecche and leerne her feith at the clergie of Goddis hool chirche in erthe; neither they as for leerning and kunning of her feith wolen obeie to the clergie or to the chirche" (109–10). Their refusal to learn their faith from the clergy relates to their belief that it is possible for them, equipped with meekness and charity rather than clerical skills in exegesis, to read the Bible independently and discover its "right and dewe litteral undirstonding" (227). These members of the Lollard textual community deny that the clergy alone "kunnen suerly enforme [them] of thilke right and dewe undirstonding" of Holy Scripture (227). They believe that the Bible provides everything we need to know about morality and belief, but they insist that we may never fully understand what it reveals to us in these respects if we continue to trust to the glosses and interpretations of the church.

The distrust of the clergy's interpretations of the Bible and the insistence on independent lay confrontation with the scriptural text are also evident in contemporary Lollard texts, such as a Lollard sermon on Matthew 10. In this text, the imperative for the laity to read the Bible for themselves and trust to themselves to find its "dewe undirstonding" relates to the way that the church—disciples of Antichrist—interpret God's law for their own purposes: "Yif men seyn that Godis lawe must nedis be soth to Godis entent, they grawnton that this is soth but the entent ligh in hem. So, as princes of preestis, and Pharisees joinede with hem, wolen interprete Godis lawe, aftur hem schal it be takon. And so her exposicion is more in autorite than is text of Godis lawe."[6] This author suggests that the church has a tendency to deceive the faithful into mistaking false interpretation for God's truth. Their interpretation reinvents the Word so that it will say something other than what God intended, and this new interpretation takes on greater authority than the Word itself in the hands of the clergy. It is not at all likely that the clergy will inform the laity of the "right and dewe undirstonding" of the text of God's law when their own interests are at stake (*BF*, 227). The Lollard writer of *De oblacione iugis sacrificii* (ca. 1413) protests that those who customarily interpret God's law on behalf of the laity have "pervertid so scripture by his fals glosis, that welny al men, lerned and lewde, taken that lawe as of litil auctorite."[7] By setting their own conclusions upon the Bible and manipulating it to agree with their own pronouncements about religious law, the clergy have brought the authority of the Bible itself under suspicion. When the authority of the biblical text is superseded by the expositions of the institutional church, the law of Christ is slandered. The implication here is that when scripture is no longer in the hands of interpretive handmaids but in the hands of ecclesiastical masters who wish to subject God's Word to their own purposes, it is time for the laity to stop trusting to the clergy's expositions.[8]

The kinds of comments that Pecock makes about the folly of the "Bible men," in their dismissal of other sources of Christian knowledge and in their suspicion of the expositions of the clergy, make it clear that the Bible will play a much different role in Pecock's own textual community. Pecock's approach to and use of the biblical text in his pedagogical works form a corrective to Lollard ideals and practices of Bible reading. His understanding of the role that the Bible should play in the lives of lay readers is informed and influenced by his perception of Lollard error: he is driven to think hard about the nature of the biblical text and the best way to ensure access to its "right and dewe undirstonding" in his efforts to correct the Lollards and bring them back to the orthodox fold, into his own textual community (*BF*, 230). Pecock's criticism of the practices and ideals of the "Bible men," however, does not lead him to deny that the Bible plays an important role in founding belief within the Christian community, or that the laity need to understand what God reveals to them in this text.

Indeed, his prologue to the *Reule of Crysten Religioun* highlights for readers the Bible's importance in grounding the truths of faith, which come to Pecock begging for textual form. In the heavenly company of universal truths that appear to Pecock, it is not just the truths of reason that wish to be freed from darkness and inscribed by him but also truths that are "bigetun" and "boren" of scripture (33). These truths that were given life by the Bible worry that the clergy's neglect of them has led to error: many "opiniouns taken as for founded in scripture misundirstonden—as is forto undirstonde scripture in propirte and in pleinnist sowning of his wordis whanne it ought be undirstonde figuratively, and ayenward forto undirstonde holy scripture figuratively whanne it oughte be undirstonde as it pleinly sowneth" (33–34). Part of the job of the *Reule* is therefore to help clear up these misunderstandings and to give light once more to the truths of faith, which originate in the Bible. It is certainly noteworthy that the eternal truths of faith *want* to be handled by Pecock; they do not countenance the notion of appearing to lay readers in the form of scripture itself. When they complain about being locked in darkness they make no mention of being released by vernacular translation of scripture. Embracing Pecock, they each grant him "a special trouthe" that he then transmits to his readers (36). Though Pecock receives these truths directly, wondering at their beautiful presence in his study, lay readers must learn about truths that originate in the Bible through Pecock's textual mediation of them (36). This passage provides us with important insights into the way that the members of Pecock's textual community are meant to access the divine truths of the Bible.

It should now be clear that the purpose of this chapter is to assess the significance and uses of scripture in Pecock's ideal, imagined textual community. If the Bible is not the sole authority on Christian truth, what importance does it have as a text that offers to readers important knowledge about things like God's moral law, the sacraments, the nature of heaven and hell, the nature of the Trinity, and the ways in which Christians can earn God's forgiveness? Members of Pecock's textual community need to understand how the Bible's authority works in comparison to other sources of authority such as church custom, the pope, oral tradition, and the book of reason. They also need to understand that there are certain ways of interpreting the Bible and certain people who must be trusted with this job: Pecock emphasizes the need for "institutional management" of the Bible in diverse ways.[9] Basically, Pecock wants the members of his textual community to have access to the truths that God reveals to them in the Bible; this access, however, must be controlled and monitored by learned clergymen like him.

Pecock was not the only churchman in late medieval England searching for effective solutions to the problems posed by the "Bible men" for orthodoxy. The Lollard belief that the Bible alone provides the key to understanding Christian belief and behavior was worrisome because it threatened to destabilize the authority of ecclesiastical traditions, canon law, and the sacraments—the entire apparatus of the church, which had been built around its central text. Responses to the claim that nothing should be believed or done without corresponding justification in the biblical text could be as direct as Hoccleve's warning to Oldcastle to stop meddling with scripture and clerical affairs;[10] other reactions, like Pecock's, were more complex and extensive, making important contributions to late medieval debates about the Bible's significance for and place in the Christian community.

It is important to study Pecock's contributions to these debates, partly because his ideas about the Bible are not well understood by scholars and partly because a close examination of Pecock's stance on these issues tells us that he had much in common with late medieval reformers who wished to stress "the importance of lay understanding of religion" while at the same time discouraging "attempts to acquire that understanding through reading the Bible."[11] John Mirk, for example, rejects Lollardy's "bibliocentric version of Christianity" by expressing his position, not directly, but "indirectly through narrative," in a way that "subtly weakens the distinction between the Bible as a unique text and the oral traditions that inform hagiographic literature, thus undermining the conception of the Bible as a uniquely true divine revelation which could serve as a standard against which all other aspects of Christianity might be measured."[12] Mirk is one of many late medieval sermon writers who find ways of strategically directing audience members toward orthodoxy and away from more radical notions about the place of the Bible in Christianity. In their studies of late medieval preaching, H. L. Spencer and Siegfried Wenzel discuss the various reactions and responses to Lollard ideals in sermons aimed at lay audiences; their studies suggest that a variety of options were considered in the effort to confirm the authority of canon law, the sacraments, and ecclesiastical tradition in the wake of Lollard claims that the Bible alone was sufficient.[13]

There was a broad range of thinking on the issue of lay access to biblical truth and a broad range of responses to Lollard bibliocentrism. Karen Winstead argues that John Capgrave did not seek to deter readers from Bible reading at the same time as he was careful to insist "that one cannot reject customs of the Church simply because they are not attested in the Bible."[14] Winstead suggests that "lay access to Scripture is one aspect of Capgrave's larger commitment to a reasoned, informed faith" and that by "making explicit the processes whereby he reasons out various linguistic, historical, and even theological controversies, Capgrave may have meant to teach lay readers how to think through similar conundra."[15] Mirk and Pecock do not go so far as to prod lay readers in the direction of the Bible, but they too show a commitment to a reasoned, informed faith. Others were much more conservative. Kantik Ghosh notes that some institutional responses to Lollard bibliocentrism included paranoia, repression, and the effort to limit the intellectual endeavors of the Lollards and the laity.[16] Translation of the Bible into English and possession of the vernacular scripture were prohibited by Arundel's Constitutions, as was reasoned discussion on the articles of faith grounded in the Bible. Pecock's observations that lay readers require a license to read the Bible and that the institutional church is interested only in delivering articles of faith to the church without "counseil therof," asking the laity to accept what is "expressely delivered" without proper understanding, suggest that teaching the truths of faith was still controversial (*Reule*, 95). Pecock's impassioned defense of the practice of giving reasonable evidences for declarations of faith, however, as well as his own practice of translating bits and pieces of scripture in his books, would suggest that Pecock does not feel himself limited by the Constitutions in these respects.

Pecock's contribution to late medieval debates about the Bible and lay Bible reading indicates that he is an important witness to a fifteenth-century reformist tradition that sought a more creative solution to the problem of Lollardy, a solution that did not involve repressing the lay intellect by refusing to get into the hows and whys of the articles of faith that were revealed to the Christian community by God's Word.[17] His contribution tells us that there was not necessarily one orthodox and one heterodox stance on these issues in the fifteenth century; rather, this was a time in which the Lollard heresy prompted a flourishing of creative thinking about what kind of book the Bible was and about the role that this book could play in the Christian community. Indeed, the range of positions that Pecock himself takes on a number of issues shows the dynamism of thought current in this era:

at times we can see him reaching for more conservative responses to the problematic prospect of lay Bible reading, while at other times we see him grappling with the same problems in new ways. Thus Pecock witnesses a transition in thinking and attitudes that occurred as late medieval intellectual and religious culture moved toward the culture of the Reformation.

Pecock responds to the notion of *sola scriptura* by directly and emphatically opposing the idea that it is possible for the Bible to ground every aspect of Christian belief and behavior. Moreover, he suggests that in matters of both faith and reason the interpretive community of the church plays a major role not simply in determining scriptural meaning but in contesting it. His notion that the Bible is more a historical document than a revelation, that its authority is not equal in all of its parts, that the truths it reveals are one source among diverse sources on Christian faith, and that its teachings on moral law are secondary to a more authoritative source indirectly discourage the laity from reading the Bible on their own by limiting the special aura and allure that scripture appears to hold for the "Bible men" and by emphasizing the difficult, complex nature of the scriptural text. His own use of the Bible in his teachings insists on the need for the interpretive authority of learned clerics.

Pecock rejects the notion of scripture's supreme authority when he discusses the way that scripture grounds the truths of faith. Truths of faith are the few truths that man's reason cannot access without the help of revelation or another man's witnessing: these truths, grounded in the Bible, are distinguished from those which "into his finding, leerning, and knowing mannis witt may by it silf aloone or by natural helpis withoute revelacioun fro God rise and suffice" (*Repressor,* 37). Examples of truths of faith include the fact that "iii persoonis ben in oon Godhede" and that "a maide bare the sone of God in his manhode" (*BF,* 136). Pecock's *Book of Faith* is an important resource for understanding his notion of the Bible's role in the Christian religion; in this work he argues that truths of faith are different from other truths because of the way we come to know them. They are not accepted into the understanding "by beholding upon the causis or effectis or circumstauncis in nature of the conclusioun or trouthe" (124). Instead, faith is what we know "for as miche as God himself immediately, or by an aungel or an apostle of God, hath affeermid by word or by writing it to be trewe, or hath in sum maner denouncid and enformed, by helpe of miracle, or in sum other maner, it to be trewe" (123–24). Our knowledge of faith comes from direct revelation, or in the form of the scriptures, or through miracle. It is important to note here that the Bible is not the unique source of truths of faith: God reveals faith not just in the Bible but also in the form of tradition. If "holy chirche this hath bileeved for feith in time of the apostlis, and fro thens continuely hiderto," this form of faith is said to be revealed by God as well (172).

The Bible is not set apart as a higher form of truth than miracle or church tradition; furthermore, though the Bible is necessary because it provides access to the kinds of truths that the human mind cannot perceive on its own, the Bible is not a uniquely revelatory text that provides direct access to God's mind. Pecock suggests that the Old Testament is a collection of writings that were passed down from the time of Ennok. Moses did not write the book of Genesis "by inspiracioun"; rather, he gathered together the writings that existed from the days of Adam himself (*BF,* 264). Ennok, who lived in the time of Adam, "wrote holy wonderful thingis of the feith" from the teachings of Adam; these writings were passed to Noah, who "kept sum and miche of this writing with him, saaf in his schippe, whilis the flood durid"; Noah delivered the written teachings on faith to his sons, and so on and so on until Moses gathered them all together into the book of Genesis (263–65). In a similar manner, Esdras "renewed not the Oold Testament in writing by gift of inspiracioun, as is comounly holde"; rather, he had a copy of "ech kinde of tho bokis" of the Old Testament, which he brought together and "maad be writen" because of his zeal that God's law must be "wel knowe" (266). Pecock provides numerous evidences and rational arguments to convince readers that the Bible is a record of the truths of faith passed down through the ages and not written by God himself "by privey miraclus inspiracioun" (270). The writing did help to stabilize the truths— Pecock suggests that the truths of faith "needis be grounded in writing, and without writing y can not see as for now in these daies eny sufficient suerte for feith" (*Reule,* 433). The special significance of the Old Testament is its role as a stable, written record of truths, which prevents the "variaunce in multiplying, in lassing, in chaunging which experience schewith to falle in talis or tidingis or eny stories or othere chauncis tolde fro persoon to persoon by mouth with oute writing" (433). In Pecock's view, the New Testament is also written by human authors rather than uniquely revealed by God; he describes the Evangelists as "persoones holy in living, simple and wel manerid," who wrote down the story of Christ from what they saw and heard (434). The New Testament is a record of events and a document that passes on Christ's teaching, instead of a supernatural kind of text allowing a special experience of God's revelation. Pecock's emphasis on the human authors and historical circumstances that produced the Bible and his emphasis that the Bible as a whole is more of a written register of certain truths than a uniquely revelatory text help to destabilize the Lollard belief in the singular authority of the book at the heart of their textual community.

Indeed, as I noted above, the account of Christian truth provided by the Bible is one source of faith among a number of diverse sources. Faith has a broad range of meanings in Pecock's understanding and includes the positive ordinances of God himself, ordinances that he specifically and directly ordered us to perform and carry out, and that, in Pecock's understanding, include the sacraments. Faith also includes the articles of belief imposed by the church on the laity: the church has the power to institute new "feithis," though not to profess that these new articles are the direct teachings of God himself (*BF*, 291). In its role as an apostolic authority, the church can institute new customs, like fasting days or holy days, and publish these new truths as faith. These new faiths will be "fer from the highnes and worthines of feithis, which God to us makith," but they must be accepted by the laity as valid truths of faith (291). Faith also includes what the church "bileeved for feith in time of the apostlis, and fro then continuely hiderto" (172). The laity must accept as faith the teachings that have been passed on orally, through church tradition, from the time of the apostles. Pecock states that "every article which the chirche in time of the apostlis helde for feith, was taught of Crist, or of the apostlis for feith; wherfore the seid article is now to be taken for feith" (173). This includes church custom, or "long uce of bileeving in the chirche" (303). Pecock also includes the Bible as one source of "kunning" of

Christ's deeds and moral life, as well as knowledge of the "positive" laws that Christ set down (*Donet*, 130–31). The test for truth of our knowledge about Christ's deeds is not recourse to the Bible alone: nothing should be granted as true "save oonly what is seen to be trewe by doom of natural resoun, or by witnesse of holy scripture, wherinne lieth oure feith, or by oolde storying and witnessing of hem that weren in time of the apostlis and heerers of the apostlis, or but eny man canne depose, undir perel of his soule, that he is siker to have it by special undoutable revelacioun, wel and wiisely examined of oold, expert, sadde and discreet men, laborid in such mater" (130). Rather than holding special revelation of the life of Christ, the Bible is one historical source among others, which range from other historical texts to the "surest private revelacioun" of modern-day mystics (131).

Pecock also suggests that scripture's authority, in some of its parts, is equal rather than superior to that of the clergy. He says, "Scripture of the Newe Testament is not, thorugh ech party of him, liik in auctorite, in worthines, and in dignite" (*BF,* 277). The clergy may "dispense with it that Scripture techith as the ordinaunce of an apostle, and may revoke it, as he may dispense with this, that Poul ordeinid a bigam to not be deken or preest" (278). The pope's authority is on a par with the apostles in his jurisdiction over the teaching of Christian faith: "The chirche now living be evene in autorite and power with sum party of Scripture" (278). The clergy does not have the same power over the "positive ordinaunce of Crist," or what Christ reveals to be the moral law or the law of faith in the Bible, but it has the power to dispense with other parts of scripture (278). Pecock describes the power that the church has over scripture in the following way: since apostolic ordinances in scripture and the clergy are "evene peers," it follows that "oon evene peer may revoke and relese that, that the othere evene peere ordeinith, or biddith to be do, or doith in dede; as we seen that oon executour revokith and relesith what the othere joined to him executour ordeinith, biddith, or doith, namelich by the lawe of Ynglond; and in this case is ech pope with ech of the apostlis" (280). Pecock suggests here that once the church has located the "right and dew" meaning of certain parts of scripture, it has the authority to decide whether this meaning is still valid (230). It is the job of the present-day apostolic authorities to ensure that the Bible speaks "to present desires."[18] In his suggestion that the church may critique and revoke practices ordained by the Bible, Pecock suggests a need for the church's intervention in the mediation of scripture to the lay community.

It is important to note that in his emphatic assertions of the authority of the pope and the modern-day clergy to revoke and create articles of faith, Pecock does not really answer Lollard arguments about the special status of biblical truth, especially considering the refusal of some Lollards to accept the pope's authority. Basing arguments on the apostolic authority of the pope and the clergy assumes that this authority is unchallenged. Basing arguments on the authority of "long uce of bileeving in the chirche" does not quite meet the Lollards head on in their refusal to accept church tradition as equal in authority to God's Word (*BF*, 303). In Pecock's textual community, lay members must accept that the church has the authority to educate the laity in the matters of faith. It is not Pecock's mission to prove to lay readers, from an analysis of relevant biblical passages, how we know that the sacraments are positive ordinances of God; instead, it is the job of learned clergymen to ensure that the laity know the truths of faith that are revealed by the Bible and mediated by the clergy.

The different relationships that lay readers and clergy have with the Bible becomes clear as Pecock discusses the way that truths of faith are to be examined. The first part of the *Book of Faith* urges fellow clerics to be better "avisid of the evidencis whiche mighten prove her bileeve of ech article" (130). Pecock's understanding of the way to prove articles of faith is especially revealing. He says that articles of faith are to be examined. Yet the method of examination is limited to "the boondis of the kinde perteining to feith" (138). This means that the labor of "arguing and examinacioun" that is undertaken to examine whether an article of faith is "trewe as feith or no" does not involve testing this truth by the rules of science or logic (133–34). Indeed, the labor of examining truths in "oure natural resoun" must not "be maad go and falle upon the natural meenis, witnessing the treuthe of thilke article to be trewe, and that thilk article oughte be bileeved as feith, as ben natural causis of the same article, or natural effectis of the same article, or natural signis or natural circumstauncis of the same article, which naturaly stonden aboute the same article" (134). I believe that

Pecock is saying here that it is not permitted to examine whether it is physically possible—by rules of natural philosophy—for Christ to rise from the dead or whether there are natural causes that explain the Immaculate Conception. The examination of truths of faith must not be made "by meene being out of the boundis longing to the kindis of feith, as if the argument be maad by meenis of philsophie, not leening to the revelacioun of God anentis the same article" (137). Faith is not the same as other forms of knowledge and therefore cannot be tested in the same way that knowledge is measured in other disciplines. Examinations of faith must be limited to determining whether God actually revealed the said article of faith. The labor of examining articles of faith "owith to be maad go and renne upon tho meenis whiche witnessen so likly God to have schewid, or have affermed thilk article to be trewe, that no meenes ben had or likely ben hopid to be had forto schewe so likly the contrarie" (134). One may examine, for example, whether it is likely that God actually revealed that "he died and roos to liif the iii day" (133). To do this, by implication, one must consult the various sources of God's revelation of faith, which Pecock has identified as the Bible, miracles, and church tradition.

Underlying this discussion of the methods of testing faith is an important and unarticulated assumption: it requires skill in biblical interpretation. Those who wish to examine the truths of faith must turn to the sources of revelation to discover whether God actually revealed them. This involves Bible study: the rational analysis of the biblical passages that are claimed as confirmation of the various truths of faith. I think it is telling that Pecock does not provide an example of how one would actually examine a truth like "the article that God is iii persoonis and oon substaunce" (*BF,* 133). If one were to argue that "God never revelid thilk article" (137), one would need access to the various biblical passages said to reveal that article, or one would need to prove that a miracle witnessing that truth was actually false, or one would need to investigate historical records to assert that the holy church had not actually believed the said article as faith "in time of the apostlis, and fro thens continuely hiderto" (137, 172). What goes unsaid in this passage is that many Lollards were applying themselves to this particular practice, in tracts like *De oblacione iugis sacrificii*, marshaling argument and biblical hermeneutics to contradict the church's teaching on the articles of faith. Showing that God never revealed a particular article means showing that the church's interpretation of a particular biblical passage is wrong and that an alternative interpretation is correct. And Pecock acknowledges that once a particular article is shown to be false, and never revealed by God, then "God forbede but that thilk argument schulde be herde of clerkis, and be assoilid, . . . yhe and but if thilk article can be proved by suche meenys or meene, he is not worthy to be holde an article of oure Cristen universal feith" (137).

This sort of examination of the truths of faith is clearly not the province of the laity, according to Arundel's Constitutions and according to Pecock himself, who stresses in subsequent passages in his *Book of Faith* that the laity's job is meekly to accept the determinations of the church even if the church should err (*BF,* 181–211). In fact, Pecock's emphasis that the laity is bound to receive the faith from the clergy and "forto obeie in mater of feith to the bischopis and preestis" (182) resembles the statements made by the character Arundel in his interrogation of William Thorpe in *The Testimony of William Thorpe.* Arguing that Thorpe has disobeyed his superiors by preaching without a license, Arundel tells Thorpe that Christian subjects are bound in obedience to their prelates, whether or not those prelates are good: "Seith not seint Poul that sogetis owe to be obedient to her sovereins, and not oonly sogettis owen to be obedient to good sovereins and virtues but also to trowantis that ben vicious men?"[19] Obedience to the clergy and acceptance of their determination of the faith are urged by Pecock in a way that echoes Arundel's appeal to the hierarchical authority of the church in directing those teaching and learning the faith. This would seem to indicate that the clergy alone may examine the articles of faith to determine whether God has actually revealed certain articles. That Pecock refuses to provide examples showing how one might do this is telling because it shows that modeling this practice could be dangerous.

What is even more telling, however, is that Pecock's discussion of the examination of faith is in the vernacular, and therefore accessible to a wide range of lay readers. While stressing to his readers that they must accept the church's teaching on the faith with obedience and respect, he informs readers somewhat obliquely about the ways in which these truths are tested and proved. There is a strong sense in this part of the *Book of Faith* that Pecock has two kinds of reader in mind: an obedient reader who will not inquire further and the type of reader who is already testing truths of faith for himself and who is ordered by Pecock to "evidently and openly without eny doute, schewe, teche, and declare that the chirche bileeveth, or hath determined thilk article wrongly and untreuly, or ellis that the chirche hath no sufficient ground for to so bileeve or determine" (181). Again, Pecock does not provide an example of how a disputatious layman might come up with evidence for his argument that the church had determined wrongly in a matter of faith. Presumably this layman would need to consult the Bible and provide a demonstration of a more correct interpretation of what God had revealed in particular passages, or that layman would need to disprove a miracle, or prove that the church had erred in its understanding of historical tradition. Such a layman would need to be learned, and he would need access to the Bible. The fact that Pecock continually warns such a reader to get his arguments ready means that such a reader existed and was in Pecock's sights. I believe that this kind of reader was the reader Pecock had in mind when writing *The Repressor*, in which he disproves heretical interpretation of biblical passages and provides orthodox interpretations in their stead. Pecock's discussion of examining truths of faith is therefore significant because it helps us to see how his understanding of faith needs to be approached as a "particular articulation of Christian faith" belonging to "particular historical circumstances."[20] Pecock's treatment of the examination of faith is characteristically both conservative and innovative, conservative in its resemblance to Arundel's decree that faith be taught without rational argumentation or analysis, and innovative in its acknowledgment that some lay readers are examining faith with rational analysis nonetheless and must be informed about the proper ways of doing so at the same time as they are carefully shepherded into the Christian fold through the invitation to disputation with other clerics. Pecock's discussion of faith shows us that "different models of faith were inextricably bound up with different models of ethics and politics."[21] His model registers the impact of conservative approaches to unifying the Christian community in the aftermath of heresy while it also looks beyond these approaches in the effort to provide a better response to the growing reality of lay engagement with the biblical text.

This discussion of how one examines the truths of faith functions, at one level, to discourage lay engagement with the Bible because Pecock does not clearly show how one might test whether God has really revealed particular articles of faith in particular biblical passages. This is one way of responding to the Lollard emphasis on *sola scriptura*. Pecock finds a more powerful and effective way (than simply asserting that laypeople are bound to receive determinations on faith from the church) to counter the Lollard notion that the Bible is the central source for Christian knowledge by suggesting that the Bible is not the most reliable source of Christian moral truth and that there is another, more reliable source. Members of Pecock's textual community have to accept another authority on moral teachings because in this domain scripture itself is not self-sufficient. Pecock starts by saying that scripture is not intended by God to provide a source or grounding for moral truths such as those extracted from the biblical text by the Lollards as a basis for their reformed belief and behavior (*Repressor*, 10–11). Pecock argues that scripture cannot ground moral texts fully because, while it may refer to moral truths, it does not provide a sufficient explanation and treatment of these truths: to act as a proper ground for any kind of truth or law, scripture "muste so teche and declare and seie out and yeve forth al the kunning upon the same vertu, governaunce, or trouthe" so that it can be "sufficiently knowen" (10). Pecock says that scripture cannot be held as a ground for moral truths because of its gaps, missing explanations, and inability to "answere and assoile alle the harde scrupulose doutis and questiouns which al day han neede to be assoilid" in everyday life (16). Pecock remarks that "ech man having to do with suche questiouns may soone se that Holi Writt yeveth litil or noon light therto at al" (16). He concludes that we cannot use scripture as a basis for arguments about the way we are to act in service to God, stressing its nature rather to exhort, commend, and remind us of our moral duties. He says, "Of no moral vertuose gouernauncis the sufficient kunning is groundid in Holy Writt, sithen al Holy Writt techith not forth the ful and sufficient and necessarie kunning of eny oon moral vertu in Goddis lawe or Goddis service, though of many of hem Holy Scripture makith schort remembrauncis to us that we schulde hem kepe and not ayens hem do" (25). Scripture makes "remembrauncis to us" of the moral points of God's law; it may witness or mention aspects of moral behavior, but it does not provide ample enough knowledge of God's moral law to act as the sole source for constructing behavioral norms and rules. Scripture is not an absolute source of God's moral message; instead, "he remembrith, or exortith, or biddith, or counseilith men upon tho vertues and gouernauncis and forto use hem, and forto flee the contrarie vicis of hem" (21). The Bible brings truths that we have already perceived into our minds; it reminds us of truths, it bids us to act according to God's law, and it motivates our ethical behavior. Such a text, intended to register moral truths printed elsewhere, and to motivate man to remember what he has learned in a more primary text, cannot be thought of as a primary, inviolate, and incontrovertible source of divine meaning. For Pecock, the only true ground for a moral law, or truth, produces "al the sufficient kunning" of that law or truth (10). He remarks, for example, that "upon sum trouthe or governaunce of Goddis lawe lenger writing muste be had, eer it be sufficiently knowe, than is al the writing of Mathewis Gospel; and yit of thilk vertu or governaunce scantly is writen in al Holy Writt ten lines" (15).

Pecock contrasts scripture with an authoritative text that does provide sufficient treatment of God's law—all the teaching on various moral points—and that can be considered a proper basis for arguments about Christian belief and behavior. He defines this text as the book of reason, the subject of the previous chapter. The book of reason, rather than scripture, provides the script that authorizes and justifies codes of conduct and patterns of moral behavior in the textual community. Pecock says, "Scripture is not ground to eny oon such seid vertu, governaunce, deede, or trouthe . . . but oonly doom of natural resoun, which is moral lawe of kinde and moral lawe of God, writun in the book of lawe of kinde in mennis soulis, prentid into the image of God, is ground to ech such vertu, governaunce, deede, and trouthe" (*Repressor*, 18). Man comes to know the "moral lawe of kinde" by the use of his rational faculties: in making man, God meant for him to seek, learn, and come to know moral truths on his own, without supernatural aid. Furthermore, because the book of the moral law of nature predates the Bible, it is more essential, for acquiring knowledge of man's service to God, than the Bible. As we saw in the previous chapter, Christ's moral precepts were not drawn from the physical text of the Bible—which was not yet written—but rather from the law of kind, written on the human soul by God: "And sithen it is so, that alle the trouthis of lawe of kinde whiche Crist and hise Apostlis taughten and wroten weren bifore her teching and writing, and weren writen bifore in thilk solempnest inward book or inward writing of resounis doom passing alle outward bookis in profite to men for to serve God . . . it muste needis folewe that noon of the seid treuthis is groundid in the wordis or writingis of Crist or of the Apostlis, but in the seid inward preciose book and writing buried in mannis soule" (31). The truths of the "lawe of kinde," which books such as Pecock's register, are even more fundamental than the truths found in the Bible: this law existed before the New or Old Testament was written, "before the daies of Abraham and of Iewis" (20).

That the Bible is secondary to the primary book of reason with regard to the moral "lawe of kinde," is suggested when Pecock writes, "Whanne euere and where euere in Holy Scripture or out of Holy Scripture be writen eny point or eny governaunce of the seide lawe of kinde, it is more verrily writen in the book of mannis soule than in the outward book of parchemin or of velim; and if eny seming discorde be bitwixe the wordis writen in the outward book of Holy Scripture and the doom of resoun, write in mannis soule and herte, the wordis so writen withoutforth oughten be expowned and be interpretid and brought forto accorde with the doom of resoun in thilk mater" (*Repressor*, 25). Pecock goes so far as to suggest that any conflict between moral knowledge provided by the Bible and that provided by our doom of reason must be resolved in favor of the doom of reason. Pecock provides an example of this kind of interpretive activity in the *Donet* when he notes that we must not believe everything we are told by the prophet Isaiah. We must fill out what "Isaie" tells us about what Christ ate when he lived on earth because Isaiah does not tell the whole story. Isaiah "makith mensioun how that Crist schulde ete buttir and hony, and he makith there no mensioun of eny othire mete which Crist schulde ete; and yitt if eny man wolde make him so curiose that therfore butter and hony comprehendid and conteined alle metis which Crist ete, and alle the metis which we oughte to ete, he were to moche curiose and to moch ful of vanite" (*Donet*, 117). Just as we must infer that Christ ate more kinds of food than Isaiah mentions, we must infer that the seven gifts that Isaiah tells us "weren in crist" cannot possibly "comprehende and conteine alle virtues and alle oure goostly governauncis" (*Donet*, 116). When we are puzzling over God's meaning in passages like this one, knowledge and training in the doom of reason are essential. Pecock says, "Without the leerning and kunning of the seid lawe of kinde and of doom of resoun, Holy Scripture may not be sufficiently and dewly undirstonde and expowned in no place where he spekith of lawe of God not being positiif lawe of feith" (*Repressor*, 44). Pecock writes that his books, and others like them, are "so necessarie forto expowne or interprete or glose dewly and treuly Holi Scripture in alle placis where he spekith of Goddis lawe and service" (*Repressor*, 47). Before he can properly interpret God's meaning in scripture, in reference to his moral law, man must first contemplate God's meaning, given to him in the book of reason. Pecock's notion that God's meaning is given primarily in the book of reason is a powerful refutation of the Lollard belief that the Bible alone provides direct access to God's mind and therefore provides the sole, authoritative basis for determining Christian belief and behavior.

The notion that God's moral law is given primarily in the book of reason, and not in the Bible, also constitutes a powerful refutation of the Lollard belief that the laity do not need the clergy's expositions of biblical meaning. As we have seen in the previous chapter, Pecock secures an important role for the clergy as the learned interpreters of the book of reason: their training in logic and moral philosophy sets them apart from those who have not spent long years of study honing skills of syllogistic reasoning. Those who are skilled in deciphering God's moral law in the book of reason have the authority to determine the meaning of scripture in passages rehearsing moral truths. Trained clergymen have the requisite "leerning and kunning of the seid lawe of kinde and doom of resoun" that enables them to expound the places in "Holy Scripture" in which God's law is discussed (*Repressor*, 44). These learned members of the clergy are the natural authority, therefore, over moral matters in scripture. In theory, the moral passages of scripture should be open and clear to a layman who has trained himself completely in Pecock's books. However, the education that Pecock offers, in the skills and methods needed for reading God's moral law, does not necessarily prepare readers with the full training they need to recognize God's moral truths by reading scripture on their own. It is noteworthy that Pecock does not offer readers much in the way of strategies for interpreting difficult passages of scripture, nor does he spend a great deal of space modeling exegetical procedures. In the *Donet*, he confirms that his intention is not for lay readers to read the Bible directly, even if they possess its interpretive key (in terms of their skill in apprehending God's moral law in the book of reason). He mentions that he has written another book that will fill out his teaching on God's moral law in his system of four tables. Instead of consulting scripture, Pecock's readers will be able to access the relevant passages witnessing and rehearsing God's moral teaching in the book of reason by reading a book called "the witnessing of the iiii tables." Pecock's system of the four tables, comprising man's moral duty toward God, self, and neighbor, provides the most extensive treatment of God's moral law available. Each point of each table is "witnessed in holy scripture," in both the "oolde testament and in the newe"; indeed, Pecock states that scripture speaks "ful moche" of the points of his four tables, in terms of scripture's "litteral undirstonding." The rehearsals or witnessings that scripture offers, of God's moral law, will be laid out in the book called "the witnessing of the iiij tables" as well as in a cheaper, shorter book called "the provoker," or "the forth caller of Cristen men," which is necessary because the "witnessing of the iiij tables" is "ful longe, and, peraventure, ouer costiose to pore men." The shorter version is made "into the esement of pore men" who cannot afford the longer original. This will make it possible for all men to see "wherinne ech point of the iiii seid tables of Goddis lawe schal be by scripture at the leest oonis y-witnessid in general" (*Donet*, 177). These books, both the longer and shorter versions, will bring to the eyes and ears of lay readers the relevant passages in scripture that make "remembrauncis" of the precepts of God's moral law. Once Pecock has educated readers in this moral law with books like the *Reule*, the *Donet*, and the *Folewer to the Donet*, he will bring to their attention the passages in scripture that can be interpreted and understood according to the book of reason. Once they are equipped with the interpretive key for these passages in scripture, they can see for themselves the various ways in which scriptural passages, mediated by Pecock, remind us of God's moral law.

Pecock does acknowledge the possibility that members of the laity will read the biblical text itself, as opposed to texts like the "witnessing of the iiij tables," which provide only bits and pieces of scripture, but he emphasizes that this reading practice necessitates the supervision of the learned clergy. Laymen should be able "forto reede in the Bible and forto studye and leerne ther in, with help and counseil of wise and weel leerned clerkis and with licence of her governour the bischop" (*Repressor*, 37). Those who are most expert in God's moral law, and therefore adept in reading the book of reason, will teach the members of the laity the correct understanding of the Bible. The clergy are in charge not only of the licensing process, which polices lay access to the Bible, but also of the Bible's interpretive key, since they have the strongest foundation in philosophical principles and rules of logic. Though the concept of the book of reason as an interpretive key for understanding God's moral law in scripture is inherently democratic, opening up scriptural interpretation to all who possess the faculty of reason, it is the learned clergy who will instruct laymen in ways of arriving at the right interpretations of the book of reason and thus in the book of God's Word. Pecock repeats this idea later on, suggesting that the stability of biblical interpretation depends on the laypeople's recognition of the need for these learned clerks and their awareness that they require a rational training in the doom of reason to confront the Bible:

> Ful weel oughten alle persoones of the lay party not miche leerned in moral philsophy and lawe of kinde forto make miche of clerkis weel leerned in moral philsophy, that tho clerkis schulden helpe tho lay persoones forto aright undirstonde Holy Scripture in alle tho placis in which Holy Scripture rehercith the bifore spoken conclusions and treuthis of moral philsophy, that is to seie lawe of kinde. Forwhy withoute tho clerkis so leerned in moral philsophy and with oute her direccioun the now seid lay per- soones schulen not esily, lightly, and anoon have the dew undir- stonding of Holy Scripture in the now seid placis. (*Repressor*, 46)

The layman's easy, light, and immediate understanding of scripture is linked directly to his acceptance of the interpretation of learned clerks, who will help him to "aright undirstonde" the Bible in relevant passages. For Pecock, the uniformity and stability of biblical interpretation—in bringing to light its "dew undirstonding"—depends on the mutual cooperation of clergy and laity. The lay members of his textual community must voluntarily seek out learned clerks and "make miche" of them as resources, asking questions about the best way to understand difficult biblical language. This scenario for the teaching of the interpretation of the Bible gives authority and power to the clergy in their assessment of scripture's "dew undirstonding." Though laymen have the mental capacity to undergo the same sort of training in moral philosophy as clerks, as I pointed out in the previous chapter, and are thus inherently capable of learning how to interpret God's moral law in scripture for themselves, they lack the training in scriptural exegesis that permits the clergy to arrive at the correct meaning of difficult passages in the Bible. This picture of the layman and cleric working side by side, puzzling together through scripture, constitutes an effort to place control over scripture's interpretation with the clergy. The fact that Pecock does not provide extensive guidance, in his books, on strategies for biblical exegesis shows that he felt that it would be safer for this guidance in interpreting the Bible to be a "hands-on" experience.

Pecock's notion of the role of the doom of reason in teaching us to interpret scripture's meaning, in passages relating to moral law, suggests the possibility that these learned clerics may read the Bible in a disinterested way. Pecock's system for right reading of moral truth in the Bible resembles, to some degree, the Lollard idea of right reading as one that subsumes the individual and negates the possibility of perverse interpretations; indeed, his notion that the interpretations made by authorities such as the church fathers must also be carefully investigated and reduced to their rational principles shows an affinity with the Lollard distrust of human readings of the Bible guided by personal assumptions and ideals rather than rational procedures. The notion that we can perceive God's meaning, and ideas, prior to our encounter with the language of scripture has major implications for the interpretive community that Pecock imagines: if we approach scripture with rational preconceptions of the meaning it will hold for us, then our interpretation will be carefully guided by these preconceptions. The kind of interpretive community that Pecock has in mind is tightly controlled, so that only readings confirmed or based in the authoritative book of reason are acceptable.

Learning to read the book of reason therefore plays an important role in explicating the passages of scripture relating to God's moral law: the book of reason essentially constitutes an interpretive key to scripture. By providing a fuller treatment of his moral law in the book he imprints on man's soul, God invites man to have a major part in determining scripture's meaning in rational, systematic ways: Pecock erodes faith in the possibility of open access to God's meaning through moral preparation when he claims that scriptural meaning must be resolved with recourse to the truth that man finds through his reason. Once we have developed skill in learning to perceive moral truths through the use of the rational faculty, and through the understanding of philosophical principles, we are prepared to recognize these truths in the biblical text. If God printed his image on man's soul to help man see, by himself, the moral truths that would guide his actions, then he intended man's perceiving mind to play a key role in arriving at the meaning of those truths in the sacred text of scripture. Meekness alone will not suffice to complete this divinely ordained task. On the other hand, the institutional authority of the church is not equipped to locate the divine meaning either if its exegetical practices are not guided by knowledge acquired from the doom of reason. Reading the natural "law of kinde" (*Repressor*, 18) in the book of reason, before we encounter scripture, prepares us to judge the validity of arguments made about God's law based on readings of scripture.

For Pecock, it is impossible for us to avoid bringing this common frame of reference to our reading of the biblical text because it is our moral duty to seek out these truths before we seek their rehearsal and confirmation in the Bible; therefore, it is also impossible to conceive of a meaning arising from the biblical text without the agency of the "perceiving intellect and its analytical categories."[22] When we resolve contradictions in scripture according to the doom of reason, and when we interpret scripture according to the moral law of philosophy, we bring to the text our own cognitive perceptions that participate in the creation and shaping of relevant meaning. It is important, however, to qualify this idea of the perceiving intellect helping to construct, shape, and produce meaning—Pecock suggests, not that the individual reader actually constructs the Bible's meaning, but that the individual reader who has acquired knowledge in the book of reason will already be familiar with God's intention and will therefore bring this divine "analytical category" to the reading of the Bible. For Pecock, the shaping of meaning is not an individual or subjective experience; rather, members of the interpretive community will bring to their reading of the text common assumptions about universal truths and their understanding of the divine intention, acquired through study in the book of reason.

Through his notion of the interpretive key of reason, Pecock proposes a different kind of disinterested reading: while our reading of the Bible will be informed by our common cultural experience, our social rules and customs, and our specific ways of thinking—our own prerogatives and analytical categories—this reading will not vary from individual to individual. For Pecock, readers who have become expert in God's most authoritative book of reason bring their own analytical categories to the Bible and therefore can be said to participate in the construction of meaning, but these analytical categories are divine. The way that we construct the Bible's meaning, as we interpret it according to our doom of reason, will be informed, not by our personal, subjective experience, but by an experience common to our humanity, which is ordered by God. The likelihood of variation of meaning is decreased by the controls within the doom of reason, by which we find truths essential and common to us all. Meaning is predetermined by the constraints of the interpretive community; interpretation is controlled by our common ground in the divinely ordained doom of reason. With this notion that the interpretive grid of reason provides the framework for uniform and stable readings of the Bible, Pecock implicitly rehabilitates the practice of exegesis. In response to the Lollard claim that disinterested reading is possible through meekness and charity, Pecock suggests that when an interpretive community is grounded in reason and united in common beliefs, assumptions, and norms based on universal truths and experiences, a disinterested reading of God's intention is indeed possible. This theory rehabilitates traditional exegesis because it claims that the interpretive grid of readers is natural and God-given.

The way that Pecock defines a form of disinterested reading, in accordance with the interpretive grid of reason, echoes to some extent the Lollard criticism of self-interested readings, as well as their cautions about an overreliance on church authority and exegetical tradition for interpretations of God's meaning. Pecock recommends a reading practice that insists on the authority of the individual to recognize moral truths, rather than the authority of traditional exegetical responses to prescribe truth, but at the same time he establishes an ideal reading practice that has no room for self-interested readings. If individual readers perform correct, rational readings of the biblical text, those readers will arrive at a uniform meaning. In her study of the culture of reading in the later Middle Ages, Laurel Amtower suggests that there is a clear divide between reading practices that afford a private response and reading practices in which institutional conditions dominate private response. She says that the scholastic reading process "was completed less through the intuitive inner sense of the individual reader than through adherence to customary function and the imposition of typological meaning overtop the strata of common lived experience." The individual was not encouraged to respond in a personal way to a text: "By means of the exegetical method, individual responsiveness or responsibility must be universalized to deemphasize the particularized experience of the reader."[23] Amtower argues that the scholastic approach was founded "on an insistence upon authority outside the individual for recognizing and stating moral or ethical 'truths.'"[24] What is interesting about Pecock's ideal reading practice is the way that he negates this opposition between a personal, individual reading and an institutionally imposed response: for Pecock, the person who is properly equipped with training in the interpretive grid of reason will arrive at the universal response that the institution, working from the same grid, will also hold to be authoritative. In this way, Pecock allows more room for the particular experience of the reader, as long as that experience involves the reader fully realizing and bringing to perfection the image of God printed on his soul. Pecock's systematic development of a model for a reading practice rooted in the doom of reason illuminates his awareness of the danger posed by heretical and erroneous interpretations of the Bible based on "'interior understanding' of God's word," or on misunderstandings of moral truths.[25] For Pecock, a Lollard can err as easily as a clerk or a learned authority like Jerome if methods of reading are not firmly founded on the doom of reason. The stability of uniform interpretation cannot be located in the authoritative institutional church or the tradition of exegetical commentary because of the potential for error; a firmer foundation for a united interpretive community exists in the interpretive grid of reason.

Pecock's implied notion of an interpretive community united by the doom of reason can be illuminated by reference to the work of Stanley Fish on interpretive communities. Fish bases his reader-oriented hermeneutics on the notion that there is "no independent text to constrain our reading of it."[26] Rather, what constrains and determines our reading of certain texts is the interpretive community, "made up of those who share interpretive strategies not for reading (in the conventional sense) but for writing texts, for constituting their properties, and assigning their intentions. In other words, these strategies exist prior to the act of reading and therefore determine the shape of what is read, rather than, as is usually assumed, the other way around." Fish speaks of a stability not in the text itself but in "the makeup of interpretive communities. . . . Of course this stability is always temporary (unlike the longed for and timeless stability of the text)."[27] The stability of a community's interpretation of a text is guaranteed, as Mary McClintock Fulkerson points out, by "communal convictions and the deeply embedded habits that constrain them" rather than by "private whim."[28] As Stephen Moore cautions with a quotation from Steven Rendall's opinion of Fish's theory, "Fish's position is *not* "that 'there's nothing out there, it's all in your head,' but rather that what we perceive is always given its shape and meaning by interpretive acts."[29] Fish's concept of the importance of the interpretive community's role in constituting the meaning of the text invites investigation of "interpretive rules, stratagems, and traditions by which we appropriate [the text]."[30] Because meaning, for Fish, is "constrained by communal rules for reading, and not by some 'objective' perspicuous sense contained within a text,"[31] the object of our inquiry should be the operation of the interpretive community in developing and dictating the meaning of a text.

As James Simpson points out, Fish's work helps us see that "all interpretive traditions, whether they recognize it or not, do this: they all posit an opaque ground of meaning that is apparently illumined by the work, but that in reality illuminates the work. For the ground of meaning evidently stands *a priori* to interpretation of the work." Simpson points out that some interpretive traditions frankly admit this hermeneutic strategy while others keep it quiet. Augustine's rules for reading according to charity, for example, openly admit of a "prejudice in favour of a predetermined reading."[32] In his notion of an interpretive community governed by reason, Pecock similarly posits a kind of "hermeneutic tradition [that] is quite explicit about the *a priori*, prejudicial status of the meanings at which interpretation must arrive."[33] This distinguishes him from the Lollards, whose positivistic call for the right reading of the text according to God's intention locates meaning in the text and therefore "might seem to minimize the powers of the interpretive community."[34] Pecock belongs instead to a tradition of theorists who "frankly recognized the ways in which the Bible needs to be remade by human intervention" and who "justified the reader's active intervention in the remaking of the biblical text."[35] Pecock's notion that discrepancies between the Bible and the doom of reason must be resolved in favor of the doom of reason implies that the way we find God's intention is by first looking outside the biblical text, at the world around us, with the aid of our rational intellect. If we can find God's intent by reading it in the book that he writes on our souls, then we have safely found a reliable strategy (safer than meekness or moral rectitude) for locating predetermined readings in the Bible, according to God's sense. Because of Pecock's vision of an interpretive community guided by an a priori awareness of God's divine meaning, we must apply Fish's arguments with caution: Fish's argument that "everything about a text, its very making in some profound sense, is constructed by the interpretive community" and his repudiation of "all attempts to locate something outside, prior to and constraining the operations of that community" stand in contrast to Pecock's notion that God's sense is written on our soul, in his image, and that we are meant to find his truths through our rational intellect.[36]

Fish's focus on the strategies of interpretive communities in the activity of writing, rather than reading texts, is useful for contemporary scholars who wish to relocate attention "from the Bible itself to the site of interpretive communities and their conventions": such an examination focuses on "the institutional and larger socio-economic and political forces that support the interpretive grids of communities."[37] These kinds of studies work from the understanding that "reading and interpretive strategies are socially, politically, and institutionally situated, and that they draw their energy and force from the subject positions of readers and interpreters."[38] For Pecock, members of the interpretive community constitute the text as God directs them; he suggests that a group of readers educated in the doom of reason both through rational training (in tools like the syllogism) and through observation and sensory experience of God's universal truths in the mundane world will arrive at the same, correct interpretation of God's moral law in the Bible. The interpretive grid of the reading community that Pecock envisions is supported, from his perspective, not by institutional, socioeconomic and political forces but by God's universal laws; although modern readers might view Pecock's ideal, rational reader as a situated reader, working from a certain subject position, Pecock would view this reader's interpretive agency as natural and God-given. What Pecock aims to do is to create an educated community that will consistently produce unanimity and correct meaning; what in fact happens is that this meaning is situated and supported by what modern readers would see as institutional, socioeconomic and political forces, in terms of the philosophical principles and moral truths that Pecock sees operating in the mundane world in the hierarchical relationships in the social order between knights and servants, between gift givers and receivers, between husband and wife, and between children and adults. In his rehabilitation of glossing, Pecock claims that the interpretive grid of a community of rational readers, with their minds working in the way that God has intended, is universal and free of bias or corruption. His analogies suggest to modern readers, however, that the interpretive actions of the community can never be this objective: "Accounts of what is in the text are extensions of deeply embedded interests, articulations of the world, and . . . constraints that include relations of power."[39] For Pecock, the accounts provided by readers trained in the doom of reason are extensions of God's universal, divinely ordained truths, natural structures, and essential realities.

For Pecock, the stability of biblical meaning is guaranteed by the stability of the "interpretive rules, stratagems, and traditions by which we appropriate [the text]."[40] However, given that Pecock feels that these interpretive rules and stratagems by which we read the biblical text are not self-interested but rational and God-given, he might object to the notion that interpretive communities are only temporarily stable. For Pecock, the condition of the interpretive community surrounding the biblical text is not "fragile" because it is governed by the laws of reason, decreed by God, which are neither temporary nor fragile.[41] Even if he were willing to admit that over time human reason must reevaluate traditional assumptions and values, leading men to reinterpret the biblical text so that it remains meaningful for human societies, he would still place human reason at the center of the interpretive community.

In theory, then, laity and clergy alike have the tools to train themselves for a productive encounter with divine meaning in the Bible. In practice, however, independent reading of the Bible, however much it is preceded by study of moral philosophy, is not part of Pecock's educational scheme for the laity.[42] Pecock's use of the Bible in his *Repressor* and the *Reule of Crysten Religioun* shows that even when he is presenting excerpts of biblical passages to his readers he is always in control of their interpretation. In the *Reule*, for instance, a book that teaches the truths of reason and of faith, it is clear that the members of Pecock's textual community are not to learn the truths of faith from analyzing biblical language. Pecock's discussion of the truths of faith in the *Reule* centers on the biblical meanings exposed and brought to light by Pecock, emblematizing the idea that the control over the Bible's interpretation rests with the clergy.

Throughout the *Reule*, Pecock shows caution in treating scripture and attempts to prevent readers from focusing their attention directly on scriptural language. For example, rather than highlighting the scriptural passages that reveal to us the truths of faith and thus opening these passages to lay inquiry, Pecock's method of teaching faith in the *Reule* tends to mix together truths that we know from the Bible and truths that we know through reason. Rather than isolating biblical passages for treatment, Pecock blends biblical truths with his own teaching, making his own interpretation of the Bible the reader's focus. In his treatment of God's benefits and punishments, the second and third matters of the seven covered in the *Reule*, Pecock notes that some benefits are known only by faith, whereas others are known by a "miztioun" of reason and faith (*Reule*, 202). The Bible alone tells us that God is our "supernatural eend and best supernatural good." We cannot know, from reason alone, that God intends for us a "myche higher" reward and end than "oure natural eende and oure natural best good." The Bible reveals to us this truth that we cannot know "by eny certeinte neither by eny greet likelihode of resoun leening to the mater in it silf" (106). Once this truth has been discovered by faith, however, our reason can discover the benefits that relate to our final end, or our heavenly reward, such as what happens to the soul at death, what happens to the soul in heaven, and whether our supernatural reward will be in proportion with the labor we endured to receive it. Our reason can derive other truths relating to the soul's immortality and the relationship of body to soul in heaven (110). Because faith— our knowledge that God is our supernatural end and greatest good— is "presupposid" and "requirid" before we can start to rationalize about the nature of our heavenly reward, the truths that we arrive at in this way are "not purely and hooly and fully profis of resoun, but they ben rather for her myztioun to be seid profis of feith" (202).

In his treatment of the truths that proceed from the first truth concerning God as our heavenly reward, such as the separation of the soul from the body, Pecock reveals that these truths are also witnessed and confirmed by holy scripture. For instance, the Bible tells us that "oure soule in his hool and ful substaunce is departable from oure body by deeth maad in the body, withoute eny hurting of the soulis substaunce and withoute eny apeirement of his resoning and his will-ing." We can come "to the knowing of this trouthe" by reading pas-sages in the Gospel of John and the Gospel of Matthew. It is important to note, however, that Pecock supplies these passages in Latin and does not comment on them or direct the reader's attention to their interpretation. His reference to the Bible looks like this: "It is writen Johan x chapter thus: 'Bonus pastor animan suam ponit pro ouibus suis,' et parum post, 'et animam meam pono pro ouibus meis'; Also Johan x chaptiter thus: 'ProPterea me pater deligit quia ego pono animam mean et iterum sumam eam. Nemo tollit eam a me sed ego pono eam a me ipso; Potestatem habeo ponendi eam et potestatem habeo iterum sumendi eam'; Also Mathew x chapter thus: 'Nolite timere eos qui occident corpus, animam autem non possunt occidere, sed pocius enim timete qui potest corpus et animan perdere in gehennam'" (*Reule*, 110). Throughout this entire section on God's benefits and punishments, the biblical passages are supplied in Latin; this is not consistent in the rest of Pecock's teaching on the seven matters. Sometimes he provides translations, and sometimes he simply cites the passage without supplying the biblical words. In this case, providing the quotation in Latin, without a translation or a gloss, does not give much food for his reader's meditation. Though he acknowledges that this truth is presented to us in the Bible, Pecock does not focus his reader's attention on the biblical text.

Instead, Pecock directs readers to the way that we know this same truth by reason, and he spends a great deal more time and attention on the way that we can come to "knowing of this trouthe" by reason (*Reule*, 110). If Pecock were interested in training readers to read the Bible, why would he not supply a gloss, modeling correct exegetical practice? If this truth is revealed to us by these biblical passages, why is it necessary to spend more time showing how this truth can also be known by reason? I suggest that Pecock is directing readers away from the exact words of the Bible and toward his rational proofs, hoping to engage the reader's intellect in a safer manner. He goes on to argue that we can be sure that the soul is not injured in death because we know "by experience" that the soul is not hurt "in her instrumentis" when the body is sick; we know that the soul's faculties of reason and will are not impaired at death because we have all seen that "ful ofte in siiknes and in point of dying the soule hath clerer undirstonding of al maner of trouthis" (111). Pecock draws his readers' attention to truths that are evident to their reason, asking them to bring their experience to bear on this truth rather than asking them to puzzle out the meaning of scripture. By prioritizing the arguments from reason in these passages, spending more time and effort on rational evidences, Pecock indicates that only the rational arguments that follow from truths of faith are up for debate; the biblical passages themselves receive scant critical attention. The Bible's function is to generate truths that are revealed to the laity by scholars like Pecock; the text ceases to be the object of attention once these truths are brought into the consideration of the doom of reason.

By blurring distinctions between the biblical text and the rational proofs that follow from what the Bible tells us, Pecock controls his readers' access to the Bible. In his treatment of God's benefits that we know by faith alone, to which "natural resoun may not atteine by certeinte neither by eny strong probabilnes," he supplies citations to passages in the Bible (*Reule*, 202). He goes on to preview the kind of interpretive strategies he will use to clarify the meanings of the relevant scriptural passages. He states that in his "rehercels of these articles of benefetis" grounded in scripture, he will not let the words of scripture stand alone. He cautions, however, that "though in the rehercels of these articles of benefetis more schal be said thane what therof is expressed in holy scripture, yitt not more schal be rehercid than what is expressed in holy scripture and thane folewith lightly and nigh by doom of resoun nedisly or likely of it which is expressed in holy scripture" (202–3). Everything that Pecock will say, even that which is "over it which is expressely in holy scripture," will "longith to feith." What is noteworthy about Pecock's interpretive method is that it is not always possible to distinguish the actual scriptural truth from that which follows "nedisly" from scripture and that which follows "oonly likely or probabily" from an article of scripture (203). This is partially because Pecock does not actually supply the words of scripture in the passages that follow. For example, in his teaching on Satan's temptation of Eve, Pecock paraphrases the biblical texts and concludes his treatment with statements like "as is writun genesis iii chapiter," or "as may be had Johan xv chapiter" (205). He does not provide the exact biblical wording, nor does he draw the reader's attention to the distinction between what we know about the loss of paradise from scripture itself and what we know about the Fall from the doom of reason.

It is particularly interesting that Pecock uses this method when he is discussing truths of faith, such as the sacraments, that are controversial. Pecock treats the sacraments as one of the ways in which we win salvation and forgiveness, and hence one of the benefits or gifts of God. He treats the sacraments of baptism, the Eucharist, and penance under the topic of God's benefits that we know by faith alone, saying, for example, that once man has sinned he can be "clensid and be recouncilid ayen to grace by repentaunce and knowleching or schrifte." We know this from what is written in "ii Petri iii chapiter, i Johan i capitulo, tite iii chapiter, James v chapiter" (*Reule*, 206). Pecock does not supply the actual biblical wording that confirms the need for shrift, nor does he refer to current controversies among the Lollards about the necessity of confession to a priest. By omitting the biblical passage and simply citing it, he refuses to supply for his reader's analysis the texts that were interpreted in different ways by different people. He also avoids specifics by stating that the Bible reveals to us the need for confession without getting into details about whether this means confession to a priest. He merely asserts that these passages in the Bible tell us about the need for confession, without providing a proper explanation of how biblical language justifies or authorizes sacramental practices.

Pecock does provide biblical quotations confirming the need for penance, however, in an earlier discussion of confession as one of God's benefits that we know through both faith and reason. In this section, he teaches the importance of "knowleching" of sin, or "confessioun or purpos and wil forto it knowleche" (*Reule*, 161). The necessity of the second part of penance, or confession, is revealed by several passages in the Bible: "'Josue seid to nachor sinner thus: 'fili mi, da gloriam domino deo Israel, et confitere, atque indica quid feceris, ne abscondas.' Respondit que achar Josue et dixit ei: 'Vere eto peccaui domino deo Israel, et sic et sic feci.' Also xxxj psalm thus: 'Dixi, confitebor aduersum me injusticiam meam domino et tu remisisti impietatem peccati mei'; Also Job xxx chapiter it is writun thus: 'Si abscondi quasi homo peccatum meum quasi dixisset non': Also Isaie xliij chapiter: "Narra siquid habes ut justificeris'" (162). Again, the recourse to Latin here indicates that Pecock is reluctant to direct the attention of his lay readers to the exact wording of the Bible—words that might produce varying interpretations. The absence of a gloss similarly fails to highlight for readers anything but the most general statement on confession that the church presents as an article of faith. Pecock treats the biblical passages that justify the ordination of the priesthood and the sacrament of the Eucharist in similar ways, telling readers that God has ordained these as "positiife lawis" by "voluntarie assignementis" but failing to provide further information on how biblical language has made this clear (309–17). Pecock does not focus readers' attention on anything beyond the basic information that God has given as justification for sacramental practices in certain biblical passages, passages that take on almost a symbolic value as Pecock refuses to engage with them and thus with the controversy that surrounded the sacerdotal functions of priests in late medieval England. Instead, he directs readers to his rational assessment of the need for these positive laws and ordinances, arguing that man would have instituted the sacraments and the priesthood regardless of God's direct orders (317–18). If readers are to engage in thinking about current controversial issues surrounding the priesthood and the sacraments, they are to do so with the faculty of reason as their guide instead of the Bible.

The foregoing analysis of Pecock's use of the Bible in his teaching on faith in the *Reule* suggests that Pecock does not wish to encourage readers to seek out the truths of faith for themselves in the Bible. His method in the *Reule* is to declare the meaning of a certain biblical passage, to provide either a reference to this passage or to provide it in its entirety in Latin, and to move on quickly to rational evidences and arguments that prove the same truth. He does not model, for readers, the interpretive strategies that have enabled him to derive the Bible's "right and dew undirstonding" (*BF,* 230). Though he is careful to refer readers to the relevant biblical passages, he does not engage in analysis of the way that these passages confirm the church's articles of faith. It is important to note, however, that though he does not provide opportunities or training for readers who wish to apply their intellects to the exposition of scripture, Pecock is determined to permit the laity to think rationally about the truths of faith rather than simply to accept articles of faith delivered to them by the church. In his view, telling the laity what to believe, by delivering an article of belief "in his owne naked forme as articles of believe ben woned be delivered to the lay peple," is not as effective as the provision of evidences that help to constrain the reason of "every competently wittid man" (*Reule*, 91). So even if Pecock is not willing to provide extensive translations of biblical passages that have given rise to controversy among the Lollards, it is significant that he is willing to reason with lay readers about these controversial issues. For example, he provides a host of arguments proving that prayers of "friends," especially those that are paid for, do not help us to earn God's favor. Selling the benefits of God is a fruitless endeavor because "no man may sille eny thing save which is his owne," and God's friendship is his own to offer (*Reule*, 189). The kinds of rational arguments that Pecock marshals against the selling of spiritual goods could be powerful in the hands of a layman; even if these arguments against clerical corruption did not draw on biblical passages, they would permit a lay reader to challenge a cleric through the evidence of reason. Pecock therefore gives readers the tools to challenge the clergy in powerful ways, and he implies that the learned clergy must prepare themselves for these kinds of discussions. Issues like the sacraments, the endowment of the priesthood (*Reule*, 328–33), and clerical corruption are not off limits to lay readers; discussing them will not provoke independent, dangerous thought if the laity is properly trained in rational modes of thought and argumentation.

The way that Pecock gives textual form to the truths of faith in his books insists that interpretive control over the Bible belongs in the hands of the learned clergy. His notion that the book of reason provides an interpretive key to scripture similarly carves out an important role for clerical exegesis. It is one thing to pile up arguments that reinforce the need for scripture to be mediated by clerics to the laity; it is another things entirely, however, to convince lay readers who are eager to get their hands on the Bible that they should let others tell them what it means. The vehemence with which the Lollard texts cited in the introduction to this chapter link the modern-day church with Antichrist because of its self-interested glosses of the Bible indicates that it would take a lot to win back the trust and faith of these "yvel disposid men of the lay partie" (*Reule*, 19). To encourage readers to trust to clerical expositions of scripture, Pecock stresses the long hours of study and extensive labor that clerics have undergone to gain expertise in reading the Bible. Pecock emphasizes that interpreting the Bible is a highly specialized task, requiring particular skills and training, by likening the trained clergy to professionals in the "kingis lawe," who have experience and special training in reading statutes and legal documents (*BF*, 228). Clerics possess specialized knowledge, from "long before going scole in logik, and in philsophie, and aftirward by liik long labour in divinite," that enables them to acquire "righte and dewe undirstonding of the highe and hard writing of oure bileeve in the Bible." Laypeople are not incapable of developing the same specialized skills—there is no innate intellectual distinction between them and the clergy—but the reality is that they have "slepid fro such studie, and laboure, and fro alle the sleightis forto helpe hem therinne" (*BF*, 229). The learning of the clergy, rather than their status as ordained priests, makes them rightful interpreters of scripture, and the laity should leave this task to the professionals.

Pecock shows some awareness, however, that emphasizing the training, knowledge, and skill of the clergy may not be enough to overcome the distrust that has grown up among the "lay partie" of clerical expositions of scripture. He realizes that the clergy have to win over the laity and that their learning only goes so far in convincing the laity to accept their authority. The members of the laity who "protesten and knowlechen that they wolen not fecche and leerne her feith at the clergie of Goddis hool chirche in erthe; neither they as for leerning and kunning of her feith wolen obeie to the clergie or to the chirche" need to be reassured of the good intentions of the clergy (*BF*, 109–10). The clergy needs the respect and admiration of the laity, a point that Pecock emphasizes continually throughout his corpus. Pecock acknowledges the powerful role that emotional bonds between clergy and laity can play in the struggle to win the laity's allegiance and obedience when he suggests that lay people fell into error, not because Wyclif convinced them with rational arguments, but because of the "affeccioun whiche the comoun peple hath" for Wyclif and his followers, and because of their "truste to the leving of thoo persoonis" (*Reule*, 96). Affection, respect, and trust are important weapons in the struggle to reinforce the authority and power of the learned clergy; Pecock's realization of this, and his attempts to harness these weapons for the defense of orthodoxy, are the subject of the next chapter.

s e v e n

Lay-Cleric Relations in
the Textual Community

As we saw in the last chapter, Pecock reinforces the authority of the
learned clergy in a variety of ways, attempting to convince lay readers
to "fele how necessarie and nedeful it is to hem, that substancial
clerkis be in scole of logic, philsophie, and divinte." He stresses that
his lay readers are to be "enformed and directed by tho clerkis," who
will prevent them from wandering "a side fro the eeven right wey of
trouthe" (*BF*, 119). Though the reader of the *Book of Faith* is to learn
to accept his dependency on the clergy, Pecock changes tack slightly
in the *Repressor*, claiming that lay readers must take a more active role
in their religious education. He describes a curate's responsibility to
educate his lay subjects, saying: "Euen as a nurisch or a modir is not
bounde forto alwey and for evere fede her children and putte meete in
her mouthis, but sche muste teche hem that they fede hem silf, (and in
liik maner doun foulis to her briddis,) so a curat may not neither
oughte forto alwey ringe at the eeris of hise suggettis; but he may so
biginne, and afterward he oughte teche hem that they leerne by hem
silf and practize meenis into leerning of good living by hem silf"
(*Repressor*, 219). The curate's job is to teach the layman to fend for
himself—to give him skills and tools in interpretation and argument, for
example, rather than encouraging him to rely constantly on the clergy
for the ready provision of information. In its emphasis on the lay

reader's self-direction and autonomy, this metaphor sits uncomfortably with Pecock's statements throughout the *Repressor* and the *Book of Faith* that emphasize the lay reader's dependency on learned clerics. In fact, many passages in Pecock's corpus display a similar tension, asking readers to envision on the one hand a model of hierarchical relations between authoritative, learned clergy and the laymen who depend on them for knowledge and on the other a picture of an empowered, educated laity gaining the kinds of interpretive skills and expertise that enable them to evaluate their clerical superiors and participate in clerical intellectual activities.

In this chapter, I examine the range of Pecock's thinking on the matter of lay-cleric relations. The variety of positions that he takes on this issue shows a shift in attitudes within Pecock's very corpus of vernacular theology, making Pecock an important witness to the broader transitions in thinking on this subject in late medieval England. Pecock's ideas about the nature of lay-cleric relations witness a larger shift in ideas in late medieval England about the differences between the clerical and lay worlds, the nature of the hierarchy that has structured the interactions of their members, and the power dynamics between those who possess the keys to God's knowledge and those who wish to gain access.

In his efforts to encourage lay agency and spiritual autonomy on the one hand and to reinforce clerical authority and control on the other, Pecock is not alone. In her recent study of Mirk's *Festial*, the most popular and widely used orthodox sermon collection in late fourteenth- and early fifteenth-century England, Judy Ann Ford brings to light one of the problems that orthodox writers faced both during and after the emergence of the Lollard heresy, which sought to invest the layperson with spiritual autonomy and "abolish" or at least diminish "clerical sacerdotal authority."[1] Helen Barr explains that without the "bedrock" of sacerdotal authority the distinction between lay and clerical worlds begins to blur: "With the denial of transubstantiation in the sacrament of the Eucharist, and the belief that auricular confession is unnecessary since contrition alone is necessary to wipe out sin, sacerdotal authority is eliminated and the dividing line between clerical and lay removed."[2] In Lollard ideology, as the lay believer gains more control and authority in his spiritual life, the authority of the clergy diminishes; as the practices that bolster clerical sacerdotal authority are taken over by the laity, this growth of lay agency and independence is tied directly to the erosion of clerical control.

Orthodox writers like Mirk and Pecock had to offer lay readers or audiences an alternative to what Ford describes as "a heretical ideology which set lay agency and clerical authority in opposition."[3] Orthodox writers sought a kind of "ballast" against this ideology,[4] and their search led in a number of directions. The orthodox church responded to this ideology in numerous ways, and these different responses can be positioned on a kind of spectrum ranging from conservative to creative: some authors took several steps back and tried to reinforce traditional hierarchical distinctions between clergy and laity in a way that denied the possibility of lay agency and autonomy, while others took several steps forward by finding ways to foster lay agency without disrupting clerical authority. For the latter, the acquisition of religious knowledge by the laity was not necessarily "a zero-sum game wherein every gain by the laity is registered as a loss for clerical authority."[5] At one extreme end of the spectrum we can situate the work of those representing the most conservative reaction of the institutional church to the threat of lay agency in spiritual education and practices, typified by the work of Nicholas Love. Love offers lay readers a way to conceptualize their place within Christian society that limits their agency and capacity. He assigns his readers to a state of spiritual immaturity by encouraging them to identify themselves as "simple readers the whiche as childryn haven nede to be fedde with milke of lighte doctrine and not with sadde mete of grete clargie and of hie contemplacion."[6] This positioning of the lay reader can be seen as an appeal to traditional, "'proper' models of lay/clerical interaction," which are described by Fiona Somerset in her examination of the way that various works written in late fourteenth-century England disrupt and renegotiate "normal expectations of lay/clerical interaction." Somerset provides a definition of a "common model of what 'proper' lay/clerical interaction would consist in," such as the assumption that "the clergy and laity are entirely distinct and have their own separate spheres," the notion that "each can be viewed as a seamless, consistent, unified whole," and the idea that "Latin literacy, competence in argumentation, and information the clergy have as a consequence of the kind of education they receive are equally their own particular reserved province."[7] Works that disrupt this model might challenge the fiction of lay uniformity—that all members of the laity can be seen as a homogenous class subordinated to the clergy— or they might show a layperson wielding clerical skills in argumentation thought to be the preserve of the clergy, blurring the traditional separation of clerical and lay capacities and roles. Works that reinforce traditional models of lay-cleric interaction exploit it to uphold the clerically dominated status quo.

Further away from the conservative end of the spectrum are works that reaffirm the clerically dominated status quo at the same time as they make space for the development of lay agency. James Simpson's analysis of John Audelay's "Marcol and Solomon" places it in this category, in terms of the way that it "challenges the consensus" and "directly and critically addresses ecclesiological issues."[8] The criticisms of clerical practice in this poem, highlighting clerical corruption and greed, are an effort not to destabilize or restructure the clerical hierarchy but to reform it: the poem is "a defense of the necessity of orthodox protest against ecclesiastical abuse" rather than a more clearly Lollard protest against the clerical establishment.[9] The criticism of the establishment in this poem is safely contained by the way that Audelay preserves "a clear division of power between clerical and lay institutions" and encourages "traditional relationships of respectful charity between lay and ecclesiastical institutions."[10] While dissent is expressed against the clergy, this dissent is not permitted to erode the power and control of the clerical institutions or destroy the traditional model of "proper" lay-clerical interaction.

The author of the Longleat sermons expresses even harsher criticism of the clergy in a text that was intended for a lay audience, but this criticism is also well contained and prevented from disrupting the "powerful clerical ideology of universal lay subservience to the whole of the clerical hierarchy."[11] Frequently throughout this collection of sermons, preachers are condemned for neglecting their duty of feeding the souls of the laity with "the bred of Goddis word," for being corrupt and greedy, for refusing to censure the upper echelons of society who provide them with luxury and comfort, for preferring to sing in the tavern rather than in holy church, and for sleeping on their

watch over God's flock.[12] However, the Longleat author's interpretation of Christ's distribution of the loaves and the fishes to the Christian
people shows that this text can be read in the same way as Simpson
reads Audelay's "Marcol and Solomon," as a work that promotes "the
reform, but not the restructuring, of the existing institution of the
Church."[13] The Longleat author compares the loaves and the fishes
given by Christ to the spiritual feeding of Christ's flock by preachers,
saying: "With these lovis and these fischis prelates and prechouris
schuldin fedin Cristene peple and settin it aforn hem and thou here
prechinge be nought sufficient to the peple leet hem clepin to Crist
and he schal so multiplin it in the herris of the peple and yevin hem
swiche savour therinne that they schul ben fed sufficiently though the
prechour be unsufficient and feble."[14] For the author of these sermons, "One bad priest does not destroy the priesthood, and does not
demand root and branch restructuring."[15] Though one priest may be
corrupt or unskilled in his duties, the clergy's position as a whole is
not weakened or threatened; rather, it remains entirely distinct from
and superior to the laity and can still be viewed as a consistent whole.
The Longleat author pronounces firmly on the natural hierarchical
position of the clergy in terms of knowledge processes when he suggests that the angel announcing Jesus' birth appeared to shepherds "in
tokene that prelates of holy cherche and lordis and lederis of the peple
whiche wakin besily in good governaunce of here soggettis ben worthy to sen the heghe thingis of God and han the mor grace to knowin
the wil of God." This clear hierarchy between those who are worthy
to contemplate higher mysteries and God's will and those who must
wait to receive this knowledge in turn is emphasized by the message
gleaned by Paul from this story: "Obeyith to youre prelates and to
youre sovereinis and be ye soget and meke to hem for they wakin in
gret besinesse as they schul yevin answere for youre soulis."[16] While
the Longleat preacher may be free with his criticisms of clerical practices and failings, he is careful to emphasize the distinct separation of
the clergy from the laity in terms of function and capabilities. Despite
all of his calls for clerical reform, the Longleat preacher reminds his
lay audience that as a whole the clerical class is above their censure: he
is hesitant to give his lay readers and listeners actual voices with which
to judge and condemn their clerical superiors.

Other orthodox writers sought to integrate certain aspects of the heretical ideology, such as its emphasis on lay spiritual autonomy, in their position on lay-cleric relations. Judy Ann Ford describes Mirk's gentle balancing act between images of lay agency and images of clerical control through this collection of sermons aimed at a rural lay audience: "The laity of Mirk's sermons pursue paths of their own choosing, but all roads leading to salvation run unswervingly through a church in which the ability to perform essential sacraments is held by the clergy alone."[17] In many of the exempla studied by Ford, Mirk offers lay readers "narratives which seem almost Lollard in the amount of agency conferred on lay characters. . . . The *Festial* invites its audience to embrace compelling images of lay agency and spiritual autonomy while at the same time carefully enfolding in those images a far less visible endorsement of the clerically dominated ecclesiological *status quo*."[18] Mirk's efforts to claim for his lay readers a degree of autonomy and control over their spiritual lives, while being careful not to go as far as the Lollards by challenging the hierarchical relationship between laity and clergy, indicate that the emergence of the Lollard heresy necessitated a rethinking of traditional models for lay-cleric interaction in Christian society.

Ford suggests that scholars can better understand this shift in attitudes to the subject of lay-cleric relations by examining the kinds of images offered by prescriptive ecclesiastical literature to lay readers—images such as Pecock's metaphor of the curate as a mother bird encouraging its offspring to become independent. Ford says that if texts like Mirk's sermons

> emphasized images of a passive, obedient laity under the authority of mediating priests, monks and friars, then the autonomy exercised by lay people in their everyday practice of religion may be presumed to have run contrary to the ideological content of the ecclesiology they were taught. If, on the other hand, images of an autonomous, independent laity with direct access to the divine, such as the woman who conversed with Christ in Mirk's story, were typical, then the notion of an oppressive late medieval church posited by the conventional interpretation of the English reformation would be far more difficult to maintain.[19]

Pecock's image of the lay reader as a bird's offspring, learning to find nourishment independently, represents the lay reader's dynamic, self-directed, active pursuit of divine religious knowledge. His choice of this image therefore shows an affinity between his own vision of lay agency and that of Mirk. The tension between Pecock's attempt to bolster the authority of the clergy and his attempt to foster the desire of the laity for a more active role in their education and salvation shows that he is actively seeking, like other orthodox writers, to find a better way to understand the relationship between the laity and the clergy in the Christian community.

Once the idea of lay autonomy had developed troubling implications for clerical authority in Lollard ideology, orthodox writers had to find new ways of conceptualizing and representing the relationship between lay and clerical members of the Christian community. In his attempt to bolster the control and authority of the learned clergy, Pecock sometimes reaches for conservative options, particularly when he reinforces hierarchical distinctions between the laity and clergy that make it clear where authority lies. Subtle shifts in thinking throughout Pecock's works, however, show him reaching for other ways to understand the relationship between the laity and the clergy. Perhaps the most noteworthy aspect of Pecock's vision of lay-cleric relations in his ideal, imagined textual community is his effort to reinforce the authority of the clergy by shifting emphasis away from the concept of hierarchy founded on essential differences, distinctions, and distance between members at each level and toward a concept of hierarchy founded on the willful decision of each member to participate in the community in the name of the common profit. Pecock's ambitious lay readers are not bound and obligated to revere their clerical superiors; instead, they are strongly compelled to respect and honor the clerical hierarchy. Pecock attempts to foster harmonious relations between a powerful, authoritative clergy and an ambitious, autonomous laity by suggesting these two groups are bound to each other by emotional ties of friendship and love.

As I noted in the previous chapter, Pecock reinforces the interpretive controls of the clergy over the Bible in a number of ways. As well as emphasizing the learning and skill of the clergy, and encouraging his lay readers to trust to their expositions of the Bible, Pecock reminds them of their inferior place in the hierarchy that God has put in place: "God hath ordeined and assigned thee forto obeie in bileeving to the clergie, and forto fecche thy feith at hem" (*BF,* 214). By appealing to the notion that there is a natural hierarchical difference between the function and nature of a cleric and a layman, Pecock shuts down notions of lay agency and reinforces the idea that laypeople are ultimately dependent on their clerical teachers for spiritual knowledge. Pecock informs his lay readers that they are "bounden, undir peine of dampnacioun," to believe the articles of faith delivered to them by the church, employing Dionysian hierarchies to emphasize his point (182): just as God made the "chirche of aungels in hevene" with a "disposicioun, and a reule, and an ordre" so that "the netherer and lower aungels" should "take her leerning and informacioun of the othere aungels overer to hem," as Dionysius teaches, so the church on earth is made with a "disposicioun and an ordre to be hadde bitwixe parties and persoones of the same, so that the lower persoones, in thilk disposicioun and ordre, oughten receive her leerning and her informacioun of the overer persoonis to hem, and oughten obeie therinne to thilk overer persoonis to hem" (185). The laypeople are bound to accept the teachings of the ecclesiastical hierarchy, and those who refuse to do so, or who have "rebelled ayens the ierarchies in the chirche and disturble the ierarchiing of the chirche," constitute an "abhominable filthehede in the chirche" (193). It is an utter perversion of God's order for the laity to reverse the proper chain of command by disobeying their clerical superiors—by preferring their knowledge to that of the church.

This analogy puts the concentration of power in the hands of the institutional church instead of affirming the possibility of initiative and agency of the laity. In these passages in the *Book of Faith,* the position of priests as the natural teachers and "superiors" to laymen is divinely ordained: the use of the Dionysian hierarchy in this passage helps justify the doctrine of social difference between cleric and layman. Pecock's remarkably conservative position on this matter mirrors that of orthodox, institutional figures who fought against vernacular translation of the Bible in the early years of the fifteenth century, such as the friar William Butler.[20] In his *determinatio* against Bible translation, Butler draws upon the same Dionysian hierarchies to emphasize the laity's dependency on the clergy for knowledge. He argues that it would be against God's ordained and natural order for the lay folk to read the Bible for themselves, just as it would be against the natural order for the inferior orders of angels to demand information from the superior orders. In their use of these kinds of analogies, both Butler and Pecock exploit a conventional model for lay-clerical inter-action in a way that does important "ideological work": they appeal to what Fiona Somerset labels traditional, "'common models of 'proper' lay/clerical interaction," such as the assumption that "the clergy and laity are entirely distinct" and function in completely separate spheres with different capabilities and roles, as well as the notion that "each can be viewed as a seamless, consistent, unified whole."[21] Communi-cating this ideology through these kinds of analogies constitutes an attempt to convince members of the laity that their dependence on the clergy and their distinct difference from the clergy are natural. This reference to Dionysian hierarchies exposes the power relations that exist in any "pedagogic action" that takes place in Pecock's en-visioned textual community.[22] Pecock's use of Dionysian hierarchies to describe the process of knowledge distribution in the Christian community is a kind of "representation of legitimacy," in the terms of Pierre Bourdieu, that makes a considerable contribution "to the exer-cise and perpetuation of power."[23]

Though he suggests in the *Book of Faith* that God has instituted clear divisions between the clergy and the laity, Pecock is careful in the *Reule* to make it clear that God has not invested the clergy with powers that exceed that of a layman. He clarifies the limits to the sac-erdotal authority of the clergy by stating that the priest's consecration of the Host is "not a deede above kinde" (*Reule*, 314). The priest does not have the power to constrain Christ to appear in the sacrament: it is God's grace that works "forto putte there verily and presently his verry body and blood by covenaunt which he makith that whanne ever such a sacrament is made he wole so worche over what the preest may by nature do" (313). The priest, by nature, can do no more than a layman can to produce Christ's real presence in the sacrament: his job is limited to "preying and blessing and in speking of wordis, whiche deedis ben not above kinde" (315). Pecock does not suggest that a layman could perform the sacraments, but he insists that the priest does not possess a supernatural kind of authority that sets him above everyone else. Pecock makes it clear that "the power of preesthode as fer as his power strecchith to make the sacrament of the auter is not above kinde" (314), insisting that there is no natural, innate difference between the power of a layman and the power of a priest.

Pecock breaks down absolute barriers between the laity and the clergy in other ways as well. When he is eagerly discussing the potential of the lay intellect to grapple with texts in the same way as more learned clergymen, Pecock suggests to his lay readers that they share the same capacity for intellectual work as their clerical superiors, in a way that blurs the boundary between clerical and lay mental worlds. He suggests in his *Folewer* that he should not be faulted for providing difficult matters for lay readers, since clerics must often labor with difficult texts: though the Bible in Latin "in many of his parties passith the capacite and the power of ful many grete clerkis and of grete and kunning doctouris," these clerks do not therefore "cast aside the bible"; instead, those who have greater "leiser and lust" than others "wrastlen so long therwith til thei gete competent undirstonding therof." In the same way, laymen will wrestle with hard and dark matters in Pecock's corpus until they achieve comprehension (7). It is up to the lay reader to decide if a certain passage is too difficult for him; if he meets with such difficulty, he should seek the counsel of a learned cleric. If the matter is still too hard for him to digest, he should "overleap" it and return to it after "feeding" himself on other matters (30).[24] Those who abandon the task entirely, however, at the first sign of difficulty, are cowardly. Pecock says, "It is ful profitable ech man forto use him and aqueinte him with sumwhat to him hard and derk maters, and forto not be over mich coward to leve of the leerning of a mater or of a book for hardnes to his witt in the biginning; ffor certis his witt schal therby take in maner now seid a greet upreising" (15). Pecock declares that the more a man labors to learn difficult truths, the more "is his resoun lifted and ablied and cleerid" (15). He who does not shy away from a challenge will witness a transformation in his mental capacity. Indeed, by engaging in this intellectual labor, laymen can cultivate their wits in the same way as their clerical teachers. Pecock suggests that greater mastery of texts is tied not to innate intellectual superiority but to the amount of time one dedicates to study and the depth of desire one has to achieve comprehension. *Clergie* does not exist independent of training—clerics do not have some inherent ability to understand the Bible that sets them apart from the laity.

Pecock wants his lay readers to play a much more active role in their religious education—in a way that calls for a restructuring of the traditional "mediation process whereby the clerically educated inform the uneducated."[25] Pecock suggests that in the process of acquiring knowledge and working toward intellectual challenges, lay readers should decide for themselves when they are ready to move on from lighter fare to denser sustenance. He says that his corpus of educational materials provides a plenteous feast at which readers can satisfy themselves:

> And if it be seid to me ferther thus, that to this purpos mighte suffice miche lasse and lightir doctrine to be deliverid by writing than is the quantite of alle the now bifore rehercid bokis, y seie ayen that God is the feest fro which men risen with relefis, after hem leeving of more than they mowe take, in reward of the feest fro which men risen hungry and desiren to ete more than it is wherwith they be servid. Also y may seie thus, that where plente of eny thing or mater is, there sum man may take therof what is to him ynough, and he may leeve what is to him more than ynough for othere men which ben of greeter capacite to take it than is he which is therof the lever; even right as men going to a comoun welle drawen of the water how miche is to hem necessarie, and leeven al the gretter deel for othere men which wolen after hem make therof the drawing; and as men going into her comoun forest taken such timbir as is necessarie and mooste meete to her owne smal bilding, and leeven miche gretter and substancialer timber to be takun of othere men into her gretter bilding. (*Reule*, 20)

Rather than writing books of light doctrine and simple truths, Pecock wants to provide an educational corpus that can accommodate all levels and all capacities of learners. A feast of knowledge awaits his readers, requiring each to take as much as he needs, working at his own level and his own pace. Pecock's notion of "who may take, take he" (*Reule,* 21) suggests that laymen have a kind of innate tendency to monitor for themselves whether they are ready to receive milk or bread. Just as the man using a well takes with him only as much water as he can carry, or as much as he needs for his own purposes, so Pecock's reader will be able to decide for himself what is too much for him to attempt to understand. Pecock attributes independence and agency to readers in determining their own intellectual capacity.

Pecock imagines his lay readers participating in the same intellectual practices as the clergy when he encourages readers in his *Book of Faith* to develop their analytical tools. When he says that readers must take "longe leiser, forto sadly and oft overrede tho bokis, unto time they schulen be wel aqueintid with tho bokis, and with the skilis and motivis therinne writen," he suggests that lay readers must participate in the same kind of reading practices as the clergy, engaging in deep reflection and study on his text (116–17). He warns that a "light, superficial overreding or heering oonly" will not suffice for proper understanding of the "skilis and motivis" or the foundations of the text's arguments (116). Readers must apply themselves with the goal not simply of passively absorbing or acquiring the knowledge provided by the text but of actively understanding the basic premises of argument and the reasoning processes of the author. He also blurs distinctions between the reading practices of the laity and those of the clergy by using metaphors likening the ingestion and digestion of food, typical of monastic descriptions of reading practices, to point to the intellectual reading processes that the laity must use.[26] He indicates that readers must thoroughly digest his works when he says that at first the books will be "unsavery, though aftirward they schulen be ful delectable" (116). He indicates that lay readers must appropriate the deep study or rumination of the monastery, rather than digesting the pre-assembled tidbits of knowledge, such as those provided by traditional manuals of religious instruction. Pecock's recommendations that his readers absorb the text as deeply as possible rather than engaging in superficial reading practices shows his notion that the lay intellect is just as capable of systematic study as the clerically trained mind. He encourages his readers to study his books until they become delectable and sweet and until they are incorporated into the self in the way that food is taken into the body. In the *Book of Faith*, Pecock expands on this comparison between reading and ingestion:

> Forsothe, summe of the kunnyngist men of youre soorte, aftir that they han red of summe of these spokun bokis, and han take, by notable time, assaie and acqueintaunce in hem, han hungrid and thirstid, forto have hadde the copie and the continuel uce of tho bokis to hem, as moche as ever they hungriden and thirstiden aftir mete and drinke. Though peraventure, at the first blusch of reding of hem, tho bokis apperiden not to be such, for in sodein chaungis from oon mete to an other mete, and from oon drinke into an othere drinke, being moche diverse, yhe, from eny oon custom longe bifore continued into an other custom moche diverse, men oughten not truste to her first into hem coming semingis; but they musten abide and continue by counsel of resoun, til a newe seming be brought forth. (206–7)

Deep reflection and long hours of study make these books more nourishing as the lay reader benefits more and more from the spiritual knowledge offered by the text. Pecock describes the reading process as one that trains the layman or woman and stimulates intellectual growth; with each new reading, something different enriches the soul and the mind. Deep reflection and careful reading enable the reader to obtain greater spiritual fruits in the same way that deep rumination on the Bible within the monastery yields fruit in meditation and prayer.

Pecock blurs the boundary between clerical and lay worlds by indicating that intellectual capacity is the same for both. As Mishtooni Bose has shown, Pecock describes an intellectual affinity between members of the clergy and members of the laity, both of whom bring the same mental equipment of rational skills to their studies and learn in similar ways.[27] Bose notes that through his discussion of the innate syllogistic powers of the laity Pecock emphasizes "the closeness between clerical and lay mental worlds."[28] Pecock shows his confidence in the natural intellectual capacity of the laity when he says that although many men would wonder if he were to argue that "the lay peple han in her undirstonding naturaly the same logic whiche clerkis han craftily or doctrinaly . . . yit if this be wel considered, it wole be founde for trewe" (*Folewer*, 38). With this statement, Pecock indicates that the skills in reasoning that clerics hone through years of study are already at work instinctively in the layman's mind; the logic that clerics use in their studies of doctrine presumably could be marshaled with equal skill by a layman. Pecock's remarks thus dismiss the existence of an intellectual hierarchy between clergy and laity based on innate reasoning powers.

All of this leveling of the lay and clerical worlds in Pecock's corpus comes from his faith in the potential of the lay intellect, his dedication to lay education, and what can only be described as his excitement about the prospect of teaching the laity to think for themselves about the fundamentals of their faith. Like Mirk, therefore, Pecock provides images of an "autonomous, independent laity" rather than a "passive, obedient laity under the authority of mediating priests, monks, and friars."[29] However, Pecock also realizes, like Mirk, that this image of a self-directed, independent lay reader must be contained to a certain degree; while Mirk enfolds within "compelling images of lay agency" a "far less visible endorsement of the clerically dominated ecclesiological *status quo*," Pecock finds a different way to prevent his image of the autonomous lay reader from totally disrupting the clerical hierarchy.[30] He asks his readers to envision themselves as members of a kind of common-profit community where values of fellowship and friendship link clergyman and layman; he safely contains lay agency and autonomy by binding his lay readers to the clergy in new ways. This forms a contrast to the way that Mirk, writing about four decades earlier, contains compelling images of lay agency by reinforcing clerical control over such things as the performance of the sacraments. Instead of reinforcing traditional images of clerical authority and power in order to maintain the clerically dominated status quo, Pecock appeals to an emotional bond between clergy and laity, which he hopes will do even more powerful ideological work.

For example, in the *Book of Faith* Pecock outlines a complex scheme, for distributing his books to all kinds of laypeople, in which he carves out a new model for lay-cleric relations: he recommends that "prelatis and othere mighty men of good" show their "great zele and devocioun" to prevent the laypeople from error by distributing and lending books to those in need. These prelates and wealthy men must not only produce these books "at her owne cost" but also encourage the members of the laity with "ful moche tiring and provoking" to study them frequently and to spend their own money, in the future, "into so profitable a thing to them." Pecock describes the publication and distribution of his books as a charitable activity, saying: "Wel were the man which hadde ricches, and wolde spende it into this so greet goostly almes, which passith ful miche the deling abrood of clothis to greet multitude of pore persoonis, notwithstonding that bothe kindis of almes ben good" (117). Pecock's book-lending scheme works from the idea that wealthy men and clerics should infuse any supplementary riches or goods back into the community for the common profit. The loan or provision of the book is based on need, and the plan reflects the notion of knowledge as common property over which no one—not even the clergy—has full rights of ownership. Wendy Scase has identified Pecock's system of bookmaking and distribution as a development of the common-profit book scheme in fifteenth-century London.[31] This plan for the sharing of knowledge among prelates, wealthy men, and the laity provides insight to Pecock's notion of how to reform and rethink models for "proper" relations between clergy and laity. Though Pecock makes no plans for what will happen to the books after they have been delivered to needy laypeople, and though he makes no mention of the need for the recipients to pray for the souls of the donors, his plan for the provision of books among the poorer people of the London community disrupts traditional hierarchical systems of knowledge exchange by enabling unprecedented access to books through unprecedented means.

Pecock's scheme for book distribution provides a perspective on the kind of relationship that should exist between laity and clergy in a textual community, as *clergie* is transferred between them. At the basis of the system of book production and circulation is what Pecock envisions as an ideal magisterial and hierarchical relationship between clergy and laity that is founded, not on the traditional clerical ideology of universal lay subservience to the whole of the clerical hierarchy, but on something different: mutual respect, fellowship, and a common desire to seek divine truth together. If readers apply themselves to the study of his books, if they "wolen rede diligently, and attende therto studiosely, and be wel acqueintid with hem, and not forto take an hasty smel or smatche in hem, and soone leie hem aside," they will gain a healthy respect for the labor and skill that men like Pecock have spent on books of great learning. They will learn to trust to the "wittis and kunning of clerkis" and to "seche bisily to have her helpe and counseiling in tho maters," learning a kind of dependency for and admiration of the learned clerks who can write or explain such books (*BF*, 205). Lay readers engaging in difficult studies will learn to "love clerkis of the chirche, and seche aftir her comuning." Pecock predicts that in return clerics "schulen love you, and teche you in tho bokis, and moche ese and joie and good lif schal come therby, and moche vice, which cometh inne for defaute of suche goostly occupacioun, schal be eschewid" (206). Pecock asks his readers to see themselves as participants in this ideal imagined reading community, in a relationship of fellowship among men seeking the knowledge of God together.

Pecock's model of a kind of common-profit book-lending scheme attempts to unify the clergy and the laity by creating bonds of love and friendship between them. If we consider the book exchange as a kind of social practice of gift exchange, then we can see more clearly the way that this interaction binds the layman to his clerical brother. Andrew Galloway's work on the concepts of gratitude and "kynde-nesse" in late medieval England offers some useful ways of thinking about the development of social bonds between clergy and layman that could be facilitated by informal systems of charitable book giving.[32] Galloway argues that in this period ingratitude becomes associated with "unkyndeness," or a violation of natural order: the recipient who does not show thanks to the giver is seen as perverse and antisocial. Galloway suggests that "by blending nature with reciprocation, Middle English 'kyndenesse' shifts religious and social bonds away from hier-archy and toward affinity, and the exploitation of these lexical possibil-ities may easily be aligned with the many distinctive late-medieval forms of community or corporate identity in which reciprocation and close affinity or ideas of such affinity cohere."[33] Someone who is ungrateful is "unkynde" and therefore violates natural ethics; the lay recipient of one of Pecock's books who abuses the clergy or challenges his authority would therefore be seen as perversely violating natural order.

By linking clergyman and layman in his system of book exchange, Pecock ties them through a natural bond predicated on reciprocity, emphasizing the social bonds of community that exist between clergy and laity. In this way he echoes Langland, who is similarly worried about conflict between laity and clergy and who extrapolates from the idea of natural reciprocity "a powerful concept of communal identity."[34] For instance, Galloway posits that Langland's Samaritan, "that epitome of social charity," "presents immediate social exchanges as more important for defining a sacred community than any institutional religious forms or practices."[35] The social exchange between clergyman and layman that occurs when the clergyman provides, at his own cost, a book of religious instruction to a member of the lay community could be just as important for defining a sacred community as sacerdotal practices. Pecock suggests that the best way to engender the laity's respect and cooperation is through mutually productive interactions in which the laity have the "helpe and counseiling" of the clergy in their pursuit of the "leerning of Cristen religioun" (*BF,* 205).

Galloway's sense of "changing notions of social adhesion" is based on his observation that by the end of the Middle Ages the concept of what made social relations "natural" was different.[36] As he points out, the traditional way to think about relations between members of society was in terms of hierarchical order, in which difference and distance between social realms were emphasized. As we have seen, William Butler and Pecock himself at times represent this way of thinking in their appeal to Dionysian hierarchies to explain relations between clergy and laity. Galloway argues that writers like William Langland begin to question whether a social order defined by difference and distance between members is indeed natural and whether there is a more natural basis for social relations in mutuality, commonality, affinity, and reciprocity. Galloway's study of the importance of keywords such as *gratitude* helps him to show that when writers describe "gratitude" as a natural phenomenon they are beginning to see that the "natural" or "given" basis of a community is not social difference but personal bonds of unity and fellowship. Pecock's own vision of layman and cleric working side by side indicates that "natural" social relations between them are based more on mutuality than on hierarchical degrees of separation.

Anne Middleton discusses the development of a similar conception of social relations in her study "The Idea of Public Poetry in the Reign of Richard II."[37] Middleton says that Ricardian public poetry gives expression to the social values and ideals that distinguished men like the Lollard Knights and conscientious public servants like Gower and Usk: this poetry exemplifies "an ideal of communal responsibility founded not primarily in an estates conception of one's duties, but in an altruistic and outward-turning form of love that might be called 'common love' . . . [which] defined man as a social being, and, unlike its private counterpart, was turned outward to public expression."[38] In this "ideally conceived worldly community," man does not see himself in relation to other members of his society according to his difference from them and the distance between his social group and another; instead, he imagines himself to be part of a community founded on values of mutuality and common understanding.[39] The basis for his actions is not his understanding of what is appropriate for his place in society but his desire to act for the common good. "Natural" social relations in this kind of community are governed by a sense of kinship rather than a sense that each member of the social order is essentially different from the others and must fulfill the responsibilities of his particular station.

The emergence of this idea that social differences may not be inevitable and natural, and the growth of a concept of communal identity rooted in collaboration and unity, can be illuminated by an understanding of changing ideas about nature and the definition of what is "natural" during this period. Butler's vision of an orderly society in which members do not step over the boundaries of their prescribed, ordained role is founded on the notion that social difference and hierarchical order are given and ordained. This idea about the way that social order should work corresponds to ideas about "nature," which Barbara Newman describes as "one of the foundational categories of Western thought."[40] Newman suggests that artistic representations of nature "sprang up side by side with scholastic ideas about human nature, natural, law, and natural sexuality," so that ideas about the natural order of things in society were linked to poems and myths that featured the personification of nature.[41] Butler's idea of "natural" social order stands side by side with artistic representations of nature in works such as Bernardus Silvestris's *Cosmographia* and Alan of Lille's *Plaint of Nature*. In these poems, nature is God's vicar on earth, a "mediatrix between God and the world."[42] Newman says that nature's "intervention sets the cosmogony in motion, and her perpetual labour assures the orderly process of *creatio continua* through procreation."[43] In the *Cosmographia*, when Nature asks the divine figure, Noys, for permission to give order to the confused state of primal matter, she pleads, "The elements come before you, demanding forms, qualities, and functions appropriate to their causal roles, and seek those stations to which they are almost spontaneously borne, drawn by a common sympathy."[44] She asks for the imposition of order and form; this appeal defines the natural as that which follows principles of order and that which assigns the various elements to their appropriate places. In the *Cosmographia*, Nature's creative process will ensure that the order of human society is patterned on divine order, showing "the completeness with which divine reality pervades and gives meaning to all life."[45] As Winthrop Wetherbee points out, the representation of nature in the *Cosmographia* gives expression to the idea "that the events of earthly life were governed and predetermined by the orderly disposition and activity of the heavenly bodies and could, in part, be foreknown through the careful analysis of celestial phenomena."[46] The divine pattern of the universe is mirrored in natural creation, in the order of society, so that the hierarchical levels of the heavens become a pattern for the hierarchical order of society in which each person is assigned to his proper place and function. According to this conception of nature, what is "natural" is the existence of a hierarchical relationship between the various parts of society that conduces toward a state of order; social differences are ordained and given, and the "natural" basis of social order is rooted in the distance rather than the affinity between social realms.

By the end of the Middle Ages, however, writers such as Chaucer and Christine de Pizan were beginning to question the natural quality of social order. As Galloway's article shows, what is "natural," given, and ordained about the social order for authors like Langland is not social difference but reciprocation, affinity, mutuality, and bonds of fellowship between social realms. When envisioning natural social order, Langland does not see an "iron curtain between the social classes" or natural distances between social realms; instead, he sees harmony as a natural force that unites the disparate social realms, and cultural unity as the "natural" or "given" basis of a community.[47] This questioning of the "natural" basis for hierarchical order in society emerges (as Newman points out) in Chaucer's *Parliament of Foules*, in which the figure of Nature is internally conflicted: on the one hand she is "the embodiment of all that is simple, joyful, instinctual, and fertile," as suggested by the "lower-class birds flying off in unproblematic pairs," and, on the other hand she represents hierarchical social order, as suggested by the aristocratic birds who form the social elite of the parliament and who insist on ordering the procreative process with rules that insist on class privilege.[48] By linking Nature to the tercels, who "feel compelled to cloak their political desire in the language of erotic desire" rather than to act instinctively, like the lower-class birds, Chaucer represents the idea of the "natural" that is expressed by Butler:[49] the hierarchical social order is natural, given, and essential. But Chaucer destabilizes this idea by representing another idea of the "natural" that conflicts with this, suggesting a good deal of skepticism about whether hierarchical relationships can be defended on the basis of their "natural" origins. As Barbara Newman points out, Christine de Pizan expresses a similar skepticism about whether it is natural for women to be excluded from certain areas of life, such as the realm of learning. Both authors are uneasy with the idea that the social hierarchy and social differences have a natural, given origin, suggesting instead that this way of conceptualizing social order may be a human construct.

Pecock also blends ideas about the natural with values of kinship and affinity: he combines love, fellowship, friendship and the natural order in a similar way to the Ricardian poets. Rather than emphasizing the inevitability or "naturalness" of social differences, Pecock emphasizes the inevitability and "naturalness" of emotional bonds between the social realms. The ideal of kinship as a natural force in the social order emerges in numerous fifteenth-century sources: Galloway cites an example of taxation documents, in which royal taxes were described as "benevolences" given to show "fondness" to the king. The relationship between the king and the taxpayers was one of "loving kindness" in which each cherished the other: in this description of social relations, each member participates in the exchange, not because of the imperative to obey, but because of a willingness to be a part of a personal relationship in the name of social cohesion.[50] In this context, one fulfills one's duty to the king, not because of a sense of what is appropriate to one's place in society, but because of a sense of communal responsibility founded in a public form of love and fellowship. For Pecock, the amount of learning and study undertaken by clerics defines their role as teachers and guides, and laypeople must show respect and gratitude toward their clerical peers out of willingness rather than the imperative to obey their clerical superiors. Submerging the "naturalness" of social differences and stressing instead the "naturalness" of social cohesion, Pecock suggests that relations between these members of the social order are based not on an estates conception of one's duties but on a desire to participate willingly in an intimately unified society. Though at times he reminds his readers of their particular place in society, Pecock also guides them toward the expression of that public love of Ricardian poetry, which Middleton defines as "an emotional and ethical force" that is "powerful and fundamental to human life."[51] Just as the poetry of Langland and Gower "envisions a society composed of members whose differing stations, functions, and ways of life yield different perspectives on the common world" and works to bring these various members "to mutual awareness" or into "common understanding," Pecock seeks to bring the various members of his fifteenth-century London society into a common textual community, engaged in a mutual quest for religious understanding.

When Pecock's project is viewed in this way, in terms of its similarity to the public poetry defined and examined by Middleton, it makes sense that he would use certain metaphors to describe his work of authorship. In the *Donet*, for example, Pecock likens himself to a merchant who works for the common profit and who wishes to bring precious goods to each member of his audience. He discusses the need to advertise his textual wares in the following way: "How schulde a man bring peple of Englonde into wil forto bye or to freely receive and have precious and profitable chaffre, which he had fett fer from othire cuntrees biyonde the see for her profite and eese, but if he wolde denounce and proclame that he had such chaffre, and which were the preciosite and the profitableness of hit, for love and zeel whiche he had into her good and availe?" (*Donet*, 83). Pecock depicts himself as a merchant who must advertise and sell his wares to make a living but who prioritizes the "good and availe" of his customers above his own profit. His great zeal to benefit his readers motivates his sales. This emphasis on public service echoes the claims of the writers of public poetry described by Middleton, whose task is "to find the common voice and speak for all" in the pursuit of secular harmony.[52] Pecock's use of this metaphor to describe his textual activities stresses the social rather than the spiritual goal of his project and the way that he envisions the power of the educational experience (mutual study of his own texts) to foster social harmony and unity.

Pecock encourages the development of a sense of group identity among his readers by focusing on the need for greater respect among laypeople for their better-educated clerical peers. He discusses relations between laity and clergy in terms of fellowship: prominent in Pecock's works are references to a kind of brotherhood of Christian fellowship that should exist among clergy and laity. For example, he says that he aims to foster good relations between the clergy and the laity by making his books so difficult that lay readers will have to call upon the clerical peers for help: "And so by occasioun herof that my writingis maad to lay men ben so hard in many processis to lay men, grettir frendschip, love, and good acqueintaunce and felawlik comunicacioun and good spending of time schulen rise and continue bitwix clerkis and lay men, than if such hardnes in tho writingis were not" (*Folewer*, 8). This kind of fellowship resembles the brotherhood of the clergy more than the hierarchical relationship of clergy and laity: Pecock envisions Christian society as a kind of common fraternity united by the same project of doctrinal inquiry. For Pecock, the education of the laity in complex theological matters and in sophisticated clerical skills of interpretation and argumentation is a viable way to maintain the status quo in terms of the laity's respect and deference to the clergy; training the laity in difficult matters, instead of simply passing on to them the most essential, basic truths, will never make the clergy redundant, but it will create an interpretive community that fosters the laity's respect and feeling of need for the clergy, and it will unite clergy and laity in the search for religious knowledge. Pecock realizes that maintaining the hierarchical relationship between clergy and laity depends not on making lay readers feel completely inferior and intellectually weak next to their clerical teachers but on making lay readers feel an intimate bond with clerics who can help them ascend on their path to divine knowledge.

Fostering bonds between clergy and laity in this way can be a potent way of affirming the authority of the clergy. In Pecock's ideal textual community, founded on the values of friendship, fellowship, reciprocity, and affinity, dissenting voices are seen as unnatural or perverse: those who would turn their learning against the clergy for polemical ends are seen as breaking intimate bonds of friendship in a way that is unnatural or "unkynde." In Pecock's *Repressor*, a defense of the clergy against the heretical charges of the lay party, Pecock describes lay judgment of and accusations against the clergy as a "horrible abhominacioun and a vile stinking presumpcioun" (149). Such accusers are to be ashamed of their "folie and of her unwisdom and pride" and should be forbidden access to the Bible—they should be excluded from the group of friends engaged in learning together (149–59). Here Pecock minimizes the possibility for dissent and difference: in this structure, laypeople who challenge their clerical superiors in fundamental ways are perceived as betraying bonds of friendship and violating social ethics. Through the exclusion from the community of those who challenge the authority of the clergy, Pecock seeks to control the consequences of his own experiment in inviting lay readers to participate meaningfully in discussion about doctrine and morality: while readers must exercise a degree of agency in developing rational modes of thought and argument, this agency never extends to questioning the clergy.

Pecock shows us what productive exchanges between laity and clergy look like when he describes amicable discussions that he has had with men of the "lay partie" who are "contrarie to the chirche." Pecock is able to embrace these dissidents in the textual community by engaging them in rational argument and showing them their error through his "motives," or proofs. He says: "I have spoke oft time, and by long leiser, with the wittiest and kunningist men of thilk seid soort, contrarie to the chirche, and which han be holde as dukis amonge hem, and which han loved me for that y wolde paciently heere her evidencis, and her motives, without exprobacioun. And verily noon of hem couthe make eny motive for her party so stronge as y my silf couthe have made therto" (*BF*, 202). Pecock emphasizes his patience and openness in dealing with these disputatious laymen when he relates his own experience of listening quietly, without scorn or reproach, to the arguments of these most respected and "wittiest" members of the lay party. He stresses the strong bond of affection between himself and these laymen when he tells us that he was able to engender their love and admiration by treating them seriously. It is important to note that Pecock does not constrain the consent of the "lay partie" by emphasizing his clerical authority and the distinction between his state and that of the laity. It is also important to note that the mutual respect shown in this exchange is just as potent as the power of reason to bring about harmony and agreement.

Pecock encourages readers to develop a sense of group identity rooted in common respect and feelings of mutuality and affinity. In her article entitled "Small Groups: Identity and Solidarity in the Middle Ages," Miri Rubin discusses the way in which the construction of "community" is "neither obvious nor natural, its boundaries are loose, and people in the present, as in the past, will use the term to describe and construct worlds, to persuade, to include, and to exclude."[53] In Pecock's ideal, imagined reading community of fellowship, "shades of tension, distance, and difference" are certainly whitewashed by the overarching values of brotherhood, friendship, and love.[54] Pecock is not alone in the way that he offers to his readers a way of conceiving the structure of their society that minimizes dissent, disagreement, and difference; Alan Fletcher notes that a fifteenth-century sermon on the three estates, for the twentieth Sunday after Trinity, also offers its listeners a way of conceiving the structure of their society that limits their independence and agency to a certain degree.[55] Fletcher writes that the author's desire to preserve harmony and limit discord motivates him to "construct, out of largely traditional parts, an unusual example of estates theory, and one whose adjustments may perhaps be understood as a public recognition and implicit curtailment of particular fifteenth-century lay aspirations. Viewed in these terms, the sermon becomes an interesting essay in social control, and evidence of the possible tension involved in any attempt to reconcile and yet maintain social differences."[56] According to Fletcher, "The diminution of the orthodox view of priesthood by the Lollards would also have tended to blur some of the traditional distinctions between clergy and laity."[57] The author of this sermon on the three estates, who keeps the laity in their place by limiting their knowledge to the Ten Commandments, "would have found such blurring abhorrent."[58] The way that Pecock asks his readers to envision their own relationship with the clergy certainly does not diminish their "lay aspirations" toward a more active, fulfilling religious life, but it does limit the extent to which they can challenge and disagree with their clerical brothers. Pecock's development of a common-profit scheme for book distribution based on mutual responsibility and fellowship between laity and clergy also reflects the traditional ideology of the harmonious interactions between the members of the three estates, and in particular the notion that each member of society must keep to his place. Pecock's scheme highlights "clearly defined roles for clergy and laity to play" in which one state does not overlap into the other.[59] Pecock's plan for "felawlik comunicacioun" between lay readers and clerics does not involve any overstepping of boundaries by the laity: clerics are in control of setting up the framework and the terms for argument and debate, and the laity can participate only if they agree to play by the clergy's rules and submit their ideas for correction.

Pecock's picture of an interpretive community united by ties of fellowship, friendship, and love in the common search for divine truth shows one way of rethinking traditional boundaries between clerical and lay worlds. His emphasis on the need to cultivate emotional connections between these two estates maps out new rules for interactions between clergy and laity in a kind of brotherhood; though there are still masters and students in this interpretive community, their relationship pivots on mutuality, reciprocity, and affinity. His description of "felawlik comunicacioun" shows the extent to which Wycliffite pedagogy has brought to the fore the reality that divisions between clergy and laity are on the whole artificial—that there are no inherent divisions between clergy and laity on the basis of mental capacity or pedagogical practices. His emphasis on love and respect shows the extent to which this blurring of the boundaries between clergy and laity requires new ideas about the most productive way for clergy and laity to relate with one another. Once the closeness between clerical and lay mental worlds has been recognized, relations between clergy and laity must change to reflect this: Pecock's attempts to preserve clerical authority by fostering harmony and encouraging a mutual quest for the common profit provide one solution.

Other solutions to this problem of either reinforcing or reformulating proper relations between clergy and laity are provided by a range of texts in the fifteenth century, revealing that this was a topic on the minds of many writers of Pecock's time. Indeed, Sarah Rees Jones has recently argued that *The Book of Margery Kempe* is essentially a clerical response to this problem of how the clergy should deal with threats to their authority posed by ambitious lay folk like Margery Kempe: Rees Jones suggests that if we view Kempe's text as a book that was written "by clergy, for clergy, and about clergy," rather than as an autobiography, we can read it as a text that serves as a warning to lower clergy of the "potential dangers to which they are exposing the church through their moral laxity and inability to adapt to the needs of a demanding laity."[60] Through Margery's dealings with the lower clergy in this text, clerical readers are shown that they are endangering the church's authority by the weakness of their pastoral care and their inability to respond to people like Margery, who is represented as "a challenging subject, whose beliefs and behaviour defy conservative clerical ideas of 'correct' devotion."[61] Rees Jones argues that the compilers of the *Book* "used it to illustrate a series of threats to the authority of the clergy that needed to be recognized and accommodated in their pastoral work."[62] Read in this way, the *Book* provides a clerical audience with advice and instruction on how to adapt their pastoral approach when faced with growing demands for lay autonomy and increasing threats to clerical control: if they do not improve their pastoral care, they will fail to maintain or reinforce clerical authority. Clerics must correct themselves and put an end to moral laxity to ensure that they are beyond the reproach of the pious laity. Rees Jones's argument shows how pervasive this issue had become by Pecock's time and how important it had become to develop creative solutions for adapting to a new religious landscape in which ambitious laypeople were attempting to cross the boundary between lay and clerical worlds.

Like other writers across the orthodox spectrum, therefore, Pecock had to think creatively to provide a kind of "ballast" against a heretical ideology that set lay agency and clerical authority in opposition.[63] Pecock's emphasis on lay intellectual autonomy and his vision of a blurred boundary between lay and clerical mental worlds show the influence of Wycliffite notions of lay agency; however, his construction of social bonds between cleric and layman shows an effort to find a balance between lay agency and clerical authority. Pecock's ideal, imagined textual community founded on friendship and reciprocity mitigates the dangers of transferring *clergie* to the laity. In a community in which the laity feels an emotional connection to the clergy rather than inferiority, endowing the laity with the clerical skills and tools of academic argumentation does not necessarily come at a cost to clerical control and power. The varying solutions found by Pecock, Butler, Love, Mirk, the Longleat author, Audelay, and others show that a good deal of creative thinking was going on during and in the aftermath of Wycliffite activity, geared toward finding novel ways of unifying the Christian community.

Conclusion

Understanding Pecock's Cultural Practice

In discussions about the production of vernacular theology after 1409, Reginald Pecock often appears as a man who was ahead of his times, a "tolerant man in an age of intolerance" whose rational, nonviolent response to heresy set him apart from other representatives of the institutional church who sought to uproot heterodox belief with censorship, repression, and fiery punishments.[1] Editors of Pecock's works describe him "as one opponent of the Lollards who was not bloody-minded" (*Reule*, xviii), citing Pecock's own advice to "by cleer witt drawe men into consente of trewe feith otherwise than by fier and swerd and hangement" (*BF*, 139). Indeed, Pecock's visionary and creative plan to protect orthodoxy by educating the laity properly in theological matters places him in contrast to representatives of the church who fear that engaging the laity in the pursuit of *clergie* will open up dangerous ways of thinking about controversial topics, like the role of the church in society, the place of the laity and the clergy in the spiritual hierarchy, or the grounding of clerical practices like monasticism in the Bible. Pecock's attempts to convert the "yvel disposid men of the lay partie" through the transfer of theological and philosophical *clergie* to the laity indicates that the prospect of lay-people discussing and thinking about religious matters was much less troubling for him than it was for some ecclesiastical authorities (*Reule*, 19). The contrasts that scholars draw between Pecock's response to the Lollard heresy and that of the ecclesiastical establishment after 1409 often tend toward a description of Pecock that emphasizes his enlightenment, his sense of humanity, and even his "kinship" with "the humanists of early Tudor England."[2]

Pecock's approach to vernacular theology looks forward in many ways, anticipating the changes that were to sweep across Christian society with the Reformation. Certain emphases in his teaching also reveal the influence of earlier traditions of theological teaching in the scholastic era and earlier traditions of pastoral teaching since Archbishop Pecham's initiatives of 1281. The balance of two impulses in Pecock's corpus of vernacular theology makes him a fascinating transitional figure. First, his emphasis on education as the key to the reform of the individual and the church anticipates the humanist insistence on the importance of education for forming and strengthening faith and devotion at the level of the individual and the level of society as a whole. Pecock looks back, however, to scholastic disciplines of moral philosophy rather than looking to the Bible as the true source of Christian and moral knowledge. Indeed, his notion that the individual's confrontation with the book of reason, rather than the Gospels, is the pivotal experience for the learning of the Christian way of life shows him fighting against the very movement that would define the Reformation.

Pecock's sense that the most important theological work is practical in nature, rather than abstract and speculative, aligns him with both the theological trends in fifteenth-century Oxford and the pastoral tendencies of Reformation theology, which focused to a great degree on questions of how to live a good life in the world and how to gain salvation. Pecock's interest is not in working out a position on academic debates about the fundamental doctrines of the Trinity, for example, but in working out clear systems of basic moral teaching and fundamental philosophical principles about the nature of virtue and sin. Whether or not subsequent theologians would have agreed that sophisticated teachings on meenal and eendal moral virtues was as relevant to the ethical education of the ordinary Christian as Christ's moral teachings in the Gospels, however, is another question. In any event, Pecock's sense that his moral teaching is vital to the everyday life of the ordinary Christian situates him firmly within fifteenth-century academic culture as well as situating him within the movement toward Reformation.

In his movement toward the idea that no absolute barrier separates the clerical and lay estates, Pecock anticipates Luther's priesthood of all believers. His notion that what separates clergy from laity is training and study, rather than innate qualities, and his demystification of theology, through the idea that theology requires a certain set of professional skills, vocabulary, and "know-how" (a common approach to talking about the things of God), indicates that the laity is capable of participating, alongside the learned clergy, in the pursuit of spiritual truth. Pecock's emphasis on the clergy's role as educators, rather than as mediators of God's divine power through the sacraments, implies there is no true difference between the clergy and laity that justifies assigning the clergy a position within a social hierarchy that is closer to God. Furthermore, Pecock's frequent admonitions and cautions to the clergy, advising them to attend more carefully to their own learning and education, combined with his stress on the importance of lay education, suggests that reform in the Christian community depends on the clergy's efforts to share knowledge. At times Pecock does insist that there is more separating the clergy and laity than training and long years of study, by reminding readers that God himself ordained the priesthood as a divine institution and by describing the clergy's elevated position within Christian hierarchy, when he is thinking specifically about the problem of lay Bible reading. On the other hand, however, his comments in the *Book of Faith* that the clergy now living does not have the same "kunning and power" that the church of the apostles had shows Pecock anticipating the movement toward a conception of the ecclesiastical hierarchy as a human institution and away from a conception of the ecclesiastical hierarchy as a state completely distinct from the secular (*BF*, 274).

Finally, in his observances of the diversity of belief that can be seen by those who "wole walke amonge the peple now living in Ynglond fer and neer," Pecock witnesses doctrinal diversity in his own cultural context, not simply in terms of the appearance of the Lollard heresy, but in terms of the variances within orthodoxy and heterodoxy that resulted in the splintering of the Christian church in the next centuries. His impulse to do everything possible to bring stability and unity back to the Catholic Church by creating a centralized, formalized system of teaching shows how seriously he considered the problem of new forms of faith and piety that threatened to shatter the unity of Christendom. His attempt to take a step back from this movement toward doctrinal plurality by embracing laity and clergy, and heretic and faithful alike within one, singular system of Christian pedagogy that incorporates certain strains of Lollard thinking (in his development of a kind of transparent form of biblical exegesis, for example) foreshadows later attempts by reformist Catholics to find common ground within a system that accommodated new impulses toward reformation that were important to Protestants and Catholics alike, such as an emphasis on the authority of scripture.[3]

An important way in which Pecock anticipates the cultural changes of the Reformation is in his impulse to contract and limit discursive possibilities within the field of vernacular theology: his corpus represents an attempt to make uniform and stable the field of vernacular theology within a singular body of writing. Pecock's sense of the need to centralize the cultural practice of vernacular theology, in the face of the threat of "diversitees" in the "conceitis" of people all across England (*BF*, 109), suggests that his work has a great deal in common with revolutionary cultural practice, as defined by James Simpson in his study of the distinctions between late medieval and early modern literature and culture. Simpson's models of reformist and revolutionary cultural practice are useful in understanding Pecock's cultural practice. Simpson draws attention to the intersection between literary practice and significant transformations within the political and social sphere, suggesting that "institutional simplifications and centralizations of the sixteenth century provoked correlative simplifications and narrowings in literature."[4] Social and political shifts provoke changes in literary culture or literary production. Working out the way that Simpson's concept helps us to make sense of certain aspects of Pecock's work necessitates quoting Simpson in full:

> "Cultural revolution" has been used to imply the wide range of cultural practices characteristic of those moments, sometimes actual, sometimes imagined, in which power is suddenly centralized. Legitimation of such newly centralized power demands both repudiation of the old order and a vigorous affirmation of novelty. Because accretive reception of texts implies historical continuity, a

revolutionary order must repudiate such reception; it must institute in its place the possibility of complete textual recovery of a
founding text in its originary purity, whether that text be the
Aeneid or the Bible. A revolutionary order must also stress its own
unity, a unity that flows from a central, organizing source. In literary practice the effects of this will be disciplined observation of
stylistic and discursive coherence. Above all, revolutionary texts
tend to stress central intelligence and initiative: whether in politics
or theology, the first half of the sixteenth century witnessed a
newly conceived transcendence of power.[5]

Now, it is clear that Pecock himself does not represent an entire revolutionary order, since he is just one man attempting to create a new
tradition of religious teaching. However, his body of work does propose a kind of cultural revolution in the sense that it aims to simplify
and centralize the cultural practice of vernacular theology, which in
Pecock's view is too incoherent and disorganized, leading to superstition and error rather than to a common consensus on truth. Pecock's
project, though wide-ranging within itself, proposes a kind of narrow-
ing of discursive possibilities for those wishing to impart *clergie* to lay
audiences by suggesting that certain kinds of approaches, such as
teaching moral virtue through figurative language, are inappropriate.
Simpson himself notes that Pecock's writings fit within the definition
of revolutionary cultural practice when he draws attention to Pecock
as an "extreme example of discursive sobriety and caution."[6] "Stability
and consistency of utterance" are key aspects of revolutionary literary
practice, and Pecock consistently strives for these.[7] Pecock shapes his
corpus to make his own teaching uniform and discursively stable,
treating the same subjects from different angles, demonstrating the
same points in numerous ways to ensure that readers cannot possibly
misunderstand him. He phrases and rephrases arguments in multiple
ways, providing numerous examples, to limit the possibility that readers
will interpret his words in a way that he does not intend. The three
characteristics of Pecock's body of work that are illuminated by Simpson's definition of revolutionary cultural practice are the following:
Pecock's appeal to the authority of the originary text of the book of
reason; Pecock's sense of the need for a uniform, universal system of

pedagogical teaching; and Pecock's repudiation of an old order of teaching, structured on the seven deadly sins, the Ten Commandments, and other groupings.

One of the ways in which Pecock's corpus of religious instruction fits within the category of revolutionary cultural practice is in his claim that he is returning to a source of Christian truth that is pure and primary: the majority of his teachings throughout his oeuvre are not of his own invention but are merely the witnessing and transmission of truths that he has found in the most supremely authoritative book of reason: the "inward book or inward writing of resounis doom passing all outward bookis in profite to men for to serve God" (*Repressor*, 31). This book, "the largist book of autorite that ever god made" (*Folewer*, 10), accessible to all mankind through the faculty of reason, is available in material form through Pecock's writings in the way that he teaches moral governances, deeds, truths, and virtues that exist in the book of reason and can be seen with the help of proofs, demonstrations, and arguments (*Repressor*, 40). As we have seen in chapter 5, this founding text of the book of reason is more extensive and hence more useful than other sources of knowledge on Christian conduct, most notably the Bible.

Another aspect of Pecock's revolutionary cultural practice is his plan to invigorate and reshape the Christian community by making lay religious education uniform, formal, and universal. One single and standardized system—rather than a diverse supply of teaching aids— is needed for teaching orthodox doctrine, and that system is Pecock's. His corpus is consistent within itself, providing a basis or foundation of material that is continually reworked in more sophisticated ways. Moreover, that system must be made available for the study of "alle thy cristen peple" (*Reule*, 13). Pecock outlines a variety of ways, described in this book, to ensure that his works "preche and teche continuely and perpetualy into the worldis eend" (*Reule*, 392), including formal systems of charitable book production and book lending. One way to get his books to all kinds of people is to set up controlled systems of book production and distribution (*BF*, 117); another way is to provide cheaper extracts—like Pecock's *Pore Mennis Myrroure*—of some of the larger works. A third way is to put Pecock's books on the curriculum of schools and universities. This will ensure that "clerkis or leernid men be brought up into leerning and kunning forto edifie and to teche othere in the vii principal maters of this present book." Pecock's ambition is for his "fruiteful treticis and bookis" to act as the foundation of the pedagogical system and the source of religious knowledge and discourse in the Christian community: his texts and his particular approach will play a central role in making religious knowledge and practice uniform and standard (*Reule*, 363). Of course, we will never know the degree to which Pecock was successful in circulating his teaching widely: we do know that after his trial for heresy, in 1457, numerous searches had to be done to root out his books, testifying, in the view of historian Wendy Scase, to "continuing anxiety concerning the circulation of writings by Pecock," by calling for "renewed zeal in pursuing those who are adherents by reason of their possession and reading of Pecock's books."[8]

The third way in which Pecock's project of theological teaching fits within the model of revolutionary literary practice is his representation of his cultural practice as the demolition of an old order and the replacement of that old order by something new: Pecock intends to replace traditional forms of teaching with a theological system that provides more clarity, stability, and consistency. In his *Reule of Crysten Religioun*, *Donet*, and *Folewer to the Donet*, Pecock overhauls the teaching of Christian belief and behavior and replaces current systems of teaching with his own. He provides his four tables in the place of the Decalogue because the "comoun foorme of the x comaundementis is noon such foorme that therby and therinne we mowe se, recorde, and remember and reporte sufficiently as is nedeful to alle Cristen men, the hool summe of Goddis comaundementis" (*Donet*, 144). His system of seven matters comprises all a Christian needs to know in order to ensure salvation. He rewrites the Lord's Prayer with "setting to of othire wordis and othire processis" to make this prayer "peraventure, . . . so riche, so swete, and so preciose" that his reader "schalt desire aftir noon othire" (*Donet*, 204). He also claims to have rewritten the Divine Office itself, since in its current form it is "unstabil and so not firme neither strong neither fers, intense or highe in his kinde" (*Reule*, 406). Pecock's liturgical forms, in contrast, which run upon "cleer to be undirstonde and upon worthy and digne maters of thy nobiltees, of thy benefetis and of thy lawis," would make the occupations of praise and prayer in monastic houses "miche higher and plesauntir" (*Reule*, 416). Pecock also criticizes the customary approach of the clergy to religious instruction—the delivering of articles of belief in their "naked forms"—as opposed to delivering truth to their "resoun" with evidence, enabling that truth to be "lightir received and perceived" (*Reule*, 91). Finally, his lack of citations to the authoritative tradition of theology, and his cautions that the findings of theological *auctores* must always be resolved into rational grounds and principles, show a bold attitude toward the traditions that precede him. Received texts are to be tested for validity, while Pecock's new texts offer a more sufficient, relevant, and updated approach to the teaching of Christian doctrine and morality. Readers need look no further than his texts, with their teaching of the seven matters, which are "so ful and sufficient to almankinde that more kunning than is conteined in hem sevene nedith no man to loke aftir or to laboure or to studie fore, as for sufficient goostly philosophie and Cristen divinite" (*Reule*, 35). In his restructuring of the way that Christianity is taught, Pecock strives above all for stability and clarity. The revitalization of the Christian community requires a complete overhaul: a standard approach to teaching doctrine and morality will make it impossible to find meaning that diverges from orthodoxy.

It is important to note, however, that Pecock also represents his replacement of old forms of teaching as reformist. Simpson's model of reformist cultural practice includes the following features: "a sense of long and continuous histories, an accretive reception of texts, where the historicity of the reader receiving the old text is not at all suppressed; clearly demarcated and unresolved generic, stylistic, and/or discursive divisions within texts; and, above all, an affirmation of the possibility of human initiative, whether in politics or theology."[9] Though Pecock states that his works are so sufficient that readers do not need to look elsewhere for alternative reading material, implying that his new works replace traditions of didactic and theological writing, he does visualize his own contribution to moral teaching as part of a long and continuous history of teaching, led by scholars who continually search to find truth and to bring it to others. Pecock sees himself as part of a tradition of "ministris and enserchers of treuthe of resoun, and as pupplischers and schewers forth therof to othere" (*Reule*, 464). Moreover, if we look closely at the language that Pecock uses to describe his replacement of the Decalogue with his own system of moral teaching, it becomes clear that his point is not to cast away the Decalogue entirely but to expand its commandments. The main problem that Pecock identifies with teaching on the Decalogue is the common opinion, or common pretension among both laity and clergy, that all moral law is included within it: God did not intend for the whole range of his moral law to be contained in the Decalogue, for the form of the Decalogue to be man's "ful reule of al that God biddith him to do, and of al that God forbedith him to do" (*Donet*, 135). Pecock rebukes this foolishness, saying that "alle the clerkis in the worlde mowe not defende that thilk tables of Moyses to teche sufficiently Goddis comaundis and alle oure necessarie governauncis anentis God ben sufficient" (*Donet*, 123).

The Decalogue was given to man as a starting point for a tradition of moral teaching: Moses's tables were "not delivered to Moises as for a ful and a sufficient summe and reule of alle thy comaundementis, neither to hem neither to us, but as an hondful of the hool summe of thy comaundementis to biginne therwith al" (*Reule*, 365). This means that the task of Pecock and other learned clerics is not to cast away this primary form of teaching but to expand it, to fill it out, to rework it as part of a reformative cultural practice. The Ten Commandments allow man to see part of God's moral law, and Pecock's teaching will expand this view: the form of Pecock's tables will do "good" to each man because "it schal opene abrood the foorme of the seid x comaundementis, that he schal the broder and the wiider se in his foorme of the x comaundementis by the foorme of the seid iiii tablis than he schulde se and knowe, if he had not this foorme of iiii tablis, neither eny other liik to it" (*Donet*, 135). The tradition of teaching was initiated by God's assignment of the moral rules of the Decalogue, but he also gave his moral law in other forms to man, in moral philosophy and through Christ's own teaching, which were to be added to the truths known from the moral law given in the Decalogue: "how fer thilk tables ben from the cleer, sufficient, ful and compendiose treting of moral virtues and of moral vertuose dedis, taught by Crist and hise apostlis, and conteined scateringly here and there in the newe testament and in moral philosophie, and gaderid to gider by doctouris and othire clerkis into bokis and treticis of moral virtues, clenly thereupon formed and writen, so fer ben tho tables from the cleer, sufficient, ful, and compendiose teching and treting of the commaundementis and counseilis of God" (*Donet*, 20). Pecock's task in the construction of the four tables is to bring all traditions of moral teaching together into one system that is eminently logical and rational: his task is not to design something entirely new but to fill out and improve on the forms of teaching that already exist but are insufficient in themselves. He is therefore above all else an innovator, not a revolutionary. Other approaches to teaching the moral law of God are extended and expanded by Pecock, who makes it clear that other men's teaching on the seven deadly sins, for example, is "comprehended and conteinid" within his own system in a way that makes teaching on sin sufficiently known: "Othire mennis foormes, taking upon hem forto teche and trete goddis comaundementis and lawis, ben insufficient and inconvenient to thilk purpose" (*Donet*, 81). Aquinas's *Summa* is one such source that differs from Pecock's in structure but resembles Pecock's in content: I explore the relationship between Aquinas's moral teaching and Pecock's elsewhere, but it is important here to note that Pecock does not throw out the baby with the bathwater. He borrows significantly from the tradition of scholastic teaching on moral philosophy, renewing and revitalizing this tradition in the vernacular and in a new structure. Pecock is not creating a new moral law but gathering together all the moral truths of God's law, from various sources, including the works of other philosophers and from the Bible itself, into a comprehensive system. His approach is renovatory rather than destructive.

There are ways, therefore, in which Pecock's literary practice seems to straddle these two models of revolutionary and reformist literary practice. On one hand, he seeks to open up discursive possibilities in the field of vernacular theology by inviting the laity to think about religion and faith in entirely new ways. He is particularly encouraging when it comes to exploring the truths of reason; as I suggest in chapter 5, Pecock's faith in the powers of human reason leads him to open up controversial subjects to lay inquiry, such as the selling of spiritual goods and the endowment of the clergy. He has such confidence in the power of the syllogism to bring clarity to the learning of God's moral truths that he invites his lay readers to explore God's moral law with a great deal of freedom. Though more tentative in his treatment of the truths of faith, he still opens up areas of inquiry that are forbidden by Arundel's Constitutions, encouraging lay readers to think through his rational evidences for articles of faith, including the value of confession to a priest and the ordination of the clerical hierarchy. On the other hand, however, Pecock attempts to seal up the category of vernacular theology itself by suggesting that his approach should stand alone and that it should replace other forms of moral teachings. Mishtooni Bose notices this tension within Pecock's corpus, suggesting, for example, that though his work opens up new ways of conceiving of lay and clerical roles within the religious community by emphasizing the importance of "argumentation in exchanges between clergy and laity," he also seeks to "control the consequences of such an experiment."[10] This attempt to control the consequences of his own experiments in changing the way knowledge is exchanged in the religious community is visible in the careful way that he structures his pedagogical system to ensure that lay initiative and agency never threaten clerical control. Pecock seems caught between a desire to foster the lay intellect by encouraging readers to wrestle with difficult and dense matters of *clergie* formerly restricted to the clerical domain and an anxiety about the kind of independent thought that this transmission of *clergie* might enable.

The attempt to control the consequences of his own experiment in opening up and expanding the discursive space of vernacular theology, particularly in matters of Christian faith, can be seen in the way that Pecock limits the rational capacity of readers to learning to recognize, receive, and see difficult, complex truths of faith presented by the clergy, rather than to examining these truths with a critical eye. As he argues that the truths of the Trinity are suitable content for his vernacular books, and "esili aweeldable of ech competently wittid lay man if he wolde take bisines therto," Pecock seals up the discursive freedoms of his readers at the very same time that he opens up new areas of inquiry for their consideration (*Reule*, 93). In the introduction to the *Reule*, he defends the capacity of the lay intellect to receive and understand complex truths by suggesting that the mercers of London and men who are "well learned in the kingis lawe of ynglond" use "so miche sotilte and heighte of witt" in their own occupations that they surely will apply themselves—or "bisette their grete, highe and sutel witt"—all the more to the matters of his *Reule*, which will be "lightir to be undirstonden, to be leerned and to be takun into the resoun" (21). Indeed, the truths about the Trinity that Pecock presents through rational argument are "perceivable" not only by these literate, skilled men of the world but by "ech competently wittid man" (90). What stands out from these kinds of declarations of faith in the capacity of his readers' intellect is Pecock's notion of how this intellect is to be applied in a passive way: the lay reader uses his great "capacite and receivabilnesse" to take in truths (*Folewer*, 13); to "see the cleer proofis of hem" (*Reule*, 87); and to "soone perceive" these truths to be true and to "receive [these truths] . . . into her feith" (*Reule*, 90). Clerics like Pecock formulate truths with careful, rational demonstrations and deliver or present to lay folk these truths that are "to be perceived and to be received of hem into consent" (*Reule*, 90). What is required of the lay reader is his acceptance, his assent to the truths of faith that are carefully laid out by the author.

Pecock distinguishes this kind of receiving action of the lay intellect from independent thinking when he argues that this deliverance of truths about the Trinity should not automatically prompt his lay readers to "sutele ferther in her owne resoning upon the leerning and the knowing of tho seid trouthis" (*Reule*, 88). There is a difference, apparently, between applying one's wits in consideration of the truths that Pecock presents and applying one's wits in uncharted territory. Pecock makes it clear that a lay reader who thinks outside the box of what is provided for his reflection is not part of his pedagogical system when he assures any objectors to his vernacular treatment of the Trinity that his readers will not respond to this discussion by thinking beyond the matters that he has laid out: "The lay peple wole holde hem weel paied with so miche deliveraunce as there is maad to hem of the trinite, and they wole be ful glad ther of and weel cherid and joied therby, and they wole lefir stond therto withoute ferther encerching and driving in her resoun than forto labore eny ferther biyonde tho same trouthis in resoning" (*Reule*, 98). This activity of "driving in her resoun" or "ferther encerchyng," of inferring, reasoning, and thinking beyond the knowledge they are given is clearly impertinent behavior: it is appropriate to consider the rational basis of Pecock's argument, and to examine the grounds and foundations of his principles and conclusions, but it is inappropriate for the "lay peple" to think in ways that Pecock has not directed on paths that he has not laid. This passage emblematizes a fear about the prospect of lay people using the rational skills and training that he has offered to them on matters outside the boundaries of his control; Pecock cannot guarantee what might happen if a lay reader applied the same analysis to truths that he had not carefully presented, broken down, and mapped out.

Pecock acknowledges the possibility that lay readers will apply their wits in unsupervised ways, however, when he goes on to state that even if a layman were to "drive in resoun folewyngly upon eny article of feith" there would be no real harm in his developing erroneous beliefs as long as he did not obstinately cling to them in the face of reason (*Reule*, 96). Pecock cannot deny that a reader may fall into error through the failure of his "craft of resonyng and of drivyng," but he cautions his readers that this assurance—that independent thinking leads to heresy only if a man obstinately cleaves to "false trowyng"— should not be seen as an invitation to "enserche ferther upon the seid maters of the trinite than is to hem delivered in this present book" (96–97). With this statement, Pecock allows that lay readers are quite capable of "enserchyng" further, beyond what is presented to them in his substantial treatment of Christian faith, but that they must *choose* to hold themselves "weel paied" with the knowledge he provides (97–98). Readers should be content with the doctrine delivered to them.

What is most important in this passage is the negative spin that Pecock puts on the activity of searching or reasoning further: he makes a clear connection between those who "stande and reste fro ferther enquering and resonyng upon the seid maters of the eukarist whiche ben delivered to hem by the chirche" and those who deserve to be "cherid and joied" by the truths of the Trinity (*Reule*, 97–98). The kind of reader that is competently "wittid" to understand the high matters of Pecock's works is not the kind of reader who is apt to let his thoughts run wild, outside the jurisdiction of Pecock's stable treatment of Christian faith. Though he does not quite succeed in convincing us that lay people are naturally just not prone to questioning or reasoning beyond what they are told, he does denigrate this activity enough to convince his readers that resisting speculative thought in matters outside his books makes them good readers. The development of the lay reader's intellect, therefore, in this context, is limited to honing the capacity to receive and consent to truths that have been driven out "and concluded forth in laboure and discours of resoun" by people with clerical training (*Reule*, 94). This serves to limit the jurisdictions of vernacular theology by putting certain topics out of bounds and ensuring that readers apply their intellectual faculties only to Pecock's carefully constructed arguments.

This passage shows that Pecock's faith in and stimulation of the lay intellect is at times in tension with his attempt to discipline and direct that lay intellect to safe lines of inquiry and stable modes of thought. Despite his best attempts to guarantee the orthodoxy of lay readers, he is ultimately creating the possibility that his readers will choose to exercise their carefully cultivated rational faculties in ways that he himself cannot foresee or prevent. If we look past Pecock's confident assurances about the mental powers of the laity and his blurring of lay and clerical mental worlds, we can detect throughout his corpus a degree of anxiety about the potential effects of transferring theological *clergie* into the vernacular—the same anxiety that Fiona Somerset detects in writers who worked decades before Pecock, such as Langland and Trevisa.[11] It is important, therefore, to pay attention not only to his ambitious plans for the education of laypeople but also to the way that the careful construction of his system of vernacular theology at times helps to guard against the kind of independent thought that the ecclesiastical institution hoped to wipe out through censorship and restrictive legislation. I would propose that if Pecock is generating his own system for enforcing orthodoxy, for controlling discursive possibilities, and reinforcing productive relations between clergy and laity, then perhaps we can see his body of work as one response among many to the Lollard heresy, as different voices became involved in the making of orthodoxy in the fifteenth century. This kind of analysis of Pecock's system depends on thinking about

Pecock, not as a defiant rebel, working on an ambitious project that attempted to open up discursive space in the face of ecclesiastical censorship, but in the way that he asks us to think of him: as an authoritative representative of the church, a powerful bishop, whose job was to ensure the health and vitality of the Christian community by promoting orthodoxy and shutting down the possibilities for heretical belief.

Appendix A

*Other Books Possibly
in Pecock's* Oeuvre

There are numerous references to these books throughout Pecock's works. It is possible that some of these may refer to the same book, as in the case of *The Lasse Book of Cristen Religioun* and *The Grettir Book of Cristen Religioun*. It is likely that *The xii Avauntagis of Tribulacioun* is not by Pecock himself: it is the only book he continually refers to as "a tretise." After each title, I have provided one reference in case readers are interested in viewing these book titles in context; there are, however, many more throughout his corpus.

Bifore Crier [*Reule*, 20]
The Book of Baptym [*Reule*, 375]
The Book of Counceils [*Reule*, 365]
The Book of Divine Office for Alle the Times of Yeere [*Donet*, 203]
The Book of Faith, Hope, and Charite [*Donet*, 37]
The Book of Lay Mennis Books [*Folewer*, 7]
The Book of Leerning [*Donet*, 177]
The Book of Making of Creaturis in General [*Donet*, 181]
The Book of Matrimonie [*Reule*, 276]
The Book of Ordris and Pastoral Care [*Reule*, 338]
The Book of Penaunce [*Donet*, 193]
The Book of Preesthode or of Preestis Power [*Reule*, 214]
The Book of Questiouns [*Donet*, 181]
The Book of Sacramentis [*Reule*, 364]

The Book of Sentence of Cristen Religioun [*Reule*, 297]
The Book of the Chirche [*Folewer*, 78]
The Book of Usure [*Donet*, 69]
The Book of Worschiping or of Signes [*Reule*, 364]
The Enchiridion or Manuel [*Donet*, 204]
The Filling of the Foure Tablis [*Reule*, 18]
The Grettir Book of Cristen Religioun [*Donet*, 42]
The Inproving of Mennis Insufficient Foormes [*Donet*, 81]
The Just Apprising of Doctouris [*Folewer*, 11]
The Just Apprising of Holy Scripture [*Reule*, 18]
The Lasse Book of Cristen Religioun [*Donet* 21]
The Proof of Cristen Feith [*BF*, 133]
The Provoker of Cristen Peple, or *The Forth Caller of Cristen Men* [*Donet*, 177]
The Spreding of the iiii Tablis [*Reule*, 365]
The Witnessing of the iiii Tablis [*Donet*, 177]
The xii Avauntagis of Tribulacioun [*Donet*, 56]

Appendix B

Pecock's Four Tables of
Thirty-One Virtues

The following points are covered briefly in Pecock's *Donet* and at length
with examples in Pecock's *Reule*.

Table 1
To live to God leerningly
To live to God preisingly
To live to God dispreisingly
To live to God preiyngly
To live to God thankingly
To live to God worshipingly
To live to God disworshipingly
To live to God sacramentaly

Table 2
To live to God goostly
To live to God obediently
To live to God rightfully or justly
To live to God mekely
To live to God trewly
To live to God beningnely
To live to God largely

Table 3
To live to oneself goostly
To live to oneself fleischely
To live to oneself worldly
To live to oneself clenly
To live to oneself honestly
To live to oneself paciently
To live to oneself doughtily
To live to oneself largely

Table 4
To live to our neighbour goostly
To live to our neighbour attendauntly
To live to our neighbour rightwisly or justly
To live to our neighbour mekely
To live to our neighbour accordingly
To live to our neighbour treuly
To live to our neighbour beningnely
To live to our neighbour largely

Notes

Introduction

1. S. Kelly and Perry, "'Hospitable Reading,'" 1.
2. See Kerby-Fulton, *Books under Suspicion*.
3. Doyle, "Survey of the Origins," 1.
4. Robertson, "Introduction," 78.
5. Georgianna, "Vernacular Theologies," 87. Kate Crassons also discusses the "capaciousness" of vernacular theology. See Crassons, "Performance Anxiety," 95.
6. Georgianna, "Vernacular Theologies," 91.
7. I. Johnson, "Vernacular? Theology?"
8. Georgianna, "Vernacular Theologies," 87.
9. Crassons, "Performance Anxiety," 95; Georgianna, "Vernacular Theologies," 89.
10. Brockwell, *Bishop Reginald Pecock*. See also Green, *Bishop Reginald Pecock*.
11. Scase, "Reginald Pecock" [1996], 75–146.
12. See Catto, "King's Government," 203.
13. See, for example, Bose, "Vernacular Philosophy," 73–99; Ghosh, "Bishop Reginald Pecock," 251–65; Scase, "Reginald Pecock" [1992], 261–74; Simpson, "Reginald Pecock," 271–87.
14. Watson, "Censorship and Cultural Change," 822–64.
15. Barratt, "Works of Religious Instruction," 415.
16. See Watson's "Censorship and Cultural Change," 822–64, for the wording of the individual decrees; for the Latin text, see Wilkins, *Concilia magnae*, 314–19.
17. See Somerset, "Professionalizing Translation," 145–58.
18. See McSheffrey, "Heresy, Orthodoxy," 47–80.

19. See Gillespie, "Chichele's Church."

20. Crassons, "Performance Anxiety," 98.

21. Scase, "Reginald Pecock" [1996], 102.

22. Scase, "Reginald Pecock" [1996], 104. See also Catto, "King's Government," 201–22.

23. On the temporal authority making an example of Pecock, see Scase, "Reginald Pecock" [1996], 116.

24. M. Johnson, "Accomplishment," 90.

25. Cobban, *Medieval English Universities*, 170.

26. Catto, "Theology after Wycliffism," 276.

27. On Pecock at Oxford, see Scase, "Reginald Pecock" [1996], 76–80. On the curriculum at Oxford's faculty of theology, see Courtenay, "Programs of Study," 325–50.

28. Catto, "Theology after Wycliffism," 264.

29. Catto, "Theology after Wycliffism," 269.

30. Catto, "Theology after Wycliffism," 266.

31. Baule, "Encountering the Word," 47.

32. Baule, "Encountering the Word," 47.

33. Baule, "Encountering the Word," 47.

34. Baule, "Encountering the Word," 48.

35. Baule, "Encountering the Word," 47. Pecock describes "felawlik comunicacioun" in *Folewer*, 8.

36. Baule, "Encountering the Word," 55.

37. Baule, "Encountering the Word," 50 n. 8.

38. Winstead, *John Capgrave's Fifteenth Century*, 20–21.

39. Winstead, *John Capgrave's Fifteenth Century*, 21.

40. Stock, *Listening for the Text*, 151.

41. Riddy, "Reading for England," 315. Riddy says, "I have taken the phrase 'textual community' from Brian Stock's *The Implications of Literacy*, but I do not use it in his sense. He applies it to people who know themselves to be a group. I intend by it the community of people who read the same text, who are brought together simply by the act of reading (or hearing); a community which the text itself creates insofar as it seeks an audience" (315).

42. Stock, *Listening for the Text*, 23, 153.

43. Stock, *Listening for the Text*, 23.

44. Stock, *Listening for the Text*, 156.

45. Stock, *Listening for the Text*, 23.

46. Stock, *Listening for the Text*, 158.

47. Stock, *Listening for the Text*, 157.

48. Strohm, "Writing and Reading," 466.

49. See Scase, "Reginald Pecock" [1996], 115. Scase notes that during the decades following his death, the University of Oxford "came under suspicion of harbouring his books and followers" (79). As Scase writes, the survival of six of his books suggests that Pecock's writings "remained a channel of his influence" (117). She notes that some fragments of his works survive, postulating that "little works, the *opuscula* which are mentioned so often in the trial documents," likely remained a source of influence (117).

50. Stock, *Listening for the Text*, 150.

51. Stock, *Listening for the Text*, 23.

52. Stock, *Listening for the Text*, 39.

53. McSheffrey, "Heresy, Orthodoxy," 48–49.

54. McSheffrey, "Heresy, Orthodoxy," 49.

55. Stock, *Listening for the Text*, 158.

56. Stock, *Listening for the Text*, 155.

Chapter 1   Pecock's Audience

My comments on Pecock's use of the corporate voice in this chapter are adapted from a conference paper, "Revolutionary Reading: Reginald Pecock's Books," presented at the New Chaucer Conference in Swansea, Wales, in July 2008. I am grateful to James Simpson for inviting me to speak in the session entitled "Reading," and I thank the audience and James for the helpful discussion that followed.

1. Strohm, "Chaucer's Audience(s)," 137.

2. Scase, "Reginald Pecock" [1996], 113–14.

3. Jauss, *Toward an Aesthetic*, 22.

4. Strohm, "Chaucer's Audience(s)," 140.

5. Iser, *How to Do Theory*, 57.

6. Scase, "Reginald Pecock" [1996], 92.

7. Sutton, *Mercery of London*, 166.

8. On the book trade, see Christianson, "Evidence for the Study," 102; on the provision of schools for children, see Sutton, *Mercery of London*, 169, and Barron, "Expansion of Education," 219–45; on the Guildhall Library, see Smith, "Library at Guildhall," 2–9; on records of book ownership, see Sutton, *Mercery of London*, 168–79.

9. Barron, "Expansion of Education," 229.

10. Pearsall, *"Canterbury Tales,"* 96.

11. Scase shows with various kinds of evidence that "Pecock's associations with a London-based circle of clergy, courtiers, and citizens evidently continued after his translation to the see of Chichester" in "Reginald Pecock" [1996], 101.

12. Pearsall, *"Canterbury Tales,"* 103.

13. Scase, "Reginald Pecock" [1996], 86.

14. Barron, "Richard Whittington," 199.

15. Sutton, *Mercery of London*, 160.

16. Imray, *Charity of Richard Whittington*, 15 and 9. See 9–15 for the respective roles of Whittington himself and his executors in conceiving of and instigating these charitable foundations.

17. Sutton, *Mercery of London*, 162. See Imray, *Charity of Richard Whittington*, for more detailed history of both foundations. On the college of priests, see Reddan, "Whittington's College," 225–26.

18. Barron, "Richard Whittington," 232.

19. Sutton, *Mercery of London*, 162.

20. Scase, "Reginald Pecock" [1996], 82.

21. Scase, "Reginald Pecock" [1996], 86.

22. Sutton, *Mercery of London*, 165.

23. Sutton, *Mercery of London*, 166.

24. Sutton, *Mercery of London*, 165.

25. Scase, "Reginald Pecock" [1996], 89.

26. Scase, "Reginald Pecock" [1996], 84.

27. Gillespie, "Haunted Text," 154.

28. Sutton, *Mercery of London*, 13.

29. Catto, "Theology after Wycliffism," 272.

30. Sutton, *Mercery of London*, 163.

31. Sutton, *Mercery of London*, 184–85.

32. Barron, *London*, 138.

33. Barron, *London*, 143, 138.

34. Barron, *London*, 147.

35. Scase, "Reginald Pecock" [1996], 95.

36. "Abbreviatio Reginaldi Pecok," in *Repressor*, 615.

37. Hudson, "Which Wyche?" 221–37.

38. Hudson, "Which Wyche?" 226.

39. Von Nolcken, "Richard Wyche," 143.

40. Sutton, *Mercery of London*, 179.

41. Sutton, *Mercery of London*, 169.

42. Sutton, *Mercery of London*, 169.

43. Wendy Scase, "Reginald Pecock" [1992], 261.

44. See Connolly, "Books," 170–81.

45. S. Kelly and Perry, "'Hospitable Reading,'" 2.

46. Sutton, *Mercery of London*, 170–71.

47. Sutton, *Mercery of London*, 168.

48. For the booklist, see Appendix 1 in Brewer, *Memoir*, 121–30.

49. Brewer, *Memoir*, 123.

50. Brewer, *Memoir*, 124.

51. Brewer, *Memoir*, 128.

52. Brewer, *Memoir*, 128.

53. See Seneca, *Dialogues and Essays*, 18–52 and 85–111.

54. Brewer, *Memoir*, 130.

55. See Vincent of Beauvais, *Speculum morale*.

56. Jauss, *Toward an Aesthetic*, 20, 22.

57. S. Kelly and Perry, "'Hospitable Reading,'" 3.

58. Jauss, *Toward an Aesthetic*, 23.

59. Compare Pecock, *Reule*, 248–52, with Aquinas's *Summa theologiae*, Secunda Secundae, article 84.

60. Jauss, *Toward an Aesthetic*, 22.

61. Riddy, "'Publication' before Print," 38.

62. Riddy, "'Publication' before Print," 40.

63. Sutton, *Mercery of London*, 165.

64. Scase, "Reginald Pecock" [1992], 261–74.

65. Scase, "Reginald Pecock" [1992], 262.

66. Scase, "Reginald Pecock" [1992], 265.

67. Gillespie, "Haunted Text," 129–72; Edwards, "Contexts of Notre Dame 67," 107–28.

68. Gillespie, "Haunted Text," 157.

69. Gillespie, "Haunted Text," 157, 136.

70. Gillespie, "Haunted Text," 136.

71. Gillespie, "Haunted Text," 133.

72. Gillespie, "Haunted Text," 150.

73. Gillespie, "Dial M for Mystic," 252.

74. See also Pecock, *Reule*, 295.

75. Wiethaus, "Thieves and Carnivals," 210.

76. For more on the *Liber albus*, see Barron, "Richard Whittington," 214; Kellaway, "John Carpenter's *Liber Albus*," 67–84; Lindenbaum, "London Texts," 294–96.

77. See Appleford, "Good Death," for more on this particular aspect of London religiosity.

78. Iser, "Indeterminacy," 8.

79. Iser, "Indeterminacy," 12–13.

80. Ingarden, *Literary Work of Art*, 262–64; Iser, "Indeterminacy," 10.

81. Iser, "Indeterminacy," 11.

82. The function of the corporate voice that utters both prayer and praise to God in Pecock's *Reule* can be illuminated by comparison to other texts in which readers are invited to appropriate the voice of the text. See Brantley, *Reading in the Wilderness*, 143–65. In her study of the performance of reading in British Library MS Additional 37049, Brantley argues that the "conflation of speaker and reader" implies or even creates the social framework of a Christian community.

Chapter 2   The Religious Education of the Laity

A version of this chapter has been published as "Reginald Pecock and the Religious Education of the Laity in Fifteenth-Century England," *Studies of Philology*, Winter 2010.

1. Barratt, "Works of Religious Instruction," 415.

2. Gillespie, "Vernacular Books of Religion," 317.

3. Beckwith, *Christ's Body*, 2.

4. Gillespie, "*Doctrina* and *Predicacio*," 36.

5. Gillespie, "*Doctrina* and *Predicacio*," 36, 46.

6. Barratt, "Works of Religious Instruction," 415.

7. Orme, *Education and Society*, 154.

8. Barratt, "Works of Religious Instruction," 415.

9. Holmstedt, *Speculum Christiani*, 2.

10. Hudson, *Works of a Lollard Preacher*, 53.

11. See Nelson, *Myrour*, 71.

12. Aquinas, *Summa contra Gentiles*, 4.

13. Gillespie, "*Lukynge in haly bukes*," 5.

14. Huot, "Polytextual Reading," 210.

15. See, for instance, Pecock, *Folewer*, 8.

16. Horstmann, "*Orologium sapientiae*," 326.

17. See chapter 5 for more on Pecock's book of reason.

18. Denley, "Elementary Teaching Techniques," 226. Denley describes various devices for instruction in pastoral manuals and religious didactic literature popular with the laity: among these teaching devices she includes the method of question-and-answer exchanges that lead to rote learning rather than to comprehension. Denley provides as an example a passage from Mirk's *Instructions for Parish Priests* in which the

preacher "breaks up the intimidating bulk of the Creed into manageable bits" that help to facilitate memorization (229). The technique of facilitating learning through repetition or mnemonic verse contrasts sharply with Pecock's technique of facilitating learning through comprehension of philosophical principles, such as the nature of sin, the nature of virtue, and the nature of the soul. Instead of memorizing the Creed, lay readers must understand where the teaching on the Creed fits within Pecock's theological system.

19. Gillespie, "*Doctrina* and *Predicacio*," 37; Barratt, "Works of Religious Instruction," 425.

20. I treat this approach (and its contrast to the mnemonic teaching methods) in more detail in chapter 5.

21. For extensive background on medieval elementary education, see the following studies: Moran, *Growth of English Schooling*; Orme, *Education and Society*; Orme, *Education in the West*; Orme, *English Schools*; Orme, *From Childhood to Chivalry*; Orme, *Medieval Schools*. At the elementary level, pupils at least seven years old would progress from learning the alphabet to learning to identify and pronounce the Latin words (at first without comprehension) of the core texts of the church service: the Pater Noster, the Creed, and the Hail Mary. Instruction in literacy therefore was combined with instruction in the basic prayers and doctrines deemed necessary for all to know, and church service books formed the basis for the standard reading curriculum.

22. Orme, *English Schools*, 62.

23. Orme, *English Schools*, 62–63.

24. Moran, *Growth of English Schooling*, 41–43.

25. Erler, "Devotional Literature," 495–96.

26. Moran, *Growth of English Schooling*, 43–46.

27. Orme, *English Schools*, 62.

28. Nelson, *Myrour*, 71.

29. McMahon, *Education*, 41.

30. McMahon, *Education*, 41–43.

31. McMahon, *Education*, 41–42.

32. Orme, *English Schools*, 60.

33. Orme, *English Schools*, 77–79, 118, 194. It may be significant that Pecock does not connect the endowment of schools with the founding of a chantry. Orme notes that most endowed schools in the fifteenth century were associated with chantries: "Education was a growing interest of the age, but it was still eclipsed by the popularity of the mass. . . . The founder of the school thus stood to gain spiritual benefits of a powerful

and effective kind if he made the master a priest whose daily masses would include perpetual intercessions for his soul. . . . Hardly anyone seems to have thought of founding a mere school whose master would simply be a schoolmaster" (196). For Pecock to regard the foundation of a school as an end in itself is radical.

34. Swanson, *Church and Society*, 304.

35. Moran, *Growth of English Schooling*, 43.

36. Nicholas Orme also discusses the education of girls in *English Schools*. He points out there were "at least a few schoolmistresses, whose duties must have been meant for young children of both sexes" (54).

37. For the activities of various Lollard communities during Pecock's time, see McSheffrey, *Gender and Heresy*.

38. *Wlatsum* is defined as disgusting, repugnant, repulsive, abominable in the *MED*, 14:798.

39. Hudson, *Premature Reformation*, 190 (see also Hudson, *Lollards and Their Books*); Hudson, *Premature Reformation*, 186–87.

40. Hudson, *Premature Reformation*, 206, 205.

41. See Hudson's section on Lollard education in *Premature Reformation*, 174–227, and Copeland's study of Lollard pedagogy in *Pedagogy, Intellectuals*.

42. Hudson, *Premature Reformation*, 192.

43. Hudson, *Premature Reformation*, 182.

44. Hudson, *Premature Reformation*, 194.

45. Hudson, *Premature Reformation*, 181.

46. Hudson, *Premature Reformation*, 182.

47. Hudson, *Premature Reformation*, 193.

48. Barratt, "Works of Religious Instruction," 413.

49. Barratt, "Works of Religious Instruction," 413.

50. Gillespie, "*Doctrina* and *Predicacio*," 38–39. See also Catto, "Religion," 43–55. Catto observes "an increasing tendency to diversification among surviving books of devotion" rather than a consistency of contents: books of hours bear "the stamp of individual character" and testify to "a more individual, humanized and intimate expression of religious sentiment" (49).

51. Orme, *From Childhood to Chivalry*, 128–29.

52. Orme, *From Childhood to Chivalry*, 128.

53. Orme, *From Childhood to Chivalry*, 133.

54. Orme, *Education and Society*, 156.

55. Orme, *Education and Society*, 174–75.

56. Copeland, *Pedagogy, Intellectuals*, 124.
57. Denley, "Elementary Teaching Techniques," 224.
58. Denley, "Elementary Teaching Techniques," 225.
59. Denley, "Elementary Teaching Techniques," 226.
60. Swanson, *Church and Society*, 304.
61. Orme, *From Childhood to Chivalry*, 128–29.
62. Copeland, *Pedagogy, Intellectuals*, 124.
63. Orme, *From Childhood to Chivalry*, 128.
64. See, for example, Pecock, *Reule*, 94–95, 252.
65. Wendy Scase, "Reginald Pecock" [1996], 93.

Chapter 3   Theological Training and the Mixed Life

1. Gillespie, "Vernacular Books of Religion," 317.

2. For a detailed discussion of the various definitions of action and contemplation, the ways these terms were distinguished from each other, and the ways they changed throughout the medieval period, see Constable, *Three Studies*.

3. *Carkful* is defined in the *MED* as "solicitous, anxious" (2:63). For a broad survey of ideas about the active life in Middle English literature, see Steele, *Towards a Spirituality*.

4. According to Constable, various writings that advocate the mixed life emphasize the benefits, value, and fruitfulness of active life in contrast to contemplative life. The positive valuation of the active life that Constable finds in these kinds of writings is often directly related to the context: bishops, for example, can be praised for abandoning the heights of contemplation for the more meritorious life of charity toward others. Constable observes that action gains more prestige in the later Middle Ages, but the examples that he provides of works that praise the active life over the contemplative while recommending a kind of mixed life are relatively few in comparison to those works that tend to praise the contemplative life. The strongest assertion of the superiority of Martha in a mixed life is typified by Master Eckhart's notion, in the fourteenth century, of contemplation as preparation for action in the world. For Eckhart, "Mary was only at the beginning of the mystic fulfilment which involved work, asceticism, and apostolic activity as well as contemplation, and Martha was closer to God" (Constable, *Three Studies*, 116). What is most interesting about the way Pecock describes Mary is that he

recommends her as a model for a lay reader, while others recommend the path from contemplation to action for prelates and churchmen who abandon the heights of contemplation for the active life serving God through ministry and education. As I show later in this chapter, Pecock is similar to Hilton in the way he makes this kind of mixed life a model for the laity.

5. Watson, "Fashioning the Puritan Gentry-Woman," 180.

6. Rice, *Lay Piety*, 56.

7. McCarthy, *Book to a Mother*, 20.

8. Rice, *Lay Piety*, ix.

9. In other works, contemplative life is described as an ascending path to God. The ascent also can be described as a progression through three stages: purgative, illuminative, and unitive. See Hogg, "Unpublished Texts," 241–84, for a printed brief tract on active and contemplative lives from a manuscript that comes from a Carthusian monastery. In this tract on active and contemplative lives, the contemplative begins with the purgative stage, cleansing his soul through nightly meditation on his sins and trespasses, meditation on the Passion, prayers to Mary, and prayers to the Lord for forgiveness; after the purgative comes the illuminative stage, in which the individual calls his thoughts and desires together and focuses them on God so that he may be ready to receive "the light of the godly beme" (280). The mind and the will are trained on God, while the individual waits meekly for the time when the Lord chooses to ravish his mind "abowne itself to be fedde with the fayr foode of angels" (280). The experience of illumination enables the individual to understand scripture and to receive "mony lightnynges of grace" (281). The third stage is unitive, in which the individual soul is joined in marriage to God; the two are knit together in grace to become one spirit.

10. Gillespie, "*Lukynge in haly bukes*," 1–27.

11. Hodgson, "Ladder of Foure Ronges," 101.

12. Gillespie, "Vernacular Books of Religion," 317.

13. Hodgson, "Ladder of Foure Ronges" 102.

14. Gillespie, "*Lukynge in haly bukes*," 4. For the adaptation and transformation of the treatise "A Ladder" for a wider audience, in the treatise *Gratia Dei*, see Keiser, "'Noght how lang man lifs,'" 145–59. For instance, Keiser describes the way the adapter aims to "bring his reinterpretation of the monastic and contemplative ideal to a wide audience" by blurring the careful distinctions that Guigo makes among meditation, prayer, and contemplation (158).

15. Huot, "Polytextual Reading," 205.

16. Huot, "Polytextual Reading," 202.

17. Gillespie, "Mystic's Foot," 207.

18. Connolly, *Contemplations*, 40. Margaret Connolly's analysis of the ownership of the fifteenth-century copies indicates that the text reached its intended audience of laity and was also owned by various religious: "The text largely reached the audience for which it was written" (7).

19. Connolly, *Contemplations*, 7.

20. Connolly, *Contemplations*, 25.

21. Consacro, "Author of *The Abbey*," 20.

22. Consacro, "Critical Edition," 1.

23. Consacro, "Critical Edition," 31.

24. Consacro, "Author of *The Abbey*," 15.

25. Rice, *Lay Piety*, 17, 26.

26. Consacro, "Critical Edition," 19, and Rice, *Lay Piety*, 26–27.

27. Rice, *Lay Piety*, x–xi.

28. Rice, *Lay Piety*, xi.

29. Kempster, "Question of Audience," 259.

30. Refer to Constable, *Three Studies*, for the history of similar advice aimed at an ecclesiastical audience. Constable says that writers like Augustine defined the ideal Christian life as a combination of charitable works with inner meditation: "No one should be so tranquil that in his tranquility he neglects his neighbour's need, nor should he be so busy that he does not need the contemplation of God" (Constable, *Three Studies*, 19, citing Augustine's *City of God*). Constable finds evidence in early writings that the mixed life was portrayed as the ideal for all Christian people, whether religious or lay (especially in works that praised important laypeople such as noblewomen who embraced both lives), but scholars of Hilton's works agree that his is the first instance of an English work designed for a lay reader that sets out with great care and detail the kinds of practical instructions for mixing the two lives that were previously given only to bishops, monks, and clerics.

31. Hilton, *Walter Hilton's Mixed Life*, 34–35.

32. Hilton, *Walter Hilton's Mixed Life*, 25–26.

33. Hilton, *Walter Hilton's Mixed Life*, 26.

34. Hilton, *Walter Hilton's Mixed Life*, 36.

35. Hilton, *Walter Hilton's Mixed Life*, 38–39.

36. Hilton, *Walter Hilton's Mixed Life*, 14.

37. Hilton, *Walter Hilton's Mixed Life*, 33.

38. Hilton, *Scale of Perfection*, 35–36.

39. Glasscoe, "Time of Passion," 145.

40. Hilton, *Scale of Perfection*, 38.

41. Hilton, *Scale of Perfection*, 39. See also Russell-Smith, "Walter Hilton," 182–97; Baker, "Active and Contemplative Lives," 85–102; and Clark, "Action and Contemplation," 258–74, for different views about the ambiguity in Hilton's treatment of the subject.

42. I borrow this metaphor from George Perry's comments on St. Edmund's *Mirror* in *Religious Pieces*, xi.

43. Kempster, "Question of Audience," 258, 268.

44. Carey, "Devout Literate Laypeople," 370.

45. For a detailed account of Cicely's devotions, see Armstrong, "Piety of Cicely," 68–91.

46. Keiser, "'To Knawe God Almyghtyn,'" 103, 114. Thornton was the scribe of British Library MS 31042 and Lincoln Cathedral Library MS 91.

47. Carey, "Devout Literate Laypeople," 361.

48. Carey, "Devout Literate Laypeople," 370.

49. See chapter 7 of this study for a closer examination of Pecock's plans to distribute his books to all members of the laity.

Chapter 4   Ritual Reading and Meditative Reading

1. Hussey, "Petitions of the Paternoster," 8.

2. Love, *Nicholas Love's Mirror*, 10.

3. See Bernard of Clairvaux, *On the Song of Songs*, 1.

4. Flanigan, Ashley, and Sheingorn, "Liturgy as Social Performance," 652.

5. Flanigan, Ashley, and Sheingorn, "Liturgy as Social Performance," 641.

6. Flanigan, Ashley, and Sheingorn, "Liturgy as Social Performance," 637.

7. Zieman, "Playing Doctor," 308.

8. Zieman, "Playing Doctor," 320.

9. *Obsecraciouns* is defined in the *MED* as "a prayer of supplication" or "an entreaty" (7:30).

10. Duffy, "Elite and Popular Religion," 141.

11. Erler, "Devotional Literature," 495, 497.

12. Erler, "Devotional Literature," 495–96.

13. Erler, "Devotional Literature," 497.

14. Saenger, "Books of Hours," 148. See Marjorie Curry Woods, "Shared Books," 177–89, for the circulation of primers and their use as a basic reading text.

15. Saenger, "Books of Hours," 153.

16. Saenger, "Books of Hours," 155.

17. Duffy, "Elite and Popular Religion," 152.

18. Duffy, "Books of Hours," 153.

19. Blunt, *Myroure*, 2.

20. Blunt, *Myroure*, 70.

21. Blunt, *Myroure*, 71.

22. Blunt, *Myroure*, 71.

23. Bryan, *Looking Inward*, 85.

24. Bryan, *Looking Inward*, 85.

25. Schirmer, "Reading Lessons," 347.

26. Schirmer, "Reading Lessons," 358.

27. Schirmer, "Reading Lessons," 355.

28. Schirmer, "Reading Lessons," 359.

29. Bazire and Colledge, *Chastising*, 221.

30. Saenger, "Books of Hours," 148–49.

31. Schirmer, "Reading Lessons," 360; Bazire and Colledge, *Chastising*, 222.

32. Glasscoe, "Time of Passion," 145.

33. Gillespie, "*Lukynge in haly bukes*," 2.

34. Ward, *Prayers and Meditations*, 43–44.

35. *Currauntli* is defined in the *MED* as "quickly, with facility" (2:795).

36. Aston, *Lollards and Reformers*, 119.

37. The book of reason is examined in chapter 5 of this book.

38. On Edmund of Abingdon, see Lawrence, "Edmund of Abingdon," 213–29; on the Latin text, see Forshaw's edition (Edmund of Abingdon, *Speculum religiosorum and Speculum ecclesie*) and her articles "New Light" and "St Edmund's *Speculum*."

39. Forshaw's introduction to Edmund of Abingdon, *Speculum religiosorum and Speculum ecclesie*, 16.

40. Edmund of Abingdon, *Mirror*, 21.

41. Edmund of Abingdon, *Mirror*, 21.

42. Forshaw's introduction to Edmund of Abingdon, *Speculum religiosorum and Speculum ecclesie*, 18.

43. Edmund of Abingdon, *Mirror*, 21.

44. Edmund of Abingdon, *Mirror*, 23.

45. Edmund of Abingdon, *Mirror*, 40.

46. See Hilton, *Walter Hilton's Mixed Life*, 51–58, for a similar list: "Sumtyme thenke on thy synnes bifore doon, and of thi freeltees that thou fallest inne eche dai, and aske merci and for3yuenesse for hem. . . . Haue mynde of the manhede of oure lord in his birthe and in his passioun, or in ony of his werkes, and feede thi thou3t with goostli ymaginacions of it for to stire thyne affecciouns more to the loue of him. . . . Thenke of the wrecchidnesse, myscheues and perilis, bodili and goostli, that fallen in this liyf, and aftir that for to thenke of the ioies of heuene, hou moche blisse there is and ioie."

47. Edmund of Abingdon, *Mirror*, 20.

48. Hirsh, "Prayer and Meditation," 55–66.

49. Hirsh, "Prayer and Meditation," 57.

50. Hirsh, "Prayer and Meditation," 60.

51. Hirsh and others who study the compilation of late medieval devotional manuscripts or anthologies also note, however, that order is often random and depends on availability of material for inclusion.

52. Edmund of Abingdon, *Mirror*, 21.

53. Edmund of Abingdon, *Mirror*, 46.

54. Edmund of Abingdon, *Mirror*, 49.

55. For one example of a Passion meditation that resembles the kind used by spiritually ambitious laypersons who observed the canonical hours and pursued a mixed life outside the cloister, see Hennessy, "Passion Devotion," 213–56. See also Glasscoe, "Time of Passion," 141–60, in which Glasscoe discusses the affinity between the liturgy and the meditations on the Passion that were used by members of the laity.

56. *Stertmele* is defined in the *MED* as "irregularly, fitfully, by starts" (11:686).

57. Edmund of Abingdon, *Mirror*, 48.

58. Edmund of Abingdon, *Mirror*, 48–49.

59. Glasscoe, "Time of Passion," 145.

60. Colledge and Walsh's introduction to Guigo II, *Ladder of Monks*, 24, 40.

61. Hodgson, *Ladder of Foure Ronges*, 109.

62. Hodgson, *Pistle of Preier*, 48–59 and 56–57.

63. Hodgson, *Pistle of Preier*, 56.

64. Glasscoe, "Time of Passion," 145.

65. Salter, *Nicholas Love's Myrrour*, 176.

66. Keiser, "'To Knawe God Almyghtyn,'" 119.

67. For evidence of book ownership within the London merchant community, see Kempster, "Question of Audience," 257–89; and Carey, "Devout Literate Laypeople," 361–81.

68. Gillespie, "Mystic's Foot," 202.

69. Gillespie, "Mystic's Foot," 202–3.

Chapter 5   The Book of Reason

1. See Briggs, "Teaching Philosophy," 99, on the translation of moral philosophy, which was "the branch of the school curriculum deemed by Latinate *literati* and readers of the vernacular alike as the most useful for a lay audience," as the "vulgarization of an extensive and varied literature loaded with complex and difficult-to-comprehend philosophical concepts." In Pecock's view, God has established for Christians a moral law that should govern their behavior, actions, and interactions: to properly follow this law, Christians need an understanding of the principles of moral philosophy. Pecock's emphasis on moral philosophy—on teaching readers about human actions, human behavior, and human relationships through instruction on subjects like the soul, the will, the intellect, the passions, the various workings of virtue and vice, the various differences between virtuous or moral works performed for the benefit of others, and the governances and rules of God's moral law—reveals his notion that the best way to educate the laity in religion is to start with a grounding of moral philosophy.

2. Mulder-Bakker, introduction to *Seeing and Knowing*, 4.

3. Mulder-Bakker, introduction to *Seeing and Knowing*, 4.

4. I borrow the phrase "talking about the things of God" from Riddy, "Women Talking," 104–17.

5. Pantin, "*Instructions*," 399.

6. "What euer lay man schal rede this book and, aftir longe studi and aftir help takun of clerkis, sum parcel therof he schal not mowe vndirstonde, he hath therin no wrong neither hurt, for he may ouer lepe thilk parcel and fede him in othire parties whiche he may with competent labour and counseil with clerkis undirstonde. Ffor so doon clerkis in dyuynyte, and so thei musten needis do, and ellis in bookis of dyunyute thei schulden neuer thryue."

7. *Ourning* is defined in the *MED* as "adornment, decoration" (7:385).

8. Kenny and Pinborg, "Medieval Philosophical Literature," 28.

9. Kenny and Pinborg, "Medieval Philosophical Literature," 28.

10. Serene, "Demonstrative Science," 496.

11. Serene, "Demonstrative Science," 498.

12. Serene, "Demonstrative Science," 513.

13. Haines, "Church, Society and Politics," 143.

14. Haines, "Church, Society and Politics," 146–47.

15. Wenzel, *Latin Sermon Collections*, 243.

16. Harvey, "Ymage of Love," 745.

17. Harvey, "Ymage of Love," 745.

18. Harvey, "Ymage of Love," 746.

19. Delany, "Late-Medieval Attack," 36.

20. Bonaventure, *Mind's Road to God*, 2.2, quoted in Delany, "Late-Medieval Attack," 36.

21. Rosemann, *Understanding Scholastic Thought*, 92.

22. Rosemann, *Understanding Scholastic Thought*, 94.

23. Mulder-Bakker, introduction to *Seeing and Knowing*, 16.

24. Mulder-Bakker, introduction to *Seeing and Knowing*, 4. See Somerset, *Clerical Discourse*, for a detailed discussion of the way that various intellectuals, working in the late fourteenth century and early fifteenth century, share Pecock's views of the ability of the laity to both understand and use clerical arguments. Somerset's study does not extend to the mid–fifteenth century and therefore does not consider Pecock's contribution to this discussion. However, where Pecock stands in relation to writers like Langland, Thorpe, and Trevisa can be summarized in the following way: while these earlier writers are engaged in thinking about the issue of lay appropriation of clerical argument and the lay invasion of the clerical stronghold, Pecock actually maps out systematic strategies to enable his readers to work through clerical arguments. Getting lay readers to understand clerical forms of argument is now a necessity in his educational program, rather than a controversial idea or project. Of course, many of Pecock's orthodox contemporaries would have disagreed with him on this point; his faith in the lay intellect and his desire to educate the laity set him apart from those who wished to ensure orthodoxy by limiting the agency and autonomy of the lay intellect. In Pecock's view, handing the laity the tools of clerical argument is a way to ensure orthodoxy by equipping the laity with the ability to understand and defend their faith.

25. See M. Johnson, "Accomplishment," 85–103; Flannery, *Acts amid Precepts*.

26. See Aston, *Lollards and Reformers*, 128. Aston describes this sermon collection of ninety-five addresses, "which purports to have been de-

livered day by day in some kind of homilectic marathon," as a vernacular sequence that appears to have been aimed at "mainly ordinary country people who were reminded of their duty to render tithe, and to whom religion was presented in terms of shovel and spade." See also Brandeis, *Jacob's Well*.

27. McCarthy, *Book to a Mother*, 57.

28. McCarthy, *Book to a Mother*, 58.

29. Siegfried Wenzel discusses the preaching of *pastoralia* in *Latin Sermon Collections*, 346–53.

30. *Gibilet* is defined in the *MED* as either the "edible entrails of a fowl" or "a gratuitous addition, or odds and ends" (4:103).

31. When Pecock says that "alle cristen peple owen to be scolers" in "dyuynyte," this forecasts, in important ways, the stress on the individual lay believer by early modern figures such as Erasmus and Luther—the vitality of the Christian community lies with its lay believers, and the job of the clergy is to act as educators.

Chapter 6   The Bible

1. Pecock labels the Lollards as "Bible men" in *Repressor*, 36.

2. Gradon, *English Wycliffite Sermons*, 2:59.

3. Gradon, *English Wycliffite Sermons*, 2:60–61.

4. Gradon, *English Wycliffite Sermons*, 2:372.

5. Hudson, *Premature Reformation*, 228.

6. Gradon, *English Wycliffite Sermons*, 2:60.

7. Hudson, *Works of a Lollard Preacher*, 161.

8. For the notion that exegesis must be a handmaid to the Bible, see Wyclif, *On the Truth*, 114.

9. Simpson, *Reform and Cultural Revolution*, 498.

10. Hoccleve writes, "Lete holy chirche medle of the doctrine / Of Crystes lawes and of his byleeue, / And lete alle other folke therto enclyne, / And of our feith noon arguments meeue," in "To Sir John Oldcastle," in *Hoccleve's Works*, 12.

11. Ford, *John Mirk's Festial*, 113.

12. Ford, *John Mirk's Festial*, 113, 116.

13. Spencer, *English Preaching*, 134–95; Wenzel, *Latin Sermon Collections*, 370–94.

14. Winstead, *John Capgrave's Fifteenth Century*, 59.

15. Winstead, *John Capgrave's Fifteenth Century*, 60.

16. Ghosh, *Wycliffite Heresy*, 19.

17. On this reformist tradition, see Gillespie, "Chichele's Church."

18. Simpson, *Reform and Cultural Revolution*, 462.

19. Hudson, *Two Wycliffite Texts*, 46.

20. Aers, "Faith, Ethics, and Community," 350.

21. Aers, "Faith, Ethics, and Community," 358.

22. Ghosh, *Wycliffite Heresy*, 39.

23. Amtower, *Engaging Words*, 80.

24. Amtower, *Engaging Words*, 82.

25. Amtower, *Engaging Words*, 84.

26. Moore, "Negative Hermeneutics," 708.

27. Fish, *Is There a Text*, 171.

28. McClintock Fulkerson, "Is There a (Non-sexist) Bible," 228.

29. Moore, "Negative Hermeneutics," 710.

30. Moore, "Negative Hermeneutics," 717.

31. McClintock Fulkerson, "Is There a (Non-sexist) Bible," 225.

32. Simpson, "Faith and Hermeneutics," 218.

33. Simpson, "Faith and Hermeneutics," 218.

34. Simpson, "Faith and Hermeneutics," 231.

35. Simpson, *Reform and Cultural Revolution*, 463.

36. Quotations from Simpson, "Faith and Hermeneutics," 232.

37. McClintock Fulkerson, "Is There a (Non-sexist) Bible," 228

38. Castelli, "Feminist and Womanist Criticism," 267.

39. McClintock Fulkerson, "Is There a (Non-sexist) Bible," 228.

40. Moore, "Negative Hermeneutics," 717.

41. On interpretive communities as "fragile," see Fish, *Is There a Text*, 171.

42. For an alternative perspective, see Winstead, *John Capgrave's Fifteenth Century*, 83, as well as Taylor, "Translation, Censorship," 143–60.

Chapter 7   Lay-Cleric Relations in the Textual Community

1. Ford, *John Mirk's Festial*, 33.

2. Barr, "Wycliffite Representation," 205.

3. Ford, *John Mirk's Festial*, 150. For instance, in Lollard accounts of lay confession, agency belongs with the penitent, who communicates directly with God, rather than through a priest. In the Lollard sermons edited by Gloria Cigman, the lay sinner is assured that God will "neyheth" to a penitent soul and "for3eueth him his synnes" despite the ab-

sence of a clerical authority. See this quotation in Ford, *John Mirk's Festial*, 38; see Cigman, *Lollard Sermons*, 3.

4. Ford, *John Mirk's Festial*, 150. Rita Copeland suggests that the blurring of the dividing line between clergy and laity also occurs in a theory of pedagogy that is radically different from traditional notions about the relationship between teacher and student. The Wycliffite project of leveling magisterial hierarchies is depicted by Copeland in her *Pedagogy, Intellectuals*, 99–140.

5. Georgianna, "Vernacular Theologies," 89.

6. Love, *Nicholas Love's Mirror*, 10.

7. Somerset, "As just as is a squyre," 193.

8. Simpson, "Saving Satire," 388; see also Simpson, "Constraints of Satire," 11–31.

9. Simpson, "Saving Satire," 394.

10. Simpson, "Saving Satire," 397.

11. Somerset, "As just as is a squyre," 205.

12. Quotation from Longleat MS 4, Folio 6va.

13. Simpson, "Saving Satire," 397.

14. Longleat MS 4, Folio 41va.

15. Simpson, "Saving Satire," 396.

16. Longleat MS 4, Folio 9vb.

17. Ford, *John Mirk's Festial*, 33.

18. Ford, *John Mirk's Festial*, 14.

19. Ford, "Autonomy of Conscience," 7.

20. See Butler, "William Butler's Determination," 399–418; Hudson discusses the Oxford translation debate in the chapter "The Debate on Bible Translation" in *Lollards and Their Books*, 67–84.

21. Somerset, "As just as is a squyre," 193.

22. Bourdieu, *Reproduction in Education*, 4.

23. Bourdieu, *Reproduction in Education*, 5.

24. "What euer lay man schal rede this book and, aftir longe studi and aftir help takun of clerkis, sum parcel therof he schal not mowe vndirstonde, he hath therin no wrong neither hurt, for he may ouer lepe thilk parcel and fede him in othire parties whiche he may with competent labour and counseil with clerkis undirstonde. Ffor so doon clerkis in dyuynyte, and so thei musten needis do, and ellis in bookis of dyunyute thei schulden neuer thryue."

25. Somerset, "As just as is a squyr," 205.

26. For examples of the model of meditative reading, adapted by some writers of late medieval English religious texts, see Wogan-Browne

et al., *Idea of the Vernacular*, 209–310. See especially an excerpt from the fourteenth-century devotional text *A Talking of the Love of God*, which invites readers to find "swete fruit" in meditation on its contents; this work was probably written for nuns but circulated among aristocratic readers (223). See also the Middle English translation of Guigo II's *Ladder of Monks*, which is discussed and cited in chapter 2 of this study. In this text, reading, prayer, meditation, and contemplation are described in the following way: "Lesson puttyth as it were hole mete to the mouth; meditacion chewith & brekith it; prayere fyndith savoure; contemplacion is the liking swettnes that so myche comfortith" (Hodgson, *Ladder of Foure Ronges*, 101).

27. Bose, "Vernacular Philosophy," 73–99.

28. Bose, "Vernacular Philosophy," 91.

29. Ford, "Autonomy of Conscience," 7.

30. Ford, *John Mirk's Festial*, 14.

31. Scase, "Reginald Pecock," [1992], 261–74. On common-profit books, see also Moran, "'Common Profit' Library," 17–25, and H. Bennett, "Production and Dissemination," 167–78.

32. Galloway, "Making of a Social Ethic," 365–83.

33. Galloway, "Making of a Social Ethic," 374.

34. Galloway, "Making of a Social Ethic," 380.

35. Galloway, "Making of a Social Ethic," 381.

36. Galloway, "Making of a Social Ethic," 366.

37. Middleton, "Idea of Public Poetry," 94–114.

38. Middleton, "Idea of Public Poetry," 96.

39. Middleton, "Idea of Public Poetry," 95.

40. Newman, *God and the Goddesses*, 51–52.

41. Newman, *God and the Goddesses*, 52.

42. Newman, *God and the Goddesses*, 53.

43. Newman, *God and the Goddesses*, 53.

44. Bernard Silvestris, *Cosmographia*, 68.

45. Bernard Silvestris, *Cosmographia*, 6–7.

46. Bernard Silvestris, *Cosmographia*, 9.

47. Galloway, "Making of a Social Ethic," 378.

48. Newman, *God and the Goddesses*, 114.

49. Quotation from Newman, *God and the Goddesses*, 114.

50. Galloway, "Making of a Social Ethic," 383 n. 48.

51. Middleton, "Idea of Public Poetry," 97.

52. Middleton, "Idea of Public Poetry," 99.

53. Rubin, "Small Groups," 134. Rubin's bibliography on the historiography of the use of "community" is extensive. See also the extensive

bibliography and discussion on scholarly use and abuse of the notion of "community" in Wogan-Browne, "Analytical Survey 5," 229–97.

54. Rubin, "Small Groups," 134.

55. Fletcher, "Unity of the State," 103–37. In this article, Fletcher describes the three manuscripts in which this sermon is copied and hazards that they are all written by the same scribe and directed toward a lay audience.

56. Fletcher, "Unity of the State," 109.

57. Fletcher, "Unity of the State," 135 n. 42.

58. Fletcher, "Unity of the State," 135 n. 42.

59. Scase, "Reginald Pecock," [1992], 267.

60. Rees Jones, "'*Peler of Holy Cherch*,'" 391, 389.

61. Rees Jones, "'*Peler of Holy Cherch*,'" 389.

62. Rees Jones, "'*Peler of Holy Cherch*,'" 391.

63. Ford, *Mirk's Festial*, 150.

Conclusion

1. Haines, "Reginald Pecock," 125.

2. Ferguson, "Reginald Pecock," 162.

3. See Wooding, *Rethinking Catholicism*. Wooding writes, for example, that the efforts to keep the English Catholic Church together during the ascent of Protestantism led to the development of a new "strain of Catholic thought" that shared a great deal with humanism and even with aspects of English Protestantism such as the concentration on the authority of scripture (8). Wooding argues that the "experience of the Henrician Reformation had given new dimensions to English Catholicism, widening the possibilities of an ideological tradition already dynamic and diverse" (113). She suggests that reformed Catholic understanding absorbed "the imperatives of the Henrician reformation" (80).

4. Simpson, *Reform and Cultural Revolution*, 1.

5. Simpson, *Reform and Cultural Revolution*, 559.

6. Simpson, *Reform and Cultural Revolution*, 343.

7. Simpson, *Reform and Cultural Revolution*, 343.

8. Wendy Scase, "Reginald Pecock" [1996], 115.

9. Simpson, *Reform and Cultural Revolution*, 558.

10. Bose, "Reginald Pecock's Vernacular Voice," 234–35.

11. Somerset, *Clerical Discourse*.

Bibliography

Manuscripts

Longleat MS 4, Longleat House, Wiltshire. Quotations from Longleat MS 4 are included by permission of the Marquess of Bath, Longleat House, Warminster, Wiltshire, Great Britain.

Medieval Works

Aquinas, Thomas. *The Summa contra Gentiles*. Edited by English Dominican Friars. London: Burns Oates and Washbourne, 1924.

———. *Summa theologiae*. Edited by Thomas Gillby et al. 60 vols. London: Blackfriars, 1963.

Arntz, Sister Mary Luke, ed. *Richard Rolle and the Holy Boke Gratia Dei: An Edition with Commentary*. Elizabethan and Renaissance Studies 92:2. Salzburg: Institut für Anglistik und Amerikanistik, 1981.

Barnum, Priscilla, ed. *Dives and Pauper*. 2 vols. EETS, o.s., 275 and 280. Oxford: Oxford University Press, 1980.

Barratt, Alexandra, ed. *The Boke of Tribulacyon Edited from MS Bodley 423*. Middle English Texts 15. Heidelberg: Carl Winter, 1983.

Bazire, Joyce, and Eric Colledge, eds. *The Chastising of God's Children*. Oxford: Blackwell, 1957.

Bernard of Clairvaux. *On the Song of Songs*. Translated by Kilian Walsh. Vol. 2 of *The Works of Bernard of Clairvaux*. Cistercian Fathers Series 4. Spenser, MA: Cistercian Publications, 1971.

Bernard Silvestris. *The Cosmographia of Bernardus Silvestris: A Translation with Introduction and Notes by Winthrop Wetherbee*. Edited by Winthrop Wetherbee. New York: Columbia University Press, 1973.

Blunt, John Henry, ed. *The Myroure of Oure Ladye*. EETS, e.s., 19. 1873. Reprint, Millwood, NY: Kraus Reprint, 1973.

Bonaventure. *The Mind's Road to God*. Translated by George Boas. New York: Liberal Arts Press, 1953.

Brandeis, Arthur, ed. *Jacob's Well*. EETS, o.s., 115. 1900. Reprint, New York: Kraus Reprint, 1973.

Butler, William. "William Butler's Determination against Biblical Translations." In *The Lollard Bible and Other Medieval Biblical Versions*, edited by Margaret Deanesly, 399–418. Cambridge: Cambridge University Press, 1966.

Cigman, Gloria, ed. *Lollard Sermons*. EETS, o.s., 294. Oxford: Oxford University Press, 1989.

Connolly, Margaret, ed. *Contemplations of the Dread and Love of God (Fervor amoris)*. EETS, o.s., 303. Oxford: Oxford University Press, 1993.

Consacro, Peter. "A Critical Edition of *The Abbey of the Holy Ghost* from All Known Extant English Manuscripts." PhD diss., Fordham University, 1971.

Deanesly, Margaret, ed. "The Holi Prophete David Seith." In *The Lollard Bible and Other Medieval Versions*, edited by Margaret Deanesly, 446–56. Cambridge: Cambridge University Press, 1966.

Edmund of Abingdon. *Speculum religiosorum* and *Speculum ecclesie*. Edited by Helen P. Forshaw. Auctores Britannici Medii Aevi 3. London: Oxford University Press, 1973.

Gradon, Pamela, ed. *English Wycliffite Sermons*. Vol. 2. Oxford: Clarendon Press, 1988.

Guigo II. *The Ladder of Monks: A Letter on the Contemplative Life; and Twelve Meditations by Guigo II*. Edited and translated by Edmund Colledge and James Walsh. New York: Image Books, 1978.

Hilton, Walter. *The Scale of Perfection*. Edited by Thomas H. Bestul. Kalamazoo, MI: Medieval Institute Publications, 2000.

———. *Walter Hilton's Mixed Life Edited from Lambeth Palace MS 472*. Edited by S. J. Ogilvie-Thomson. Elizabethan and Renaissance Studies 92:15. Salzburg Studies in English Literature. Salzburg: Institut für Anglistik und Amerikanistik, 1986.

Hoccleve, Thomas. *Hoccleve's Works: The Minor Poems*. Edited by Frederick J. Furnivall. EETS, e.s., 61. 1892. Reprint, London: Oxford University Press, 1970.

Hodgson, Phyllis, ed. *A Ladder of Foure Ronges by the Which Men Mowe Wele Clyme to Heven*. In *Deonise Hid Diuinite, and Other Treatises on Contemplative Prayer Related to the Cloud of Unknowing: A Tretyse of the*

Stodye of Wysdome That Men Clepen Beniamyn; A Pistle of Preier; A Pistle of Discrecioun of Stirings; A Tretise of Discrescyon of Spirites, 100–117, Appendix B. EETS, o.s., 231. London: Oxford University Press, 1958.

———. *A Pistle of Preier.* In *Deonise Hid Diuinite, and Other Treatises on Contemplative Prayer Related to the Cloud of Unknowing: A Tretyse of the Stodye of Wysdome That Men Clepen Beniamyn; A Pistle of Preier; A Pistle of Discrecioun of Stirings; A Tretise of Discrescyon of Spirites*, edited by Phyllis Hodgson, 48–59. EETS, o.s., 231. London: Oxford University Press, 1958.

Holmstedt, Gustaf, ed. *Speculum Christiani: A Middle English Religious Treatise of the 14th Century.* EETS, o.s., 182. 1933. Reprint, New York: Kraus Reprint, 1971.

The Holy Bible: Made from the Latin Vulgate by John Wycliffe and His Followers. Edited by Josiah Forshall and Frederic Madden. Oxford: Oxford University Press, 1850.

Horstmann, Karl, ed. "*Orologium sapientiae* or The Seven Poyntes of Trewe Wisdom aus MS Douce 114." *Anglia* 10 (1887): 333–89.

Hudson, Anne, ed. *Two Wycliffite Texts: The Sermon of William Taylor 1406; The Testimony of William Thorpe 1407.* EETS, o.s., 301. Oxford: Oxford University Press, 1993.

———, ed. *The Works of a Lollard Preacher: The Sermon Omnis plantacio, the Tract Fundamentum aliud nemo potest ponere and the Tract De oblacione iugis sacrificii.* EETS, o.s., 317. Oxford: Oxford University Press, 2001.

Kempe, Margery. *The Book of Margery Kempe.* Edited by Barry Windeatt. New York: Longman, 2000.

Kirchberger, Clare, ed. "The Cleansing of Man's Soul." *Life of the Spirit* 4 (1949): 290–95.

Love, Nicholas. *Nicholas Love's Mirror of the Blessed Life of Jesus Christ. A Critical Edition Based on Cambridge University Library Additional MSS 6578 and 6686.* Edited by Michael G. Sargent. New York: Garland, 1992.

McCarthy, Adrian James, ed. *Book to a Mother: An Edition with Commentary.* Elizabethan and Renaissance Studies 92. Salzburg Studies in English Literature. Salzburg: Institut für Anglistik und Amerikanistik, 1981.

Mirk, John. *Mirk's Festial.* Edited by Theodor Erbe. EETS, e.s., 96. 1905. Reprint, Millwood, NY: Kraus Reprint, 1987.

Moon, Helen, ed. *The Lyfe of Soule, an Edition with Commentary*. Elizabethan and Renaissance Studies 75. Salzburg Studies in English Literature. Salzburg: Institut für Englische Sprache und Literatur, 1978.

Nelson, Venetia, ed. *A Myrour to Lewde Men and Women: A Prose Version of the "Speculum vitae," ed. from B.L. MS Harley 45*. Middle English Texts 14. Heidelberg: Carl Winter, 1981.

Pecock, Reginald. *Book of Faith*. Edited by J. L. Morison. Glasgow: James Maclehose and Sons, 1909.

———. *The Donet*. Edited by Elsie Vaughan Hitchcock. EETS, o.s., 156. 1921. Reprint, New York: Kraus Reprint, 1971.

———. *The Folewer to the Donet*. Edited by Elsie Vaughan Hitchcock. EETS, o.s., 164. 1924. Reprint, New York: Kraus Reprint, 1981.

———. *The Poore Mennis Myrrour*. Appendix to *The Donet*. Edited by Elsie Vaughan Hitchcock. EETS, o.s., 156. 1921. Reprint, New York: Kraus Reprint, 1971.

———. *The Repressor of Overmuch Blaming of the Clergy*. 2 vols. Edited by Churchill Babington. Rerum Britannicarum Medii Aevi Scriptores 19. London: Longman, Green, and Roberts, 1860.

———. *The Reule of Crysten Religioun*. Edited by William Cabell Greet. EETS, o.s., 171. 1927. Reprint, Millwood, NY: Kraus Reprint, 1987.

Perry, George, ed. *Religious Pieces in Prose and Verse Edited from Robert Thornton's MS (Circa 1440)*. EETS, o.s., 26. 1914. Reprint, New York: Kraus Reprint, 1981.

Purvey, William. "Purvey's Epilogue to His Comment on S. Matthew's Gospel." *The Lollard Bible and Other Medieval Versions*, edited by Margaret Deanesly, 457–61. Cambridge: Cambridge University Press, 1966.

Seneca, Lucius Annaeus. *Dialogues and Essays*. Translated by John Davies. Oxford: Oxford University Press, 2007.

Swinburn, Lilian Mary, ed. *The Lanterne of Li3t*. EETS, o.s., 151. 1917. Reprint, New York: Kraus Reprint, 1988.

Trevisa, John. *Dialogus inter militem et clericem, Richard fitzRalph's Sermon: "Defensio curatorum" and Methodius: "The Bygynnyng of the World and the Ende of Worldes" by John Trevisa, Vicar of Berkeley*. Edited by A. J. Perry. EETS, o.s., 167. 1925. Reprint, New York: Kraus Reprint, 1971.

———. "Trevisa's Original Prefaces on Translation: A Critical Edition." Edited by Ronald Waldron. In *Medieval English Studies Presented to George Kane*, edited by E. D. Kennedy, R. Waldron, and J. S. Wittig, 285–99. Woodbridge, Suffolk: Brewer, 1988.

Vaissier, J. J., ed. *A Devout Treatyse Called the Tree and Twelve Frutes of the Holy Goost*. Groningen: Wolters, 1960.

Vincent of Beauvais. *Speculum morale sive Speculum maius*. Graz: Akademische druck—U. Verslagsanstalt, 1964.

Wilkins, David, ed. *Concilia magnae Britanniae et Hiberniae*. Vol. 3. Oxford: Clarendon Press, 1964.

Wyclif, John. *John Wyclif: On the Truth of Holy Scripture*. Edited and translated by Ian Christopher Levy. Consortium for the Teaching of the Middle Ages. Kalamazoo: Medieval Institute Publications, Western Michigan University, 2001.

Secondary Sources

Aers, David. "Faith, Ethics, and Community: Reflections on Reading Late Medieval English Writing." *Journal of Medieval and Early Modern Studies* 28 (1998): 341–69.

Akbari, Suzanne. "The Family Tree in Pecock and *Benjamin Minor*." Paper presented at the International Congress on Medieval Studies, Kalamazoo, MI, May 4–7, 2006.

———. "Nature's Forge Recast in the *Roman de Silence*." In *Literary Aspects of Courtly Culture*, edited by Donald Maddox and Sara Sturm-Maddox, 39–46. Cambridge: Brewer, 1994.

Alford, John A. "The Idea of Reason in *Piers Plowman*." In *Medieval English Studies Presented to George Kane*, edited by Edward Donald Kennedy, Ronald Waldron, and Joseph S. Wittig, 199–215. Woodbridge, Suffolk: Brewer, 1988.

Amtower, Laurel. *Engaging Words: The Culture of Reading in the Later Middle Ages*. New York: Palgrave, 2000.

Appleford, Amy. "The Good Death of Richard Whittington." In *The Ends of the Body: Identity and Community in Medieval Culture*, edited by Suzanne Conklin Akbari and Jill Ross. Toronto: University of Toronto Press, forthcoming.

Armstrong, C. A. J. "The Piety of Cicely, Duchess of York: A Study in Late Medieval Culture." In *For Hilaire Belloc, Essays in Honour of His Seventy-first Birthday*, edited by Douglas Woodruff, 68–91. New York: Greenwood Press, 1942.

Aston, Margaret. *Lollards and Reformers: Images and Literacy in Late Medieval Religion*. London: Hambledon Press, 1984.

Baker, Denise. "The Active and Contemplative Lives in Rolle, The *Cloud*-Author and Hilton." In *The Medieval Mystical Tradition, England, Ireland and Wales: Papers Read at Charney Manor, 1999, Exeter Symposium VI*, edited by Marion Glasscoe, 85–102. Cambridge: Brewer, 1999.

———. *Julian of Norwich's Showings: From Vision to Book*. Princeton: Princeton University Press, 1994.

Barr, Helen. "Wycliffite Representation of the Third Estate." In *Lollards and Their Influence in Late Medieval England*, edited by Fiona Somerset, Jill C. Havens, and Derrick G. Pitard, 197–216. Woodbridge, Suffolk: Boydell Press, 2003.

Barratt, Alexandra. "Works of Religious Instruction." In *Middle English Prose: A Critical Guide to Major Authors and Genres*, edited by A. S. G. Edwards, 413–29. New Brunswick: Rutgers University Press, 1984.

Barron, Caroline M. "The Expansion of Education in Fifteenth-Century London." In *The Cloister and the World: Essays in Medieval History in Honour of Barbara Harvey*, edited by John Blair and Brian Golding, 219–45. Oxford: Clarendon Press, 1996.

———. *London in the Later Middle Ages: Government and People, 1200–1500*. Oxford: Oxford University Press, 2004.

———. "Richard Whittington: The Man behind the Myth." In *Studies in London History Presented to P. E. Jones*, edited by A. E. J. Hollaender and William Kellaway, 197–248. London: Hodder and Stoughton, 1969.

Baule, Cynthia. "Encountering the Word: Reading the Union in John Capgrave's *Life of Saint Katharine*." *Sewanee Medieval Studies* 11 (2001): 47–63.

Beadle, Richard. "'Devoute Ymaginacioun' and the Dramatic Sense in Love's *Mirror* and the N-Town Plays." In *Nicholas Love at Waseda: Proceedings of the International Conference, 20–22, July 1995*, edited by Shoichi Oguro, Richard Beadle, and Michael Sargent, 1–17. Cambridge: Brewer, 1997.

Beckwith, Sarah. *Christ's Body: Identity, Culture, and Society in Late Medieval Writings*. London: Routledge, 1993.

Bennett, H. S. "The Production and Dissemination of Vernacular Manuscripts in the Fifteenth Century." *Library*, 5th ser., 1 (1947): 167–78.

Bennett, Michael J. "Education and Advancement." In *Fifteenth-Century Attitudes: Perceptions of Society in Late Medieval England*, edited by Rosemary Horrox, 79–96. Cambridge: Cambridge University Press, 1994.

Benson, C. David. "Salvation Theology and Poetry in *Piers Plowman.*" *English Language Notes* 44 (2006): 103–7.

Bose, Mishtooni. "Reginald Pecock's Vernacular Voice." In *Lollards and Their Influence in Late Medieval England*, edited by Fiona Somerset, Jill C. Havens, and Derrick G. Pitard, 217–36. Woodbridge, Suffolk: Boydell Press, 2003.

———. "Vernacular Philosophy and the Making of Orthodoxy in the Fifteenth Century." *New Medieval Literatures* 7 (2005): 73–99.

Bourdieu, Pierre. *Reproduction in Education, Society and Culture.* 2nd ed. Newbury Park, CA: Sage Publications, 1990.

Brantley, Jessica. *Reading in the Wilderness: Private Devotion and Public Performance in Late Medieval England.* Chicago: University of Chicago Press, 2007.

Brewer, Thomas. *Memoir of the Life and Times of John Carpenter, Town Clerk of London.* London: Arthur Taylor, 1856.

Briggs, Charles F. "Teaching Philosophy at School and Court: Vulgarization and Translation." In *The Vulgar Tongue: Medieval and Postmedieval Vernacularity*, edited by Fiona Somerset and Nicholas Watson, 99–111. University Park: Pennsylvania State University Press, 2003.

Brockwell, Charles F. *Bishop Reginald Pecock and the Lancastrian Church: Securing the Foundations of Cultural Authority.* Texts and Studies in Religion 25. Lewiston, NY: Edwin Mellen Press, 1985.

———. "The Historical Career of Bishop Reginald Pecock, D.D.: The Poore Scoleris Myrrour or a Case Study in Famous Obscurity." *Harvard Theological Review* 74 (1981): 177–207.

Bryan, Jennifer. *Looking Inward: Devotional Reading and the Private Self in Late Medieval England.* Philadelphia: University of Pennsylvania Press, 2008.

Bynum, Caroline Walker. *Jesus as Mother: Studies in the Spirituality of the High Middle Ages.* Berkeley: University of California Press, 1982.

Carey, Hilary M. "Devout Literate Laypeople and the Pursuit of the Mixed Life in Later Medieval England." *Journal of Religious History* 14 (1987): 361–81.

Castelli, Elizabeth. "Feminist and Womanist Criticism." In *The Postmodern Bible: The Bible and Culture Collective*, edited by George Aichele, 225–71. New Haven: Yale University Press, 1995.

Catto, Jeremy. "The King's Government and the Fall of Pecock, 1457–58." In *Rulers and Ruled in Late Medieval England: Essays Presented to Gerald*

Harriss, edited by Rowena E. Archer and Simon Walker, 201–22. London: Hambledon, 1995.

―――. "Religion and the English Nobility in the Later Fourteenth Century." In *History and Imagination: Essays in Honour of H. R. Trevor-Roper*, edited by Hugh Lloyd Jones, Valerie Pearl, and Blair Worden, 43–55. London: Duckworth, 1981.

―――. "Theology after Wycliffism." In *The History of the University of Oxford*, vol. 2, *Late Medieval Oxford*, edited by J. I. Catto and Ralph Evans, 263–80. Oxford: Clarendon Press, 1992.

Christianson, C. Paul. "Evidence for the Study of London's Late Medieval Manuscript-Book Trade." In *Book Production and Publishing in Britain, 1375–1475*, edited by Jeremy Griffiths and Derek Pearsall, 87–107. Cambridge: Cambridge University Press, 1989.

Clark, J. P. H. "Action and Contemplation in Walter Hilton." *Downside Review* 97 (1979): 258–74.

Cobban, Alan B. *The Medieval English Universities: Oxford and Cambridge to c. 1500*. Aldershot: Scolar Press, 1988.

Cole, Andrew. "Chaucer's English Lesson." *Speculum* 77 (2002): 1128–67.

Connolly, Margaret. "Books for the 'helpe of euery persoone that thenkith to be saued': Six Devotional Anthologies from Fifteenth-Century London." *Yearbook of English Studies* 33 (2003): 170–81.

Consacro, Peter. "The Author of *The Abbey of the Holy Ghost*: A Popularizer of the Mixed Life." *14th Century English Mystics Newsletter 2*, no. 4 (1976): 15–20.

Constable, Giles. *Three Studies in Medieval Religious and Social Thought: The Interpretation of Mary and Martha, The Ideal of the Imitation of Christ, The Orders of Society*. Cambridge: Cambridge University Press, 1995.

Copeland, Rita. *Pedagogy, Intellectuals, and Dissent in the Later Middle Ages: Lollardy and Ideas of Learning*. Cambridge: Cambridge University Press, 2001.

Courtenay, William J. "Programs of Study and Genres of Scholastic Theological Production in the Fourteenth Century." In *Manuels, programmes de cours et techniques d'enseignement dans les universites médiévales: Actes du Colloque International de Louvain-la-Neuve*, edited by Jacqueline Hamesse, 325–50. Louvain-la-Neuve: Institut d'Études Médiévales de l'Université Catholique de Louvain, 1994.

Crassons, Kate. "Performance Anxiety and Watson's Vernacular Theology." *English Language Notes* 44 (2006): 95–102.

Davenport, W. A. "Patterns in Middle English Dialogues." In *Medieval English Studies Presented to George Kane*, edited by Edward Donald Kennedy, Ronald Waldron, and Joseph S. Wittig, 127–45. Woodbridge, Suffolk: Brewer, 1988.

Davidson, Clifford. "Northern Spirituality and the Late Medieval Drama of York." In *The Spirituality of Western Christendom*, edited by Rozanne Elder, 125–51. Kalamazoo, MI: Cistercian Publications, 1976.

Davies, R. G. "Lollardy and Locality." *Transactions of the Royal Historical Society*, 6th ser., (1991): 191–212.

De Hamel, Christopher. "Books of Hours: 'Imaging' the Word." In *The Bible as Book: The Manuscript Tradition*, edited by John L. Sharpe III and Kimberly Van Kampen, 137–43. London: British Library, 1998.

Delaisse, L. M. J. "The Importance of Books of Hours for the History of the Medieval Book." In *Gatherings in Honour of Dorothy E. Miner*, edited by Ursula E. McCracken, Lilian M. C. Randall, and Richard H. Randall Jr., 203–25. Baltimore: Walters Art Gallery, 1974.

Delany, Sheila. "The Late-Medieval Attack on Analogical Thought." *Mosaic* 5 (1972): 31–52.

Denley, Marie. "Elementary Teaching Techniques and Middle English Religious Didactic Writing." In *Langland, the Mystics, and the Medieval English Religious Tradition: Essays in Honour of S. S. Hussey*, edited by Helen Phillips, 223–41. Cambridge: Brewer, 1990.

Donoghue, Daniel. "The Tremulous Hand and Flying Eaglets." *English Language Notes* 44 (2006): 81–86.

Doyle, A. I. "Survey of the Origins and Circulation of Theological Writings in English in the 14th, 15th, and Early 16th Centuries with Special Consideration of the Part of the Clergy Therein." PhD diss., University of Cambridge, 1953.

Duffy, Eamon. "Elite and Popular Religion: The Book of Hours and Lay Piety in the Later Middle Ages." *Studies in Church History* 42 (2006): 140–61.

———. *The Stripping of the Altars: Traditional Religion in England, 1400–1580*. New Haven: Yale University Press, 1992.

Edwards, A. S. G. "The Contexts of Notre Dame 67." In *The Text in the Community: Essays on Medieval Works, Manuscripts, Authors, and Readers*, edited by Jill Mann and Maura Nolan, 107–29. Notre Dame: University of Notre Dame Press, 2006.

Erler, Mary. "Devotional Literature." In *The Cambridge History of the Book in Britain*, vol. 3, *1400–1557*, edited by Lotte Hellinga and J. B. Trapp, 495–525. Cambridge: Cambridge University Press, 1999.

Evans, G. R. *The Language and Logic of the Bible: The Road to Reformation*. Cambridge: Cambridge University Press, 1985.

———. "Wyclif's Logic and Wyclif's Exegesis: The Context." In *The Bible in the Medieval World: Essays in Memory of Beryl Smalley*, edited by Katherine Walsh and Diana Wood, 287–300. Oxford: Blackwell, 1985.

Ferguson, Arthur B. "Reginald Pecock and the Renaissance Sense of History." *Studies in the Renaissance* 13 (1966): 147–65.

Fish, Stanley. *Is There a Text in This Class? The Authority of Interpretive Communities*. Cambridge, MA: Harvard University Press, 1980.

Flanigan, C. Clifford, Kathleen Ashley, and Pamela Sheingorn. "Liturgy as Social Performance." In *The Liturgy of the Medieval Church*, 2nd ed., edited by Thomas J. Heffernan and E. Ann Matter, 635–52. Kalamazoo, MI: Medieval Institute Publications, 2005.

Flannery, Kevin L., S.J. *Acts amid Precepts: The Aristotelian Logical Structure of Thomas Aquinas's Moral Theory*. Washington, DC: Catholic University of America Press, 2001.

Fletcher, Alan. "'The unity of the state exists in the agreement of its minds': A Fifteenth-Century Sermon on the Three Estates." *Leeds Studies in English* 22 (1991): 103–37.

Ford, Judy Ann. "The Autonomy of Conscience: Images of Confession in Mirk's *Festial*." *Renaissance and Reformation* 23 (1999): 5–27.

———. *John Mirk's Festial: Orthodoxy, Lollardy and the Common People in Fourteenth-Century England*. Cambridge: Brewer, 2006.

Forshaw, Helen. "New Light on the *Speculum ecclesie* of St Edmund of Abingdon." *Archives d'Histoire Doctrinale et Litteraire du Moyen Age* 38 (1971): 7–33.

———. "St Edmund's *Speculum*: A Classic of Victorine Spirituality." *Archives d'Histoire Doctrinale et Litteraire du Moyen Age* 39 (1972): 7–40.

Galloway, Andrew. "The Making of a Social Ethic in Late-Medieval England: From *Gratitudo* to 'Kyndenesse.'" *Journal of the History of Ideas* 55 (1994): 365–83.

Georgianna, Linda. "Vernacular Theologies." *English Language Notes* 44 (2006): 87–94.

Ghosh, Kantik. "Bishop Reginald Pecock and the Idea of 'Lollardy.'" In *Text and Controversy from Wyclif to Bale: Essays in Honour of Anne Hudson*, edited by Helen Barr and Ann Hutchison, 251–65. Medieval Church Series 4. Turnhout: Brepols, 2005.

———. "Eliding the Interpreter: John Wyclif and Scriptural Truth." *New Medieval Literatures* 2 (1998): 205–24.

———. "Nicholas Love." In *A Companion to Middle English Prose*, edited by A. S. G. Edwards, 53–66. Cambridge: Brewer, 2004.

———. *The Wycliffite Heresy: Authority and the Interpretation of Texts.* Cambridge Studies in Medieval Literature 45. Cambridge: Cambridge University Press, 2002.

Gillespie, Vincent. "Anonymous Devotional Writings." In *A Companion to Middle English Prose*, edited by A. S. G. Edwards, 127–49. Cambridge: Brewer, 2004.

———. "Chichele's Church: Vernacular Theology after Thomas Arundel." Paper presented at the 42nd International Congress on Medieval Studies, Kalamazoo, MI, May 10–13, 2007.

———. "Dial M for Mystic: Mystical Texts in the Library of Syon Abbey and the Spirituality of the Syon Brethren." In *The Medieval Mystical Tradition*, edited by Marion Glasscoe, 241–68. Cambridge: Brewer, 1999.

———. "*Doctrina* and *Predicacio:* The Design and Function of Some Pastoral Manuals." *Leeds Studies in English*, n.s., 11 (1980): 36–50.

———. "The Haunted Text: Reflections in *A Mirror to Devout People*." In *The Text in the Community: Essays on Medieval Works, Manuscripts, Authors, and Readers*, edited by Jill Mann and Maura Nolan, 129–72. Notre Dame: University of Notre Dame Press, 2006.

———. "*Lukynge in haly bukes: Lectio* in Some Late Medieval Spiritual Miscellanies." In *Spätmittelalterliche Geistliche Literatur in der Nationalsprache*, Analecta Cartusiana 106, edited by James Hogg, 1–27. Salzburg: Institut für Anglistik und Amerikanistik, 1984.

———. "Mystic's Foot: Rolle and Affectivity." In *The Medieval Mystical Tradition in England: Papers Read at Dartington Hall, July 1982*, edited by Marion Glasscoe, 199–230. Exeter: Short Run Press, 1982.

———. "Vernacular Books of Religion." In *Book Production and Publishing in Britain, 1375–1475* edited by Jeremy Griffiths and Derek Pearsall, 317–44. Cambridge: Cambridge University Press, 1989.

Glasscoe, Marion. "Time of Passion: Latent Relationships between Liturgy and Meditation in Two Middle English Mystics." In *Langland, the Mystics, and the Medieval English Religious Tradition: Essays in Honour of S. S. Hussey*, edited by Helen Phillips, 141–60. Cambridge: Brewer, 1990.

Gray, Douglas. "London, British Library, Additional MS 27049." In *Text and Controversy from Wyclif to Bale: Essays in Honour of Anne Hudson*, edited by Anne Barr and Anne Hutchison, 99–116. Medieval Church Series 4. Turnhout: Brepols, 2004.

Green, V. H. H. *Bishop Reginald Pecock: A Study in Ecclesiastical History and Thought*. Cambridge: Cambridge University Press, 1945.

Haines, Roy M. "Church, Society and Politics in the Early Fifteenth Century as Viewed from an English Pulpit." *Studies in Church History* 12 (1975): 143–57.

———. "Reginald Pecock: A Tolerant Man in an Age of Intolerance." *Studies in Church History* 21 (1984): 125–37.

Harvey, Ruth. "The Ymage of Love." In *The Complete Works of Thomas More*, Appendix A, vol. 6, *A Dialogue Concerning Heresies*, edited by T. M. C. Lawler, G. Marc'Hadour, and R. C. Marius, 729–59. New Haven: Yale University Press, 1981.

Hasenohr, Genevieve. "Religious Reading amongst the Laity in France in the Fifteenth Century." In *Heresy and Literacy, 1000–1530*, edited by Peter Biller and Anne Hudson, 205–21. Cambridge Studies in Medieval Literature 23. Cambridge: Cambridge University Press, 1994.

Hennessy, Marlene Villalobos. "Passion Devotion, Penitential Reading, and the Manuscript Page: 'The Hours of the Cross' in London, British Library Additional 37049." *Mediaeval Studies* 66 (2004): 213–56.

Hirsh, John. "Prayer and Meditation in Late Medieval England: MS Bodley 789." *Medium Aevum* 48 (1979): 55–66.

Hogg, James. "Unpublished Texts in the Carthusian Northern Middle English Religious Miscellany, British Library MS Additional 37049." In *Essays in Honor of Erwin Sturzl on His 60th Birthday*, Salzburger Studien zur Anglistik und Amerikanistik 10, 1:241–84. Salzburg: Institut für Englische Sprache und Literatur, 1980.

Hudson, Anne. *Lollards and Their Books*. London: Hambledon Press, 1985.

———. *The Premature Reformation: Wycliffite Texts and Lollard History*. Oxford: Clarendon Press, 1988.

———. "Some Problems of Identity and Identification in Wycliffite Writings." In *Middle English Prose: Essays in Bibliographical Problems*, edited by A. S. G. Edwards and Derek Pearsall, 81–90. New York: Garland, 1981.

———. "Which Wyche? The Framing of the Lollard Heretic and/or Saint." In *Studies in the Transmission of Wyclif's Writings*. Aldershot: Ashgate Variorum, 2008. Originally published in *Texts and the Repression of Medieval Heresy*, edited by C. Bruschi and P. Biller, 221–37. York: York Medieval Press, 2003.

Hudson, Anne, and Helen Spencer. "Old Author, New Work: The Sermons of MS Longleat 4." *Medium Aevum* 80 (1983): 220–38.

Huot, Sylvia. "Polytextual Reading: The Meditative Reading of Real and Metaphorical Books." In *Orality and Literacy in the Middle Ages: Essays on a Conjunction and Its Consequences in Honour of D. H. Green*, edited by Mark Chinca and Christopher Young, 202–22. Turnhout: Brepols, 2005.

Hussey, Maurice. "The Petitions of the Paternoster in Medieval English Literature." *Medium Aevum* 27 (1958): 8–16.

Imray, Jean. *The Charity of Richard Whittington: A History of the Trust Administered by the Mercers' Company, 1424–1966*. London: Athlone, 1968.

Ingarden, Roman. *The Literary Work of Art: An Investigation on the Borderlines of Ontology, Logic, and Theory of Literature*. Translated by George G. Grabowicz. Evanston: Northwestern University Press, 1973.

Irvine, Martin. "Interpretation and the Semiotics of Allegory in Clement of Alexandria, Origen, and Augustine." *Semiotica* 63 (1986): 33–71.

Iser, Wolfgang. *The Act of Reading: A Theory of Aesthetic Response*. Baltimore: Johns Hopkins University Press, 1978.

———. *How to Do Theory*. Oxford: Blackwell, 2006.

———. *The Implied Reader: Patterns of Communication in Prose Fiction from Bunyan to Beckett*. Baltimore: Johns Hopkins University Press.

———. "Indeterminacy and the Reader's Response in Prose Fiction." In *Aspects of Narrative: Selected Papers from the English Institute*, edited by J. Hillis Miller, 1–45. New York: Columbia University Press, 1971.

Jacob, E. F. *Essays in Later Medieval History*. Manchester: Manchester University Press, 1968.

Jambeck, Thomas. "The Dramatic Implications of Anselmian Affective Piety in the Towneley Play of the Crucifixion." *Annuale Mediaevale* 16 (1975): 110–27.

Jauss, Hans Robert. *Toward an Aesthetic of Reception*. Translated by Timothy Bahti. Theory and History of Literature 2. Minneapolis: University of Minnesota Press, 1982.

Johnson, Ian. "Vernacular? Theology? Vernacular Theology?" April 8, 2008, Geographies of Orthodoxy: Mapping English Pseudo-Bonaventuran Lives of Christ, 1350–1550, www.qub.ac.uk/geographies-of-orthodoxy/discuss/2008/04/08/vernacular-theology-vernacular-theology.

Johnson, Mark. "An Accomplishment of the Moral Part of Aquinas's *Summa theologiae*." In *Essays in Medieval Philosophy and Theology in Memory of Walter H. Principe, CSB*, edited by James R. Ginther and Carl N. Still, 85–103. Aldershot: Ashgate, 2005.

Joliffe, Peter. "Middle English Translations of *De exterioris et interioris hominis compositione*." *Mediaeval Studies* 36 (1974): 259–77.

Jones, E. A. "The Compilation(s) of Two Late Medieval Devotional Manuscripts." In *Text and Controversy from Wyclif to Bale: Essays in Honour of Anne Hudson*, edited by Anne Barr and Ann Hutchison, 79–97. Medieval Church Series 4. Turnhout: Brepols, 2004.

Keiser, George. "The Holy Boke Gratia Dei." *Viator: Medieval and Renaissance Studies* 12 (1981): 289–317.

———. "'Noght how lang man lifs; bot how wele': The Laity and the Ladder of Perfection." In *De cella in seculum: Religious and Secular Life and Devotion in Late Medieval England*, edited by Michael Sargent, 145–59. Cambridge: Brewer, 1989.

———. "'To Knawe God Almyghtyn': Robert Thornton's Devotional Book." In *Spätmittelalterliche Geistliche Literatur in der Nationalsprache*, Analecta Cartusiana 106, 103–29. Salzburg: Institut für Anglistik und Amerikanistik, 1984.

Kellaway, William. "John Carpenter's *Liber albus*." *Guildhall Studies in London History* 3 (1978): 67–84.

Kelly, Henry Ansgar. "Uniformity and Sense in Editing and Citing Medieval Texts." *Medieval Academy News* 148 (Spring 2004): 8–9.

Kelly, Stephen, and Ryan Perry. "'Hospitable Reading' and Clerical Reform in Fifteenth-Century London." April 24, 2009. Geographies of Orthodoxy: Mapping English Pseudo-Bonaventuran Lives of Christ, 1350–1550, www.qub.ac.uk/geographies-of-orthodoxy/discuss/2009/04/24/hospitable-reading-and-clerical-reform-in-fifteenth-century-london.

Kempster, Hugh. "A Question of Audience: The Westminster Text and Fifteenth-Century Reception of Julian of Norwich." In *Julian of Norwich: A Book of Essays*, edited by Sandra McEntire, 257–89. New York: Garland, 1998.

Kenny, Anthony. *A New History of Western Philosophy*. Vol. 2. Oxford: Clarendon Press, 2005.

Kenny, Anthony, and Jan Pinborg. "Medieval Philosophical Literature." In *Cambridge History of Later Medieval Philosophy*, edited by Norman Kretzmann, Anthony Kenny, and Jan Pinborg, 11–42. Cambridge: Cambridge University Press, 1982.

Kerby-Fulton, Kathryn. *Books under Suspicion: Censorship and Revelatory Theology in the Literature of Late Medieval England*. Notre Dame: University of Notre Dame Press, 2006.

Knowles, David. *The Evolution of Medieval Thought*. London: Longmans, 1962.

Kurath, Hans, and Sherman M. Kuhn, eds. *Middle English Dictionary*. Ann Arbor: University of Michigan Press, 1964–81.

Lawrence, C. H. "Edmund of Abingdon." *Month* 215 (1963): 213–29.

Lindenbaum, Sheila. "London Texts and Literate Practice." In *Cambridge History of Medieval English Literature*, edited by David Wallace, 284–309. Cambridge: Cambridge University Press, 1999.

Little, Katherine C. "'Bokes ynowe': Vernacular Theology and Fourteenth-Century Exhaustion." *English Language Notes* 44 (2006): 109–12.

MacFarlane, K. B. *Lancastrian Kings and Lollard Knights*. Oxford: Clarendon Press, 1972.

McClintock Fulkerson, Mary. "Is There a (Non-sexist) Bible in This Church? A Feminist Case for the Priority of Interpretive Communities." *Modern Theology* 14, no. 2 (1998): 225–42.

McGrady, Deborah. "Reading for Authority: Portraits of Christine de Pizan and Her Readers." Paper presented at the Conference on Medieval Authorship, Vancouver, British Columbia, November 12–13, 2004.

McKeon, Richard. "Poetry and Philosophy in the Twelfth Century: The Renaissance of Rhetoric." *Modern Philology* 43, no. 4 (1946): 217–34.

McMahon, Clara P. *Education in Fifteenth-Century England*. Johns Hopkins Studies in Education 35. Baltimore: Johns Hopkins University Press, 1947.

McSheffrey, Shannon. *Gender and Heresy: Women and Men in Lollard Communities, 1420–1530*. Philadelphia: University of Pennsylvania Press, 1995.

———. "Heresy, Orthodoxy and English Vernacular Religion, 1480–1525." *Past and Present* 186 (2005): 47–80.

———. "Literacy and the Gender Gap in the Late Middle Ages: Women and Reading in Lollard Communities." In *Women, the Book, and the Godly*, edited by Lesley Smith and Jane H. M. Taylor, 157–70. Cambridge: Brewer, 1995.

Middleton, Anne. "The Idea of Public Poetry in the Reign of Richard II." *Speculum* 53 (1978): 94–114.

Minnis, Alastair. "'Authorial Intention' and 'Literal Sense' in the Exegetical Theories of Richard Fitzralph and John Wyclif: An Essay in the Medieval History of Biblical Hermeneutics." *Proceedings of the Royal Irish Academy* 75C (1975): 1–31.

———. "Langland's Ymaginatif and Late-Medieval Theories of Imagination." *Comparative Criticism* 3 (1981): 71–103.

———. "Medieval Imagination and Memory." In *The Cambridge History of Literary Criticism*, vol. 2, *The Middle Ages*, edited by Alastair Minnis and Ian Johnson, 239–74. Cambridge: Cambridge University Press, 2005.

———. "The Trouble with Theology: Ethical Poetics and the Ends of Scripture." Paper presented at the Conference on Medieval Authorship, Vancouver, British Columbia, November 12–13, 2004.

Minnis, Alastair, and A. B. Scott. *Medieval Literary Theory and Criticism, c. 1100–c. 1375: The Commentary Tradition*. Oxford: Clarendon Press, 1988.

Moore, Stephen D. "Negative Hermeneutics, Insubstantial Texts: Stanley Fish and the Biblical Interpreter." *Journal of the American Academy of Religion* 54, no. 4 (1986): 707–19.

Moran, Jo Ann Hoeppner. "A 'Common Profit' Library in Fifteenth-Century England and Other Books for Chaplains." *Manuscripta* 28 (1984): 17–25.

———. *The Growth of English Schooling, 1340–1548: Learning, Literacy, and Laicization in Pre-Reformation York Diocese*. Princeton: Princeton University Press, 1985.

Morrison, Stephen. "Lollardy in the Fifteenth Century: The Evidence from Some Orthodox Texts." *Cahiers Elisabethains* 52 (1997): 1–24.

Mulder-Bakker, Anneke B. Introduction to *Seeing and Knowing: Women and Learning in Medieval Europe, 1200–1550*, 1–20. Turnhout: Brepols, 2004.

Murtaugh, Daniel. *Piers Plowman and the Image of God*. Gainesville: University Presses of Florida, 1978.

Newman, Barbara. *God and the Goddesses: Vision, Poetry and Belief in the Middle Ages*. Philadelphia: University of Pennsylvania Press, 2003.

Olson, Paul A. "*The Parlement of Foules*: Aristotle's *Politics* and the Foundations of Human Society." *Studies in the Age of Chaucer* 2 (1980): 53–69.

Orme, Nicholas. *Education and Society in Medieval and Renaissance England*. London: Hambledon Press, 1989.

———. *Education in the West of England, 1066–1548*. Exeter: University of Exeter, 1976.

———. *English Schools in the Middle Ages*. London: Methuen, 1973.

———. *From Childhood to Chivalry: The Education of the English Kings and Aristocracy, 1066–1530*. London: Methuen, 1984.

————. *Medieval Schools from Roman Britain to Renaissance England.* New Haven: Yale University Press, 2006.

Owens, Joseph. "Faith, Ideas, Illumination, and Experience." In *The Cambridge History of Later Medieval Philosophy, 1100–1600,* edited by Norman Kretzmann, Anthony Kenny, and Jan Pinborg, 440–59. Cambridge: Cambridge University Press, 1982.

Pantin, William. *"Instructions for a Devout and Literate Layman."* In *Medieval Learning and Literature: Essays Presented to Richard William Hunt,* edited by J. J. G. Alexander and M. T. Gibson, 398–402. Oxford: Clarendon Press, 1976.

Parkes, M. B. *Scribes, Scripts and Readers: Studies in the Communication, Presentation, and Dissemination of Medieval Texts.* London: Hambledon Press, 1991.

Patrouch, Joseph F. *Reginald Pecock.* New York: Twayne, 1970.

Pearsall, Derek. "The *Canterbury Tales* and London Club Culture." In *Chaucer and the City,* edited by Ardis Butterfield, 95–108. Cambridge: Brewer, 2006.

Peikola, Matti. *Congregation of the Elect: Patterns of Self-Fashioning in English Lollard Writings.* Anglicana Turkuensia 21. Turku, Finland: University of Turku Press, 2000.

Pollard, William F. "Mystical Elements in a Fifteenth-Century Prayer Sequence: 'The Festis and the Passion of Oure Lord Ihesu Crist.'" In *The Medieval Mystical Tradition in England, Papers Read at Dartington Hall, July 1987, Exeter Symposium IV,* edited by Marion Glasscoe, 47–61. Cambridge: Brewer, 1987.

Raymo, Robert R. "Works of Religious and Philosophical Instruction." In *A Manual of the Writings in Middle English, 1050–1500,* vol. 7, edited by Albert E. Hartung. New Haven: Connecticut Academy of Arts and Sciences, 1986.

Reddan, M. "Whittington's College." In *The Religious Houses of London and Middlesex,* edited by Caroline M. Barron and Matthew Davies, 225–26. London: University of London Institute of Historical Research, 2007.

Rees Jones, Sarah. "'*A peler of Holy Cherch*': Margery Kempe and the Bishops." In *Medieval Women: Texts and Contexts in Late Medieval Britain: Essays for Felicity Riddy,* edited by Jocelyn Wogan-Browne et al., 377–91. Turnhout: Brepols, 2000.

Rice, Nicole. *Lay Piety and Religious Discipline in Middle English Literature.* Cambridge: Cambridge University Press, 2008.

Riddy, Felicity. "'Publication' before Print: The Case of Julian of Norwich." In *The Uses of Script and Print, 1300–1700*, edited by Julia Crick and Alexandra Walsham, 29–49. Cambridge: Cambridge University Press, 2004.

———. "Reading for England: Arthurian Literature and National Consciousness." *Bibliographical Bulletin of the International Arthurian Society* 43 (1991): 314–31.

———. "Women Talking about the Things of God: A Late Medieval Subculture." In *Women and Literature in Britain, c. 1100–1500*, edited by Carol Meale, 104–27. Cambridge: Cambridge University Press, 1993.

Robertson, Elizabeth. "Introduction." *English Language Notes* 44 (2006): 77–79.

Rosemann, Philipp W. *Understanding Scholastic Thought with Foucault.* New York: St. Martin's Press, 1999.

Rubin, Miri. "Small Groups: Identity and Solidarity in the Late Middle Ages." In *Enterprise and the Individual in Fifteenth-Century England*, edited by Jennifer Kermode, 132–50. Stroud: Alan Sutton, 1991.

Russell-Smith, Joy. "Walter Hilton." In *Pre-Reformation English Spirituality*, edited by James Walsh, 182–97. Bronx, NY: Fordham University Press, 1965.

Saenger, Paul. "Books of Hours and the Reading Habits of the Later Middle Ages." In *The Culture of Print: Power and the Uses of Print in Early Modern Europe*, edited by Roger Chartier and translated by Lydia G. Cochrane, 141–73. Princeton: Princeton University Press, 1989.

———. *Space between Words: The Origins of Silent Reading.* Stanford: Stanford University Press, 1997.

Salter, Elizabeth. *Nicholas Love's Myrrour of the Blessed Lyf of Jesu Christ.* Analecta Cartusiana 10. Salzburg: Institut für Englische Sprache und Literatur, 1974.

Sargent, Michael. "Minor Devotional Writings." In *Middle English Prose: A Critical Guide to Major Authors and Genres*, edited by A. S. G. Edwards, 147–75. New Brunswick: Rutgers University Press, 1984.

Scase, Wendy. "Reginald Pecock." In *Authors of the Middle Ages*, edited by M. C. Seymour, 8:1–146. Aldershot: Variorum, 1996.

———. "Reginald Pecock, John Carpenter and John Colop's 'Common-Profit' Books: Aspects of Book Ownership and Circulation in Fifteenth-Century London." *Medium Aevum* 61 (1992): 261–74.

Schirmer, Elizabeth. "Reading Lessons at Syon Abbey: The *Myroure of Oure Ladye* and the Mandates of Vernacular Reading." In *Voices in Dialogue: Reading Women in the Middle Ages*, edited by Linda Olson and Kathryn Kerby-Fulton, 345–94. Notre Dame: University of Notre Dame Press, 2005.

Serene, Eileen. "Demonstrative Science." In *The Cambridge History of Later Medieval Philosophy*, edited by Norman Kretzmann, Anthony Kenny, and Jan Pinborg, 496–517. Cambridge: Cambridge University Press, 1982.

Simpson, James. "Confessing Literature." *English Language Notes* 44 (2006): 121–26.

———. "The Constraints of Satire in 'Piers Plowman' and 'Mum and the Sothsegger.'" In *Langland, the Mystics, and the Medieval English Religious Tradition. Essays in Honour of S. S. Hussey*, edited by Helen Phillips, 11–31. Cambridge: Brewer, 1990.

———. "Faith and Hermeneutics: Pragmatism versus Pragmatism." *Journal of Medieval and Early Modern Studies* 33, no. 2 (2003): 215–39.

———. *Reform and Cultural Revolution: 1350–1547*. Vol. 2 of *The Oxford English Literary History*, general editor Jonathan Bate. Oxford: Oxford University Press, 2002.

———. "Reginald Pecock and John Fortescue." In *A Companion to Middle English Prose*, edited by A. S .G. Edwards, 271–87. Cambridge: Cambridge University Press, 2004.

———. "Saving Satire after Arundel's *Constitutions*: John Audelay's 'Marcol and Solomon.'" In *Text and Controversy from Wyclif to Bale: Essays in Honour of Anne Hudson*, edited by Helen Barr and Ann Hutchison, 387–404. Medieval Church Series 4. Turnhout: Brepols, 2005.

———. *Sciences and the Self in Medieval Poetry*. Cambridge Studies in Medieval Literature 25. Cambridge: Cambridge University Press, 1995.

Smalley, Beryl. "The Bible and Eternity: John Wyclif's Dilemma." *Journal of the Warburg and Courtauld Institutes* 27 (1964): 73–89.

———. "Gospels in the Paris Schools: Peter the Chanter, Hugh of St. Cher, Alexander of Hales, John of La Rochelle." *Franciscan Studies* 40 (1980): 298–369.

Smith, Raymond. "The Library at Guildhall in the 15th and 16th Centuries." *Guildhall Miscellany* 1 (1952): 2–9 and 6 (1956): 2–6.

Somerset, Fiona. "'As just as is a squyre': The Politics of 'Lewed Translacion' in Chaucer's *Summoner's Tale*." *Studies in the Age of Chaucer* 21 (1999): 187–207.

———. *Clerical Discourse and Lay Audience in Late Medieval England*. Cambridge: Cambridge University Press, 1998.

———. "Professionalizing Translation at the Turn of the Fifteenth Century: Ullerston's *Determinacio*, Arundel's *Constitutiones*." In *The Vulgar Tongue: Medieval and Postmedieval Vernacularity*, edited by Fiona Somerset and Nicholas Watson, 145–58. University Park: Pennsylvania State University Press, 2003.

———. Review of Copeland's *Pedagogy, Intellectuals, and Dissent*. *Medium Aevum* 72 (2003): 140–41.

———. "Wycliffite Spirituality." *Text and Controversy from Wyclif to Bale: Essays in Honour of Anne Hudson*, edited by Anne Barr and Ann Hutchison, 375–86. Medieval Church Series 4. Turnhout: Brepols, 2004.

Spencer, H. L. *English Preaching in the Late Middle Ages*. Oxford: Clarendon Press, 1993.

Staley, Lynn. "The Penitential Psalms and Vernacular Theology." *English Language Notes* 44 (2006): 113–19.

Steele, F. J. *Towards a Spirituality for Lay-Folk: The Active Life in Middle English Religious Literature from the Thirteenth Century to the Fifteenth*. Lewiston, NY: Edwin Mellen Press, 1995.

Steiner, Emily. *Documentary Culture and the Making of Medieval English Literature*. Cambridge: Cambridge University Press, 2003.

———. "Lollardy and the Legal Document." In *Lollards and Their Influence in Late Medieval England*, edited by Fiona Somerset, Jill Havens, and Derrick Pitard, 155–74. Woodbridge, Suffolk: Boydell, 2003.

Stock, Brian. *The Implications of Literacy: Written Language and Models of Interpretation in the Eleventh and Twelfth Centuries*. Princeton: Princeton University Press, 1983.

———. *Listening for the Text: On the Uses of the Past*. Baltimore: Johns Hopkins University Press, 1990.

Strohm, Paul. "Chaucer's Audience(s): Fictional, Implied, Intended, Actual." *Chaucer Review* 18 (1983): 137–45.

———. "Writing and Reading." In *A Social History of England, 1200–1500*, edited by Rosemary Horrox and W. Mark Ormrod, 454–72. Cambridge: Cambridge University Press.

Sutton, Anne. *The Mercery of London: Trade, Goods, and People, 1130–1578*. Aldershot: Ashgate, 2005.

Swanson, R. N. *Church and Society in Late Medieval England*. Oxford: Oxford University Press, 1989.

———. "Literacy, Heresy, History and Orthodoxy: Perspectives and Permutations for the Later Middle Ages." In *Heresy and Literacy,*

1000–1530, edited by Peter Biller and Anne Hudson, 279–93. Cambridge: Cambridge University Press, 1994.

Taylor, Andrew. "Translation, Censorship, Authorship and the Lost Work of Reginald Pecock." In *The Politics of Translation in the Middle Ages and the Renaissance*, edited by Renate Blumenfeld-Kosinski, Luise von Flotow, and Daniel Russell, 143–60. Ottawa: University of Ottawa Press, 2001.

Von Nolcken, Christina. "Richard Wyche, A Certain Knight, and the Beginning of the End." In *Lollardy and the Gentry in the Later Middle Ages*, edited by Margaret Aston and Colin Richmond, 127–54. Stroud: Sutton; New York: St. Martin's Press, 1997.

Wailes, Stephen L. "Why Did Jesus Use Parables? The Medieval Discussion." *Medievalia et Humanistica*, n.s., 13 (1985): 43–64.

Ward, Benedicta. *The Prayers and Meditations of St. Anselm*. London: Penguin, 1973.

Watson, Nicholas. "Censorship and Cultural Change in Late-Medieval England: Vernacular Theology, the Oxford Translation Debate, and Arundel's Constitutions of 1409." *Speculum* 70, no. 4 (1995): 822–64.

———. "Conceptions of the Word: The Mother Tongue and the Incarnation of God." *New Medieval Literatures* 1 (1997): 85–124.

———. "Cultural Changes." *English Language Notes* 44 (2006): 127–37.

———. "Fashioning the Puritan Gentry-Woman: Devotion and Dissent in *Book to a Mother*." In *Medieval Women: Texts and Contexts in Late Medieval Britain, Essays for Felicity Riddy*. Medieval Women: Texts and Contexts 3, edited by Jocelyn Wogan-Browne et al., 169–84. Turnhout: Brepols, 2000.

Wenzel, Siegfried. *Latin Sermon Collections from Later Medieval England: Orthodox Preaching in the Age of Wyclif*. Cambridge: Cambridge University Press, 2005.

Wiethaus, Ulrike. "Thieves and Carnivals: Gender in German Dominican Literature of the Fourteenth Century." In *The Vernacular Spirit: Essays on Medieval Religious Literature*, edited by Renate Blumenfeld-Kosinski, Duncan Robertson, and Nancy Bradley Warren, 209–38. New York: Palgrave, 2002.

Winstead, Karen A. *John Capgrave's Fifteenth Century*. Philadelphia: University of Pennsylvania Press, 2007.

Wogan-Browne, Jocelyn. "Analytical Survey 5: 'Reading Is Good Prayer': Recent Research on Female Reading Communities." *New Medieval Literatures* 5 (2002): 229–97.

Wogan-Browne, Jocelyn, Nicholas Watson, Andrew Taylor, and Ruth Evans, eds. *The Idea of the Vernacular*. University Park: Pennsylvania State University Press, 1999.

Wooding, Lucy E. C. *Rethinking Catholicism in Reformation England*. Oxford: Clarendon Press, 2000.

Woods, Marjorie Curry. "Shared Books: Primers, Psalters, and the Adult Acquisition of Literacy among Devout Laywomen and Women in Orders in Late Medieval England." In *New Trends in Feminine Spirituality: The Holy Women of Liège and Their Impact*, edited by Juliette Dov, Lesley Johnson, and Jocelyn Wogan-Browne, 177–89. Medieval Women: Texts and Contexts 2. Brepols: Turnhout, 1999.

Yoshikawa, Naoë Kukita. "The Role of the Virgin Mary and the Structure of Meditation in the *Book of Margery Kempe*." In *The Medieval Mystical Tradition: England, Ireland and Wales, Papers Read at Charney Manor, July 1999, Exeter Symposium VI*, edited by Marion Glasscoe, 169–92. Cambridge: Brewer, 1999.

Zieman, Katherine. "Playing Doctor: St. Birgitta, Ritual Reading, and Ecclesiastical Authority." In *Voices in Dialogue: Reading Women in the Middle Ages*, edited by Linda Olson and Kathryn Kerby-Fulton, 307–34. Notre Dame: University of Notre Dame Press, 2005.

———. *Singing the New Song: Literacy and Liturgy in Late Medieval England*. Philadelphia: University of Pennsylvania Press, 2008.

Index

KIRSTY CAMPBELL

is professor of English at John Abbott College in Montreal, Canada.